# Who Is God, *Really?*

## Two Scientists Discuss Their Faith

Dr. Victoria Lim
Dr. Stephen Robinson

Cover photo by Daniel Leone on Unsplash.[1]

---

[1] unsplash.com/photos/g30P1zcOzXo

# CONTENTS

# PROLOGUE

On August 10, 2017, Victoria Lim, a PhD student in computational chemistry at the University of California, Irvine sent her former physics professor, Steve Robinson of Belmont University,[1] an email. The subject line read, "What was Schrödinger's favorite movie genre?" This joke setup[2] was in reference to Erwin Schrödinger, winner of the 1933 Nobel Prize in Physics "for the discovery of new productive forms of atomic theory"[3] and was fitting in that Victoria was in four of Steve's classes: two introductory courses and two courses on quantum mechanics, the theory of small-scale physics. From that single email, a deep discussion of Everything Important unexpectedly ensued and continued over the next 3+ years. This book is that discussion, and one may view it properly from several perspectives.

At its most basic level, it is a dialogue (never an argument) between two scientists with different worldviews. As you will read, we both strongly believe that hard introspection—and even doubt—are healthy steps toward a pursuit of the answers to life's biggest questions. This "always questioning" attitude is what led both of us into scientific careers; thus, we are both open to external and self-criticism of our default—and often deeply held—perspectives. It is both that willingness to hear from each other and our scientific training in how to properly question and answer that allowed this book to blossom.

On another level, this book touches on numerous defenses and difficulties of Christian theology. That is, if one removed the personalities of the authors, one might find an apologist's handbook in these pages. However, apologetics without people brings to mind the apostle Paul's warning:

> If I speak in the tongues of men or of angels, but do not have love, I am only a resounding gong or a clanging cymbal. If I have the gift of prophecy and can fathom all mysteries and all knowledge, and if I have a faith that can move mountains, but do not have love, I am nothing. (1 Cor 13:1–2)

If those of us who call ourselves followers of Christ seek only the goal of winning an argument, we have indeed forgotten the mission of Christ:

---

[1] Victoria and Steve are grateful for the opportunities to work and speak freely at their respective workplaces, but this book is in no way endorsed by either the University of California or Belmont University. The contents herein are the views of the authors alone.

[2] Keep reading for the punchline.

[3] "Erwin Schrödinger," *The Nobel Prize*, www.nobelprize.org/prizes/physics/1933/schrodinger/biographical/.

*"I have come that they may have life, and have it to the full."* (Jn 10:10b)

Thus, this book brings apologetics down to a personal level. Our pursuit of answers herein has real consequences for two real people desperately searching for meaning and purpose in a seemingly mechanistic and/or random universe. We believe the personal nature of this book will lend a hand to those struggling with cold theological questions.

Finally, this book can be viewed as simply a conversation between friends who both want to understand each other and offer new perspectives. Given the busyness of life, it is difficult to maintain a conversation like this one without an underlying care for the other person. Theodore Roosevelt (possibly) expressed it nicely: "Nobody cares how much you know until they know how much you care." In that light, this conversation becomes a story in which we work through our own questions and doubts, continually landing in unforeseen destinations. By questioning each other, we have both come to new understandings of ourselves, each other, and humanity.

Wherever you are on the spectrum of belief—skeptic, doubter, indifferent, believer, apologist, evangelizer—or whatever your motivations are for picking up this book—debating, pondering, learning, entertainment—we believe you will find your time perusing these pages fruitful. To help you get a glimpse of what we each brought into this conversation, we will begin with who we are. In the epilogue, we will discuss who we have become and where we're heading.

### STEVE

I was born into a middle-class, rural, white family of five in the southeastern United States, also known as the Bible Belt. Both of my parents grew up in nominally Christian cultures, but both became followers of Christ as adults (before I was born). As a child, church attendance was regular and mandatory for me, and I was personally unaware of *anyone* who would not identify as a Christian. That may have been the result of the small-world picture that all children have, but it is unmistakable that the Bible Belt produces cultural expectations unlike any other part of the United States.

Although I attended church regularly, most of my time in a church service was spent goofing off in the back row of our sanctuary with my friends. I was "confirmed" by my church at the age of 12, which was supposed to give an indication that I understood basic Christian theology, but it honestly still wasn't there. Later that year, my oldest brother Tracy, who had been the first of our local extended family to attend a four-year college, helped me understand for the first time that I was a sinner in need of savior, and I became a Christian at that point.

In middle and high school, it became apparent that I would choose a career in math or science and entered North Carolina State University to pursue engineering. I met my wife Windee there,[4] and her solid faith

---

[4] She was not my wife when I met her.

provided a boost for mine. However, as my faith increased, so did my understanding of science, and the two were headed for a collision course. Over the next several years, through graduate school at the University of Illinois at Urbana-Champaign, I wrestled mightily with reconciling modern science (cosmology, evolution, geology, paleontology, neuroscience, etc.) with my (what I now know as a wooden, literal) interpretation of scripture. The doubts produced in me shook my foundation enough that the mental, financial, and spiritual stress of being a husband, student, researcher, and now parent of three had nowhere to rest. I fell into a deep depression for about 18 months, in which *everything* became a challenge, and my faith was hanging on by a thread.

Unknown to me, God was faithful behind the scenes, and he was working in me through my despair. Over those many months, with the help of my wife, friends, and church, three verses kept me going:

*I say to the LORD, "You are my Lord; apart from you I have no good thing."* (Ps 16:2)

*For the LORD your God is a consuming fire, a jealous God.* (Deut 4:24)

*Though he slay me, yet will I hope in him.* (Job 13:15a)

The new perspective I was gaining in meditating on these verses was that nothing can satisfy me apart from God, he is refining me for my own benefit and glory, and thus, whatever he does to me, I will accept. God was forcing me to submit until I was willing to submit.

Eventually emerging from this depression, my worldview had been violently shaken. First, I knew that God alone was responsible for healing my mind. Second, I suddenly had a new understanding of difficulties that others face, as I had previously been a fairly judgmental person. Third, for the first time, I began to understand that all the things I had been striving for in life (family, education, career, money, morality, health, etc.) were worthless in comparison to pursuing and knowing God:

*But whatever were gains to me I now consider loss for the sake of Christ. What is more, I consider everything a loss because of the surpassing worth of knowing Christ Jesus my Lord, for whose sake I have lost all things. I consider them garbage, that I may gain Christ.* (Phil 3:7–8).

This realization led to a further amateur study of theology to get a grasp on what life is all about. Simultaneously, I felt a strong call to minister to the college students at my work and church, because I know that many of them are going through the same types of difficulties that I went through. In retrospect, these difficulties I faced were the best thing that ever happened to me:

*Not only so, but we also glory in our sufferings, because we know that suffering produces perseverance; perseverance, character; and character, hope.* (Rom 5:3–4)

My discussion with Victoria (I call her "Vickie") is a result of those difficulties. In those classes from 2012–2014, she showed herself to be the best student I've ever had. I don't think she liked me as a professor at first, but she continually showed up in my office hours to work on problems I hadn't assigned and aced just about everything I put in front of her. She was extraordinarily bright and ambitious but tempered it all with humility: the kind of student that keeps teachers sane.

After she left Belmont, we kept in touch through letters of recommendation and general friendly conversation about how she was progressing through graduate school. After a couple of years of this, I felt that Vickie and I had grown close enough in friendship to pry into her life a little, so in December 2016, I asked her about her faith, and she responded, "I'm not religious, and I believe in God (but it's a belief I'm not sure I understand). Have you always been Christian, Dr. Robinson?" I then responded with an entire page detailing my beliefs and finished with "Your turn."[5] The next time I heard from Vickie was eight months later. I thought I had offended and/or lost a friend, so I was happy to get her email in August. We exchanged our usual pleasantries with no reference to the previous email. However, I was still curious about what she believed, so in discussing what I was up to, I bluntly asked her the first question you'll read in Chapter 1.

## VICTORIA

I am a second-generation immigrant, born in the United States from parents who escaped Vietnam during the war. My parents are ethnically Chinese, and they hold traditional views from Chinese culture such as honoring one's elders, valuing education, and practicing Buddhism. I inherited some of these beliefs myself, although somewhat diluted due to my surrounding community.

Born and raised in a suburban area of Tennessee, I knew no other Asians outside my family. Without knowing others like me, I unconsciously associated my family's beliefs with Asian culture in general. Likewise, I associated my friends' beliefs with White American Culture. That was how I came to assume that one's religion depended on one's ethnicity and that I was Buddhist "by default." In actuality, even the Buddhist beliefs and practices were not a strong component of my family's lifestyle. This may be due to the lack of Buddhist communities in the area, but that notwithstanding, religion never seemed to have much practicality as my parents worked hard to raise a family of five on a single blue-collar income.

---

[5] I don't recommend this approach.

Given its absence throughout my childhood and formative years, I came to believe that religion was not essential in life. Carving out time to go to a temple or church, not to mention expectations of tithing and service, seemed like a waste of limited resources. I didn't think people with spiritual beliefs were necessarily wrong or uninformed; however, I saw religion as a salve for widespread psychological crutches or emotional weakness. I labeled myself an "agnostic atheist" during my high school and college years, although I was better characterized as religiously apathetic.

My decision to attend Belmont University was orthogonal to its identity as a Christian university. I chose Belmont due to my scholarship, the low student-teacher ratio, and its proximity to home. I didn't mind attending a Christian university; if anything, I figured I would learn something about the beliefs of a majority of the world's population.

College was a transformative time in my life. One area of transformation was developing intellectual curiosity. Before college, I was overly practical in doing what it took to succeed academically and not wasting my time on other subjects. In college, I pursued interests beyond my primary field of study (chemistry) such as sociology, economics, and religion. I started to learn about the history, foundation, and even culture of Christianity, independent of a pressure to convert.

Throughout my learning and exposure to Christian principles and people at Belmont, I remained politely distant whenever the conversation became personal. I respected others having their beliefs, and I expected others to respect my (lack of) belief. Surprisingly, the person who challenged me most during my time at Belmont was not my *Understanding the Bible* professor or friends who started their own Bible study; it was my differential equations professor. He raised the topic when I went to office hours and later gave me a number of books to read and consider. Over the following several months, I read through *Mere Christianity*, *The Case for Christ*, and part of the Gospels. I felt that I gave Christianity a serious consideration, but I wasn't convinced enough to upend my life and take on a completely new lifestyle.

After graduating from Belmont, I moved to Orange County, California, to start my Chemistry PhD at the University of California, Irvine. During the transition, a thought crossed my mind about how leaving the Bible Belt also meant leaving behind any Christian influences. Additionally, although I had long since abandoned my naïve view of correlating ethnicity and religion, I never saw science and Christianity as being wholly compatible. I subconsciously assumed that one would have to compromise scientific integrity to be Christian or vice versa. I was mildly intrigued, then, upon learning that one of my PhD advisors was Christian, but I didn't think much of it beyond my initial surprise.

Throughout graduate school, I kept in touch with Steve (I call him "Dr. Robinson"). He was one of my recommendation letter writers for graduate school and graduate fellowships. This was partly because I never faced so much difficulty in any other class than his two calculus-based physics courses. I worked unbelievably hard to get an A in those classes, and that also meant getting over my worry about bothering him at nearly every available office hour session. I grew to respect him as an educator and a rational thinking scientist throughout my time at Belmont, and also as a friend in the years following.

When Dr. Robinson asked me about my beliefs, I was caught unaware and didn't know how to answer. So, I procrastinated my response to that email, and "later" turned into "never." I felt bad about my lack of response. I just didn't know what to say about being generally nonreligious and not having strong or well-thought-out views one way or the other. My stance at the time was that I had no need for religion, and I didn't see inherent purpose or meaning in life. However, I also believed in personal growth, and I saw self-awareness and open-mindedness as contributors to growth. I was glad when Dr. Robinson followed up on his question despite my prolonged silence. Mentally prepared the second time around, I dove into the conversation. I had no expectations going in, only a receptiveness to new ideas and just enough humility to consider that I could be wrong.

## FORMAT

As our email replies became too large and unwieldy, we quickly moved to typing in an online document. We never intended this conversation to end up in a book, but besides needed (yet relatively rare) clarifications and having to correct our casual grammar, this is the exact conversation we had. Unlike an in-person conversation, we had the ability to discuss many subjects at once. Thus, while there is a generally linear progression of thought from the beginning to the end, you may occasionally find yourself saying, "Didn't they already discuss that?" In those instances, the first mention of a topic may have inspired us to revisit a former topic in a new light. We've done our best to clear up confusion and not turn this into a time-travel book. In addition, we discussed and referenced a number of hyperlinks throughout this conversation, a few of which have since expired. If you wish to pursue any of these references, we respectfully refer you to the Internet Archive (archive.org), which will hopefully have a saved snapshot of the website.

If you've made it this far, you deserve the original email's punchline: ΨΦ. (These are two Greek letters often used in quantum mechanics: psi and phi. Together, they are often pronounced the same as "sci-fi.") Sorry, it gets better from here.

# CHAPTER 1: BEYOND THE NATURAL WORLD

**Steve**: So I started doing ministry at my church with college students, and it's pretty cool, but I have to be sociable, which is really hard for me. What faith or lack thereof do you subscribe to, Vickie?

**Victoria**: I never know how to answer that. I grew up in a household that was Buddhist by name. That means we mostly did the religious things on Chinese New Year and when someone passed. It never meant much to me, and I would've labeled myself to be somewhere between agnostic and atheist when asked. In hindsight, it was more non-religious than anything. I was mildly curious about Christianity while at Belmont, and I remember taking a class there that talked about it from a historical standpoint. I really enjoyed learning about it, though I mostly took it all in from an intellectual, detached point of view. Dr. Biles[1] and I also had some conversations about Christianity, and he gave me a couple of books to read. I liked Lewis' *Mere Christianity*,[2] and logically it seemed sound, but the feeling of detachment was always present. There weren't any specific objections I had; just a lack of emotional investment. This has all led me to believe that there's probably something out there, maybe benevolent, and not really involved.

**Steve**: You should know that I consider you a friend regardless of what you believe or whether you agree with me. I'm really interested in hearing your thoughts on lots of questions I have about faith. I like talking through hard questions with smart people, so would you be willing to have an honest email discussion with me about our beliefs? There is zero chance you could offend me with honest answers and pointed questions since I am an emotionless robot. (It also wouldn't offend me if you thought that was the worst possible thing we could ever do.)

**Victoria**: Thanks, Dr. Robinson! I appreciate the sentiment and your open-mindedness. Yes, I'm definitely interested in starting an email discussion! At the very least, I think it'll reveal insight one way or another. Also, I think your being an "emotionless robot" would probably help, because I find that people are sometimes taken aback by my seemingly-critical-but-really-just-curious questions.

**Steve**: So here go the first questions. You said that you "believe that there's probably something out there, maybe benevolent, and not really involved." 1) What leads you to believe that anything supernatural (probably) exists? [To the reader: the second question begins Chapter 2.]

---

[1] Dr. Daniel Biles, a Belmont University math professor. He's Victoria's former teacher, Steve's friend, and an all-around great guy.

[2] C. S. Lewis, *Mere Christianity* (New York: HarperCollins, 2015).

**Victoria**: The more I learn about science, the more I see the intricate conditions crucial for life to exist; for example, the gravitational constant. It's also remarkable how "nature does it best," such as regarding the strong but light nature of Teflon, modeled after spider silk, or the incredible efficiency and specificity of these tiny molecular machines that we call proteins. We humans spend decades of research to figure out how to understand/build this kind of stuff.

**Steve**: I agree; the universe, life, and consciousness are quite compelling lines of evidence for god(s).

**Victoria**: How compelling do you/others find this? I know for some, that's enough proof for the existence of god(s). For myself, I see this as an inkling, but not to the level that it's wholly compelling.

**Steve**: A) I know of no philosophy or physical theory which allows a thing to create itself. The universe (multiverse?) cannot have created itself, nor could the physical laws from which the universe sprang. (An eternal being would, by definition, never have been "created," and would thus be exempt from such a rule.)

B) Human consciousness does not clearly follow from any known physical law or possible physical law. You don't give conscious properties to the molecules you simulate because they don't have them, and yet we are made from such molecules and have consciousness. Emergence (e.g., water is wet, but a water molecule is not "wet") is an idea I've heard floated around to explain this, but it seems to be a huge stretch to me.

These two things are unquestionably the most compelling arguments for the existence of god(s) in my mind. I would love to hear how those things are not compelling to you, because I can't seem to get around them.

**Victoria**: I don't disagree with your reasoning. Perhaps this ties into the other questions, but the argument from first cause suggests to me that there *existed* this force, perhaps some god or perhaps some non-corporeal thing, that led the universe to form. Does this force still exist? Does it have properties of omniscience, omnipotence, and omnibenevolence? I don't know. Why is emergence a huge stretch for you regarding human consciousness?

**Steve**: You bring up a great question. I'm not sure there's a great argument to be made for the continued existence of god(s), except to say that I cannot imagine a scenario in which it/they would cease to exist. There's certainly no analog to biological death that we could imagine. I would probably put it in the category of "probability by absurdity" (I made that phrase up) in that, if everything we know of only exists because of god(s), it seems unfathomable that such a being could itself cease to exist. I suppose it's possible, but I would put the burden of proof on a skeptic to lead to that conclusion. The ability to create a universe would seem to require omnipotence (at least practical omnipotence), and omnipotence would seem to imply omniscience (i.e., an omnipotent being would have the power to create omniscience, right?). Omnipresence and omnibenevolence are maybe a little harder to assume.

As for emergence, the "wetness of water" follows pretty clearly from hydrogen bonding. So while the whole has an emergent property, it is understandable and reducible to a more fundamental law. How could reducible consciousness be a thing?

**Victoria**: Maybe this is a wild question and in the "probability of absurdity," but if the universe and everything we know only exists because of god(s), could the god(s) simply leave and create other universes completely distinct from ours? This is getting into physics much beyond me. It's interesting that you say, "I would put the burden of proof on a skeptic to lead to that conclusion," because I commonly hear that argument reversed to say that those who believe in god(s) have the burden of proof regarding existence. I can agree with your statement on omnipotence and omniscience. Why can't reducible consciousness be a thing (like something hinted at by this article.[3])?

**Steve**: A) If the creator of space and time can't change because it's outside of time, I don't think it could "leave" because it's also outside of space. But it certainly could've created a multiverse in which ours is one of many. We have absolutely no evidence that such a thing happened, but I'm open to it. The multiverse hypothesis was formulated to explain the extreme fine tuning (e.g., the inflexibility of the cosmological constant[4] to 1 part in $10^{120}$) of our universe for life.[5]

B) I hate brains. Of course we need neurons for consciousness. But neurons themselves do not have this property. No one understands this, so it seems that we have two options. 1) Consciousness and free will are illusions. I don't discount this possibility from any scientific or philosophical position. But for all the people who claim to believe it, I've never seen any live it out. For example, Richard Dawkins spends considerable energy trying to convince me (well, OK, not me personally) that God doesn't exist. If he has no free will in doing so, why should I (or how *could* I) believe his collection of molecules? (Also, "believing" doesn't exist.) And if I have no free will in whether I believe him, why

[3] Bec Crew, "A Giant Neuron Has Been Found Wrapped Around the Entire Circumference of the Brain," *Science Alert*, February 15, 2017, www.sciencealert.com/a-giant-neuron-has-been-found-wrapped-around-the-entire-circumference-of-the-brain. Synopsis: a large neuron in a mouse's brain was discovered that connects so many parts (and thus, functions) of it that it could help explain the origin of consciousness.

[4] "Cosmological constant," *Wikipedia*, en.wikipedia.org/wiki/Cosmological_constant.

[5] Jonathan Borwein and David H. Bailey, "When science and philosophy collide in a 'fine-tuned' universe," *Phys.org*, April 3, 2014, phys.org/news/2014-04-science-philosophy-collide-fine-tuned-universe.html.

should I (or how *could* I) try? (Also, "trying" doesn't exist.) There's no point in protesting white supremacy. There's no point in trying to feed the hungry. There's no point in caring about anything. In this paradigm, things just "are," but literally no one lives like that. Most atheists I know are good people who care deeply about important issues and work hard to make society better (in *their* minds, at least). So, a big reason I don't believe it is because I don't think that anyone in this mindset really believes what they say they believe. (And wow, they could certainly say the same thing about many/most Christians! But many/most is not all, and our failure is a moral one, not a philosophical one.) 2) God somehow uses neurons to impart consciousness to humans (or all animals in some sense). I can't fathom how that could possibly work at all, but it's what I believe because I find the alternative untenable.

**Victoria:** A) That's reasonable regarding the creator not changing because of being outside of space and time. If the creator had the power to create this uni/multiverse, why would fine tuning even be necessary? If the creator is omnipotent and omniscient, it should only take one try, right?

B) 1) There was a thought-provoking article in the Atlantic[6] I read sometime last year on how there's no such thing as free will. I would agree that there is no point in anything if free will doesn't exist. That being said, I wouldn't deny that consciousness and free will don't exist, i.e., that they are indeed illusions. From a practical standpoint, seeing as my actions seem to have a direct consequence, I'll keep living as if I do have some sort of free will. Tangentially, what do you mean that people could say the reverse statement of not believing what they say they believe regarding Christians? Does that mean those people are hypocrites, for lack of a better word? 2) That's a valid option. 3) This doesn't discount emergence then. You said earlier that this seems to be a huge stretch to you. Why is this a huge stretch, and B.2 not a huge stretch?

**Steve:** A) The multiverse argument says that with gazillions of universes coupled with an atheistic or deistic worldview, there are bound to be a few via random chance that sustain life, so it's not a surprise that we exist. So fine tuning does not exist in the multiverse hypothesis, whereas it seems much more likely in a single universe and would indeed take one try from a theistic perspective.

B) 1) So are you saying you don't believe in free will, but you're *choosing* to act as if it existed? Isn't that proof that free will exists? As far as the Christian thing, yes, I do mean that Christians, and everyone probably, is guilty of hypocrisy at some level. (But being a Christian, it's especially convicting to me to point ourselves out.) 3) Emergence of consciousness is a stretch to me in terms of my own personal experience

---

6 Stephen Cave, "There's No Such Thing as Free Will," *The Atlantic*, June 2016, www.theatlantic.com/magazine/archive/2016/06/theres-no-such-thing-as-free-will/480750/.

and human observation; i.e., it *feels* very immaterial. But it's not a stretch to me for any scientific reasons, and I can sympathize with an argument that complexity with feedback begets coherence, so I agree that I can't completely discount it. I suppose B.2 is congruent with other assumptions I've made: namely, that god(s) explain the unexplainable. That's a terrible way to come to faith and do science,[7] but for that issue in particular, I don't feel we have a better option. (As an aside, there are also theists who would argue that we don't really have free will. So, my faith in god(s) doesn't hinge on consciousness; rather, I would say that god(s) provide the best explanation for it.)

**Victoria**: A) So nothing rules out the possibility of a multiverse in an atheistic/deistic worldview? Does that mean the multiverse, theism, and fine tuning don't really go together, either? It seems that based on what you're saying, the possibilities for theism are: universe and theism or multiverse with theism without fine tuning?

B) 1) I wouldn't say I believe in free will with 100% certainty, but I do live my life with the belief in free will with 100% certainty. I don't know if that's proof that free will exists, though. Nothing tells me that I am making this choice completely of my own volition, or rather that it was just part of some deterministic picture in which I muse about free will and then chose to decide that it exists. What happens if/when one commits hypocrisy when it comes to Christianity? What does this mean in the larger picture? Is that "sinful"? 3) Hmm, okay, so it's life context that makes B.2 more reasonable to you than B.3. I suppose that's as far as I can think of to take this particular topic, as I don't see things in that context and therefore find it harder to accept that a reason for the existence of god(s) is to explain the unexplainable. (The aside was worth mentioning, thanks.)

**Steve**: A) I think the impossibility of a multiverse coming into existence without a creator rules out the multiverse/atheistic worldview, but not the multiverse/deistic worldview. The multiverse hypothesis wasn't designed to explain everything, only the existence of our particular universe. The multiverse and fine tuning aren't mutually exclusive, but the fine tuning would happen at the multiverse level instead of the universe level. I don't believe theism is greatly affected by the multiverse hypothesis. I personally have no problem with god(s) creating a multiverse without fine tuning, waiting for life, and then interacting with it. On a side note, the particulars of the physical realm in which we live are not extremely important; rather, I would say that theism/deism arises from a broader question: "Why is there something instead of nothing?"

B) 1) I agree that it is probably impossible to know with certainty that free will exists. With regard to hypocrisy, I wouldn't narrow it down to Christianity; hypocrisy in any worldview is a problem. But if we must,

---

[7] "God of the gaps," *Wikipedia*, en.wikipedia.org/wiki/God_of_the_gaps.

yes, it would be considered sinful in Christianity to make claims that one is a Christian and yet act in a way or believe things that are contrary to what Christianity stands for. For example, the Ku Klux Klan has sometimes claimed to be a Christian organization, but their entire philosophy runs counter to the central claims of Christianity. 3) Fair enough, but a central idea of deism/theism is that god(s) are an explanation for things we believe have no other explanation, so I'm not sure how to avoid it in some capacity once one accepts the idea of a supernatural creator. I don't like brains.

**Victoria**: A) By impossibility, do you mean improbability? So, if deism could be an option, why not that? Is that what the other questions address? I'd agree that the particulars of our physical world are more tangential. It also seems that regarding that broader question, we're on the same page that some supernatural force must exist.

B) 1) That's a very understandable example. What about the finer details? For example, addictions/drug/sex/alcohol? I suppose if someone were living a life in reverence to this greater force and chose to live a "cleaner" life, then sure. Why might this greater power be concerned with such relative minutiae? 3) Certainly. I think this particular topic might be representative of a broader question of how much god(s) explain the unexplainable. Perhaps deism might align more with the emergence side, and theism might align more with the God-imparting-consciousness-via-neurons side. (Maybe you'll like this image.[8]) But on a more serious note, is there more reason to your not liking brains? Or is it just because of this "source of consciousness" stuff?)

**Steve**: A) I suppose I don't have the authority or knowledge to say impossible, so yes, you're probably right. But I've never heard a credible argument for a creatorless uni/multiverse from any angle, so it's at least impossible in my mind. Also, yes, I think the other questions address the deism/theism option better than creation does.

B) 1) The central claim of Christianity is as follows. All people are sinners (even much worse than we think we are), and yet we exist in the presence of a perfectly good God (I'm moving to capital G here) who holds us to his (God is not a male, but this is common Christian parlance to reveal God's relationality) perfect standards because of his very nature. Helpless to meet those standards, God took the form of a man, Jesus, who suffered and died on a cross to take the just punishment for our sins. He then rose from the dead two days later and ascended into heaven. All God asks of Christians is that we believe these things to be true, and then we are effectively made good by his standards. So to your question: Christians are not better moral people than anyone else (and

---

[8] Julie Besonen. "What Awaits in New Haven? Pizza, Yes, and Brains in Jars," *The New York Times*, May 25, 2017, www.nytimes.com/2017/05/ nyregion/what-awaits-in-new-haven-pizza-yes-and-brains-in-jars.html.

are often more immoral people who realize their hopelessness), so if a Christian struggles with addictions/drugs/sex (outside of marriage)/ alcohol (in excess), that certainly would not disqualify him/her from being a Christian in principle (God alone could know whether someone believes what they claim to believe). But since we (attempt to) live morally out of gratitude for what God has done for us, then if someone embraces such a lifestyle, it may be an indication that he/she never believed in the first place. As far as why god(s) would be concerned with the relative minutiae of moral living in humans, I'm not sure any person of any faith has a great answer for that. From a Christian perspective, it is indeed baffling that God would have done what he did through Jesus. We would interpret that as incredible love for his creation and his desire for that creation to enter into relationship with him. (Think about your cat. It has no idea why you love it and take care of it, but you know that you do it out of love, affection, relationality, and kindness. Now multiply that by a gazillion and pretend that you created your cat.) [To the reader: this comment spawned Chapters 5–12, so it will not be directly addressed by Victoria in this chapter. Stay tuned.] 3) I would agree with your deism/theism analysis of the brain. Brains are squishy and gross, so that's 10% of it. But it's 90% "What the heck is going on?"

**Victoria**: A) This is a wild idea, but do you think there's a possibility that the creation of the uni/multiverse could somehow be explained given more information in the far future, and that, until then, that creation concept is what leads many to think there is a creator?

**Steve**: A) Yes, there is that possibility. But the question, "Why is there something instead of nothing?" seems to be outside of what science can or will ever aim to do. In other words, it's a nonscientific question. But science has done a lot, so I can't discount the possibility.

**Victoria**: A) Ah, okay. It's definitely plausible in my mind for science to someday explain creation, but probably not something within the grasp of many lifetimes (if humans survive that long).

# CHAPTER 2: DOING THE RIGHT THING

**Steve**: Is it possible for something to be simultaneously benevolent and uninvolved?

**Victoria**: Hmm, I suppose; why not? According to Merriam-Webster, *benevolent* means "kind and generous; organized to do good things for other people." By that definition, though, I would say "no," something can't be both benevolent and uninvolved. For example, I care about my cat Mia and want good things for her, so that leads me to be involved for making her life better. I suppose something could be *inclined* toward doing good but not necessarily *do* good. In that case, something could be simultaneously benevolent and uninvolved, though this is a moot argument since the connotation of benevolence is predicated upon action. If one had good intentions but never did a thing, I wouldn't think of them as benevolent. This leads me to the question: Could there be a supernatural entity who isn't benevolent? [To the reader: this question starts Chapter 3.]

**Steve**: I agree. It does seem that a benevolent god would necessarily be involved and that we would necessarily see its effects in some way. The fact that goodness seems to exist leads me to believe that a good god also exists.

**Victoria**: Can goodness not exist without a good god?

**Steve**: Human-defined goodness, subject to changes in environment, evolution, technology, society, etc., can most certainly exist. But that kind of goodness appears to simply be pragmatism to me, subject to change at some future point. For true, objective, real goodness to exist, it must again come from something other than the molecules you simulate, because they don't have goodness, either. And the fact that most of us around the world agree on what fundamental goodness is leads me to believe that altruism exists at a level that evolution can't explain; i.e., that we have some common inherent definition of goodness from another source.

**Victoria**: I can't wrap my mind around why the common definition of goodness would necessarily come from another source. Can it not be rationalized? For example, people are good because they grow up learning right from wrong. "Faulty" upbringing by parents or society can lead to lapses in judgment of "good"—however that's even defined. Let's say a boy was brought up by wolves. Would "goodness" within him not be reflective of survival instinct, such as a mutualistic relationship between member and wolf pack?

**Steve**: It's clear that we define good/bad differently in animals than in humans. I would be in prison or a psychiatric hospital if I did what my dog and cat have done. But I think Wolf Boy would probably still have a different definition of good/bad than his wolf friends because he has a wildly different conscience. But perhaps that's pure conjecture, so let me approach this from a different angle. Was the Holocaust bad?

**Victoria**: It does seem like conjecture. Yes, I'd say the Holocaust was bad.

**Steve**: Why?

**Victoria**: I think the motives were ill-conceived, and this led to the destruction of many due to the folly of a few.

**Steve**: Why is destroying people bad?

**Victoria**: Because it exerts an unfair power to end another's everything. Why should some person have power over another person's life or death?

**Steve**: Why is exerting an unfair power over another being a bad thing?

**Victoria**: My answer might be circular, but I think it's bad *because* it's unfair. My life shouldn't be in the power of another person to take away (barring exceptional circumstances). I would be more upset and indignant about dying if someone murdered me compared to if someone accidentally ran me over. In the former case, that person knowingly exerted a power over me that they don't have the right to have. Only I should have that right, though some might say even I shouldn't have that power.

**Steve**: So maybe we're getting somewhere. I would posit that human-defined morality is always 1) circular and 2) relative. In fact, it is pretty evident that the Nazis strongly believed that what they were doing was in the best interest of humanity. So would you say that the Nazis were 1) actually, objectively wrong or 2) just wrong in your opinion, and it was OK for them to have their own opinion?

**Victoria**: Sure, I can believe that human-defined morality is circular and relative. Other topics are too, though. (Borrowing from *Wikipedia*: "The probability for a 'fair' coin is..." "A 'fair' coin is defined by a probability of...) Does that mean these concepts are necessarily externally sourced? To answer your question, I would say half of the second answer. It's my opinion that they're 100% wrong, but I don't think it's valid for them to have their own opinion if they exert their power in such a way. There's no way I can know everything enough to say objectively without a doubt. Is one class of humans better than another? I say no, but how do I really know?

**Steve**: Human language requires us to define things circularly (the dictionary itself is Exhibit A), so I don't discount circular definitions outright. But if the idea of human-based morality is to help us define justice and make hard ethical decisions, it seems contradictory for humans to not see the need for a higher standard. For example, the vast majority of Americans would say that it was right for us to enter World War II and kill Nazis. But if we can't say that Nazis and their ideals needed defeating, why were we killing them? Or more personally, if you went to your car and saw someone slashing your tires, would you report them to the police, or would you say, "Who am I to say that what he's doing is wrong?" I know the answer, so what in your heart makes you demand justice for something for which you have no objective basis? Maybe the guy had a great, justifiable reason in his mind (it's probably someone you taught!). So, I don't see morality as something I can prove to anyone, and I don't claim that there are always black-and-white answers to moral questions. Rather, I view humans as acting in every way as if an objective standard existed (e.g., our entire justice system) but then denying it with their mouths. In other words, I think we know that objective standards exist (for others), but we don't want them to exist (for ourselves). I do think that you really, deep down, believe that one class of humans is not better than another. So, in the face of not being able to prove it to yourself, you should consider why you believe it. And if the answer is something like upbringing, society, evolution, or "it could come back to hurt me," then try to stop believing it since you now know better. I don't think you can. (Yeah, I know: one could claim that's due to a lack of free will.)

**Victoria**: This reminds me a lot of the trolley problem.[1] I would also agree that killing Nazis is bad but may be a "necessary evil" to prevent the potentially greater destruction of much more if their power went unchecked. In the tire-slashing scenario, I would demand justice because it's a harm done to my property. Yes, the guy could have a great, justifiable reason that would lead anyone else in his position to do the same thing. But perhaps the basis of all of these actions is selfishness? They seem to all fit the criteria of everyone looking out for his or her own self-interest, maybe merely for the principles of survival and passing on one's genes.

Regarding whether "objective standards exist," okay, right, I do believe that no single class of humans is better than another. I still can't make the connection as to why this indicates the existence of objective standards. Maybe morality isn't something that can be proven, but then why do I find objective morality hard to believe? I don't know; lack of convincing evidence?

**Steve**: I agree that the basis of human-defined morality is ultimately selfishness, but we all agree that selfishness is immoral! I agree (as mentioned above) that selfish evolutionary forces are huge influences in our behavior, but if that was it, wouldn't we embrace selfishness as the highest standard of morality rather than shunning it? And how does evolution explain someone like Mother Teresa? Why do we think she was good instead of foolish?

As to the last point, we could probably find data that shows small average distinctions between races and/or nationalities (e.g., intelligence, work ethic, athleticism, ideology, economics, crime,

---

[1] "Trolley problem," *Wikipedia*, en.wikipedia.org/wiki/Trolley_problem. Synopsis: Is actively killing one person better than doing nothing and letting several die?

altruism, freedom, etc.).[2,3] In that light, the connection to objective moral standards is that you (and I) believe something to be true (i.e., there is no "best" class of humans) without (or possibly against) evidence. In other words, you and I have an inherent, heartfelt idea about what "not better" means (probably "deserving of equal treatment") that isn't based on any other standard you can think of. That's objective morality.

**Victoria**: Oh, I didn't think about it that way—that the seemingly common thread of selfishness would imply that selfishness was the basis for the highest standard of morality. That sounds pretty absurd. I actually don't know what to think about Mother Teresa. I always associated her with good but then remember seeing articles that depicted her more controversially.[4] Suspending this uncertainty, helping others is interpreted as something that is good. Sacrificing or devoting one's life to help others can even be interpreted as noble. Thinking back to the big picture, acts of goodness may seem to trace their roots back to a selfish nature, but it's generally understood that selfishness itself is bad. Even if selfishness is in human nature (evolutionary forces or whatnot), we dishonor this trait. It wouldn't make much sense to say that people dishonor it in others for their own benefit (but, for argument's sake, why not?), so that may imply that there must be something objective and externally derived as a source of morality.

Regarding the second part of your statement, I had to reread that three times to understand the connection, but it makes sense. Even though evidence might suggest that one class of humans might be better than another, I have an inherent understanding otherwise, suggesting the existence of objective morality. But objective reality can't be person-dependent, as there are people who don't believe the same as I do. Is there some sort of analogous proof by induction to say that objective morality exists, regardless of any one person's particular beliefs?

**Steve**: I only brought up Mother Teresa as an example of someone who clearly did *some* good things against her own earthly best interest and evolutionary instinct. In reality, whether those accusations are true or not, she's undoubtedly as inherently sinful as all of us. I do think that people dishonor selfishness in others for their own benefit. If we have ice cream at my house, my two sons will go to great lengths to point out

---

[2] Kai Chan, "The World's Smartest Countries," *Insead Knowledge*, July 12, 2017, knowledge.insead.edu/leadership-organisations/the-worlds-smartest-countries-6631.

[3] Rachel Dicker, "The 10 Most Athletic Countries in the World," *US News*, February 24, 2016, www.usnews.com/news/best-countries/articles/2016-02-24/the-most-athletic-countries-in-the-world-ranked.

[4] "What's going on with this Mother Teresa being a bad person?" *Reddit*, March 3, 2013, www.reddit.com/r/explainlikeimfive/comments/19m7rc/eli5_whats_going_on_with_this_mother_teresa_being/.

how selfish the other one is in taking too much. Why? Because they want more for themselves. It's obvious for adults to see it in kids, but trickier for us to see it in ourselves. There are certainly people who don't believe that all people are equal, but I think they have to dissuade themselves of the notion of equality or be taught otherwise:

> "No one is born hating another person because of the color of his skin, or his background, or his religion. People must learn to hate, and if they can learn to hate, they can be taught to love, for love comes more naturally to the human heart than its opposite."[5]

(Even still, I'm not sure I fully agree with Mandela's sentiment here. I think the evolutionary instinct to hate and kill and be tribal is very strong and inborn. But I do agree that we also have a moral compass (from God) and that we must actively choose against that compass to begin hating.) I don't think there's a logical proof for objective morality, but the human demand for justice is clear evidence to me that we all think it exists whether we openly admit it or not.

**Victoria**: It's interesting to me that you said, "she's undoubtedly as inherently sinful as all of us." Recalling what we talked about earlier about how a sin is a sin is a sin no matter the degree of severity, does that mean that every single person has the same amount of sinfulness (except for babies, I guess)?

If people dishonor selfishness in others for their own benefit, how does this support the existence of objective morality? One could stand by the statement that all we are motivated by is surviving and passing down our genes. That would explain why we consider selfishness to be bad—because deep down we are *that* selfish. Wouldn't that also explain the human demand for justice, if we as humans ultimately just look out for ourselves and our own kind?

I like that quote from Mandela. To really see if everyone comes with a moral compass for God, one would have to assess how the sense of right and wrong develops with and without societal influences, right? I think we mentioned something along those lines earlier (Wolf Boy), but it seems like an unethical experiment to intentionally carry out.

I did a quick Google search of where our sense of right and wrong come from and came across a fascinating hypothesis by a Harvard biologist that "people are born with a moral grammar wired into their neural circuits by evolution."[6] This guy, Marc Hauser, talks about snap decisions made in life-or-death situations that the conscious mind has

---

[5] Nelson Mandela, *Long Walk to Freedom: The Autobiography of Nelson Mandela* (Boston: Back Bay Books, 1995).
[6] Nicholas Wade, "An Evolutionary Theory of Right and Wrong," *The New York Times*, October 31, 2006, www.nytimes.com/2006/10/31/health/psychology/31book.html.

no time to process. Religion is also mentioned in the sense that this hypothesis suggests that religion isn't the source of the moral code but rather a social enforcer of this instinctive moral behavior. He's not the only one with those theories of innate morality.[7] (Apparently even babies have an innate moral sense?! The latter article also talks about babies having biases of "us" versus "them.") Given what the science may seem to suggest about the existence of innate morality, this could support the view that God provides this moral compass, analogous to the existence of consciousness.

**Steve**: From a human standpoint, of course there are different amounts of sin that each person has committed. From God's standpoint, though, yes, you're right; we all have the same standing before God with regard to our sin. (Clearly, this is not due to God's ignorance, but to the nature of sin from his perspective.) As far as babies, toddlers, and the mentally disabled, the classic Christian response is basically that they are not capable of having chosen or rejected God, and that he most likely responds to them (e.g., if they die early) with mercy and love. But it doesn't surprise me that babies might have an inborn moral compass.

"If people dishonor selfishness in others for their own benefit, how does this support the existence of objective morality?" To selfishly dishonor selfishness is like trying to make sure no one invades your country by destroying it in advance to make it uninvadable or killing someone in advance to make sure they don't murder anyone. It's nonsensical, and you've removed any ability to judge rightly by doing the same thing yourself:

> *"How can you say to your brother, 'Let me take the speck out of your eye,' when all the time there is a plank in your own eye? You hypocrite, first take the plank out of your own eye, and then you will see clearly to remove the speck from your brother's eye."* (Mt 7:4–5)

That standard of judgment then must be external to the situation for it to be valid.

I'm not fundamentally opposed to some level of innate, biological, evolutionary morality, but I do have three general objections: 1) Evolutionary explanations of morality or social behavior are forever untestable. One can literally apply any sort of reasoning as to why early humans evolved socially in the way they did, but it's all conjecture and always will be. This is very different than looking at the evolution of fossils and DNA, which are concrete and measurable. So I take lots of these explanations with a grain of salt. 2) These explanations always start with the implicit assumption that evolution is the only possible

---

[7] Emily Esfahani Smith, "As Babies, We Knew Morality," *The Atlantic*, November 18, 2013, www.theatlantic.com/health/archive/2013/11/as-babies-we-knew-morality/281567/.

explanatory mechanism, and then use evolution to explain the behavior. I understand that science (often unavoidably) works that way, but evolution is a fundamentally quantifiable/physical/chemical/biological phenomenon, and it's being used to explain the unquantifiable/ unphysical domain of the mind and society, thousands/millions of years after the fact. On what basis? 3) Most importantly, these theories start with assumptions about what good and evil are to begin with, and then use evolution to explain them. Where did the researchers get their ideas as to what counts as good/bad? If morality is an entirely natural phenomenon, then A) there can't be good/bad; there can only be what "is," and B) the researchers are implicitly claiming they have transcended their own evolutionary instincts to tell us what is good/ bad. How could they possibly do such a thing? Even if we were to agree that "good" meant something quantifiable like "higher survival rate," we still have no foundation upon which we can say that is a "good" thing; it just "is." So I don't see how morality could possibly be fully explained naturally; there still must be some objective, external source.

**Victoria**: The first part is congruous with my understanding, so no further questions there. On the next part, I don't fully understand your response on selfishly dishonoring selfishness. I see how the three examples you provided are nonsensical and how the concept of dishonoring selfishness for one's own gains *could* sound absurd, but just because it doesn't make sense doesn't mean it couldn't be true. The connection to objective morality is ambiguous to me.

For the last part, good answers! I like point 3 especially. Clarifying a minor detail: when you say that we'd still have no foundation upon which something can be deemed good even if it could be quantified, how is this so? If it could be quantified, can't you say that state A is more or less better than state B? Or, do you mean "no foundation" as in, this line of thinking would mean that goodness is relative, and it can't be relative because ... ?

**Steve**: If we dishonor selfishness in others because of our own selfishness, we end up in a never-ending recursive loop. Let's say I think you are a bad person for not paying taxes because it makes me have to pay more taxes. The problem is that my motivation (saving money for *myself*) is exactly the same as yours! (Why does motivation matter? Suppose I grabbed your arm and made you stab someone to death. Now suppose you decided on your own to make the exact same motion with your arm to stab someone to death. One is prosecutable (for you); one is not. The only difference is motivation.) From a practical/human standpoint, we usually can't judge based on motivation, but only on action, so that's where the loop breaks. We most often prosecute based on the first external action committed and ignore our own selfish motivations for doing so (e.g., I want "bad" people locked up, away from me). (By the way, I think this is completely necessary for a society to exist and believe the Bible agrees at some level.) Not so with God: from his standpoint, my greed 1) is no different than your greed because he sees our motivations and 2) made me commit another sin by judging you while ignoring my own problem. We may be able to flounder along as a society this way (i.e., without any clearly stated objective morality), but it's merely pragmatism. I'm more concerned with what's *actually* right and wrong, not what makes our justice system work. Or to put it another way, the only thing that differentiates me from someone in prison isn't morality, but opportunity. The connection to objective morality is that if we *actually* want to know right from wrong apart from how it selfishly affects us, we have to use some higher standard external to ourselves; otherwise, it's not really morality but pragmatism.

As to your last question, if you decide to quantify morality, you have to decide whether a big number or small number is good (e.g., child abuse rate or donation dollars to charity). There's nothing inherently good or bad about those numbers (e.g., 3.9% or $4 billion), so we have to assign value to them. On what basis do we assign value to anything? We can't start with the assumption that "humans are valuable" and then say that they get to assign value. That's a huge unfounded assumption! So if I want to say that 3.9% is a good or bad number, I need someone to tell me that I am a valuable valuer to begin with. That's God's role.

**Victoria**: I'm not sure I follow on the never-ending recursive loop... Yes, I can see that both motivations of greed end up being the same, but that means we'd both be at the same starting point, not continually referring back to something. I think you're saying that objective morality exists because motivation matters? You said, "The connection to objective morality is that if we actually want to know right from wrong apart from how it selfishly affects us, we have to use some higher standard external to ourselves..." I think the premise of this statement is what I'm questioning. What evidence is there that right vs. wrong *isn't* decided from how it selfishly affects us? For your last part, this seems to be addressing morality from an absolute standpoint, such as if 3.9% is a good or bad number. What if goodness is a relative quantity? For example, let's say you donated $x in one year but donated $x + $100 the next; therefore, the second year was a better year in that regard.

**Steve**: I'm not doing a great job here, but I'll keep trying. If I truly believe that cheating on one's taxes is wrong, I need a standard by which to make that judgment. If that standard is "It ultimately hurts *me* when *you* cheat on *your* taxes," then I have said that my hurt outweighs the hurt that someone else might feel in paying taxes (for any reason ranging from hating the government to needing money to support a starving family). So by acting/thinking in such a way, I have made the implicit assumption that my values/ethics/reasons are more important than others'. But on what basis? We do this with everything in our judicial system and, again, I agree that it must be run that way. For example, we must decide as a society that keeping people alive is a higher value than a murderer's ardent convictions for his actions (as murderers often have). But this alone doesn't make it *right* to prosecute a murderer. It only makes us pragmatic for our own selfish gain. If I want to know whether murdering is *wrong*, I need some other standard: some external objective morality that gives me that information. The problem *is* that we're at the same starting point and that's why we need to continually refer back to something. For example, suppose a company were comprised of only two equal-rank employees. If one wanted to fire the other, they would have no basis to do so unless there were some kind of founding document that outlined fireable offenses: an external objective source that delineates between acceptable and unacceptable behavior. Likewise, on what grounds could I, a selfish human, accuse another selfish human of wrongdoing unless a non-selfish human tells me how to do that? Perhaps a person or society wants to say, "We're going to do whatever we need to do to make people live the longest, healthiest, most educated lives." (That seems to be how our country makes our laws, which are ethical, moral decisions by definition.) OK, fine, but why are those good things? "Well, because of X, Y, and Z." OK, fine, but why are X, Y, and Z good things, etc.? I see the moral argument a lot like I see the creation argument. What created us? "The universe." What created the universe? "God(s)." What created those, etc.? There has to be some Moral Lawgiver in the same way there must be some First Cause *if* one believes that right and wrong actually exist. If one believes that right and wrong do not actually exist, all of this is out the window. But you believe that right and wrong do exist on their own (e.g., treating everyone equally even though they may not be "equal"), so I'm coming at it from that angle. All things being equal, it might seem on the surface that giving $x + $100 is better than giving $x to a charity. But who's to say that the charity you support is "good?" (For example, suppose I wanted to give $x + $100 to the Kim Jong-un Charity that goes straight into his bank account.) Who's to say you shouldn't have given the money to some other cause? Who's to say that "giving" or "money" or "people" are good? If we live in a meaningless world, who's to say that living longer is good? So if one doesn't have a clue what "good" is because there's nothing to tell them, quantitatively ramping it up certainly isn't going to help.

**Victoria**: I think I'm starting to grasp what you're saying. It makes more sense for me to think about this as "one moral reality is not truer than another" rather than "morality is objective," even if they're saying the same thing. Tim Keller's argument against absolute relativism helped me think about this further:

> In his book *A Rumor of Angels* [sociologist Peter L.] Berger recounts how the twentieth century had uncovered "the sociology of knowledge," namely that people believe what they do largely because they are socially conditioned to do so. We like to think that we think for ourselves, but it is not that simple. We think like the

people we most admire and need. Everyone belongs to a community that reinforces the plausibility of some beliefs and discourages others. Berger notes that many have concluded from this fact that, because we are all locked into our historical and cultural locations, it is impossible to judge the rightness or wrongness of competing beliefs.

Berger goes on, however, to point out that absolute relativism can only exist if the relativists exempt themselves from their own razor. If you infer from the social conditionedness of all belief that "no belief can be held as universally true for everyone," that itself is a comprehensive claim about everyone that is the product of social conditions—so it cannot be true, on its own terms. "Relativity relativizes itself," says Berger, so we can't have relativism "all the way down." Our cultural biases make weighing competing truth-claims harder, yes. The social conditionedness of belief is a fact, but it cannot be used to argue that all truth is completely relative or else the very argument refutes itself. Berger concludes that we cannot avoid weighing spiritual and religious claims by hiding behind the cliché that "there's no way to know the Truth." We must still do the hard work of asking: which affirmations about God, human nature, and spiritual reality are true and which are false? We will have to base our life on *some* answer to that question.[8]

I'll have to muse on this further as my understanding is pretty tenuous.

"If one believes that right and wrong do not actually exist, all of this is out the window." A worthwhile mention!

---

[8] Timothy Keller, *The Reason for God: Belief in an Age of Skepticism* (New York: Dutton, 2008), 9–10.

# CHAPTER 3: WHAT GOD IS LIKE

**Victoria**: Could there be a supernatural entity who isn't benevolent?

**Steve**: Assuming you mean "malevolent," yes, because there is clearly badness in the world also. I think we have a few possibilities in that scenario.

A. Good God is not all good and has some bad traits. But that seems really unlikely to me; why wouldn't such a powerful being remove its own bad traits? Or why couldn't Good God simply define everything it did to be good? Perhaps Good God is simply finite and not in absolute control. But that seems to contradict the creation of an insanely huge uni/multiverse and being supernatural in principle.

B. There are two (or more) equal Good and Bad Gods. But how could such a situation exist apart from a higher being creating them each simultaneously? That would bring us back to one god.

C. There are unequal good and bad supernatural beings, one of which created the other. That seems weird, but if the lesser being was created good and then chose to become bad (analogous to the human experience), that would seem possible to me (and is what I believe).

Assuming instead that you mean "indifferent," that is a tenable stance in my mind, but as you mentioned, the intricacy, efficiency, and specificity of creation and life would seem to contradict that as well.

**Victoria**:

A. To the first part, it seems you're saying that there can't be a God who is both good and bad. Regarding why such a powerful being wouldn't remove its own bad traits, is that something human reasoning could question or fathom? Making an attempt to connect to a human level, there are people who have bad traits, know it, and likely even have the power (along with considerable effort) to remove those traits. Why can't the same line of thought be applied? To the latter part, I'd agree that the creation of this world precludes a God with finite power in the same world.

B. Agreed.

C. I don't doubt that is a possibility.

Regarding indifference, maybe the god created while *not* in an indifferent state and then later became indifferent. People's passions fade, and projects die. What if "world creation" was just another project someone lost interest in?

**Steve**:

A. I agree that it is probably impossible for a human to ascribe good/bad traits to a god unless that god has defined good/bad for us. It seems that, absent from some higher source of ethics (impossibly above god), whatever that god was like is how we would define "good." In fact, the etymology of the word "good" is indeed "god."[1] Or in other words, a conflicted god would cease to be a god, whereas it's entirely natural in finite beings like us.

We change because our circumstances and knowledge change. A god who created space and time could not possibly receive any new information by which to change. So in the same way, a god whose fundamental characteristics change could also not be god.

**Victoria**: So you're saying the creator is "good" because that's how good is defined. Features in opposition to that of the creator are defined as "bad." Then it seems like the most straightforward answer to the original question "Could there be a supernatural entity who isn't benevolent?" is "No, because that's how we define benevolence." Am I interpreting that correctly? This relates back to our earlier discussion, but then how do we know this god even has emulable qualities of benevolence at all?[2]

Additionally, why would a conflicted god cease to be a god? Can't a god choose to change characteristics at will? Why do you say that an entity whose fundamental characteristics can change cannot not be a god?

**Steve**:

A. If god/force exists or did exist at some point (which we seem to agree on), then if we claimed to be able to define this god as good/bad/both, we would necessarily be using an ethic higher than or outside of god. By what authority could we do such a thing? Wouldn't that ethic itself necessarily be a higher god/force?

B. Under what circumstances would this god change? If it created time itself (and lives outside of time itself), I don't think the word "change" even makes sense. In other words, if a god could see that it would "change" a billion years from now, wouldn't it have already "changed" in some sense? Or better stated: how could a god who fills an entire timeline at once change at all? It just "is." (In addition, if I believe that a god can't really change, it certainly can't stop existing; i.e., ceasing to exist implies being in time as well.)

---

[1] This is wrong; more precisely, it is correct in letter but not spirit. The Modern English word "good" comes from the Old English word "god," which does not mean "god" in Modern English. Still, the surrounding argument is unaffected.
[2] This question was not fully addressed, but it is certainly true that God has many qualities that cannot be emulated (aseity, immutability, simplicity, etc.). In addition, it is reasonable to believe that God has divine attributes that we cannot comprehend, emulate, or even describe. In this case, however, as with some other adjectives we use to describe God, we say that we can emulate an omnibenevolent God by just removing the *omni*.

**Victoria:**

A. The reasoning behind that makes sense: that there'd have to be some "highest" power from which we could claim thing X as good/bad/both. What if there's nothing to claim about this god, though? As an example, I don't think of gravity as being a force that's good/bath/both. It just is.

B. I can see what you're saying. If this god created and was beyond time itself, change wouldn't really make sense. This might seem silly, but what if the god *wanted* to change, such as trying out a different look or being more sarcastic? Can a god get bored having the same exact identity forever? Maybe I'm over-anthropomorphizing this god. I suppose if there is only "one right answer" for a perfect god (unlike many possible forms and personalities of humans), then any change from that would lead to an imperfect god. So even though this god could change, it wouldn't need or want to. Okay, now I wonder about the omnipotence of this god. The universe is always changing, and entropy is always increasing. Presumably, an omnipotent god is also beyond the laws of thermodynamics, else one could argue again that this god may be constantly changing. Is this god beyond the laws of thermodynamics?

**Steve:**

A. Gravity can do no other than what it does. God, I believe by definition, has a will to do this or that. As soon as a choice is involved, it allows "can" to turn into "should." And if "should" is allowed, a distinction between good and bad naturally follows. What specifically "counts" as good or bad would depend on the definer of good and bad.

B. If god(s) were subject to any physical law, those physical laws would necessarily be higher than god(s) and be gods themselves.

**Victoria:**

A. Hmm, on whatever force caused our uni/multiverse to come about, why isn't it from some "natural" source like gravity? Why must this force have the will to purposefully create?

B. I don't think I follow. If some god(s) were subject to physical law, why would the laws be gods themselves? It's not that the laws are what created the uni/multiverse. Can't they just be the framework within which some god(s) acted? Oh wait, because then that would refute omnipotence, right? What if the god(s) were omnipotent within the framework of the thermodynamic laws?

**Steve:**

A. I think it has to go back to a first cause. First, how could the first physical laws come into being without a will being involved? Second, you and I have already agreed (I think) that some supernatural force exists. A supernatural force can't be a natural force.

B. How could god(s) exist within a framework? That framework would bind god(s) against their (possible) will. And if something can limit a god, isn't that thing necessarily a higher god? Maybe this will help: my definition of a god is that which nothing higher exists, an entity which has total control. I don't see how one could be omnipotent and yet constrained by any physical law just by the definition of omnipotence. Also, thermodynamics exists within space and time, whereas I've made the argument that god(s) exist outside of space and time.

**Victoria:**

A. Agreed regarding that some supernatural force exists, and that it can't be a natural force. Okay, I can see why that would lead to the original discussion this one stemmed from. To summarize, some god(s) exist and have the will to create; thus, there is good and bad. We define "goodness" in the likeness of this/these god(s).

B. "And if something can limit a god, isn't that thing necessarily a higher god?" I was thinking that a god has the power to do stuff, but the framework would not be a god because it doesn't have the will nor the power to do anything other than exist. That's a reasonable argument I can agree with regarding thermodynamics. I suppose the total control part makes sense as well.

**Steve:**

A. Yes!

B. I guess I would ask, "Who made the guidelines?" which takes us back to a first cause. Also, if guidelines don't have power, why should god(s) follow them?

**Victoria:** That's a good point. I suppose they would have to come from somewhere. But does everything require a cause? What was the cause of the god(s)? I would guess the answer is "there isn't and doesn't have to be one," but then why would there need to be a cause for the guidelines? If the guidelines don't have power, the god(s) wouldn't have to follow them. I don't really think of gravity in that way—that it has power over us—but that must be true.

**Steve:** It seems to me that the "everything requires a cause" argument works very well with everything we have experienced and could experience in this uni/multiverse. But 1), I would say that god(s), being outside of this uni/multiverse by definition, would not be subject to such logic, and 2) even if they were, I believe that "everything requires a cause" is limited to those things which have been created or come into existence in time, which by definition, would exclude god(s).

3) If we force it to, the "everything (including God) requires a cause" ends up in infinite causation, which doesn't seem tenable. It's kind of like the solution to the harmonic oscillator potential in Schrödinger's equation, where you have to cut off the infinite sum to avoid nonsense. I'm OK with no cause for the guidelines, but I think we then have to call those guidelines god(s). Gravity is certainly an inescapable guideline

(I'm laughing thinking about defining physics in terms of the Four Fundamental Guidelines of Nature) that has power over us we cannot avoid. But it seems to have no choice in what it does (making it not a god) and be subject to a more fundamental (currently unknown) natural idea (also making it not a god).

**Victoria**: Why is infinite causation not tenable? I can agree with your answer on 1) and 2). I like how you answered 3) because the analogy helped, and the breakdown on why gravity is not a god helped. (I would be amused if you slipped the "Four Fundamental Guidelines of Nature" into one of your lectures.)

**Steve**: "Infinite causation" is an oxymoron because each effect had a beginning, but there is no (even metaphysical) beginning.[3]

---

[3] William Lane Craig, "#248 Infinite Regress and the Leibnizian Cosmological Argument," January 16, 2012, *Reasonable Faith*, www.reasonablefaith.org/writings/question-answer/infinite-regress-and-the-leibnizian-cosmological-argument/.

# CHAPTER 4: BELIEF WITHOUT DIRECT EVIDENCE

**Steve**: I should state here that my faith has never been absolute certainty in anything; I don't feel I can be absolutely certain that I even exist in an objective reality. Rather, my faith is an examination of lines of evidence, determining the most probable, and altering my life to fit within those lines of evidence. I do believe some things to be true without any direct evidence, but those things must be at least congruent with the "lines of evidence" type of faith.

**Victoria**: Regarding certainty, I agree as a general paradigm. I would have a hard time saying anything is completely certain in life, but the things I "know" are just what is most probable. I'm curious as to what you mean by believing some things are true without direct evidence.

**Steve**: An example of believing something without direct evidence would be with regard to some of the doctrines in the Bible. I came to believe the Bible was and is a reliable and cohesive source, but it makes claims about things I have never experienced nor could possibly prove, such as the Trinity, heaven, and hell.

**Victoria**: Would you believe in anything else without direct evidence? I'm trying to think of any scenarios in my life that I would believe deep down inside without direct evidence, but I'm not coming up with anything. It's easier to take things at face value than to be deeply, emotionally convinced.

**Steve**: You and I both strongly believe that we are rational creatures with an ability to parse logical arguments and examine evidence, or we wouldn't be doing this. But you have no direct evidence that such a thing is true; you simply assume it a priori. Scientific research always begins with the assumption that the unknown universe is comprehensible, but we have no direct evidence of that. Neither of us has direct evidence that we even exist, but we seem to go about our day as if that's a given (but maybe that's putting Descartes before the horse).

**Victoria**: What do you mean when you say we don't have direct evidence that we're rational creatures, etc.? Shouldn't it be true based on how we define rational? Perhaps human logic is all wrong—whatever that might mean—but if we consider the basis of human consciousness, don't we have evidence of rationality based on everyday functioning and how we've done what we've done in our lives? About scientific research and our existence, I guess I would agree. (Ha ha on Descartes.)

**Steve**: I agree that our definition of rationality makes us rational via self-fulfilling prophecy. But if free will is an illusion, we can't be any more rational than our constituent molecules, and our perception of rationality would be illusory as well. No one has direct evidence on the truth of a hard-coded behavior vs. God-imparted free will.

**Victoria**: I suppose that's fair to say.

# CHAPTER 5: WHY WE NEED GOD

**Victoria**: You said earlier that we are much worse than we think we are. What do you mean by that? Do we commit sins that we don't know about? Is the magnitude of what we do minimalized in our minds?

**Steve**: I mean that the evil we see happening in the world is the condition of every human heart, and that there's ultimately no difference between hating a Nazi and being a Nazi. I think we most certainly commit sins we don't know about. It could certainly be argued that me typing this sentence right now instead of going to help the homeless guy a few hundred yards from me is direct evidence of my selfishness. While I do believe I could make a viable argument for typing this sentence instead of helping him, the fact that I desperately want to justify it tells me that something is seriously wrong with me.

**Victoria**: Why did God design the human heart with a condition to create evil? Or was this related to "the fall"? I can understand there not being a difference, ultimately, between hating a Nazi and being a Nazi. Both roles involve hate. However, since one involves acting upon the hate in order to harm, shouldn't there be a difference?

About the homeless guy and the topic of knowingly sinning, if we know it's a sin, why would we not choose to act in a way to not sin? And if we do act in a way that defies living "morally out of gratitude for what God has done for us," why is God okay with that?

Connecting back to a previous statement—"since we (attempt to) live morally out of gratitude for what God has done for us, if someone embraces such a lifestyle, it may be an indication that he/she never believed in the first place"—does it mean that purposeful sinners aren't true Christians?

**Steve**: I don't feel certain, but I would lean toward a belief that God created the universe with us in mind and let it form naturally (with maybe a few interactions like the first cell or something, but maybe not) until evolved humans appeared. God revealed himself (in various ways) to us, but we still have those strong evolutionary survival instincts that result in selfish, sinful impulses. But given God's intervention in our minds, we can choose otherwise. In practical terms, there is a difference between hating and harming someone. But ultimately, there's not; I still chose a thing over God, so it's the same sin. I think we sometimes sin knowingly and sometimes unknowingly. For example, my apathy toward and avoidance of the homeless guy would be two sins, but my apathy could make me never think about the homeless guy, so I only knowingly sinned once.

Maybe I can answer all of these questions at once. If one views sin as a thing that God doesn't like because he is using some moral code external to himself and unknown to us, then the arbitrariness of how much sin is allowed, how sorry one has to be, and whether one was intentional about it is overwhelming and debilitating. But if one views sin as simply choosing self over God, it changes the whole idea. Here's an analogy. A surgeon could have two perspectives during surgery: 1) recalling and applying the surgical techniques learned in medical school or 2) saving the patient's life. 1) without 2) is shortsighted and too rigid when things go wrong. 2) is the correct overall perspective, but we would fire a surgeon who claimed he was all about 2) but never did 1); it would reveal his real beliefs better than his words. A good surgeon lives for 2) but uses 1) as a supplement. If he sometimes messes up 1) but is all about 2), the patient might still live depending on factors too numerous to count; only the patient's status would ultimately let us know if it worked out. Now, moral behavior is 1), the worship of God is 2), and the patient is our relationship with God.

**Victoria**: Hmm, regarding why evil exists, your answer is how I've thought about God's level of involvement in general (i.e., not that involved after the world's creation and early times).

To your answer, why would evolutionary survival be at odds with living a "good" life? In your opinion, would it be feasible to have a world in which these evolutionary survival instincts didn't result in selfish, sinful impulses?

Regarding the same sin, so a person who hates and another person who acts upon their hate would pay the same price? I suppose that's a vaguely similar concept to the farmer passage[1] of people getting the same thing working different amounts of time.

Hmm, this is really reshaping the way I've interpreted sin. I like the surgeon analogy; it's relatable and understandable. What does it mean for a person to knowingly sin? Or, let's say the surgeon always did one particular operation incorrectly. The surgeon still has a strong guiding principle of saving people's lives, but every time someone comes his way and needs $x$ done, he botches it (non-fatally). He doesn't want to avoid situations of having to do $x$ (maybe he needs the numbers or wants the money). He knows he's wrong, and knows what he should do, but never brings himself to do it correctly. Can he still be considered a good surgeon?

**Steve**: I don't know of any modern society that defines "good" as ripping someone's body to shreds and eating it, but that seems pretty consistent with evolutionary survival. In fact, it seems that society and justice have evolved (no pun intended) by fighting against evolutionary instincts. But when Donald Trump and Kim Jong-un figuratively beat their chests and bare their teeth, we're just back to being our normal chimp selves again.

As far as all sins being equal, the Bible does seem to indicate this to be the case:

---

[1] Mt 20:1–16.

*"You have heard that it was said to the people long ago, 'You shall not murder, and anyone who murders will be subject to judgment.' But I tell you that anyone who is angry with a brother or sister will be subject to judgment. Again, anyone who says to a brother or sister, 'Raca,' is answerable to the court. And anyone who says, 'You fool!' will be in danger of the fire of hell."* (Mt 5:21–22)

*"You have heard that it was said, 'You shall not commit adultery.' But I tell you that anyone who looks at a woman lustfully has already committed adultery with her in his heart."* (Mt 5:27–28)

As for the surgeon analogy, I believe the surgeon would be fired and/or imprisoned for that type of behavior, whether he knew what he was doing or not; it's malpractice either way. It's because of this that the Bible doesn't allow any person to claim goodness:

*As it is written: "There is no one righteous, not even one; there is no one who understands; there is no one who seeks God. All have turned away, they have together become worthless; there is no one who does good, not even one."* (Rom 3:10–12)

**Victoria**: To phrase my question better, why do we have a world in which evolutionary instinct *is* fundamentally at odds with moral behavior? Not to question God or anything, but why couldn't survival of the fittest involve an underlying theme of being good instead of being selfish?

Regarding Mt 5:21–22, it just says "subject to judgment." But it doesn't say the level of judgment. Would they all suffer the fire of hell, but at varying degrees of the fire of hell? Mt 5:27–28 might imply otherwise for the example of lust/adultery, but why would that be so? That doesn't seem like balanced punishment. Remembering that sin is favoring something else over God, I guess things do become more black-and-white. Is it all just black and white?

On Rom 3:10–12, jeez, that sounds extraordinarily bleak. If no one can claim goodness, why even try? I suppose that might be more of a rhetorical question in light of everything we've discussed. So one should try to be righteous, understand/seek God, and do good to live in honor of an infinite God versus being swayed by the finitude of everything else.

Also, in the surgeon analogy, does that mean anyone who sins knowingly is going to hell?

**Steve**: Hmm, I've never thought about your first question before. I guess I would answer that it's the second law of thermodynamics,[2] which governs just about everything in the universe (including the mutations

---

[2] The second law of thermodynamics states that systems left to themselves will become more disordered over time.

necessary for natural selection). The universe tends toward disorder and chaos, while morality is, in a sense, "putting things back in order." It takes physical and mental energy for me to do *anything*, let alone be moral. I can't conceive of a universe in which things tended toward order while remaining even remotely similar to the one we live in. When considering God's apparent decision to let us choose him instead of being forced to follow him, Christians would say that God could've created things differently but chose the *best overall* possible universe.

Regarding "levels of judgment," the Bible tries to create a pretty clear dichotomy: one's life was either about God or it was not. When one dies, that choice continues eternally. In other words, those who wished their lives to be about God will continue to have their lives be about God forever. Those who wished their lives to be about themselves will continue to have their lives be about themselves. (C. S. Lewis makes a good argument[3] that hell is not literal fire and all that, but a separation from God that is hellish in the same way that this world with its North Koreas and famines and hatred is hellish: i.e., that it is a continuation of the self-centered lives we currently choose to live.)

Yes, Romans presents a very bleak perspective. The intention isn't to induce debilitating guilt, but to cause us to turn to God as our only hope. It's like this: suppose I fell off a boat and began drowning while sharks circled around me. You're on the boat and scream, "You're going to die! Take this life preserver!" and I respond, "Well, that's an awfully bleak perspective you have there, Vickie," instead of taking the life preserver.

The good news related to your last question is this:

> *"I give them eternal life, and they shall never perish; no one will snatch them out of my hand."* (Jn 10:28)

In other words, if we cannot come to God because of our goodness,

> *For it is by grace you have been saved, through faith—and this is not from yourselves, it is the gift of God—not by works, so that no one can boast.* (Eph 2:8–9)

then we also cannot lose him because of our badness. I still knowingly sin, and I can't imagine anyone being immune to such behavior. So I would say that continual, sinful rebellion without repentance is more a *sign* of a lack of a relationship with God than a *prohibitor* of a relationship with God. But it's never a human's job to say that any particular person is going to heaven or hell; there's just no way we could know about anyone but ourselves.

---

[3] C. S. Lewis, *The Great Divorce* (New York: HarperOne, 2015).

Regarding the surgeon, I do think he should be fired, but that's the beauty of Christianity: we stand "fired" (i.e., condemned), but God has extended an offer of mercy to us.

**Victoria**: That sounds … sound. A universe that tended toward order might even be self-destructive. I could imagine that if everyone were inherently moral and self-sacrificing, that could lead to self-erosion of the human race.

Regarding dichotomy, that's interesting. It contrasts with everything in life being a continuum. From the C. S. Lewis comment on hell being a continuation of the self-centered lives we live, I thought hell was supposed to be worse than our lives now?

Ha ha, that shark scenario. I get what you're trying to explain in that analogy, but that's a case in which there exists hope; the life preserver is presumably within reach and is graspable. The Romans bit doesn't seem to allow any hope at all, saying that no person at all does good. Hmm, let me try another interpretation. All living humans are in the water surrounded by sharks. The sharks are everything that might distract one from living a life of goodness. The end of the story can be being eaten by sharks or getting in the boat, but both scenarios involve fully conscious, non-dead humans, because presumably humans do face the effects of the afterlife (though that's something I'm still not sure about).

On the last part on knowingly sinning, I haven't heard that explanation before, at least in this context. It seems contradictory to think about, that sinning puts one further away from God, yet most people (all people?) knowingly sin. If I understand correctly, you're saying that sin prohibits a relationship with God, and continual, sinful rebellion without repentance means there isn't a relationship with God at all. Going further, even though both are bad, the former can still be with God in the end because of God's mercy, and without this no one even has a chance of making it (connecting it to the shark scenario). I think I can kind of understand this, but it also still feels contradictory, since many people can sin less if they really tried, right (like helping homeless people)?

Trying to visualize this, I imagine this super-tall clear cylinder with green liquid inside or something. The ones with "continual, sinful rebellion" have no liquid inside their cylinders. A higher level of green fluid signifies a stronger relationship with God. The cylinder is constantly draining though, so one has to actively maintain fluid levels by … doing good things or something. Doing something sinful knowingly can cause a sharp increase in drainage. (Wait, that implies that sins add up. Do they?) Even doing nothing, or living neutrally, causes the cylinder to drain (representing secular lifestyles?). Maybe a bad visual analogy, but what do you think?

**Steve**: I'll try to be as succinct as possible in an attempt to answer all of these questions at once.

1. We are all hopeless sinners at the core. On the outside, we may look good or bad for a time and may sin more or less at certain points of time, but that's inconsequential. Trying to "not sin" is like putting duct tape on the Titanic. No one can live a life of "goodness." No one gives God his "due."

2. God, being perfect/holy, is incompatible with sin. So all of our sin, whether it is intentional, unintentional, a lot, or a little (it would be difficult to clearly define any of those), severs/hurts our (potential) relationship with him (mainly because the act of sin is a statement of the unworthiness of God).

3. God, being relational and the definition of love, wants to have a relationship with us, his creation.

4. God, being just, demands punishment for sin.

5. God, being love (again), decided to take that punishment himself. Jesus came to earth to die on a cross and give us a clear, tangible picture of the seriousness of our sin and the seriousness of his love.

6. Our job is not to become better moral people. We cannot and will not because it is too ingrained in everything we do. Instead, all we do is believe 1–5 as truth. To not do so is to continue to reject God's offer of love and mercy.

7. God invites those who accept his offer of love and mercy to live with him forever; first, they can now enter his presence because their sins are forgiven; second, they have already indicated that they *want* to live with God forever (heaven). For those who choose to rely on their own goodness, God allows them to continue their delusion (hell). Yes, hell is worse than our situation on Earth because God will have withdrawn from those in hell because of their own wish to have nothing to do with him.

It seems to me that you're (understandably) stuck on the sin issue. Life is most certainly a continuum as you mentioned, but from the Christian point-of-view, it's never about how sinful one is, but whether one has chosen to accept God's way or one's own way (i.e., are we gods or are we God's?), making it fairly black-and-white. We believe that Hitler could end up in heaven and Mother Teresa could end up in hell if they ultimately and genuinely decided to accept God's mercy or not before they died. Only God could or would know such a thing. So no, I would not use an analogy of a "cylinder of righteousness" (I'm probably the first person to ever use that phrase) that moves up and down based on our actions. Rather, the cylinder is either bone dry or completely filled up based on our belief alone.

**Victoria**: That's odd to me that even the least sinful person in this world (who's capable and conscious of sinning) is still doomed as a sinner. We've discussed this from many angles, but *why* is it a dichotomy? (Once again, not to question God, but it doesn't make sense to me.) Why *shouldn't* the person who lives a more selfless life than another be favored more in the end? The flow of the logic in that list (especially 3–6) reminds me of unconditional parental love. It's definitely not at that level, but like with the interaction of any two individuals, if person A does an act of service for person B, A would typically want that to be acknowledged and appreciated. Hmm, that again makes it sound like God has an ego, but I suppose your earlier answer of how God may be the only thing worth our focus/attention/love/worship applies here, too.

I don't get what heaven would be if Hitler were there. Would that mean he is a good person from then on?

**Steve**: Through a Christian filter, your first sentence sounds like, "It's odd to me that a lightly poisoned drink still kills you." The point isn't how much poison there is, but that's it poisoned. That being said, heaven and hell are apparently not devoid of degrees,

> *"For the Son of Man is going to come in his Father's glory with his angels, and then he will reward each person according to what they have done."* (Mt 16:27)

> *But because of your stubbornness and your unrepentant heart, you are storing up wrath against yourself for the day of God's wrath, when his righteous judgment will be revealed. God "will repay each person according to what they have done."* (Rom 2:5–6)

so it's not a complete dichotomy in every sense, and it does appear that the Bible agrees with you that the person who lives a more selfless life will be favored. But the Bible is also clear that there is a heaven and a hell, so that's where the dichotomy arises. I assume you agree that someone cannot be partially licensed, married, graduated, or pregnant? Those are examples of dichotomies we live with daily, even though there are varying degrees of completeness in each one. If one thinks that one can earn his/her way into heaven or hell by being a good or bad person, your view makes complete and total sense. But that's the exact opposite of the Christian view. We didn't earn anything; we simply either believe or do not believe: hence the dichotomy.

I don't see it as God needing or wanting me to worship him, but rather that God wants me to recognize the truth. Do you think it's in Mia's best interest to know the truth of who takes care of her (because that almost certainly helps her survive), or are you an egomaniac craving attention?

No one is good but God:

> *"Why do you call me good?" Jesus answered. "No one is good—except God alone."* (Lk 18:19)

I do believe that there is no more sin in heaven, and sure, we could be called "good" in that context. But that "goodness" will always be derived from God, like a reflection instead of a source. So, yeah, Heaven Hitler (I feel uncomfortable typing that phrase) would be "good" in one sense, but it would have nothing to do with him.

**Victoria:** That's a good explanation. They seemed like separate things at first (dichotomy vs. gradation in the Christian view), but now I see how they fit together.

On Mia, wow, that's a timely comment. A week ago, I was going to take her outside (since she loves to explore but is an indoor cat), and she managed to jump out of my arms and under the apartment building. I crouched there for three frustrating hours trying to coax her out, and I remember thinking, "Why can't I just reason with a cat?! I'm trying to *provide* her the shelter that she's seeking by being under the apartment." So, right, I can see why God wants people to recognize the truth for their own good.

Okay, Lk 18:19 doesn't make sense to me. You believe that Jesus is God in a sense, so why does it sound like he's refuting the original idea of being called good? That aside, the rest of your answer reminds me of Plato's theory of Forms.[4]

**Steve:** Regarding Lk 18:19, Jesus uses the Socratic method of teaching a lot.[5] In this case, he seems to be 1) questioning the asker's assumptions of who or what is good and bad and 2) continuing to assert that people need to decide whether they believe he is God:

> When Jesus came to the region of Caesarea Philippi, he asked his disciples, "Who do people say the Son of Man is?" They replied, "Some say John the Baptist; others say Elijah; and still others, Jeremiah or one of the prophets." "But what about you?" he asked. "Who do you say I am?" Simon Peter answered, "You are the Messiah, the Son of the living God." Jesus replied, "Blessed are you, Simon son of Jonah, for this was not revealed to you by flesh and blood, but by my Father in heaven." (Mt 16:13–17)

I agree with your suggestion regarding Plato, but that God is the ultimate Form.

**Victoria:** Oh, okay. I like that approach.

---

[4] "Plato," *Internet Encyclopedia of Philosophy*, www.iep.utm.edu/plato/#SH6b. Synopsis: Ultimate reality is not found in the physical world, but in a spiritual Realm of Ideas. Forms (e.g., numbers, shapes, the "perfect" chair) are ideal concepts within that realm.

[5] "135 Questions Jesus Asked," *Monday Morning Review*, May 14, 2010, mondaymorningreview.wordpress.com/2010/05/14/137questionsjesusasked/.

# CHAPTER 6: GOD AS A PERSONAL GOD

**Victoria**: Your statement that "God is not a male" leads me to wonder: what nouns would you use to define God? The typical description that I hear mostly involves adjectives prefixed by "omni." The noun that comes to mind is "creator." Is God a "being?" "Form?" "Force?" I suppose there's the idea of the Trinity. What exactly is the "Father?"

**Steve**: Christians consider God to be a being because of his personhood (like an individual with a will.) But we have no idea what God "is." We have no idea what the Trinity "is" either, but the Father is the person of the Trinity described in the Bible as God before Jesus came (i.e., the Old Testament). He wasn't called Father a lot then (it was usually "God" or "Lord"), but when Jesus came and said he was the Son of God and appeared to speak to someone else who wasn't exactly himself, we call that person "Father." Gosh, this must sound weird to non-Christians.

**Victoria**: Okay, so God is a being. An individual with a will. A tangible, concrete being? Who has human-like characteristics, assuming man was modeled after God? Each of the Father, Son, and Holy Spirit, and the concept of the Trinity are all confounding to me. I don't understand what it means. The form of Jesus is probably the most understandable because I'm a person. But even he had superhuman powers.

**Steve**: No, not tangible and concrete:

> "God is spirit, and his worshipers must worship in the Spirit and in truth." (Jn 4:24)

But Jesus was tangible and concrete:

> For this reason he had to be made like them, fully human in every way, in order that he might become a merciful and faithful high priest in service to God, and that he might make atonement for the sins of the people. (Heb 2:17)

Yes, God has human-like characteristics (although I would be much more comfortable saying that we have God-like characteristics). Don't believe anyone who says they understand the Trinity; they're lying. But it *is* supported by the Bible and seems consistent with God's interpersonal nature (i.e., how could an eternal unitarian god have an interpersonal nature?). Honestly, I don't *like* the concept, and if I didn't greatly esteem the Bible, I would probably try to find a way to reject it outright. (But that would probably be because I don't like not understanding things, so it would be more an indication of my pride than any real argument I have against it.) So I believe it in spite of my misgivings.

**Victoria**: Umm, okay so Jesus is the only tangible, concrete being of the Trinity? What's the difference between the Father and the Spirit? I don't understand what this statement means: "How could an eternal unitarian god have an interpersonal nature?"

**Steve**: Ha ha, I love how you started with "Umm, okay..." It's weird, I know. So we believe that Jesus died, rose from the dead two days later (the "resurrection:" that's Easter) and then ascended into heaven 40 days later. He was certainly tangible and concrete then, but could I give him a high-five now and it would make a high-five sound? Well, we believe that Jesus' resurrection body was a glimpse of what we'll have in heaven one day (actual bodies that are still tangible and concrete), and that he probably still has a tangible and concrete body as well. But the Bible is honestly a little vague on the details of heaven and the afterlife, so it's hard for me to feel certain. We usually think of the Trinity by assigning different roles. The Father is generally thought of as the creator in the Old Testament, the one who personally led the Israelites around, and the giver of the Old Testament laws. The Father required punishment for sin (like our justice system does), but in the form of the sacrifice of an animal in a temple. So the Old Testament Jewish mentality was sin/repent/sacrifice/repeat until you die. With that mentality, the more closely you follow the laws, the better your standing with God. Then the Father sent his Son, Jesus, to actually be the sacrifice for our sins once and for all. Those who rely on that sacrifice to be their righteousness (i.e., Christians) have the Holy Spirit living inside them (scientifically, I have no idea what that means) to guide them in their thoughts, behavior, and understanding of scripture. Are there three Gods? Definitely not. Is it just semantics when we distinguish between the three? Maybe it is, but the Bible leans away from that interpretation; i.e., there really is some distinguishability between the three, but no one really knows what that means.

As to your last question, a "unitarian" god (as opposed to a "trinitarian" god) would be one in which there is absolute "oneness" of being. For example, in Islam, there is one God, Allah, and to say that anyone else (e.g., Jesus) could also be God is the height of blasphemy. So if we claimed that an eternal unitarian god was by nature relational, with whom did he relate for eternity past? That would seem to negate his relational qualities. A trinitarian god seems to solve that problem, but not in any way that makes it comprehensible to us.

**Victoria**: The Jesus part of the Trinity sounds magical but not unreasonable in context. (Diverging question: What evidence is there for an afterlife?) Does that mean the Father existed before the Son? And the Son came about before/around the time of the Holy Spirit? I think maybe these questions don't make sense, since God is infinite and should have always existed, so all God-related components should have always existed. Then what were the Son and Holy Spirit up to before being sent down? Oh, thinking about this in context of other answers, the Father + Son +

Holy Spirit was loving and being relational within himself. The meaning of that last statement is what you referred to as being incomprehensible to us? (Another diverging question: what do they do now? Is their work to help/guide/be relational to humans? Do non-humans believe in God? Or is faith tied to "intelligence"? Is the Holy Spirit found elsewhere other than living in Christians?) Summarizing a bit of what you said, there are not three Gods, but there also isn't one. It's a mix between the two statements of one God having three facets? This goes back to the statement of "three 'whos' and one what." [To the reader: Victoria is referring a discussion in Chapter 12: earlier in time, later in the book.] So if I understand correctly, God can't be only one "who" because 1) he has a relationship based on love for us (i.e., that he is relational), and 2) his being eternal means that he is relational always, but it wouldn't be possible to be eternally relational if there was only one who. Is that right? On the human-scale, can a person not relate to himself?

**Steve**: There's absolutely no evidence of the afterlife apart from what the Bible says (either through eyewitness accounts or teaching). Some people claim to have, say during an operation, died and gone to heaven or hell and come back to tell us what it's like. But people say a lot of things; I'm ambivalent to those "near-death experiences" outside of the Bible.

The Father/Son/Holy Spirit have always existed together:

*In the beginning was the Word, and the Word was with God, and the Word was God. He was with God in the beginning. Through him all things were made; without him nothing was made that has been made.* (Jn 1:1–3)

*The Word became flesh and made his dwelling among us. We have seen his glory, the glory of the one and only Son, who came from the Father, full of grace and truth.* (Jn 1:14)

The actual thirty-some years that Jesus lived as a man on earth were a small microcosm of his bigger, eternal perspective:

*The Son is the image of the invisible God, the firstborn over all creation. For in him all things were created: things in heaven and on earth, visible and invisible, whether thrones or powers or rulers or authorities; all things have been created through him and for him. He is before all things, and in him all things hold together. And he is the head of the body, the church; he is the beginning and the firstborn from among the dead, so that in everything he might have the supremacy. For God was pleased to have all his fullness dwell in him, and through him to reconcile to himself all things, whether things on earth or things in heaven, by making peace through his blood, shed on the cross.* (Col 1:15–20)

*All inhabitants of the earth will worship the beast—all whose names have not been written in the Lamb's book of life, the Lamb who was slain from the creation of the world.* (Rev 13:8)

(The latter one is a reference to the idea that Jesus' death on a cross was not so much focused in one instant of time and space, but that it (figuratively) spans all of time. This means that those who followed God before man-Jesus was around were restored in the same way as those who follow God after man-Jesus was around; i.e., the animal sacrifices were also a microcosm.) The Holy Spirit shows up in the Old Testament in places like these:

*"The Spirit of the LORD spoke through me; his word was on my tongue."* (2 Sam 23:2)

*Then the Spirit of the LORD came on Gideon, and he blew a trumpet, summoning the Abiezrites to follow him.* (Judg 6:34)

Granted, the theology wasn't developed at that point to distinguish between the Father and the Spirit, so Jews, like Muslims, still believe in the oneness of God.

The incomprehensibility I referred to is the idea that three things can be one thing. I just don't get it. But yes, the Trinity still works now. The Spirit does stuff like this:

*"But very truly I tell you, it is for your good that I am going away. Unless I go away, the Advocate will not come to you; but if I go, I will send him to you. When he comes, he will prove the world to be in the wrong about sin and righteousness and judgment:"* (Jn 16:7–8)

The Son does stuff like this:

*Who then is the one who condemns? No one. Christ Jesus who died—more than that, who was raised to life—is at the right hand of God and is also interceding for us.* (Rom 8:34)

The Father does stuff like this:

*"No one can come to me unless the Father who sent me draws them, and I will raise them up at the last day."* (Jn 6:44)

The Bible (and science) is completely silent on whether non-humans "believe" anything, so the silence itself would lead me to say "no." It does say that nature praises God,

*When he came near the place where the road goes down the Mount of Olives, the whole crowd of disciples began joyfully to praise God in loud voices for all the miracles they had seen: "Blessed is the king who comes in the name of the Lord!" "Peace in heaven and glory in the highest!" Some of the Pharisees in the crowd said to Jesus, "Teacher, rebuke your disciples!" "I tell you," he replied, "if they keep quiet, the stones will cry out." (Lk 19:37–40)*

but I'm assuming that's passive and not active (e.g., the complexity of the laws of nature holding a stone together reveal a creator deserving of worship).

The Bible says that the Holy Spirit lives inside of Christians:

*And I will ask the Father, and he will give you another advocate to help you and be with you forever—the Spirit of truth. The world cannot accept him, because it neither sees him nor knows him. But you know him, for he lives with you and will be in you. (Jn 14:16–17)*

But it also says that we only come to God by his calling,

*You did not choose me, but I chose you and appointed you so that you might go and bear fruit—fruit that will last—and so that whatever you ask in my name the Father will give you. (Jn 15:16)*

not by our own effort; so, at some level, God must involve himself in some way with non-believers.

On your second-to-last question regarding relationality: yes!

On your last question: Yes, a human can relate to himself (and the other persons of the Trinity are also "himself!"), but I suppose you're asking why God couldn't be "one" and still relational. I think the answer is that we're conflating the interpersonal meanings of relate, which could either be 1) to have a relationship or 2) to understand. I think I'm using the former sense and you're using the latter. With mine, no, I don't think a human can relate to himself.

**Victoria**: If there is no evidence for an afterlife apart from what the Bible says, how can people conjecture what it's like? You mentioned previously that C. S. Lewis makes a comment that hell isn't about literal fire, though that seems to be the most common depiction of hell. Also, the Bible speaks in metaphors sometimes, right? Then it would be harder to get a sense of what might be after death. That brings up another thing I don't get—all the ways that the Bible can be translated. [To the reader: this comment begins Chapter 7.]

You say that all three members of the Trinity have always existed together, but I don't understand how Jn 1:1–3 makes that same point—what's "the Word?" If the Word was with God, what does it mean for the

Word to also be God? It sounds as odd as me saying, "Dr. Robinson is with Dr. Robinson."

On Col 1:15–20, the idea of the Son as the image of the invisible God makes sense. Regarding the three entities of the single God, no one entity has hierarchy over the others, right? If this is true, why is there this nomenclature of "Father" and "Son," which does denote hierarchy?

I'm glad you added the explanation on Rev 13:8 because I certainly didn't make that connection. This relates back to my question on interpretation earlier in this reply—how can you get that understanding from the line in the Bible itself (either specifically this one, or more generally speaking)? "Will worship the beast"—what does that mean? What's the beast?

"The theology wasn't developed at that point"—doing a bit of history searching, it seems that the concept of the Trinity was never explicitly laid out in the Bible, but it gives strong implications to these three parts. How do we know it's three, then? If someone were to comb through the Bible with the preconceived idea that there's two, four, five, or *N* distinct entities of God, wouldn't it be easy to show that the Bible implies such?

On the section that the Trinity is still active now: 1) I don't understand Jn 16:7–8. I tried reading it in context, but it didn't clear up much. "Unless I go away, the Advocate will not come to you" seems to imply that the Father is not present, but then the Son will come? What part of this is the Spirit? 2) On Rom 8:34: same question as earlier on the hierarchy of the Trinity. 3) On Jn 6:44, your reference was, "The Father does stuff like this," but what exactly is the Father doing? Drawing people? Is Jesus the one raising them up? I like the concept behind "the Spirit/Son/Father does stuff like this." Could you provide additional examples? I don't quite understand the ones here.

On Jn 15:16, that's fascinating. So then God doesn't call to everyone? Why do some get chosen? Does this go back to living lives that uphold and honor God? Well, I guess that's not true by default if we're talking about non-believers who are called to God. This is weird to think about. [To the reader: This comment starts Chapter 8.]

That aside, I can understand your stance on what it means to relate; I suppose if God is omni*, it would make more sense to have distinct (but also the same?) other parts to relate to.

**Steve**: The idea of the fire of hell does seem metaphorical to me for a few reasons. First, the word Jesus often used that we translate as "hell" in the New Testament actually refers to a place near Jerusalem where lots of fire-related things happened.[1] Second, from a scientific perspective, what is the source of this combustion, and does it continually require our nerve endings to hurt, and what happens to our skin after being burnt, etc. It just doesn't seem to make sense in a literal way. Third,

---

[1] "Gehenna," *Wikipedia*, en.wikipedia.org/wiki/Gehenna.

God's character is not portrayed in the Bible as going out of his way to hurt people for fun, so C. S. Lewis' interpretation rings a little truer to me. But to your first question, I don't know how anyone could have any clue what the afterlife is like apart from some divinely-inspired religious text, but I think we can infer from God's character what heaven must be like (it's all about him) and what hell must be like (it has nothing to do with him).

Jn 1:1–3 is coupled with Jn 1:14, which explains that Jesus is the Word. So the writer of those verses is effectively saying to the reader, "Hey, do you remember that man named Jesus who caused a big controversy and was killed? Well, he was God from the beginning."

The "Father" and "Son" and "Spirit" labels were really codified by Jesus himself, so that's why we use them. While he was on Earth as a man, he voluntarily gave up some of his majesty and lowered himself to obey the Father's will. For example, at one point he says that he doesn't want to die but will do so if the Father wills it:

> "Father, if you are willing, take this cup from me; yet not my will, but yours be done." (Lk 22:42)

So I view it not necessarily as a hierarchy, but as a practical way to label something otherwise incomprehensible.

The book of Revelation is the last book in the Bible. It details the end of the world, but some think it was, in large part, predicting a near future for the Christians living in the Roman Empire around 100 AD. Some believe that perhaps it is a double prophecy for both, because it's kind of vague. It is absolutely full of metaphors and graphic imagery. So the "beast" is some kind of evil force/empire/person who opposes God. The book of Revelation has one basic message: God wins and evil is destroyed in the end. Everything else is up for debate and interpretation.

You're correct that the Bible never says, "So here's the Trinity..." But there are lots of places where the implication seems to be pretty clear:

> and the Holy Spirit descended on him in bodily form like a dove. And a voice came from heaven: "You are my Son, whom I love; with you I am well pleased." (Lk 3:22)

> When the Advocate comes, whom I will send to you from the Father— the Spirit of truth who goes out from the Father—he will testify about me. (Jn 15:26)

> who have been chosen according to the foreknowledge of God the Father, through the sanctifying work of the Spirit, to be obedient to Jesus Christ and sprinkled with his blood: Grace and peace be yours in abundance. (1 Pet 1:2)

*Therefore go and make disciples of all nations, baptizing them in the name of the Father and of the Son and of the Holy Spirit,* (Mt 28:19)

I've never heard anyone suggest that there could be $N > 3$ parts of the God, so I love that question! I agree that one could cherry-pick verses throughout the Bible to show different sides of God to make $N$ any number, but 1) that doesn't seem to be the consistent conclusion of the Bible (especially the New Testament) when read as a whole and 2) at no time has any part of Judaism ($N = 1$) or Christianity ($N = 3$) ever believed such a thing. It seems God would've revealed some truth to us in that regard if it were important, so Christians are sticking with three. Or in other words, the silence of the New Testament on anything other than those three is telling.

The "Advocate" of Jn 16:7 is the Holy Spirit. When man-Jesus left Earth, the Holy Spirit took over as the guiding force in Christians' lives, and Jesus is telling people what was getting ready to happen.

To save space and give you some other resources, here's a more thorough explanation of the Trinity than I've given.[2] And here's a clearer statement of the roles of the persons of the Trinity.[3]

**Victoria:** Your description makes heaven and hell sound like some other dimension or some other parallel universe.

Your reference to Lk 22:42 reminds me of this bit mentioned in Keller's book:

*About three in the afternoon Jesus cried out in a loud voice, "Eli, Eli, lema sabachthani?" (which means "My God, my God, why have you forsaken me?").* (Mt 27:46)

It's strange to me; if human Jesus felt/was forsaken by God, how does anyone else know that they aren't also forsaken by God?

Regarding $N = 3$, that's a pretty clear explanation! You have such a wealth of knowledge pointing to different parts of the Bible which reveal strongly consistent themes. Imagine a social experiment in which you take a group of people who had no prior knowledge/bias to Christianity or religion in general and told them to read the Bible. I wonder if they would come to the same conclusions.

Thanks for sending those links on the Trinity! This was unexpected to me: "Sometimes the Personhood of the Father and Son is appreciated, but the Personhood of the Holy Spirit is neglected. Sometimes the Spirit is treated more like a 'force' than a Person. But the Holy Spirit is not an

---

[2] Matt Perman, "What Is the Doctrine of the Trinity?" *Desiring God*, January 23, 2006, www.desiringgod.org/articles/what-is-the-doctrine-of-the-trinity.
[3] Dawson McAllister, "What is the Trinity?" *Christianity Today*, www.christianitytoday.com/iyf/advice/faithdoubt/what-is-trinity.html.

'it,' but a 'he.'" I've definitely always thought of the Holy Spirit being more of an "it." But God isn't necessarily "male," right? Or is he? Anyway, to me, the Holy Spirit seems to be the least discussed of the three, and it's the one I least understand, especially with the literal definition of "spirit."[4] Hmm, I wonder if my questions of whether God is really involved in human lives is actually a question of if the Holy Spirit exists (and how we know of his existence).

**Steve**: Regarding heaven/hell in some alternate reality/dimension/universe—sure: I have no idea!

As for Lk 22:42 and Mt 27:46, there's a lot of theology in there! The "cup" Jesus refers to in Lk 22:42 is probably a reference to the "cup of the God's wrath" in Is 51:17–23 and relatedly, this cup at the Last Supper:

> *In the same way, after the supper he took the cup, saying, "This cup is the new covenant in my blood, which is poured out for you."* (Lk 22:20)

In other words, Jesus, as a man, was quite terrified...

> *And being in anguish, he prayed more earnestly, and his sweat was like drops of blood falling to the ground.* (Lk 22:44)

because of what he knew was soon going to happen to him (i.e., single-handedly experience God's full wrath on humanity through an excruciating—look up that etymology!—death), but he decided to submit to God's will. In Mt 27:46, Jesus was actually quoting from the Old Testament:

> *My God, my God, why have you forsaken me? Why are you so far from saving me, so far from my cries of anguish?* (Ps 22:1)

So this was 1) another allusion to text written a thousand years prior, an indication of Jesus' (and in effect, Matthew's) belief that this was God's plan all along and 2) an acknowledgement that he was indeed (temporarily) experiencing God's wrath and being forsaken (both in our place) while he was on the cross. So these verses are actually indications that Jesus is taking all of that forsakenness on himself and not allowing us to experience it.

Back to the $N = 1$ vs. 3 view of God, this was the main reason (from a human perspective) that Jesus was killed. The Jews (which included Jesus in race and religion) believed (and still believe) that the idea of a man being God is blasphemy; it was punishable by death during Jesus'

---

[4] "The non-physical part of a person which is the seat of emotions and character; the soul," *Lexico*, www.lexico.com/en/definition/spirit.

time. So it was extremely difficult for the first Christians, who were almost all Jewish, to believe $N = 3$. They (as mentioned above) risked family and community excommunication, death, and God's wrath to believe what they did. It must have been quite convincing to them.

So would people in your social experiment believe? I love that question! But my first thought is the impossibility of such an experiment that could remove all extraneous variables. I will say, however, that I've spent the last 25 years of my life trying to disprove my faith, and the Bible convinces *me*, so I believe any answer I gave here would be unquestionably biased in my favor and thus, unhelpful (i.e., I would say "Of course they'd believe!" and then give all the reasons *I* believe).

Referring to the Father or Spirit as "he" can only refer to God's personhood, not sex or gender. I don't know of any Christian who thinks God has male anatomy except, of course, when referring to Jesus the man. You bring up interesting points regarding the Holy Spirit. First, there's this,

> "God is spirit, and his worshipers must worship in the Spirit and in truth." (Jn 4:24)

so we believe that all three persons of the Trinity are "holy spirits," but only one has the name "Holy Spirit." (I've never thought about that before! Weird.) Second, from a Christian perspective, yes, I agree: you are actually asking how we know the Holy Spirit exists, but the question is valid (and would have the same answers) whether we frame it that way or not. We don't have any biblical or philosophical reason to think that the Holy Spirit is different in essence (i.e., what he *is*) from the Father or Son.

**Victoria:** Wow, more new perspectives. It's usually mentioned how great, good, holy, revered, and respectable Jesus is, but he gets scared and sweats like normal people. Do you think there's at all the slightest possibility that Jesus as a person decided he didn't want to take all that forsakenness on himself? What might that look like? Either way, if he was sentenced to death, what other scenarios could've played out?

To the $N = 1$ vs. 3 view, to ask this bluntly: does that mean all Jews are going to hell because they don't believe Jesus is God?

Ha ha, I agree that such a social experiment is practically impossible. Related to the thought of initial exposures to Christianity, there are people who grow up Christian then renounce their faith, and there are people who grow up without faith and come to grasp it later in life. There are also people who are Christian in name but not in heart. This is more of an opinion question, but from your experience in who you would deem a "true" Christian, is there any majority as to how they came to believe, whether 1) growing up Christian and always believing, 2) growing up Christian and having hard doubts and then believing (like you?), or 3) not growing up Christian but then believing?

What does it mean that "'he' can only refer to God's personhood?" I only know how to think about "he-ness" in terms of sex or gender. What might it look like if God's personhood were "she?"

The Holy Spirit is something I definitely don't understand, and I think I'm even more bemused now. I think the bare bones idea of what I have is that the Holy Spirit is a "he," and he is in every person whether Christian or not (right?). I need to do some more digging myself on this.

**Steve**: Regarding Jesus deciding to not go to the cross, that's just another aspect of the free will/determinism/Calvinism/Arminianism debate. The Bible (in my mind at least) clearly points to Jesus' death before it occurs. So in that sense and in the Rev 13:8 sense mentioned earlier, it was predetermined before time began. But I could make an argument (and do believe) that God only *knew* what Jesus would choose (weird Trinity language), even though he could've chosen otherwise.

Hmm, if Jesus had chosen otherwise... Another great question (you're good at this)! I suppose from a Christian perspective (although there wouldn't be a Christian perspective if this didn't happen), we would probably have a system similar to Islam, in which we would need to earn our way to heaven via good deeds (which is impossible from a Christian perspective).

Are all Jews going to hell? Gosh, Vickie, I *always* feel very uncomfortable with this question or some related question, because it's just about impossible to make it not sound like it's just my opinion, or something I want, or some deep-seating hatred I have, or self-righteousness. But you asked, so here goes. If by "Jews," you mean people that have knowingly and actively (or even apathetically) rejected Jesus as *the* divine savior of the world and have instead chosen a system of Old Testament practices and laws as their only hope for salvation, yes, I believe the Bible teaches they will end up in hell via their own choice. But if by "Jews," you mean people of Jewish ancestry, no, of course not. Even more generally, I believe that the Bible teaches that *everyone* who has knowingly and actively (or apathetically) rejected Jesus as *the* divine savior of the world or has instead chosen *anything else* as a means of salvation has, in effect, made a statement that they do not wish to spend eternity with God and will be given what they wish: hell, which is eternal separation from God.

Regarding your question about "true" Christians, I only know them in theory, because I'm never in a place to decide who is or is not a "true" Christian. That being said, I *feel* like I personally know many "true" Christians with good probability. The answer for American Christians would be that most of us grew up in Christian homes and went to church and have believed since childhood or adolescence.[5] Any honest Christian in that category would admit to some doubts, but probably not

---

[5] "When Americans Become Christians," *National Association of Evangelicals*, www.nae.net/when-americans-become-christians/.

to the level I was at. However, in many parts of the world, especially Asia and the Middle East, Christianity is more often believed in adulthood because it is either not culturally accepted or widespread enough to be the norm.

Regarding God being a "he," all I mean is that we have three singular third-person personal pronouns: he, she, and it. "It" is not great, because it seems demeaning, distant, and impersonal: things we definitely don't relate with God. Regarding "he" vs. "she," I think this article is pretty good.[6]

Regarding whether the Holy Spirit is in everyone: no-ish.[7] Mostly "no" in the sense that the Holy Spirit is God's presence in the life of a believer. But partly "yes," because 1) if we claim that hell is "existing without God," that certainly implies that he is with everyone now in some sense, 2) as mentioned earlier, we can only come to God as he calls, so he must have been in the presence of all believers before they were believers, and 3) everyone has some innate sense of God:

> ... since what may be known about God is plain to them, because God has made it plain to them. For since the creation of the world God's invisible qualities—his eternal power and divine nature—have been clearly seen, being understood from what has been made, so that people are without excuse. (Rom 1:19–20)

I realize I'm saying "God" instead of "Holy Spirit," but as the Holy Spirit is often thought of in terms of both God's presence and the "revealer" of God,

> ... these are the things God has revealed to us by his Spirit. The Spirit searches all things, even the deep things of God. (1 Cor 2:10)

then I think it fits. I think it's also important to mention that a Christian is generally unconcerned with distinguishing between the three in daily life. For example, when I pray or worship, I don't feel like I need to point out any particular member of the Trinity or address all three except where it's obvious (e.g., "Thank you Jesus, for dying on the cross.").

**Victoria**: Those are comprehensible answers regarding Jesus going to the cross! I'd be interested in hearing more Christian perspectives on that.

The part on "what's going to happen to Jews" reminded me of this thought I had of, "Would it be easier to believe one thing or the other if

---

[6] Berni Dymet, "God—He, She or It?" *Christianityworks*, www.oneplace.com/ministries/christianityworks/read/articles/god--he-she-or-it-13962.html.
[7] "What is the indwelling of the Holy Spirit?" *Got Questions*, www.gotquestions.org/indwelling-of-the-Holy-Spirit.html.

I lived in that time period?" Then I was at a Bible study with IGSM[8] a couple of weeks ago, and they talked about how people even witnessing Jesus' doings didn't necessarily believe in him as the Son of God. So I suppose it probably wouldn't be that much more convincing if I did live in a more Bible-active setting. It seems that being born into the Jewish faith might make it harder to turn toward Christianity if you have to "un-learn" all this stuff that's been so ingrained. Sometimes I wonder about life trends that no one knows the answer to, and in this case, I wonder what the percentage is of switching between different religions, kind of like a Markov model.[9]

On "he" vs. "she" of God, I like that link you sent, when he talked about the idea of God transcending our culture, such as the patriarchal culture that was ingrained in Jesus' day and is still evidently present today. Keller reconnects to that point often in his book on how the viewpoints of humans are vastly limited in perspective and egocentric. However, regarding the article you referenced, I don't know that the point on God's actions (i.e., that he has more frequently revealed himself to us using masculine terms) is that convincing to me since it was humans who wrote the Bible; that is, humans biased by their culture. Could not God have been represented more "she-like" had the life of Jesus happened in the modern day? (I'm not bothered by this designation, but I'm asking for the sake of understanding and argument.) Something that piqued my curiosity was the line: "Had God wanted to reveal Himself differently, He could readily have chosen a different time and place to do so." Is there a good reason Jesus was on earth at that time in particular? Also, the author is pretty funny: "But my hunch is that [certain feminine descriptions of God] serve no more to reveal Him as She, than the image of God as having wings (Psalm 36:7 and elsewhere) reveals Him to be a Bird."

On the "no-ish" link, two questions. 1) "When you accept Christ as your Savior (Rom 10:9–13), the Holy Spirit takes up residence in your heart, bringing with Him an entirely new life of love, relationship, and service to the Lord." This seems counterintuitive; isn't having the Holy Spirit a prerequisite to accept Christ as Savior (though your "partly-yes" point might be relevant here)? Okay, overall, that "mostly no/partly yes" distinction does help; i.e., understanding the parts (Holy Spirit) helps to better understand the whole (Trinity). 2) Now, on the "innate sense of God" link, I've seen Rom 1:19–20 referenced a *lot* recently. I have a hard time getting/accepting it. "For since the creation of the world God's invisible qualities—his eternal power and divine nature—have been clearly seen, being understood from what has been made, so that people are without excuse." I don't think it's really all that plain to see.

---

[8] International Graduate Student Ministry at UC Irvine. See Chapter 15 for the beginning of this story.

[9] "Markov model," *Wikipedia*, en.wikipedia.org/wiki/Markov_model.

**Steve**: "Would it be easier to believe one thing or the other if I lived in that time period?" I wonder that about location, too (e.g., would I be a Christian if I was born in Pakistan?). I'm sort of at the point where I know that I could explain away even a miracle that happened right in front of me (e.g., I was hallucinating, it was a coincidence, etc.), so the fact that I continue to have faith in that context means something to me. So I don't know an answer to that question for sure, but I feel like I've already overcome many obstacles to get where I am, so I'd like to think I would come to the same conclusions no matter when/where I lived.

"Could not God have been represented more "she-like" had the life of Jesus happened in the modern day?" Yes, I suppose, but it's hard to say how well men would respond to that even today. We tend to have egos and would probably secretly resent being told what to do by a goddess, or even worse, sexualize her.[10] Also, if Jesus showed up as a man but we always called God "she," that would be weird. But if God/Jesus were even figuratively female, I suppose that would influence our picture of gender in some unknown way, which makes it hard to answer the question. All this being said, while God is pictured as male, Christianity is heavily female.[11] Is there some connection there? I don't know.

"Is there a good reason Jesus was on earth at that time in particular?" Yes, it seems so,

> But when the set time had fully come, God sent his Son, born of a woman, born under the law, to redeem those under the law, that we might receive adoption to sonship. (Gal 4:4–5)

though I'm confident God could've made it work at any time. 1) The Old Testament required Jews to sacrifice animals for the forgiveness of sins. This was the pattern for thousands of years

> Then Noah built an altar to the LORD and, taking some of all the clean animals and clean birds, he sacrificed burnt offerings on it. The LORD smelled the pleasing aroma and said in his heart: "Never again will I curse the ground because of humans, even though every inclination of the human heart is evil from childhood. And never again will I destroy all living creatures, as I have done. (Gen 8:20–21)

and became more ordered and official through the law of Moses...

---

[10] It seems that sex and fertility deities are disproportionately female: "List of love and lust deities," *Wikipedia*, en.wikipedia.org/wiki/List_of_love_and_lust_deities.

[11] "Quick Facts," *Church for Men*, churchformen.com/men-and-church/where-are-the-men/.

*Sacrifice a bull each day as a sin offering to make atonement. Purify the altar by making atonement for it, and anoint it to consecrate it.* (Ex 29:36)

and finally with the building of the temple[12] about 1000 years before Jesus. The temple (and the accompanying system) was still in place when Jesus was around, but the Romans destroyed it[13] just 35 years or so after he died, and there hasn't been a temple built since.[14] Christians believe that Jesus' sacrifice effectively replaced this system of sacrifice, but due to the timing, there was no gap in one's ability to seek God. 2) The Old Testament continually pointed to a savior/messiah/christ well before Jesus was born.[15] Jews interpreted (and still interpret) much of this under the impression that the Messiah would be the leader of an earthly government.[16] The oppression of the Jews by the Romans led many to look for a Messiah at that time (i.e., they wanted someone to overthrow the Romans)[17]. Many followed Jesus when he was around solely with that expectation:

*After the people saw the sign Jesus performed, they began to say, "Surely this is the Prophet who is to come into the world." Jesus, knowing that they intended to come and make him king by force, withdrew again to a mountain by himself.* (Jn 6:14–15)

When he made claims that it was all about God and not government or his taking care of their physical needs, many people left him:

*"Just as the living Father sent me and I live because of the Father, so the one who feeds on me will live because of me. This is the bread that came down from heaven. Your ancestors ate manna and died, but whoever feeds on this bread will live forever." He said this while teaching in the synagogue in Capernaum. On hearing it, many of his disciples said, "This is a hard teaching. Who can accept it?" Aware that his disciples were grumbling about this, Jesus said to them, "Does this offend you? Then what if you see the Son of Man ascend to where he was before! The Spirit gives life; the flesh counts for nothing. The*

---

[12] "Solomon's Temple," *Wikipedia*, en.wikipedia.org/wiki/Solomon's_Temple.
[13] "Siege of Jerusalem (70 CE)," *Wikipedia*, en.wikipedia.org/wiki/Siege_of_Jerusalem_(70_CE).
[14] Yehuda Shurpin, "Why Haven't Jews Rebuilt the Temple Yet?" *Chabad.org*, www.chabad.org/library/article_cdo/aid/3009476/jewish/Why-Havent-Jews-Rebuilt-the-Temple-Yet.htm.
[15] "356 Prophecies Fulfilled in Jesus Christ," *According to the Scriptures*, www.accordingtothescriptures.org/prophecy/353prophecies.html.
[16] "Mashiach: The Messiah," *Judaism 101*, www.jewfaq.org/mashiach.htm.
[17] "Zealots," *Wikipedia*, en.wikipedia.org/wiki/Zealots.

*words I have spoken to you—they are full of the Spirit and life. Yet there are some of you who do not believe." For Jesus had known from the beginning which of them did not believe and who would betray him. He went on to say, "This is why I told you that no one can come to me unless the Father has enabled them." From this time many of his disciples turned back and no longer followed him.* (Jn 6:57-66)

So I see the timing of Jesus' life coinciding with a great expectation of followers. When he did not fulfill those expectations, it was as if God were making a huge theological statement to all of us: life is about him in eternity, not ourselves during a few decades. 3) Not counting the apocrypha, there was about 400 years between the last written book of the Old Testament and Jesus' arrival; people had waited a long time for the Messiah.

"This seems counterintuitive; isn't having the Holy Spirit a prerequisite to accept Christ as Savior?" An unsatisfying and ambiguous answer is that the Holy Spirit *leads* us to Christ but doesn't *live* in us until we accept him. I don't think there's a way to explain that scientifically or anything, but I would interpret it as some kind of higher degree or level of God's presence (like my relationship with you vs. my relationship with my wife Windee: I'm the same person but interact with you two on different levels).

"What does it mean that 'For you are bought with a price?'" The Bible calls Christians adopted children[18] but also slaves.[19] Either perspective requires being brought into a family or under a master at some cost. The cost for that to happen was the death of Jesus who "paid our debt" to God:

*For the wages of sin is death, but the free gift of God is eternal life in Christ Jesus our Lord.* (Rom 6:23)

(Also see the parable in Mt 18:21–35.) Before Jesus, the cost was the death of an animal; it was God's way of visibly showing the seriousness of our sin.

"I don't think [God's eternal power and divine nature are] really all that plain to see." You've already admitted (I think) to believing in a supernatural, extremely powerful creator outside of time without any concrete evidence. You must've reasoned your way into that, so I would argue that you *have* plainly seen it in that context (i.e., "seeing" is figurative).

**Victoria**: I like that answer for what might it mean for God to be represented as female. I hadn't thought about the potential implication of male egos

---

[18] Rom 8:15, Rom 8:23, Gal 4:5, Eph 1:5.
[19] Rom 1:1, Gal 1:10, Eph 6:6, Phil 1:1, Col 4:12, Tit 1:1, Jas 1:1, 2 Pet 1:1, Jude 1:1, Rev 1:1.

or desires. Also, that's super interesting about Christianity being heavily female; I didn't know that before. I also wonder if that might mean that a female God would lead to even less worship by men than the current numbers.

On the timeliness of Jesus on earth, wow, your answer led me to realize how thought-provoking the question actually was as well as its relevance. I always wondered, "why not now," but apparently, "why *then*" is more insightful. Overall, the three reasons you gave are essentially: timing, to make a statement, and timing again? I don't get the purpose of the third reason. Four hundred years is already a long time; why not make it 300 or 200? Would that overthrow the first two reasons? I guess all the reasons are really about timing: timing to streamline the continued generation of followers, timing to make a statement most effectively, and timing because it had been a while. So if Jesus were born a century later, could that have significantly weakened Christianity?

"The Holy Spirit leads us to Christ, but doesn't live in us until we accept him." So believing in Christ is a positive feedback loop?

"The Bible calls Christians adopted children but also slaves." Hmm, this is a grimmer interpretation than people make it sound (e.g., compared to people who talk about Jesus being their "best friend"). It's more graspable to me though. If God were omni*, it would only make sense for humans to be slaves. If Christians are called as slaves, then non-Christians would most certainly also be slaves, but after death, non-Christians would specifically be slaves without God as a master, right? So that means that freedom is hell, and hell is freedom?

"Before Jesus, the cost was the death of an animal; it was God's way of visibly showing the seriousness of our sin." Why was this serious cost done away with via Jesus? Isn't that counterproductive since it might make sin seem more trivial?

**Steve:** "I wonder if that might mean that a female God would lead to even less worship by men than the current numbers..." Assuming you mean "a God portrayed as female" (because God having an actual sex would create an entirely different theology for Christians), that's an interesting (and unanswerable) question. It makes me wonder about the influence of religion on perceptions of gender. There's certainly a correlation (and possibly a causation) between the western world becoming post-Christian and the modern idea of gender fluidity.[20]

"I don't get the purpose of the third reason." I don't think about that one as *timing* as much as *fulfilling a promise*: God promised it would happen, so he made it happen late enough for things to "get ready," (reasons 1 and 2) but soon enough that the entire thing wasn't forgotten. In other words, waiting 100,000 years for the Messiah to come would probably make people think it's never going to happen.

---

[20] Preston Sprinkle, *Embodied* (Colorado Springs, CO: David C. Cook, 2021).

(This is also a common argument against Christianity. The Bible says that Jesus will return to earth one day,

> *"Men of Galilee," they said, "why do you stand here looking into the sky? This same Jesus, who has been taken from you into heaven, will come back in the same way you have seen him go into heaven." (Acts 1:11)*

> *"Immediately after the tribulation of those days the sun will be darkened, and the moon will not give its light, and the stars will fall from heaven, and the powers of the heavens will be shaken. Then will appear in heaven the sign of the Son of Man, and then all the tribes of the earth will mourn, and they will see the Son of Man coming on the clouds of heaven with power and great glory. And he will send out his angels with a loud trumpet call, and they will gather his elect from the four winds, from one end of heaven to the other." (Mt 24:29–31)*

but it's been 2000 years, so where is he? The Bible answers with 1) only God knows when he will return,

> *"But concerning that day and hour no one knows, not even the angels of heaven, nor the Son, but the Father only." (Mt 24:36)*

and 2) we trust him with the timing.[21]) I see it as God saying, "Here I am, doing what I said I would do; I haven't forgotten."

"Why not make it 300 or 200?" The Roman Empire, the force behind the crucifixion[22] and a catalyst for the spread of Christianity,[23] didn't exist then.

"So if Jesus were born a century later, could that have significantly weakened Christianity?" If one's belief is that God is omni*, then no; this could've happened any way imaginable and everything would've been fine. That being said, it is clear that God reveals himself and works with humans in ways they can understand,[24] and this specific timing seems to work in that regard (i.e., it makes sense to us in a way that a different time may not have).

"So believing in Christ is a positive feedback loop?" Yes, that is a summary of my life.

---

[21] 2 Pet 3.

[22] Mt 27:11–31.

[23] Jack Wellman, "How Did the Existence of the Roman Empire Help the Spread of Christianity?" *Patheos*, December 26, 2016, www.patheos.com/blogs/christiancrier/2016/12/26/how-did-the-existence-of-the-roman-empire-help-the-spread-of-christianity/.

[24] John Walton, "Does the Bible Contain Errors?" *Biologos*, October 9, 2018, biologos.org/articles/does-the-bible-contain-errors.

"If Christians are called as slaves, then non-Christians would most certainly also be slaves, but after death, non-Christians would specifically be slaves without God as a master, right? So that means that freedom is hell, and hell is freedom?" The Bible says that we are *all* slaves to something:

> "No one can serve two masters, for either he will hate the one and love the other, or he will be devoted to the one and despise the other. You cannot serve God and money." (Mt 6:24)

> Jesus replied, "Very truly I tell you, everyone who sins is a slave to sin." (Jn 8:34)

The question is what we are slaves to. The Bible paints the picture that perceived freedom leads to actual slavery...

> What then? Shall we sin because we are not under the law but under grace? By no means! Don't you know that when you offer yourselves to someone as obedient slaves, you are slaves of the one you obey—whether you are slaves to sin, which leads to death, or to obedience, which leads to righteousness? But thanks be to God that, though you used to be slaves to sin, you have come to obey from your heart the pattern of teaching that has now claimed your allegiance. You have been set free from sin and have become slaves to righteousness. I am using an example from everyday life because of your human limitations. Just as you used to offer yourselves as slaves to impurity and to ever-increasing wickedness, so now offer yourselves as slaves to righteousness leading to holiness. When you were slaves to sin, you were free from the control of righteousness. What benefit did you reap at that time from the things you are now ashamed of? Those things result in death! But now that you have been set free from sin and have become slaves of God, the benefit you reap leads to holiness, and the result is eternal life. For the wages of sin is death, but the gift of God is eternal life in Christ Jesus our Lord. (Rom 6:15–23)

while voluntarily becoming a slave to Christ leads to actual freedom:

> "So if the Son sets you free, you will be free indeed." (Jn 8:36)

(This is maybe where the biblical slavery analogy breaks down a little: we are not forced to be slaves like one imagines when they think of slavery. The picture is more related to total and absolute submission rather than forced labor.) Here are two examples (at least in my mind). 1) The "freedom" of the sexual revolution[25] led to the ubiquitous

---

[25] "Sexual revolution," *Wikipedia*, en.wikipedia.org/wiki/Sexual_revolution.

sexualization of women[26] which led to them being treated like literal[27] and figurative[28] slaves to men. (To be clear, the actions/symptoms are generally the fault of men, not women, but society as a whole has embraced the idea/disease and is reaping the consequences.) On the other hand, the bond of marriage, which seems like a restriction on the surface, was designed as a protection for women to not be treated like dirt: something that allowed for their freedom. In summary, the "freedom" we've sought as a society has led to the enslavement of millions of women as sex objects. (Yes, of course, this happened before and outside of the sexual revolution as well, but usually in the context of lawlessness/injustice rather than under the guise of freedom.) 2) The gospel (which includes many commands to "not do things" and seems restrictive) can liberate people from their own slavery to other things (e.g., substance abuse[29]). So I would say that human freedom is hell, and hell is human freedom. Slavery to Christ is actual freedom. So how does this work? Well, slavery is doing whatever one's master says you must do. If your master is drugs, you will do drugs even when you don't want to do drugs. If your master is sex, you will be someone's sex object. If your master is politics, you will be consumed by it. If your master is the First Amendment, you will be a slave to the government's application and interpretation of it. If your master is a diploma with "PhD" on it, you will spend endless hours in a lab wishing you were outside. If your master is morality, you will spend your life keeping up an image and reputation that you know doesn't exist. But if your master is Jesus, you will do whatever he says, and you will find that you don't need drugs, sex, money, the government, a degree, approval, or morality to make you happy; he will be enough. And when you don't need finite, temporal things to make you happy, that's the very definition of real freedom.

"Why was this serious cost done away with via Jesus? Isn't that counterproductive since it might make sin seem more trivial?" I would look at it two ways: 1) The serious cost was not done away with; on the contrary, it was shown to be infinitely serious when God himself died on the cross. One might say that the repetitive physical reminder of our sinfulness is gone (and I would agree), but I would argue that Christianity cannot be practiced without continual knowledge of one's own sinfulness,

---

[26] "20 Mind-Blowing Stats About the Porn Industry and Its Underage Consumers," *Fight the New Drug*, fightthenewdrug.org/10-porn-stats-that-will-blow-your-mind/.

[27] "Factsheets," *Equality Now*, www.equalitynow.org/factsheets.

[28] Doug Criss, "The (incomplete) list of powerful men accused of sexual harassment after Harvey Weinstein," *CNN*, November 1, 2017, www.cnn.com/2017/10/25/us/list-of-accused-after-weinstein-scandal-trnd/.

[29] "Success Stories," *Adult & Teen Challenge*, teenchallengeusa.org/about/success-stories.

*Godly sorrow brings repentance that leads to salvation and leaves no regret, but worldly sorrow brings death.* (2 Cor 7:10)

so that that this mindfulness doesn't (or shouldn't) disappear. 2) This goes back to the previous paragraph related to freedom. The animal sacrifice system was given to a particular race of people (Israelites) in a certain location on earth (Israel). It was a mark of their identity, which was most clearly manifested by the existence of the temple in Jerusalem. That system did not lend itself well to extension to other people in other parts of the earth. Jesus' sacrifice made the gospel more easily accessible to all people without restriction to culture or geography:

*The woman said to him, "Sir, I perceive that you are a prophet. Our fathers worshiped on this mountain, but you say that in Jerusalem is the place where people ought to worship." Jesus said to her, "Woman, believe me, the hour is coming when neither on this mountain nor in Jerusalem will you worship the Father. You worship what you do not know; we worship what we know, for salvation is from the Jews. But the hour is coming, and is now here, when the true worshipers will worship the Father in spirit and truth, for the Father is seeking such people to worship him. God is spirit, and those who worship him must worship in spirit and truth." The woman said to him, "I know that Messiah is coming (he who is called Christ). When he comes, he will tell us all things." Jesus said to her, "I who speak to you am he." (Jn 4:19–26)*

In fact, Rom 6:15 (the first verse of the reference above about "perceived freedom") basically states (using The Robinson Translation[30]): "Since the old system that focused so heavily on sin has been replaced by grace, should we not take sin as seriously? Of course not!" The reasoning given is that it doesn't make sense to run back into enslavement to things/self when that is the very thing we escaped by following Christ.

**Victoria**: "There's certainly a correlation (and possibly a causation) between the western world becoming post-Christian and the modern idea of gender fluidity." This is intriguing to think about, especially in context of other tolerances (e.g., sexual orientation). Perhaps a good baseline would be to see trends also within religion.[31]

---

[30] The Robinson Translation does not exist. It's basically Steve taking English translations and putting them in his own words. There is zero authority behind The Robinson Translation.

[31] Caryle Murphy, "Most U.S. Christian groups grow more accepting of homosexuality," *Pew Research Center*, December 18, 2015, www.pewresearch.org/fact-tank/2015/12/18/most-u-s-christian-groups-grow-more-accepting-of-homosexuality/.

I never realized before how human freedom isn't actually true freedom but rather slavery to other more worldly things such as wealth, academic/career success, social status, etc. I liked the way you concluded that paragraph: "And when you don't need finite, temporal things to make you happy, that's the very definition of real freedom."

I see. So basically, on the surface, sin might seem more trivial "because we are not under the law but under grace." But the way that we receive this grace—Jesus' death—actually indicates otherwise, that sin is very *not* trivial, since it took the life of God himself in order to pay the wages of all of our sins. Furthermore, this sacrifice was so great that it has the extent to cover all people everywhere and anytime.

# Chapter 7: Reliability of the Bible

**Victoria**: There are many different versions of the Bible ranging from word-for-word to thought-for-thought. But since translations come from humans deciding on the "original" text's interpretation, how do you know if you're getting the truth or not? Also, what does it mean when the Bible is inconsistent with itself? (There's a *Wikipedia* article[1] on that! I didn't expect that, though am not too surprised.)

**Steve**: The internal consistency of the Bible is one way we can be confident in its reliability. It was written over a period of about 1900 years by about 40 authors from very different cultures and occupations, but its basic message is the same throughout. I believe it is also the most scrutinized and criticized book in the history of the world but seems to have handled those criticisms pretty well. You're exactly right about the translation issues, but it's not as big of a deal as you might think. For example, the Quran is said to have been given directly to Muhammad by an angel in Arabic and is said to be Allah's exact message to humanity. Thus, if we found other early copies of the Quran that were not letter-for-letter identical with the Quran that we know of now,[2] that would present a problem for the historicity of that revelation to Muhammad. Neither the Bible nor Christians make such claims about the revelation of the Bible. We (or at least I) believe it was inspired/influenced by God but written by people, so that even the original words in Hebrew and Greek don't have to be letter-for-letter from God.[3] (In fact, there are times where Paul sort of steps outside of the Bible and says, "Hey I'm the writer of this, and this isn't directly from God," such as in the following passages:

> But if our unrighteousness brings out God's righteousness more clearly, what shall we say? That God is unjust in bringing his wrath on us? (I am using a human argument.) (Rom 3:5)

> To the rest I say this (I, not the Lord): If any brother has a wife who is not a believer and she is willing to live with him, he must not divorce her. (1 Cor 7:12)

> In this self-confident boasting I am not talking as the Lord would, but as a fool. (2 Cor 11:17)

---

[1] "Internal consistency of the Bible," *Wikipedia*, en.wikipedia.org/wiki/Internal_consistency_of_the_Bible.
[2] "Sana'a manuscript," *Wikipedia*, en.wikipedia.org/wiki/Sana'a_manuscript.
[3] John Walton and Brent Sandy, *The Lost World of Scripture* (Downers Grove, IL: InterVarsity Press, 2013).

The translation and copying of the Bible over the last 2000 years has *not* been perfect, but it's been good enough for us to feel very certain that we know what the original text said. Honestly, I think the fact that large parts of the Bible were written as if they were historical documents instead of divine revelations is a strength, not a weakness:

> *Many have undertaken to draw up an account of the things that have been fulfilled among us, just as they were handed down to us by those who from the first were eyewitnesses and servants of the word. With this in mind, since I myself have carefully investigated everything from the beginning, I too decided to write an orderly account for you, most excellent Theophilus, so that you may know the certainty of the things you have been taught.* (Lk 1:1–4)

**Victoria**: On the Sana'a manuscript, I was reading more about it elsewhere,[4] and it was stated that "the past existence of such manuscripts is well known to Muslims and those that did not completely agree with the Uthmanic[5] text were eliminated in various ways." Could that also be true for the Bible? That is, could the messages that differed from some consistent message have been eliminated?

**Steve**: Regarding the Quran/Bible, I think they have both undoubtedly suffered from small copying errors or additions over time, but both seem to retain a very consistent message from "then" until "now." (The Dead Sea Scrolls are good evidence of this for the Old Testament.) The difference is in what Muslims and Christians believe their books to be. Muslims believe their book to be a verbatim revelation directly from God,[6] so small textual differences between similarly-dated texts are a huge problem in my mind. Christians believe their book to be a mix of historical accounts and revelations from God which can and should be translated for everyone to read. It doesn't matter to a Christian which— if either—of these God said during Jesus' baptism,

> *And a voice from heaven said, "This is my Son, whom I love; with him I am well pleased."* (Mt 3:17)

> *And a voice came from heaven: "You are my Son, whom I love; with you I am well pleased."* (Mk 1:11)

---

[4] Jeffrey Lang, "A Response to the article, 'What is the Koran?'" *American Muslim Council*, amconline.org/publish/op/op-lang.html.

[5] Uthman (579–656) was the third caliph, under whom the Quran was compiled in its present book format.

[6] "Quran: The Word of God," *Why Islam?*, www.whyislam.org/quran/quran-the-word-of-god/.

and he certainly didn't say it in English.[7]

As to the reliability of the writings to begin with, these are my thoughts: 1) The writings of the New Testament spread pretty rapidly[8] to different parts of the world after Jesus' death, so it would be very difficult for someone to deliberately distort the message in one location and have it become universal. 2) Modern Bibles acknowledge that there are passages of scripture that do not show up in the earliest manuscripts and may not be original.[9] This acknowledgement is a strong indication that scholars feel very confident in the originality/authenticity of the rest. 3) The consistency and historicity of the biblical message from beginning to end makes it easy to spot frauds, and those frauds are well known[10] and either discounted or not important to the overall message. So, yes, Christians have systematically disallowed writings from the Bible that contradict the central message of Christianity. Of course, that begs the question of whether that central, original message is historical and/or true, but it's hard to think of a reason for people to create a teaching they knew to be false that would cost them their lives.[11] 4) Extra-biblical accounts of Jesus[12] and the early church[13] seem to corroborate the Bible. Or, to put it another way, the biblical accounts are written as criticizable history, not epic fairy tales that can't be disputed; my understanding is that it stands up to this historical scrutiny as well as any other ancient historical document. (Of course, it does make claims of miraculous events that can't be subjected to scientific or historical analysis at this point, but it would be weird if the Bible were *only* historical.)

**Victoria**: Your point about biblical frauds is striking. In the *Wikipedia* link you sent (on Apocrypha), the "Disputes over canonicity" section seems pretty murky in terms of frauds being well-known, but it seems clearer in the "New Testament apocrypha" section. There's also a section called "List of Sixty" which seemed kind of confusing.

---

[7] John Piper, "Do We Have the Exact Words of Christ, or a Paraphrase?" *Desiring God*, December 21, 2020, www.desiringgod.org/interviews/do-we-have-the-exact-words-of-christ-or-a-paraphrase.

[8] "Development of the New Testament canon," *Wikipedia*, en.wikipedia.org/wiki/Development_of_the_New_Testament_canon.

[9] "List of New Testament verses not included in modern English translations," *Wikipedia*, en.wikipedia.org/wiki/List_of_New_Testament_verses_not_included_in_modern_English_translations.

[10] "Apocrypha," *Wikipedia*, en.wikipedia.org/wiki/Apocrypha#Christianity.

[11] "Persecution of Christians in the Roman Empire," *Wikipedia*, en.wikipedia.org/wiki/Persecution_of_Christians_in_the_Roman_Empire.

[12] "Historicity of Jesus," *Wikipedia*, en.wikipedia.org/wiki/Historicity_of_Jesus.

[13] "Historical reliability of the Acts of the Apostles," *Wikipedia*, en.wikipedia.org/wiki/Historical_reliability_of_the_Acts_of_the_Apostles.

Taken out of context, your statement, "Christians have systematically disallowed…" evokes the idea of "victors writing the history books," but I suppose that isn't completely congruous with the initial widespread persecution of Christians. Still though, on the *Wikipedia* article you referenced regarding the reliability of the book of Acts, isn't it kind of unsettling to read things like, "Acts describes Paul differently from how Paul describes himself, both factually and theologically"?

**Steve**: Regarding the "well-known frauds" subject, I didn't mean to definitively state that the apocrypha are frauds, but that we knowingly and intentionally label them as apocrypha and thus treat their theological and historical significance as dubious. Think of dubious scientific theories:[14] we simply don't have enough information in many cases to definitively decide whether they are necessarily wrong, but they're certainly not something I'm going to base my knowledge or practice of physics on because there are clear, well-established alternatives. The stages of canonization relied on reasonable methods[15] of deciding what was reliable and what wasn't. Yes, this required "systemically disallowing" some disputable texts, but I don't see how that's different than what we do in science. As you mentioned, if the decisions on what was allowed in the Bible benefited those who decided, I would understand serious skepticism. But they died doing what the Bible told them to do. I'd never heard about the "List of Sixty" until I read the *Wikipedia* article. I can't find much information on it, but it seems to have been organized well after just about every canonization process we know of, so I have no idea what this refers to.

"Still though, isn't it kind of unsettling to read things like, 'Acts describes Paul differently from how Paul describes himself, both factually and theologically'?" Yes, that statement in and of itself *is* unsettling. But when I click on the source of that quote, the quote doesn't seem to exist anymore, so I'd need to see some specifics to answer the question. Just looking at the section entitled "Passages of disputed historical accuracy" in the article on Acts, they all seem to be reasonably addressed except for the last one on Acts 21:38; however, there is a good explanation of that one, too.[16] If the quote you brought up is referring to how people view themselves vs. how others view them, well, yeah, that's every person in history, and I would expect Luke's and Paul's perspectives about Paul to be different because they're different humans.

---

[14] "Alternatives to general relativity," *Wikipedia*, en.wikipedia.org/wiki/Alternatives_to_general_relativity.

[15] "How and when was the canon of the Bible put together?" *Got Questions*, www.gotquestions.org/canon-Bible.html.

[16] Mark Brighton, "The Sicarii in Acts: A New Perspective," *The Journal of the Evangelical Theological Society*, 54 (3), 547–558 (2011).

**Victoria**: Oh! Those first two sentences put it in better perspective for me as a scientist. Subconsciously, I was mistrustful of all the "baggage" tangential to what the Bible itself has, but I suppose it isn't too different from all the existence of competing hypotheses for natural phenomena. (I wonder if this is why some people are skeptical/doubtful of science.)

I did some more digging on the Paul discrepancy, following the *Wikipedia* quote. *Encyclopedia Britannica* has these:[17]

> "That an actual companion [Luke] of Paul writing about his mission journeys could be in so much disagreement with Paul (whose theology is evidenced in his letters) about fundamental issues such as the Law, his apostleship, and his relationship to the Jerusalem church is hardly conceivable."

> "Acts presents a picture of Paul that differs from his own description of himself in many of his letters, both factually and theologically. In Acts, Paul, on his way to Damascus to persecute the church, is dramatically stopped by a visionary experience of Jesus and is later instructed. In his letters, however, Paul stated that he was called by direct revelation of the risen Lord and given a vocation for which he had been born (recalling the call of an Old Testament prophet, such as Jeremiah) and was instructed by no man."

> "The account of Paul's relation to Judaism in Acts also differs from that in his letters."

*Encyclopedia Britannica* and *Wikipedia* generally say that Paul's account of his own life is generally the favored one, but *Wikipedia* also says, "prominent scholars and historians view the book of Acts as being fairly accurate and corroborated by archaeology, and in general agreement with the Pauline epistles." In the bigger picture, this might not be a crucial discussion point, but at the same time, I wouldn't say it has zero effect on the perceived credibility of the Bible. Incidentally, that article you referenced on "The Sicarii in Acts" talks about having to understand ancient Greek culture to adequately apply some New Testament passage to our everyday life since the biblical authors didn't write to a modern western world. Do normal people who are not Christian scholars actually do this?

**Steve**: So let's talk about *Encyclopedia Britannica*. "That an actual companion [Luke] of Paul writing about his mission journeys could be in so much disagreement with Paul…" I'm still not sure what the author of that statement is referring to; I'd love to know. Luke's writings (the books of Luke and Acts) are not so much theology as historical accounts.

17 "The Acts of the Apostles," *Encyclopedia Britannica*, www.britannica.com/topic/biblical-literature/The-Acts-of-the-Apostles.

Paul's writings are heavy in theology with little history. I'd need specific "disagreements" (like comparisons of two verses) to be able to address them.

"Acts presents a picture of Paul that differs from his own description of himself in many of his letters, both factually and theologically..." I don't see how the provided examples in that paragraph are different.

"The account of Paul's relation to Judaism in Acts also differs from that in his letters." How? The sentences that follow in the article don't explain.

On all of these questions, I'm not asking you to answer my concerns, per se. I did read through the article, but it's sloppy and vague in its criticisms. I seriously don't understand where they're getting their information/arguments/justifications. They even write sentences like: "These [passages in which Luke says "we"] do not, however, necessarily point to Luke as a companion of Paul—as has been commonly assumed—but are rather a stylistic device, such as that noted particularly in itinerary accounts in other ancient historical works (e.g., Philostratus' Life of Apollonius of Tyana)." That's pure conjecture. The whole article seems to be filled with baseless claims and non sequiturs to me. I'm admittedly not a Bible scholar, but I like a good debate, and *Encyclopedia Britannica* isn't even trying.

"Do normal people who are not Christian scholars actually do this?" Ha ha, no! It's completely unnecessary for belief in Christianity (and often out of my league). But in all fairness, when the Bible is criticized from a historical angle (as it should be), it inevitably becomes a debate just like any historical debate: nuanced, incomplete, and usually inconclusive. I think the main thing I get out of these rebuttals by Christian historians is not any kind of absolute super-convincing argument that my faith hinges on, but that I see that the initial criticisms themselves are not the final word and also have deficiencies. It allows me to feel certain that Christianity is—if nothing else—not irrational.

**Victoria**: "I like a good debate, and *Encyclopedia Britannica* isn't even trying." Ha ha! I suppose every reference has its flaws.

# CHAPTER 8: RESPONSIBILITY OF SALVATION

**Steve**: Jn 15:16 and several other verses have caused a schism in Christianity regarding our role in salvation. Calvinists believe that, because God is in charge of everything, every part of our salvation was predetermined by him before time began. Apparently then, God did not choose everyone. Arminians instead believe that we are responsible for our own salvation and must actively choose God, because otherwise, how could God hold us responsible? I disagree with both views and live in some middle ground.[1] An analogy would be my son playing soccer. He (not me) must play the game, but he cannot play the game unless I drive him there. Similarly, we cannot know God unless he calls us (and I believe he has called everyone in some form; it could be quite subtle), but we are responsible for choosing or rejecting him.

**Victoria**: I was reading more about Calvinism vs. Arminianism,[2] and I don't understand how your view (and most Christians' views that I come across) differs from the Arminian view. Isn't the main idea that each person is ultimately responsible for his/her outcome?

You said, "I believe he has called everyone in some form." This might be an extreme example, but what about indigenous tribes or some random person who never had exposure to this information, the Internet, or discussions on God?

**Steve**: Regarding Calvinism vs. Arminianism, there are extremes and degrees within each, so sometimes what I believe seems to line up with Calvinist wording and sometimes Arminian wording (and it depends on who wrote the wording), so I can't say for certain where I am. A lot of it reminds me of the free will discussion we had earlier, which exists in great tension in both Christianity and naturalism. (Hmm, maybe when we get down to it, all of us really want to know just two questions: "Who or what is in charge?" and "What am I supposed to do?" Free will/determinism/Calvinism/Arminianism are (possibly futile) attempts at gaining perfect clarity in that regard.) Calvinism is summed up best by the acronym TULIP[3] (there is no "official" wording), and those who agree with every letter are known as "five-point" Calvinists. I would give myself the following scores/beliefs on each letter: T = 100%, U = 80%, L = 30%, I = 50%, and P = 90%. So I'm a 3.5-point Calvinist, which might

---

[1] "Molinism," *Wikipedia*, en.wikipedia.org/wiki/Molinism.

[2] "Calvinism vs. Arminianism—which view is correct?" *Got Questions*, www.gotquestions.org/Calvinism-vs-Arminianism.html.

[3] TULIP stands for Total depravity, Unconditional election, Limited atonement, Irresistible grace, and Perseverance of the saints. For a description of each point, see the following: "The Five Points of Calvinism," *The Calvinist Corner*, www.calvinistcorner.com/tulip.htm.

make me an Arminian! This maddening debate has been going on for centuries, and I don't plan on solving it now, except to say that I've rarely found answers in any theological extremes, so I have doubts about either being fully explanatory.

As for your question about the person who's never been exposed to Christianity, Paul and Jesus sum it up in these two passages:

> *All who sin apart from the law will also perish apart from the law, and all who sin under the law will be judged by the law. For it is not those who hear the law who are righteous in God's sight, but it is those who obey the law who will be declared righteous. (Indeed, when Gentiles, who do not have the law, do by nature things required by the law, they are a law for themselves, even though they do not have the law. They show that the requirements of the law are written on their hearts, their consciences also bearing witness, and their thoughts sometimes accusing them and at other times even defending them.) This will take place on the day when God judges people's secrets through Jesus Christ, as my gospel declares.* (Rom 2:12–16)

> *"The servant who knows the master's will and does not get ready or does not do what the master wants will be beaten with many blows. But the one who does not know and does things deserving punishment will be beaten with few blows. From everyone who has been given much, much will be demanded; and from the one who has been entrusted with much, much more will be asked."* (Lk 12:47–48)

(The latter one's in the middle of a story, so you'd have to read that to see why people are being beaten!) In other words, each person will be judged by the information he/she had (possible) access to. I feel about 60% confident in that answer; this is another debate in Calvinism/Arminianism, and there are good counterarguments to my belief.[4] [To the reader: a better answer awaits in Chapter 35.]

**Victoria**: Your two questions do seem to be at the core of much of religion and philosophy.

Those TULIP percentages are unexpected to me; when I was reading the explanations it seemed like either one agrees with the point or not. Maybe I don't see the finer nuances since there's a lot I don't know.

So while I was looking for that story of the people being beaten, I came across this...

---

[4] Matt Smethurst, "What Happens to Those Who Never Hear the Gospel?" *The Gospel Coalition*, www.thegospelcoalition.org/article/what-happens-to-those-who-never-hear-gospel/.

*And everyone who speaks a word against the Son of Man will be forgiven, but anyone who blasphemes against the Holy Spirit will not be forgiven.* (Lk 12:10)

which brings up more related confusion on the Holy Spirit. What does this verse mean?

Your view that "each person will be judged by the information he/she had (possible) access to" reminds me of similar things I've heard, such as at Belmont. My initial impression of inclusivism and exclusivism is that inclusivism sounds more "good" in wanting to believe that others have a chance even if they've never heard of God or Jesus. Conversely, exclusivism sounds elitist, as if some group was privileged to know/believe, so they'll be saved, and it sucks for everyone else out there. Regarding *The Gospel Coalition* link you referenced which leans more on the exclusivist side, it says, "Humans aren't guilty because they haven't heard the gospel; they're guilty because they haven't honored their Creator." If that's so, could it be the case that people can be redeemed if they honor some random god who they believe is their creator even if they've never heard of God? I can maybe believe that "there are no innocent tribesmen," but the idea of someone who comes up with the idea of Jesus without any kind of external source of information is pretty far-fetched to me. Exclusivism seems frustratingly unfair. On the other hand, how could inclusivism account for one having to believe in Jesus and the Trinity and not, for example, just a single-sided God?

**Steve**: Yes, TULIP is finely nuanced and frustrating to pin down. I'll give you examples of my issues with ULIP (since I agree completely with T). When I said U = 80%, I completely and absolutely agree that I can only come to God as he calls me and that his calling of me has nothing to do with my merit/goodness. But I don't agree that he has specifically and intentionally called some and not others. This is related to I = 50%, because *I personally* do see God's grace as completely irresistible because of how incredible it is. But I'm a believer already, so I'm biased and not helpful to this argument. There are clearly people who have heard the gospel and reject it. A Calvinist would look at that evidence and say that God never called that person, so that's why they rejected it. An Arminian would look at that evidence and say that the person *chose* to reject it (and might even see that rejection as evidence that everyone is T = totally depraved). How can we possibly know? For L = 30%, I believe that L = 100% is the logical conclusion of believing TUIP 100%, and since I don't, I have a big problem with L because of God's ubiquitous love for humanity. For P = 90%, I agree that once a person is truly saved, that he/she will remain saved; Jesus said as much:

*My sheep listen to my voice; I know them, and they follow me. I give them eternal life, and they shall never perish; no one will snatch them*

*out of my hand. My Father, who has given them to me, is greater than*
*all; no one can snatch them out of my Father's hand.* (Jn 10:27–29)

But there's so much ambiguity about "knowing" whether someone else
is saved that I have a slight hesitation. In other words, if someone
professes to be and acts like a Christian for 80 years and then renounces
it all one day before he dies, there's no possible way for us to know if he
was really a Christian all along, so it doesn't seem very helpful in
argument (although I do see how it is very reassuring on a personal
level). So maybe I have problems with both sides, not because they're
clearly wrong but because neither is entirely compelling.

Lk 12:10 is in the context of a larger debate Jesus was having with
the Pharisees (the Jewish religious leaders), who accused him of doing
demonic work:

*Then they brought him a demon-possessed man who was blind and*
*mute, and Jesus healed him, so that he could both talk and see. All the*
*people were astonished and said, "Could this be the Son of David?" But*
*when the Pharisees heard this, they said, "It is only by Beelzebul, the*
*prince of demons, that this fellow drives out demons."* (Mt 12:22–24)

This was clearly about the worst thing you could say to Jesus (i.e.,
claiming an infinitely good God to be bad, which is the definition of
blasphemy). So in that context, this commentary from Joseph Benson
(1749–1821, hence the old-school English) on this verse seems
appropriate (he begins using the perspective of Jesus and ends in third
person):

"And whosoever, &c.—Nothing, therefore, can be more dangerous
and fatal than to oppose my cause: and yet the denying me in some
degree, may, upon true repentance, be forgiven: for whosoever shall
speak a word—Expressive of unbelief and disregard, or even of
opposition and enmity; against the Son of man [Jesus]—In this his
present state of humiliation and suffering, he may possibly
hereafter repent, and on his repentance his sins may be forgiven
him. But unto him that blasphemeth against the Holy Ghost—If a
man's denying of me rise so high that he blasphemes and reviles the
Holy Spirit, and ascribes the miracles wrought by him, in
confirmation of the gospel, to the agency of Satan, this sin shall
never be forgiven, neither is there place for repentance. And
especially he that, after my resurrection and ascension, blasphemes
the Holy Ghost, when that Divine Spirit shall have displayed his
most glorious agency as my great advocate and witness; he who
then opposes that last and most convincing and powerful method of

God's recovering grace, shall, as utterly incorrigible, be abandoned to final destruction."[5]

Your last paragraph is great. You seem to really "get" the debate, which is still linked to Calvinism/Arminianism. I think the best quote I read from the link I gave you was, "I believe the most Christian stance is to remain agnostic on this question. The fact is that God, alongside the most solemn warnings about our responsibility to respond to the gospel, has not revealed how he will deal with those who have never heard it." Here are three things I know for certain: We are terrible. God is love. God is just. The last two are in constant tension (and yet beautifully resolved on the cross). That tension has inevitably led to a lack of human understanding about how God operates. I think the problem is that we want God to operate according to a preset formula: he is *always* like this or *always* like that or deals with *everyone* like this or that. While there are certainly absolutes about his nature that he has revealed to us, carrying that line of thinking too far makes him just another law of physics, which he clearly is not. I don't have hope of this debate ever being solved because God is inherently unsolvable. Finally, everyone who has ever considered these questions *has* heard the gospel, and it is clear what God has commanded them to do:

> They replied, "Believe in the Lord Jesus, and you will be saved—you and your household." (Acts 16:31)

> Then the eleven disciples went to Galilee, to the mountain where Jesus had told them to go. When they saw him, they worshiped him; but some doubted. Then Jesus came to them and said, "All authority in heaven and on earth has been given to me. Therefore go and make disciples of all nations, baptizing them in the name of the Father and of the Son and of the Holy Spirit, and teaching them to obey everything I have commanded you. And surely I am with you always, to the very end of the age." (Mt 28:16–20)

That's a completely sufficient starting point, even in the face of uncertainty.

**Victoria**: Your interpretation of some of the nuances of TULIP cleared up much of the haziness I had. I think this would be interesting to revisit sometime later after I get a better understanding of the bigger picture, overturn subconscious misconceptions, etc.

Benson's commentary was very helpful! I think of this as similar to having the right motive for one's behavior. If one gives time, money, etc. on the outside but is miserly/reluctant on the inside, then it's not fully a

---

[5] Joseph Benson, "Luke 12:10," *Bible Hub*, biblehub.com/commentaries/luke/12-10.htm.

good deed. In this context, if one *doesn't know better* and speaks against Jesus, there's still hope; but speaking against God himself—after knowing what he has done for us—is unforgivable.

I'd agree with the agnostic stance and your statement of the problem with what humans want from God (a preset formula). I find the mention of Mt 28:16–20 interesting. When I was younger and knew almost nothing about Christianity, my impression of Christians was that they're a bunch of proselytizers, or that they were there for fitting into the culture/community. Christianity was not something I had the least bit of interest in. So, it was relieving and refreshing to me when I would meet seemingly devoted Christians who didn't immediately try to convince me that my way of life and my beliefs were all wrong (though I would also be wondering why they weren't doing that and what it meant for being a "true" Christian). It's not that I doubted who they said they were, but it made things seem more disjointed from an external and peripheral perspective. That being said, I think talking to people who are Christian and who are also people I respect as intellectuals (e.g., you and my current research advisor, David Mobley) has helped me to see more of the true idea of what being a Christian means. When I graduated from Belmont and moved away from the Bible Belt, I didn't think Christianity would be something I would give that much consideration anymore; yet, here we are.

**Steve**: As to the last paragraph, I think a true Christian *must have* come to grips with the fact that it wasn't their morality, understanding, cleverness, or effort that led them to Jesus. In that context, how could a true Christian not have an understanding of a non-believer's difficulty in becoming a Christian? It's hard to be a Christian when you already believe, but it's insanely hard to become a Christian in the first place,

> *"Enter through the narrow gate. For wide is the gate and broad is the road that leads to destruction, and many enter through it. But small is the gate and narrow the road that leads to life, and only a few find it."* (Mt 7:13–14)

especially in adulthood; there are so many reasonable doubts that have to be overcome:

> *And he told them many things in parables, saying: "A sower went out to sow. And as he sowed, some seeds fell along the path, and the birds came and devoured them. Other seeds fell on rocky ground, where they did not have much soil, and immediately they sprang up, since they had no depth of soil, but when the sun rose they were scorched. And since they had no root, they withered away. Other seeds fell among thorns, and the thorns grew up and choked them. Other seeds fell on good soil and produced grain, some a hundredfold, some sixty, some thirty. Hear then the parable of the sower: When anyone hears*

*the word of the kingdom and does not understand it, the evil one comes and snatches away what has been sown in his heart. This is what was sown along the path. As for what was sown on rocky ground, this is the one who hears the word and immediately receives it with joy, yet he has no root in himself, but endures for a while, and when tribulation or persecution arises on account of the word, immediately he falls away. As for what was sown among thorns, this is the one who hears the word, but the cares of the world and the deceitfulness of riches choke the word, and it proves unfruitful. As for what was sown on good soil, this is the one who hears the word and understands it. He indeed bears fruit and yields, in one case a hundredfold, in another sixty, and in another thirty."* (Mt 13:3–8, 18–23)

"Though I would also be wondering why they weren't..."[6] I would be a bad friend indeed if I truly thought I had incredible news and didn't tell you. I do wish that more Christians simply presented Christianity as "good news" instead of a way to convert more people to "our side." (As an aside, it's important to know that most Christians are normal people: they 1) are insecure, 2) feel like it's none of their business to get involved in someone else's beliefs, and 3) fear rejection. It takes a lot of courage to risk losing a relationship with someone by presenting Christianity, so most Christians prefer to not say anything to anyone about their faith; I believe that's clear disobedience, but that's where we are. I know it because I lived it for most of my life.)

**Victoria**: "In that context, how could a true Christian not have an understanding of a non-believer's difficulty in becoming a Christian?" True. It's kind of like some people with science. Someone can get really deep into their field and then lose touch with what the blank-slate students don't know. I had a teaching assistant who kept telling us the quantum material was trivial. (I still have no understanding of Green's functions in nonlinear spectroscopy.) I really like the parable of the sower; those are good analogies!

That's an interesting video by Penn Jillette and a really good argument for the act of proselytizing. If a person were in danger of getting hit by a truck, I would think that most, if not all, people would push the person out of the way. "I do wish that more Christians simply presented Christianity as "good news" instead of a way to convert more people to 'our side.'" I think that would affect the social connotation of Christianity for the better. The aside was a worthwhile mention! "I know it because I lived it for most of my life." Wherever this goes, I'm glad you started the conversation.

---

6 "A Gift of a Bible," *YouTube*, www.youtube.com/watch?v=6md638smQd8.

# CHAPTER 9: WHAT MAKES CHRISTIANITY DIFFERENT

**Victoria**: "All God asks of Christians is that we believe these things to be true..." Why is this so hard? Why doesn't he give more "hints," so to speak?

**Steve**: This is very difficult to put in words. I think if we completely understand a thing, it is nearly impossible to love it. The things I really love (my family, friends, students, etc.) require me to constantly drive my attention to them to attempt to gain a grasp of what they're like. On the contrary, if someone hands me a pencil, I immediately appreciate what it does, but I don't love it because it doesn't require me to pursue it to understand it. The beauty of love is in that uncertainty, no? If you knew everything about your boyfriend you could possibly know, I believe he would become an unlovable robot to you. I also feel a tinge of this with science. I love it because of the unknown, but in the end, it must—by definition—be robotic as well. I love coming home from work to my family because, unlike the couch, I have no idea what they're going to do/say/be like. It's also nice that my family loves me back unlike my couch, but that feels less important to me. Now, if we accept these premises, God is like that but again multiplied by a gazillion. I feel as if I'm pursuing an infinite, inexplicable good thing that can never be fully known by me, which makes me want to keep pursuing and trying to know that thing. And if God regularly showed up in some "five senses" kind of way, he'd just be an awesome friend, or even worse, a pencil to be studied.

**Victoria**: I completely agree regarding knowing and loving. I enjoy the process of learning, molding, and growing with those I love and the topics I love to pursue. Something completely known and predictable doesn't evoke feelings of love and respect. So I can understand how you make that connection (times a gazillion) to God. The thing is, going back to human scale, if my boyfriend went AWOL, I would probably eventually cease my love and care for him, because there would be no interchange of ideas, thoughts, anything. I think that a relationship built on love has to be dynamic and mutually involving. If there doesn't seem to be any input from the other side, and the relationship feels one-sided, how can one be convinced that they're in a loving relationship?

**Steve**: We believe that God *has* made himself evident in creation and reason. Given his other qualities—often revealed in us, such as a sense of morality—it stands that he *should* reveal himself and has, the events of which were recorded in the Bible. So, a Christian would say that God speaks to us today most explicitly through the Bible: a static and finite set of ideas about what he is like. In other words, it is mostly enough for me to examine the authenticity, consistency, and historicity of the Bible, accept it at face value, and then experience God through his interactions with biblical characters. (I say "mostly" because I do believe that I've had prayers answered, experienced supernatural things, and seen God work in the big picture in my life, but I get that there's absolutely no way to convince anyone that those things really happened.) So, in one sense, God has revealed himself to me in a way (written word) that is much clearer than I can to him when I speak to him in prayer (because of my own ignorance and inadequacy with language).

**Victoria**: "...evident in creation and reason." Is this like the idea of having to look for it to find it? How do you know what to look for? How do you know you're not fooling yourself?

As for God speaking through the Bible, this is something else I've never understood. It seems that God was once so active in the world: wars, plagues, floods, and the time that Jesus was around. Why is the Bible now past tense/static/finite? I realize that you can apply concepts and see analogies in present-day scenarios, but why was the Bible from time $x$ to time $y$? Will there ever be more to it?

"...ignorance and inadequacy with language." Is this a common thing? Or, conversely, how common do you think it is for people to feel connected to God via prayer? On that note, can you define prayer? My understanding is that prayer is communication to God that can be in a variety of forms. But I don't really understand what that means either. A common depiction is someone on their knees with clasped hands. Is that typical, and can something that isn't this "movie view" of prayer still be a prayer?

**Steve**: I guess I would give a couple of responses. 1) The atheist perspective answers a lot of questions very cleanly and clearly and satisfactorily. But it doesn't—nor can it—even attempt to answer, "Why is there something instead of nothing?" So, I think that while atheism can be very attractive, one must actively dissuade oneself from the evidence that there is a creator, rather than it being a default position. 2) The atheist position itself uses reason to argue its case, which it often does quite well. But having no basis to assume that reason is even a real thing, the atheist position is always circular at best and self-defeating at worst. So, God has made himself evident in those two areas. I like your idea, however, that at some point one must search for God to find him. After all, we have thousands of religions that say many different things, and 1) and 2) above probably aren't enough on their own to find a "winner." Maybe it could be thought of in the same way as science: i.e., it's clear that scientific principles exist, but they will remain hidden until we actively pursue them. So how would we know which religion to follow, given the assumption of god(s)? I tend to think along these lines (this is off the top of my head; I'm sure there's more):

1. Is Religion X as rational as creation appears to be?

2.  Does Religion X seem to be the natural mythical byproduct of a certain race, nationality, gender, political view, or governmental structure, or does it seem to apply to all people at all times?
3.  Is there historical evidence that the events recorded by Religion X actually happened?
4.  Has Religion X made claims about future events that seem to have come true?
5.  Do the proponents of Religion X materially benefit on earth by adhering to it, or is that of little concern to them?
6.  Does Religion X attempt to make its followers look good, or is it more concerned with telling the truth?
7.  Does Religion X reveal things about me that weren't readily obvious, but in hindsight, are (i.e., does it know me better than I know myself?)
8.  Does Religion X make sense to follow in eternity, or just right now?
9.  Does Religion X solve any problems or just tend to create a lot more?
10. Does Religion X require me to do things I can't possibly do?
11. Can Religion X use me at all, or am I just a bystander?
12. Do I want to be like the past followers of Religion X?
13. How seriously have those followers taken Religion X? Were they willing to die for it?
14. Does Religion X ask me to do things I don't want to do, or does it simply confirm what I already believe? (In other words, does it attempt to conform me to God or god to me?)
15. Can Religion X fulfill me in the face of anything that could happen to me on earth?
16. Does Religion X attempt to make clear distinctions between truth and falsehood?
17. Does Religion X survive when critically and objectively analyzed from historical, philosophical, social, governmental, and scientific grounds, or does it require the suspension of such criticism?

Regarding the static nature of the Bible: There are, depending on how you define a miracle, maybe something like 150 miracles in the approximately 2000 years recorded in the Bible. So that's, on average, one miracle *in one spot in the world* every 13 years. So, imagine that in your 80 years on earth, something like six miracles happened in random locations on earth (and we'd probably have doubts about those: I know I would). The perceived regularity of amazing events in the Bible is an incorrect perception based on our ability to scan hundreds of years in a few minutes. In fact, the ability of Jesus to perform about 40 of those (recorded) miracles in a short time frame (~3 years) makes him the exception, not the rule. In other words, the average life of the average person in biblical locations during the Old and New Testaments was like our lives: devoid of miraculous events. So, I would argue that the Bible has *always* been static/past tense/finite (even as it was being written) for 99.99% of all believers. The last book of the Bible—Revelation—

basically (but nebulously) tells us how it all ends, so I don't see much room for addition there. Once Jesus came 2000 years ago, that was pretty much the main point of everything from a Christian perspective.

I view prayer as talking to God in the same way I would talk to a friend, but it's definitely more of a one-way conversation. I can "make" God say anything I want in my head and convince myself that he actually said it, so I'm highly skeptical when people say, "God told me..." But I can't discount it. I think many would say they feel a certain internal leading to do something or speak to someone, maybe like a "gut feeling," but again, I have a very hard time with that, so I don't rely on it very much. Hands clasped/on your knees is a common way to depict prayer (and maybe for some to pray) because it indicates submission and focus, but it's not necessary or important. I do almost always close my eyes; otherwise, I'll start thinking about other things if I'm looking at them.

**Victoria**: Regarding atheism part 1), I agree. I did once claim myself as atheist for a short time, but the lack of addressing the "why" and the improbability of the "how" changed my mind. Incidentally, I think the "Why are we here?" question has different layers. In one aspect, that might be answered by, "God created man," and so on, but that is broader than the other aspect of "What's the point of anything/everything?" I think this leads into the topics we're currently discussing elsewhere. Regarding atheism part 2), do you mean that reason might not be a real thing as a subset of an earlier discussion of consciousness not being a real thing (i.e., reason implies consciousness but not the other way around)?

Going to the main idea of God making himself evident in these two areas, that makes sense for answering, "*Is there* a God who exists?" How can one see in present day that God is *still* evident, and not that he created and introduced reason and is taking a completely hands-off approach with the world? Hmm, I think this connects to earlier when we were talking about deism and theism. I'm not sure if we talked about one vs. the other directly, or if there was a clear conclusion there.

Regarding how to know which religion to follow: wow, such detail! Most of them seem sensible to me. There are some that I'm interested in in more detail:

1. Can creation really be said to be rational, as supposedly man was formed from the dust of the ground in the image of God?
6. I was a bit surprised that this is considered. What religions exist that attempt to make their followers look good?
7. How does a religion know one better than the person knows oneself? Does that mean just speaking about general human nature or about the individual specifically? If general human nature, I would also probably say that a psychologist in many ways knows me better than I know myself.

8. Also didn't expect this one. Why is this important? I think this might be more relevant if one already believed in eternity and consciousness remaining after death.

11. Hmm, a religion using its followers? Is this like proselytizing? Why is that important to consider in choosing a religion?

14. I don't understand why this is considered. I think if I were locked in a room for $x$ hours and had to think of my own questions of criteria for choosing a religion, I don't know that I would come up with this one.

15. Why is this important? What does it mean to be fulfilled in the face of something happening? The way I interpret this is if, for example, there was a traumatic event like the death of a loved one, and then religion comes into play whether for comfort, community, etc.

17. No questions here, but I just wanted to say I like this one.

Musing on this again, here's my train of thought: there is a God who has made himself evident in creation and the basis of reason, and we must actively pursue theological principles to find the truth. In this way, actively pursuing theological principles is analogous to actively pursuing scientific principles; however, many people choose not to do science (or even actively dislike it). What would motivate someone to go to such length of research (e.g., addressing one's stance on these challenging questions) to find some religion to live bound by?

For the static nature of the Bible, that's an understandable answer. If miracles still happen in the present day (as I presume they would with God's continual involvement), then why don't the more modern ones (or anything within the last two millennia) make it into the Bible? Wouldn't that make the Bible more relatable? I suppose that could be impossible in the present day (i.e., how would you convince so many people that this new addition is legitimate?).

People write to friends as in letters and such. Does that mean one could, in a sense, pray via writing letters to God, "texting" God, etc.? Presumably, the outputs of these things would just sit there, but I wonder about the intent and idea, as related to the concept of prayer. Would these be effective modes of prayer communication? Is one way better than another, given that the same message is going across regardless?

**Steve**: Yes, I mean that one cannot simply assume that one is reasonable a priori and then use reason to prove one's point. The theistic perspective assumes an external source of reason on which to ground arguments. Deism, by definition, assumes that god has not intervened in the universe after creation, so a deistic god couldn't have given us reason. So if one argues for deism, one is again assuming reason a priori and weakening/destroying one's own argument. In addition, objective morality and deism are incompatible, because objective morality also requires an external giver of something, which deism denies. On to the questions!

1. I didn't mean Creation (God's act to make the universe and us), but creation, the mechanistic laws of nature, which seem inherently rational.
6. An unfortunately large branch of Christianity follows the "prosperity gospel," the idea that God's desire for Christians is to be wealthy and healthy. But beyond that, I would argue that any religion which claims that its followers can achieve righteousness by being "good" is making just that claim.
7. Yes, I was referring to general human nature.
8. If this life is all there is, I really don't see the point. It seems like a big waste of time:

   *If only for this life we have hope in Christ, we are of all people most to be pitied.* (1 Cor 15:19)

11. Personally, I just want to be involved in important things. But from an argumentative standpoint, we seem to exist in a world that has both mind and matter components. If a religion existed only in my mind and didn't cause me to interact with the material universe in any way, that would seem to be a huge disconnect with the nature of reality.
14. Ha ha! If a religion just basically asked me to do the things I already wanted to do and believe the things I already believed, what am I worshiping? What's the point? How is that even a religion? A good religion should lead me somewhere I wasn't already going.
15. Assuming that a religion believes in the supernatural, it, by definition, contains components that are beyond this material world. So how could the material world affect such a belief system (besides convincing me that my religion is bogus)? For example, does this religion provide me with enough evidence of God's goodness that I still believe in it when *my* house is destroyed by a hurricane? If not, then I know that my faith will *eventually* be shattered, so why believe now?

"What would motivate someone to go to such length of research (e.g., addressing one's stance on these challenging questions) to find some religion to live bound by?" I wholeheartedly agree with your implication that the vast majority of humanity will never pursue these questions because of a lack of knowledge, introspection, or even interest. Most genuine Christians I personally know became Christians through years of (sometimes unintentional) immersion in surface-level theology (upbringing/culture/church) followed by a shocking realization of their own sinfulness and God's holiness. That's enough for most, but it wasn't and hasn't been enough for me (although I have also had those same shocking realizations). But I'm confident that Christianity is simultaneously simple enough for toddlers...

*And he said: "Truly I tell you, unless you change and become like little children, you will never enter the kingdom of heaven." (Mt 18:3)*

and advanced enough for scholars:

*Jesus did many other things as well. If every one of them were written down, I suppose that even the whole world would not have room for the books that would be written. (Jn 21:25)*

As far as the completeness of the Bible, it seems to have been (mostly) finalized in the 300s. There had been many stories written about Jesus and theology since his death, so church leaders had to piece together which were authentic and which were not, which were congruous with the established theological picture and which were not, etc. When the Protestant Reformation happened in the 1500s (as a response to church corruption and skewed theology), a few more "borderline" books were cut off, leaving us with 66 total books. That doesn't discount modern miracles or anything, but it's effectively a statement saying, "This is enough for us to go on:"

*"He said to him, 'If they do not listen to Moses and the Prophets, they will not be convinced even if someone rises from the dead.'" (Lk 16:31)*

Practically, it allows us to move on from constantly having to decide whether *this* or *that* is a miracle and how much it matters.

Finally, yes, I do believe that writing/texting/thinking can all be loose forms of communication with God if designed in such a way (although I'm not sure what phone number you would use for texting). However, when I write, I have to focus on the pen/paper/screen to get it done, so I feel like I would lose my focus on God, and I imagine that's why the standard form of prayer is preferred.

**Victoria**: Your comments on deism make sense. Could there exist a state somewhere in between deism and theism? Such a state might have, for example, a God who created the uni/multiverse and was the source of reason and objective morality in the first humans, and then those gifts got passed down biologically. Okay, now that I'm writing this out, I can see where the logic seems to falter; I would find it hard to believe that somehow reason and morality are somehow encoded in our beings (e.g., DNA) and can be handed down from parent to offspring. Despite this, how can one argue that God is involved and has a vested interest in people's lives (if that's what's believed), other than providing these intangible ingredients? Getting to the questions:

1. Ah, okay.
6. So you're saying that (true) Christianity is concerned with telling the truth instead of making its followers look good. And there's no

way (true) Christianity can make its followers look good, since, in context with our earlier discussion, no person can actually ever *be* good.

7. So far, we've established: "Does Religion X know me better than I know myself, as referred to general human nature?" → "Why is this important to consider for choosing a religion?" People generally wouldn't consider psychology or sociology in a fervent religious manner, though I'm sure these fields can explain how we think and behave more than we know about ourselves. Why then would this particular idea matter for Christianity?

8. Well … it does seem like a waste of time to me sometimes. This connects to our earlier discussion regarding what else there is besides life and the "why" of anything. So, I'm probably limited in my understanding here based on my lack of understanding in those other areas. I also don't understand that quote: "If only for this life we have hope in Christ, we are of all people most to be pitied." People who have hope in Christ in this lifetime only are seeing it wrong? People should have hope in Christ beyond this life? I thought beyond this life (if there's something beyond this life), one's destination is set, so why does one still need to hope?

**Steve**: I think the gist of your questions can be summed up with: How do we know God is (attempting to be) involved in our lives? Well, of course, as with anything, we can't know with absolute certainty. But from the very beginning, I've tried to argue from reason and probability, so here goes (the following numbers are unrelated to the previous ones):

1. If we've established that God is omniscient, he certainly knew that we would exist and have the ability to attempt to understand and relate to him. With that knowledge, he still decided to create the universe, so he must have done it with a relationship in mind. (Of course, *we* could be delusional and irrational, but you're asking about God.)

2. If we've established that objective morality exists and must've come from God, it follows that there are things he wants us to do or not do, which I would say is an involvement.

3. The entirety of human history has been intertwined with an attempt to relate to god(s). That seems odd if he didn't give us that desire.

4. There are good, rational people who are fully convinced that they have interacted with God and are trying to convince me of the same. I heard someone say once, "You can tell what God is doing in your life by the people he's put in your life." I agree wholeheartedly.

5. The alternative is meaninglessness, but the vast majority of humanity appears to act as if life has meaning. It would be odd if life truly had no purpose but we constantly acted as if it did.

6. The Bible presents a case of God's continued interaction with people from extremely different backgrounds and a priori beliefs as if it

were historical fact. I find it odd that people who would normally have nothing to do with each other would come together in this way.

7. There is clear extrabiblical evidence of the sacrifices, even unto humiliating death, that the first Christians were willing to endure. They gained nothing materially from their lives or beliefs, so I find it difficult to believe that so many were willing to give up their comfortable religious traditions, occupations, and family life to be killed for a delusion; i.e., they must have seen something amazing with their own eyes.

**Victoria**: I think the fact that there are such large numbers (i.e., 7+ billion people on earth) makes it hard to think about God having a personal relationship with each and every person. (But you did also mention that the Bible says that we only come to God by his calling, so does he just not call to everyone?) Also, some of these seem like less active forms of involvement by God, such as doing or not doing things as guided by morality. I guess I'm also not convinced by the indications via example (as opposed to proofs by example) of 3–7. I'm trying to figure out how one can actually say that God is actively involved in life at the present for ... everyone? Basically, what is God's level of involvement, how do we know it's still relevant today, and how do we know it's relevant for ... whomever it's relevant for. That being said, I really liked number 4 in the list and that quote especially. It touches on each of these, but not as strongly on how we know it was specifically God's doing.

If God is putting certain people in other people's lives, wouldn't he just fill each other's lives with Christians (if we set aside the call to spread God's word)? Also, I was thinking about this walking to school today in light of recent life stuff. Isn't it just a matter of perspective? The same things can happen to person A and person B; A might view these circumstances as works of God, whereas B might just see these as a series of coincidences. This is related to synchronicity[1], I think. If one's already in one camp or the other, why might they make the switch?

**Steve**: I also find it difficult to grasp God's relationship with so many people. But if I've gotten to the point where I believe he created $10^{80}$ particles in our universe (and maybe $10^{500}$ universes), that's the least of my issues. (I'll address the "calling" thing below.) I also agree that God's exact involvement in my life is very unclear most of the time. But again, if I've accepted that an invisible being created everything to begin with, ambiguity is to be expected. As stated, I'm pretty sure I can't prove to you that God is involved with us. But here are some examples in my life, one of which you might not like ... but here goes.

1. Two months ago, I bought my daughter a used car but was concerned that I wouldn't have enough to pay for a major repair. I kept "feeling" like I needed to save $500 when I had the chance (due to getting paid extra for teaching a summer class). Last week, her

---

[1] "Synchronicity," Wikipedia, en.wikipedia.org/wiki/Synchronicity.

"check engine" light came on, and the mechanic today told me it would be $502.07 to repair the car. I would give this a 10% chance of God supernaturally leading me to save money in advance and a 90% chance that I just used biblical wisdom and decent estimation techniques (using my God-given reasoning abilities) to save what I need for an event like this. Whether the truth is supernatural or mundane, I thank God for being involved in my life to help me in this scenario (even *very* indirectly).

2.  I had a toothache for about four months (I'm really stubborn) in college before I finally had to drive home (2.5 hours away) to see a dentist. The dentist looked at my teeth and saw nothing wrong. When I got to my house after visiting the dentist, my father, who had been dealing with cancer for a while, suddenly took a turn for the worse and died within a couple of hours. I got to be with him as he died, which was an incredibly important thing to me. My tooth never hurt again after his death, but if I hadn't had a toothache, I wouldn't have been with him. No toothache immediately after four straight months of a toothache? I would peg that one at 80% chance of supernatural, 20% chance of coincidence.

3.  I sent you an email on December 20 that basically detailed my faith in a pretty straightforward way and asked you to respond with your thoughts. You usually reply pretty quickly, so when you didn't, I thought I had probably gone overboard. I didn't think you were necessarily mad or anything, but that maybe I crossed a line of what you were willing to discuss. I was honestly afraid that you wouldn't ever email me back and that I had lost a friend because I was too forward. Fast forward to August 9. I was in a Bible study, and we were talking about friendship and I brought up the fact that I thought I had lost a friend and I just felt kind of bummed about it. I asked everyone to pray for my "friend in California, that I hadn't done something to hurt or offend her, and that we could restore our relationship (or that I could know that it was OK), but that I also still wanted to discuss faith with her." You literally emailed me 42 hours later after nothing for almost 8 months and now we're having this discussion. (I hope none of that is too weird or creepy for you, but you asked how I know that God is involved in my life, so it's all your fault!) So here we are. Is it possible that all of this was a coincidence? Absolutely, but I'm guessing maybe a 50% chance of supernatural, 50% coincidence on this one.

Now, if just one supernatural event were to occur in my life, that would be convincing to me that God is working in my life. The (completely made-up) probability of at least one supernatural event occurring from these three events is $1 - 0.9 \times 0.2 \times 0.5 = 91\%$. Now, over my life, I've had dozens, if not hundreds, of stories like that: none with certainty, many with very low supernatural probability, but in total, a combined very high probability that God is at work in my life. For example, if the chances were even as low as a 1% chance of a supernatural interaction in, let's say, each of 100 pretty cool coincidences in my life (2–3 per year), then there is a $1 - 0.99^{100} \approx 63\%$ chance that God has supernaturally intervened in my life, which seems good enough to go on for me. (If you ramped it up to 3% per event, you're above the 95% confidence level! Yes! I proved that God exists![2] I'm so nerdy.) So it's never been any single event, but rather my experience and reason over the course of my life that give me confidence. In addition, I never have to base something like loving my neighbor...

> *Do not seek revenge or bear a grudge against anyone among your people, but love your neighbor as yourself. I am the LORD.* (Lev 19:18)

on whether Event X was supernatural or not:

> *The Pharisees and Sadducees came to Jesus and tested him by asking him to show them a sign from heaven. He replied, "When evening comes, you say, 'It will be fair weather, for the sky is red,' and in the morning, 'Today it will be stormy, for the sky is red and overcast.' You know how to interpret the appearance of the sky, but you cannot interpret the signs of the times. A wicked and adulterous generation looks for a sign, but none will be given it except the sign of Jonah."* *Jesus then left them and went away.* (Mt 16:1–4)

(The "sign of Jonah" is related to an Old Testament story and is Jesus' prediction that he would die and then be raised from the dead). Of course, if you make all of the probabilities zero beforehand, they all add up to zero in the end. In other words, if you go through life with the a priori assumption that God cannot possibly work in your life, you'll end up with a self-fulfilling prophecy. Or like Henry Ford said, "Whether you think you can or whether you think you can't, you're right."

Yes, all of these things could be synchronicity and God could not exist and I could be delusional. If we "knew" any of these answers with absolute certainty, we wouldn't be having this discussion. But here's the thing. On what basis does one discount supernatural events (especially if one (cough) has already stated one's belief in god(s))? I get that they don't happen with clarity or predictability, but does that mean they don't happen?

---

[2] Inherent uncertainty in scientific work (the laws of physics actually *forbid* exactitude with certain types of measurements) makes it common for scientists to express a probability of confirming a hypothesis rather than declaring complete certainty. In many fields, this standard of "proof" lies at 95% or above.

"If God is putting certain people in other people's lives, wouldn't he just fill each other's lives with Christians?" No way! The Bible is full of stories of murderers/prostitutes/slimeballs (some believers, some not) that God used to fulfill his purposes. I mean, God has put people like Sigmund Freud and Josef Stalin and Neil deGrasse Tyson in my life (at least intellectually) to force me to address hard questions and draw me nearer to himself. Those types of interactions become more profound and useful the more personal those relationships become (e.g., with professors, colleagues, pastors, friends, family, etc.), and I can see—if I look to see—how God has used them all to shape me in different ways.

"If one's already in one camp or the other, why might they make the switch?" (I'm assuming your camps are "naturalism" and "supernaturalism.") My advice to someone in a camp is: Don't be in a camp. Be open-minded from the outset that both camps are possible and may even reinforce each other.

**Victoria**: This is kind of a minor point, but when you say "invisible being" referring to God creating everything, but he created man in the image of himself, he can't be invisible then, can he? (Where did you address the "calling" thing? Was that in a different question?)

Those three events … that's the kind of stuff that is referred to when they say truth is stranger than fiction. Other people have recounted similarly astounding incidents in their lives, but I never really know what's truth and what's embellishment. (I don't think you would embellish.) Even if you showed me hard evidence, I admit it's hard for me to grasp those things happening in real life (especially event two)— it calls for a suspension of rational thought based only on natural cause and effect. Event three is also pretty bizarre. I remember not knowing what I thought well enough to reply to that last email right away, and so the email just sat there for a while. And then it was hard to respond after much time had passed.

Wow, I'm amused by that "proof!" The percentage will necessarily depend on how many such potential-God events one interprets to occur in life. I think even the math of my own life would work out to be more than 50%. That's a really neat frame of reference.

"No way!" That's somewhat relieving for reasons I don't fully know how to articulate.

"Don't be in a camp." I'll try.

**Steve**: Most people think that the "image of God" is not about physical appearance, but rather a "representation of," like your mirror image is a representation of you (but that's a terrible example because it also looks just like you → sad trombone). Anyway, I don't necessarily mean that God is invisible in a "photons don't bounce off of him" way, but rather in a "we don't see him" way. (There *is* this story…

*"But," he said, "you cannot see my face, for no one may see me and live." Then the* LORD *said, "There is a place near me where you may*

*stand on a rock. When my glory passes by, I will put you in a cleft in the rock and cover you with my hand until I have passed by. Then I will remove my hand and you will see my back; but my face must not be seen." (Ex 33:20–23)*

along with many others, where God seems to take a physical form for the purpose of directly communicating to people, but it's usually interpreted as a practical thing instead of being what he "really looks like." Otherwise, we would have some major crazy questions to deal with like why God needs an anatomy and how that would relate to our own appearance via evolution.)

I remember writing that I addressed the "calling" thing, but I can't remember what I was referring to. But *now* I feel that we have talked about it with the Calvinism/Arminianism thing, in that who God calls is a point of unending debate in Christianity. (My opinion: at a minimum, he calls everyone through creation, morality, and reason, and we all have the choice/ability to reject/ignore that call.)

I think "'Don't be in a camp.' I'll try." is my favorite thing either one of us has written so far! It's like both of our lives summed up in seven words! Ha ha!

**Victoria**: Regarding the image of God, that's a reasonable concept! Do people see him after death then? Or is that considered "life after death" so people still wouldn't see him? Also, Ex 33:20 ("you cannot see my face, for no one may see me and live") kind of reminds me of Medusa. I hope that's not disrespectful.

As far as the last sentence, I'd agree with that! :)

**Steve**: I actually like the example of Medusa. It's a reminder to me that humans throughout history have had an incredible fear and awe of the gods...

*... since what may be known about God is plain to them, because God has made it plain to them. For since the creation of the world God's invisible qualities—his eternal power and divine nature—have been clearly seen, being understood from what has been made, so that people are without excuse. (Rom 1:19–20)*

but that it's been distorted:

*Although they claimed to be wise, they became fools and exchanged the glory of the immortal God for images made to look like a mortal human being and birds and animals and reptiles. (Rom 1:22–23)*

But yes, we will see God in heaven. This...

*No longer will there be any curse. The throne of God and of the Lamb will be in the city, and his servants will serve him. They will see his face, and his name will be on their foreheads.* (Rev 22:3–4)

is from the last chapter of the Bible ("face" may be an anthropomorphization and "names on foreheads" is probably a metaphor for ownership/servitude/submission/awe/worship.) I prefer to think about seeing God as awesomely vaporizing my atoms like in a nuclear blast or something, but that's just the geek in me.

**Victoria**: That's amusing! I'm glad you explained that last passage. It'd probably be useful if I actually read the Bible in full so that I can evaluate its main ideas myself. This tells me I should probably look for some kind of annotated version.

**Steve**: I agree that you should not trust anything I say at face value, and that you should study these things for yourself. I use the *NIV Study Bible*.[3] It's great.

**Victoria**: Out of curiosity, how do you in particular go about reading the Bible? Has your approach to it evolved over the years?

**Steve**: I began an attempt to read through the entire Bible for the first time while I was in college. To help me, I 1) read *Matthew Henry's Commentary*[4] alongside it, 2) attended church/Sunday school/Bible study regularly to hear the "big perspective" from other points of view, and 3) used a lot of Google searches to help explain verses I didn't understand. It took me many years going very slowly to get through the whole thing. However, I had the benefit of growing up in church and being immersed in Christian ideas, whereas you would be starting at almost zero (or even negative because I imagine you've only known a politicized and moralized version of Christianity in America). That being said, I usually tell interested readers to start with the book of John. It really gets to the heart of the matter: what Jesus did and who he claimed to be. I'd be happy to read "alongside" you if you wanted. At this point in my life, I'm much more involved in teaching rather than learning (I mean that only in the "What is Christianity about?" sense, not learning about God), so much of my study is focused on small sets of verses and trying to exegete in a historical and cultural context (e.g., looking at why a writer might have addressed believers in a certain city in a certain way). But honestly, my guiding life question has changed over the past few years from "How does God relate to me?" to "Everything is about God, so how do I live and convey that idea?" That was in great part due to two huge influences in my life: Dave Broome, the senior adults minister at my church, who led a Bible study I was in, and John Piper,

---

[3] *NIV Study Bible* (Grand Rapids: Zondervan, 2002).
[4] Leslie Church, *Matthew Henry's Commentary* (Grand Rapids: Zondervan, 1961).

whose books *Desiring God*[5] and *When I Don't Desire God*[6] have elucidated how to find purpose and joy in God alone.

**Victoria**: I'd agree with the negative starting point that you mentioned, judging by all the misconceptions you've cleared up for me already! That would be fantastic if we could read it concurrently. I was thinking about starting it shortly after my PhD advancement exam on November 16. I actually did once try to read through all the gospels (a few years ago while at Belmont), but then life got busy and I lost the purpose to continue. Would you recommend I get *Matthew Henry's Commentary* in addition to the *NIV Study Bible*? Also, I was just talking to my advisor today about how best to read the Bible, and he recommended I go through the Old and New Testaments concurrently, "else you might just get to Numbers and quit." (I like your use of the word "exegete!") Regarding your guiding life question, that's a noteworthy shift! I'm curious to hear about your experiences; can you speak more about those two influences?

**Steve**: Great! I envision maybe slowly moving through chapters, hearing your thoughts, and then giving my own (or perhaps a conventional) interpretation. It sounds like fun!

*Matthew Henry's Commentary* was great for me in that it 1) forced me to slow down (because it's huge) and 2) gave a ton of cross-references, explanations, and extra-biblical knowledge. It isn't necessary, but it is free,[7] so it can always easily be used as a good reference (and there are plenty of others[8]). So, yes, I recommend it, but not if it makes reading the Bible a chore or daunting task, which it can.

I agree with your advisor (side note: I don't like when people spell it "adviser," so I'm glad we're on the same team) that reading from the beginning of the Old Testament alone can be a challenge, but I'm not so sure that's true when reading from the beginning of the New Testament. It's definitely true that a lot of New Testament history is understood through the Old Testament, but the apostle Paul spent most of his time dealing with people who had no clue what the Old Testament even was, so it's not necessary to begin there. (Also, you won't get enough from Genesis to know everything about John anyway.) So, I'm not opposed to that idea, but again, as busy as you are, you'd have to decide whether that would be too much to begin with.

---

[5] John Piper, *Desiring God: Meditations of a Christian Hedonist* (Sisters, OR: Multnomah Publishers, 2003).

[6] John Piper, *When I Don't Desire God: How to Fight for Joy* (Wheaton, IL: Crossway Publishers, 2004).

[7] "Matthew Henry Commentary on the Whole Bible," *Bible Study Tools*, www.biblestudytools.com/commentaries/matthew-henry-complete/.

[8] Matt Perman, "What Commentaries Does DG Recommend?" *Desiring God*, January 23, 2006, www.desiringgod.org/articles/what-commentaries-does-dg-recommend.

Dave Broome joined our church in 2008 as the senior adults' pastor (a euphemism for a minister to old people). He immediately struck me as the happiest person I had ever met, so when he began leading a Bible study on Wednesday nights, I had to attend to find out how he ended up that way. (I've always been very skeptical of happy people, as if they haven't really thought about the difficult questions of life.) After spending a few years in his Bible study, I really sensed a pattern that everything in his life was about Jesus: talking about Jesus, thinking about Jesus, worshiping Jesus, loving Jesus, leading people to Jesus, seeing Jesus as the explanation and solution for everything, trying to model Jesus' behavior, etc. I learned about how difficult his life had been in many ways (e.g., having an authoritarian father, living in poverty, experiencing his wife's death, etc.) and how wrong I was to assume that happy people are shallow. I had never met anyone who seemed to really know how to pull off Christianity in the way that he did, and since then I've attempted to model his behavior.

For all that Dave Broome did for me through his example, I still lacked a strong intellectual justification for it. That's where John Piper stepped in. I began reading and listening to some of his stuff 4–5 years ago, and I've never known a theologian present such complex issues in ways that are understandable and livable. He showed me that my main purpose in life *is* to be happy, but my only hope of accomplishing that is through God. In other words, until that point, I (subconsciously) believed that glorifying God and being happy were mutually exclusive. In other words, if my entire focus were on God, it could not be on me, and if my focus were not on me, I could not do the things I needed to bring myself satisfaction. Or, if my focus were all on myself, I could not possibly have my focus on God, which I knew *should be* my ultimate goal. Piper really made it clear that my satisfaction and my worship/love/ glorification of God are the same thing: one cannot exist without the other. His ministry, *Desiring God*,[9] has the motto: "God is most glorified in us when we are most satisfied in him."[10] It's not that he said anything that isn't already clear in the Bible, but I was just missing it. My life is now about making myself as happy as I possibly can, but that almost always means doing the exact opposite of what the world says will make me happy. It simply involves attaching myself to the greatest thing ever.

**Victoria**: I have the *NIV Study Bible*! I'm down to start whenever is good for you. [To the reader: this Bible study begins in Chapter 18.]

That sound like a good contrast of role models to have. I identify with being skeptical toward people who seem overly happy, so I think it's neat that you saw a deeper life history which could lead anyone else

---

[9] *Desiring God*, www.desiringgod.org.
[10] John Piper, "God Is Most Glorified in Us When We Are Most Satisfied in Him," *Desiring God*, October 13, 2012, www.desiringgod.org/messages/god-is-most-glorified-in-us-when-we-are-most-satisfied-in-him.

to have a darker personality. Maybe it's the social and cultural contexts that give us these misconceptions—similar to my own previous thoughts on the incompatible beliefs of science and faith.

That *Desiring God* motto (and your life "goal" for lack of a better word) is beautiful in its simplicity and exhortation.

# CHAPTER 10: THE NATURE OF SIN

**Victoria**: In Chapter 1, you said that if a Christian were to struggle with some particular sin, that it wouldn't disqualify them from being a Christian. What if a Christian pursued a particular sin but it wasn't a struggle (i.e., sinning without remorse)?

This reminds me of a question I thought of years ago but never really got addressed. Earlier, you stated, "All God asks of Christians is that we believe these [foundational claims of Christianity] to be true, and then we are effectively made good by his standards." If this is true, what would prevent someone from delaying any belief in Christianity until later in life so as to not feel guilt for sinning, or so they might not be required to abstain from hedonistic pleasures? Wouldn't that allow them to have the "best of both worlds"? They could 1) live in a carefree (guilt-free, rules-free) manner for most of their life as well as 2) make the decision to convert before dying so as to spend eternity in heaven with God.

Put in a more tangible scenario: If Person A is a lifelong devout Christian who chooses to live the cleanest life he can and denies himself sinful short-term pleasures, and Person B lives a carefree life but legitimately converts to Christianity a few years before death, what does it mean for each of them for eternity? Do they both end up in the same place regardless?

**Steve**: Recognizing one's own sinfulness is essential to understanding the need for a savior, so if a person had no remorse over sinful behavior and no intention to change it, it would lead me to believe that there's something seriously wrong with his/her theology and/or relationship with God. In addition, Christians believe that the Holy Spirit functions to make our sinfulness clear and point us to Jesus, so again, the lack of a conscience with regard to sinful behavior would be an indication of a broken relationship with God or no relationship at all. I should say that from a human perspective, there would never be a time where we could look at someone and say, "He's not a Christian because he has sin in his life." For Christians, personal sin never goes away (but it should diminish); rather, the attitude toward sin is more important. That's why I would never claim to be morally superior to anyone on Earth; I am deeply aware of my own sinfulness (admittedly, though, sometimes my sinfulness manifests in not being aware enough of my sinfulness).

To your second point, Jesus addressed it here:

*"For the kingdom of heaven is like a master of a house who went out early in the morning to hire laborers for his vineyard. After agreeing with the laborers for a denarius a day, he sent them into his vineyard. And going out about the third hour he saw others standing idle in the*

*marketplace, and to them he said, 'You go into the vineyard too, and whatever is right I will give you.' So they went. Going out again about the sixth hour and the ninth hour, he did the same. And about the eleventh hour he went out and found others standing. And he said to them, 'Why do you stand here idle all day?' They said to him, 'Because no one has hired us.' He said to them, 'You go into the vineyard too.' And when evening came, the owner of the vineyard said to his foreman, 'Call the laborers and pay them their wages, beginning with the last, up to the first.' And when those hired about the eleventh hour came, each of them received a denarius. Now when those hired first came, they thought they would receive more, but each of them also received a denarius. And on receiving it they grumbled at the master of the house, saying, 'These last worked only one hour, and you have made them equal to us who have borne the burden of the day and the scorching heat.' But he replied to one of them, 'Friend, I am doing you no wrong. Did you not agree with me for a denarius? Take what belongs to you and go. I choose to give to this last worker as I give to you. Am I not allowed to do what I choose with what belongs to me? Or do you begrudge my generosity?'"* (Mt 20:1–15)

In Christianity, fairness does not seem very important to God, mainly because our standing before him has nothing to do with our effort. In fact, the whole thing seems to be designed for unfairness in our favor.

**Victoria:** "Recognizing one's own sinfulness is essential to understanding the need for a savior." What if you don't understand why some of those things are sins? It makes sense that one shouldn't treat others unkindly, but not all of them are so obvious. For example, gluttony is a sin, yet many people go to buffets.

Regarding conscience, it seems that one must have a conscience to have an unbroken relationship with God, though having a conscience doesn't mean there is that relationship at all. One must have conscience + belief + more things? Perhaps having belief is a superset of having conscience, though.

"Personal sin should diminish." How so? If the amount of sin were plotted as a function of amount of time lived, I would imagine a decent amount of fluctuations. It starts at zero, maybe climbs pretty sharply (as one grows up and learns things), maybe decreases some (as one matures) but then may fluctuate around a somewhat-constant value. When you say it should diminish, are you saying this function should go back down to zero? Is that possible?

Regarding attitude being important, I can understand that. Attitude seems to be what gets anyone anywhere in life. For example, we have rotation students in my lab that know little about computational chemistry or how to code, yet my advisor chose them to rotate because of their enthusiasm and curiosity.

Regarding the question of fairness, wow, I like that passage. Let's say someone already knew that the landowner was generous and that everyone would get a denarius regardless. Wouldn't that person just start later in the day and end up having to work the least?

**Steve**: I wouldn't say that all *sins* are clearly obvious but that everyone's *sinfulness* is clearly obvious. (Specifically, in the Old Testament, God's relationship with the Israelites is partly theocratic, and there are specific rules and regulations that God required of them that we don't consider to be universal for all people and all time; e.g., dietary restrictions.) I think you're hitting on a very common misconception of Christianity (and one that many Christians and I have personally subscribed to at some point): Christianity is *not* sin management. We do believe that 1) it is sin that separates us from God (in relationship, not spatially), and 2) recognizing and repenting of your sins is necessary for a healthy relationship with God. But at no time on earth will we ever be sinless or have our sins ordered, categorized, named, and repented of:

> *For I do not understand my own actions. For I do not do what I want, but I do the very thing I hate. Now if I do what I do not want, I agree with the law, that it is good. So now it is no longer I who do it, but sin that dwells within me. For I know that nothing good dwells in me, that is, in my flesh. For I have the desire to do what is right, but not the ability to carry it out. For I do not do the good I want, but the evil I do not want is what I keep on doing.* (Rom 7:15–19)

(That was written by someone I consider to be the "best" Christian of all time, the apostle Paul.) In fact, considering the fact that the Bible was written thousands of years ago, it could not possibly directly address modern issues (e.g., stem cell research), so there's always ambiguity and always will be. I believe that sin *should* decrease as one's relationship with God improves over time, but a poor relationship may preclude that.

Regarding your last question, Jesus speaks of it here:

> *"Then he said, 'This is what I'll do. I will tear down my barns and build bigger ones, and there I will store my surplus grain. And I'll say to myself, "You have plenty of grain laid up for many years. Take life easy; eat, drink and be merry."' But God said to him, 'You fool! This very night your life will be demanded from you. Then who will get what you have prepared for yourself?'"* (Lk 12:18–20)

In other words, how could one plan such a thing? But it addresses another misconception: Christians don't (or *shouldn't*) view heaven as an awesome place with infinite tacos or something as our goal. Our goal is to be with God forever (his presence is what makes it heaven). So if you don't want God now, why would you want him in 50 years (or a billion years), besides regret?

**Victoria**: What does it mean for sinfulness to be obvious while sins might not be obvious? If a sin isn't obvious, and one committed it, how would the sinfulness be obvious? Or is it just obvious to God? (Incidentally, why did God's relationship with people change over time? "Partly theocratic" to ... what is it now?)

"Christianity is not sin management." Hmm. Wow. It does come across as that. I think the view of Christianity as sin management evoked my "Why would God care?" question earlier, since there are all these things in my mind that are associated with Christianity, and they don't all feel like one cohesive picture. Your reframing of sin being "self over God" helped (Chapter 5).

Regarding Rom 7:15–19, that's confusing to me. I read it twice but still can't make sense of it. So Paul's saying that he doesn't understand why he wants to do evil? If he does a thing that he hates to do, why is he doing it? Does he hate it in theory but still does it because he doesn't hate it in practice due to his sinful nature? I don't even know how to interpret verse 16. How does all this relate back to your statement, "at no time on earth will we ... have our sins ordered, categorized, name, and repented of?" (Tangentially, and maybe I should ask this later because it's more of a curiosity in the middle of all this, but why do you consider Paul the "best" Christian of all time? What does that even mean?)

I also don't quite understand that part from Lk 12:18–20. I interpreted it as: don't save up your life for later because you might not have a chance to live it later? I don't know what verse 20 is trying to imply, though, or how this relates to sin going back down to zero or not. And then how does the idea of heaven fit in here? Can we take a couple of steps back? (I also don't get the idea of heaven, but I'll ask about that later.)

**Steve**: OK, let's slow down and/or take a couple of steps back! I'll just answer the first question, and maybe we can go from there. What I meant was that it's clear that we all have selfish (i.e., sinful) motivations and impulses that aren't necessarily the best for ourselves and/or others (as you mentioned before with human-defined morality), but laying those out into a clear, codified, named list of severity is impossible. It's sort of like modeling the weather: the hurricane is obviously there, but trying to pinpoint all of its causes and fluctuations is outside the realm of human ability. So saying, "Is this a sin?" or "Is that a sin?" or "Does this count?" does have meaning, but it's missing the hurricane.

**Victoria**: I see. Intuitively, I would have thought about this in the opposite manner, by which I mean something along the lines of actions speaking louder than words. It can be clear when a sin has been committed, but sinfulness can be less obvious because it's hard to know what someone's real intentions are and how sinfully they live. I'm not sure if this view is congruous with your answer; they seem to say opposite things (in terms of trends of obviousness), yet they both seem sensible.

Regarding the hurricane analogy, I guess that means the hurricane is sinfulness, and specific factors that lead to the hurricane are the sins. The sins cause the sinfulness? Here, I would've thought the opposite, that being sinful leads one to sin, which itself can worsen the sinfulness. From your previous message, I can understand that sin separates us from God and that a healthy relationship with God would necessitate recognizing and repenting of sins. I don't know where to begin to make sense of the next part, regarding sins not being ordered, categorized, etc.

**Steve**: Let's look at the physical act of murder (e.g., stabbing). One perspective is that a lump of carbon and water inserted a piece of metal into another lump of carbon and water. So with that perspective, what distinguishes that from a surgeon inserting a pacemaker into a patient? It all comes down to the motivation of the person with the metal. But, as we are extremely limited in our ability to discern motivation, we must rely on our flawed ability to interpret actions. God, on the other hand, has no such limitation and looks at the motivation. A murder is just an effect. The cause is a willful rebellion against God; that is, we do not value his creation (the victim). It is undoubtedly true that we are lumps of carbon and water, so killing one of these lumps can't be a *real* problem unless we assign value to it (and, by extension, God). That extrinsic value of human life can only come from God. So, I'm saying that it is clear to most humans that humans are sinful because we see the outward effects (the hurricane). But we cannot hope to pinpoint all of the individual causes of that sin because it remains hidden to us humans. I'm also trying to make the point here that instead of saying to people, "Don't murder, cheat, and steal," we should be saying, "View God as supremely valuable above everything, and when you do, you will fix the deeper, inner problem of wanting to murder, cheat, and steal." But since it may be difficult for some to immediately jump to that conclusion, the Bible tells us explicitly that murdering, cheating, and stealing are wrong and to not do them. Knowing *why* to not do those things takes more thought. So, yes, we should avoid sin; it's bad. But they whose focus is "not sinning" (for themselves or others) are missing the bigger, deeper, more important picture.

**Victoria**: Ah, so it's the human-view that sees the acts of sins themselves as more of the obvious incriminator (hence the legal system), whereas the God-view sees deeper to the motives to determine one's actual sinfulness. The shift in focus from "don't murder" to "view God as supremely valuable" actually makes a lot more sense, and it also more clearly distances Christianity from the association of "sin management." I then thought, "Why don't they just say outright what the bigger picture is, versus saying don't do *x, y,* and *z*?" I guess even if they did, it would probably still be hard to comprehend. It's like learning any subject. The main, overarching idea may be presented at the very beginning (such as the basic mechanistic principles in organic chemistry), but it's hard to fully understand what that means without diving into specific details (such as learning specific reaction mechanisms) and intentionally connecting them back to the main theme. Thinking about sin in the lens of self-over-God helps clarify that as well. Now I still don't fully understand how all this relates to your reference to Rom 7:15–19.

**Steve:** "Why don't [Christians] just say outright what the bigger picture is, versus saying don't do *x*, *y*, and *z*?" 1) As mentioned earlier, most Christians you will meet will be Christians in name only. They simply grew up in a "Christian country."[1] They won't know what the Bible says because they haven't read it.[2] They will believe that Christianity is completely compatible with other contradictory beliefs.[3] They will have intertwined Christianity and American politics to the point that they don't know the difference.[4] So most "Christians" have no clue what Christianity is about.[5] 2) Sin management feels good. It is easy for me to develop a set of things I probably already wanted to do and declare myself moral while condemning the things I probably already didn't want to do. It also allows me to be judgmental toward others, which makes me feel righteous. 3) Sin management is concrete and follows human nature. Most of our lives are entangled with the reward/ punishment idea for doing good/bad (e.g., work and school), so our natural inclination is to believe that when I do good, good things should happen to me, and when I do bad, bad things should happen to me. This is the basis for the vast majority of theistic, polytheistic, pantheistic, and even atheistic belief systems. So the fundamental idea of Christianity (unmerited favor from God), flies in the face of everything we believe or want to believe. Christians can easily fall into that trap as well.

As far as Rom 7:15–19, it's the testimony of the apostle Paul, whom the Bible claims had a life-transforming, miraculous meeting with Jesus, which led him from killing Christians to becoming a Christian, writing most of the New Testament on missionary journeys, and ultimately being executed. He's saying that even after his life transformation in both belief and action, he still struggled with sin *all the time*. So my point

---

[1] Mark Edwards, "Was America founded as a Christian nation?" *CNN*, July 4, 2015, www.cnn.com/2015/07/02/living/america-christian-nation/.
[2] Bob Smietana, "Americans Are Fond of the Bible, Don't Actually Read It," *LifeWay Research*, April 25, 2017, lifewayresearch.com/2017/04/25/lifeway-research-americans-are-fond-of-the-bible-dont-actually-read-it/.
[3] "Christian Beliefs about Religions," *ReligionFacts*, November 20, 2016, www.religionfacts.com/christianity/other-religions.
[4] Nigel Barber, "Why Religion Rules American Politics," *HuffPost*, July 20, 2012, www.huffpost.com/entry/why-religion-rules-americ_b_1690433.
[5] Ben Farmer, "A quarter of Christians do not believe in the resurrection," *The Telegraph*, April 10, 2017, www.telegraph.co.uk/news/2017/04/10/quarter-christians-do-notbelieve-resurrection/.

was that if Paul, the exemplar of the Christian faith, couldn't conquer sin, we cannot possibly view Christianity as sin management and hope to defeat it. Our only hope is to accept God's forgiveness through belief in Jesus, his cross, and his resurrection, and then live grateful lives that honor and glorify him with our actions (which partially includes "not sinning.")

**Victoria**: That CNN article is eye-opening! I never thought much about whether America was founded as a Christian nation or not, but always assumed it had been. The assertion that "Christian America" didn't take hold until the 1950s is surprising to me. Doesn't this article refute the idea of America being a Christian nation today? (For example, "The moment that punctuated the end of Christian America was the 1984 publication of Richard John Neuhaus' 'The Naked Public Square.'"). Anyway, that article notwithstanding, the numbers[6] do indicate a Christian America, at least nominally. Incidentally, while Googling "Christian America," I found articles that mentioned current topics of debate such as same-sex marriage and abortion. That's another thing I didn't get about Christianity. It seems that anyone can leverage the Bible in their favor; how is anyone supposed to know what to believe?

On the Lifeway Research article, there was a part I didn't get: "Those with evangelical beliefs are more likely (49 percent) to read a little bit each day than those without evangelical beliefs (16 percent)." Google defines evangelical as, "of or according to the teaching of the gospel or the Christian religion," but isn't that just Christianity in general? *Wikipedia* mentions belief in the "born again" experience; is that what evangelical beliefs are? I also found the different approaches taken to reading the Bible interesting, such as re-reading favorite parts or picking a passage at random. Is one way "more correct" than another?

On the Huffington Post article, this made me wonder: if church and state were fully separated, hypothetically speaking, would that lead to a sharper decline in religion/Christianity? One of the key underlying concepts in the article was that, in the United States, more difficult living conditions are associated with increased religiosity. If poor people in America cease "a self-defeating voting pattern," maybe America would start to rival Europe for economic security, better living conditions, etc., … and also a far lower emphasis on religion in daily life.

Not to go down too many rabbit holes with those articles; I get the overall point you're making of most Christians being so in name only. Do you have an estimate as to what the percentages are like? Can that even be researched?

Anyway, we've established that sin management is a human construct for viewing Christianity, as flawed as it may be. The thing is,

---

6 Frank Newport, "Percentage of Christians in U.S. Drifting Down, but Still High," *Gallup*, December 24, 2015, news.gallup.com/poll/187955/percentage-christians-drifting-down-high.aspx.

why would such a universal belief (good deeds lead to good things, bad deeds lead to bad things) be contradictory to, or at least not be fully consistent with, the fundamental idea of Christianity? Not sure what to think about this; it kind of reminds me of the objective morality argument in a way.

On Rom 7:15–19, oh, I see now. It was a lot clearer when I read it again after your explanation. (On verses 15–16, 19; I don't know if I've ever seen the word "do" so many times in just a few sentences.) Why was Paul the "exemplar of the Christian faith?"

**Steve**: "It seems that anyone can leverage the Bible in their favor; how is anyone supposed to know what to believe?" Yes, that is a problem. One has to read it, and we have lots of research to show that people don't read it. Conservatives watch Fox News because it confirms their biases. Liberals watch MSNBC because it confirms their biases. Conservatives love verses like this...

> *Later Jesus found him at the temple and said to him, "See, you are well again. Stop sinning or something worse may happen to you." (Jn 5:14)*

because it confirms their biases. Liberals love verses like this...

> *"Judge not, that you be not judged." (Mt 7:1)*

because it confirms their biases. The truth is that there's not a single verse in the Bible that was intended to stand alone; in fact, there weren't verse numbers in the original texts. The Bible is made of stories and letters that have to be read that way. It's nuanced and needs to be interpreted and dealt with on a case-by-case basis. For example, this...

> *Because of this, God gave them over to shameful lusts. Even their women exchanged natural sexual relations for unnatural ones. In the same way the men also abandoned natural relations with women and were inflamed with lust for one another. Men committed shameful acts with other men, and received in themselves the due penalty for their error. (Rom 1:26–27)*

says that homosexual acts are sins, even though it is apparent that some people do have homosexual tendencies. But this...

> *Therefore do not worry about tomorrow, for tomorrow will worry about itself. Each day has enough trouble of its own. (Mt 6:34)*

says that worrying is a sin, even though I personally have strong worrying tendencies. My worrying is not a lesser sin than homosexuality (and I might even argue that it's worse), so we have to step back and look at the bigger picture that the Bible presents: 1) We all have sinful tendencies, whether via nature or nurture; some may struggle more with Thing A while some may struggle more with Thing B (sounds like Dr. Seuss), but it's clear that we are all submerged in sin. 2) It's impossible to eradicate sin in our lives, but we must acknowledge it and see our need for the solution: Jesus. The liberal idea that we just pretend that things aren't sinful is clearly wrong, because without an acknowledgement of the problem, we'll never see a need for the solution. In the same way, the conservative idea that the solution is "not sinning" is also clearly wrong, because Jesus condemned those with that mindset more than anyone.[7] So I try to read the Bible as a whole, which usually means interpreting things through some "middle ground" perspective. Or as I see it, if someone's (even implicit) big picture view of the Bible is anything other than "God will and must be glorified," it's unbiblical and probably intended to benefit them in some way.

Evangelicalism is better defined by *Wikipedia*: "the belief that the essence of the Gospel consists of the doctrine of salvation by grace through faith in Jesus' atonement. Evangelicals believe in the centrality of the conversion or 'born again' experience in receiving salvation, in the authority of the Bible as God's revelation to humanity, and in spreading the Christian message."[8] Not all Christians are evangelical; I suppose it's possible to claim that the Bible is 1) more of a feel-good book about how to be a good person, and 2) that it's not really a Christian's job to tell people about Christianity (i.e., to evangelize). Both of those are mind-bogglingly wrong to me, but it does seem to be a sizable part of American culture.

Being "born again" refers to this...

> *Jesus answered him, "Truly, truly, I say to you, unless one is born again he cannot see the kingdom of God." Nicodemus said to him, "How can a man be born when he is old? Can he enter a second time into his mother's womb and be born?" Jesus answered, "Truly, truly, I say to you, unless one is born of water and the Spirit, he cannot enter the kingdom of God. That which is born of the flesh is flesh, and that which is born of the Spirit is spirit. Do not marvel that I said to you, 'You must be born again.'"* (Jn 3:3–7)

It's basically the idea that all of your ideas, beliefs, and life patterns are so radically new in Christianity that it's almost like being born into a new world.

It does seem that religion is on the decline in America for many reasons, but I think a milquetoast and/or political form of Christianity is partly (or maybe mostly) to blame.

---

[7] Mt 23:13–33.

[8] "Evangelicalism," *Wikipedia*, en.wikipedia.org/wiki/Evangelicalism.

As far as "good deeds lead to good things, bad deeds lead to bad things" (i.e., karma), its main problem is that it is clearly not true in life. Otherwise, it would imply that most everyone in the western world is "good" because life is comfortable, while most everyone else is "bad" because life is harder. I'm sure that the objective morality that I'm claiming lives in you hates that idea with a passion. 2) The Bible says that we don't know our own motivations:

> *All a person's ways seem pure to them, but motives are weighed by the* Lord. (Prov 16:2)

so even attempting to define good/bad is impossible on our own. In addition, who's to say that life is bad in a place like Haiti, or good in a place like Sweden? How could we ever know whether karma was real? That being said, Christians believe that living a biblically moral life will generally lead to a happier and "better" life, but that's certainly no guarantee, and in fact, the opposite is sometimes promised:

> *"And you will be hated by all for my name's sake. But the one who endures to the end will be saved."* (Mk 13:13)

> *"They will put you out of the synagogues. Indeed, the hour is coming when whoever kills you will think he is offering service to God."* (Jn 16:2)

**Victoria**: It makes sense to read and interpret the Bible in context.

Why would worrying be a worse sin than homosexuality? Also, I'm uncomfortable with the view that homosexuality is a sin. As you said, sinful tendencies might be nature or nurture, so couldn't one argue that homosexuality, if we assume it is a sin, was designed into one's nature so it isn't necessarily attributed to one's self-over-God intentions? And if someone naturally leans towards homosexuality but chooses to suppress those tendencies, isn't that a lose-lose situation since motivation matters, i.e., would they not still be "sinning" despite resisting the inclination to commit "sinful" acts? What's one supposed to do in that case, hypnotize oneself? (Just being facetious here.)

I'm glad you added that explanation on "born again." Would you say a "true" Christian is one who is an evangelical Christian? Are non-evangelical Christians still Christians? Or are they Christian in name only? Are there more or less evangelicals than non-evangelicals? (The *Wikipedia* article you referenced says, "A 2004 Pew survey identified Evangelicals as 26.3 percent of the population, while Catholics make up 22 percent and mainline Protestants make up 16 percent," and other data[9] makes it seem less common). I'm trying to get an idea of how to think about these roles (such as if it fits the pattern of a Venn diagram, superset/subset, etc.). (P.S. I don't know if I've ever seen "milquetoast" before. Nice word choice!)

Summarizing this main idea, the Bible/Christianity says to not do bad things, but this leads Christianity being viewed as a construction for sin management. That's because sin management feels good/concrete/natural, but there's no basis for that being a truth in life, so this helps to shift the picture of Christianity to a broader view of the importance of good intentions to live a life that glorifies God?

**Steve**: "Why would worrying be a worse sin than homosexuality?" 1) The Bible says something along the lines of "do not be afraid" *a lot.*[10] It mentions homosexuality maybe like five times.[11] It's unfortunate that we have singled that sin out as worse than others (or even labeled it as unforgivable). It seems to me that it's because it's one that most people don't struggle with, so it's easy to bash. 2) Worrying/fear are a direct affront to God's goodness, sovereignty, and care for me, while I find that the sinful things I physically do and say are "merely" impulsive, selfish, and/or misguided.

"Also, I'm uncomfortable with the view that homosexuality is a sin." 1) Me, too, but I'll take it way further. I don't like what the Bible says about me, anyone I know, or anyone I don't know:

> ... as it is written: *"None is righteous, no, not one; no one understands; no one seeks for God. All have turned aside; together they have become worthless; no one does good, not even one. Their throat is an open grave; they use their tongues to deceive. The venom of asps is under their lips. Their mouth is full of curses and bitterness. Their feet are swift to shed blood; in their paths are ruin and misery, and the way of peace they have not known. There is no fear of God before their eyes."* (Rom 3:10–18)

I usually "feel" like a pretty good person; I'm working hard for other people and haven't harmed anyone. I love God and believe that he loves everyone and that everyone is "equal." I feel like I've chosen political ideologies that work for the overall benefit of humanity. I'm kind to people. Furthermore, I could probably say that most people feel the same way about themselves. But reading the Bible over and over again (and looking at how humans *act* instead of *feel*) has completely

---

[9] Albert Winseman, "U.S. Evangelicals: How Many Walk the Walk?" *Gallup*, May 31, 2005, news.gallup.com/poll/16519/US-Evangelicals-How-Many-Walk-Walk.aspx.

[10] *BibleGateway*, www.biblegateway.com/quicksearch/?quicksearch=do+not+be+afraid&qs_version=NIV&limit=100.

[11] "Homosexuality," *OpenBible*, www.openbible.info/topics/homosexuality.

convinced me that all of that is an illusion. 2) It's a pretty easy task to show that every single person on Earth has a stronger proclivity toward certain sins than others, and those "certain sins" are different for every person. 3) It's also a pretty easy task to show that every single person's sinful tendencies have a genetic/chemical/upbringing component to them that is completely beyond his/her control. So I don't know why we have to have this debate about whether homosexual tendencies are hard-wired, based on upbringing, or a choice (I think the overall consensus is just "yes" for all three) while we ignore literally every other sin. Along those lines, if one were to say that a homosexual were compelled to be a homosexual, couldn't one, with just as much science behind them, say that a homosexual hater is compelled to be a homosexual hater? Personally, I find myself constantly battling worry, lust, anger, and pride (and a million other things, but those came to mind; I would even go so far as to say that I have inborn genetic tendencies toward adultery and promiscuity like just about every man who's ever lived.[12]) I rarely, if ever, consciously *choose* those temptations. Rather, I just find myself immersed in them despite my overall desire to not be. I know for a fact that they are hard-wired into my DNA/psyche/whatever because they are my tendencies as much as my tendency to breathe and blink. But I *can* (and must) choose not to follow where they're trying to lead me. 4) The Bible makes a pretty strong distinction between *temptation* and *sin*:

> *No temptation has overtaken you that is not common to man. God is faithful, and he will not let you be tempted beyond your ability, but with the temptation he will also provide the way of escape, that you may be able to endure it.* (1 Cor 10:13)

> *Then Jesus was led up by the Spirit into the wilderness to be tempted by the devil. And after fasting forty days and forty nights, he was hungry. And the tempter came and said to him, "If you are the Son of God, command these stones to become loaves of bread." But he answered, "It is written, '"Man shall not live by bread alone, but by every word that comes from the mouth of God.'" Then the devil took him to the holy city and set him on the pinnacle of the temple and said to him, "If you are the Son of God, throw yourself down, for it is written, '"He will command his angels concerning you,' and '"On their hands they will bear you up, lest you strike your foot against a stone.'" Jesus*

---

[12] Michael Price, "Are People 'Naturally' Polygamous?" *Psychology Today*, August 18, 2011, www.psychologytoday.com/us/blog/darwin-eternity/201108/are-people-naturally-polygamous; Shankar Vedantam, "Desire and DNA: Is Promiscuity Innate?" *Washington Post*, August 1, 2003, www.washingtonpost.com/archive/politics/2003/08/01/desire-and-dna-is-promiscuity-innate/4cc92d41-21f1-4a52-a89a-721658f096be/.

*said to him, "Again it is written, 'You shall not put the Lord your God to the test.'" Again, the devil took him to a very high mountain and showed him all the kingdoms of the world and their glory. And he said to him, "All these I will give you, if you will fall down and worship me." Then Jesus said to him, "Be gone, Satan! For it is written, '"You shall worship the Lord your God and him only shall you serve."'" Then the devil left him, and behold, angels came and were ministering to him.* (Mt 4:1–11)

*But each person is tempted when he is lured and enticed by his own desire. Then desire when it has conceived gives birth to sin, and sin when it is fully grown brings forth death.* (Jas 1:14–15)

Thus, I don't think there's anything wrong with homosexual tendencies or temptations in and of themselves, but the Bible says they should not be dwelt or acted upon. My goodness, if sexual temptation disqualified people from heaven, there might be like three women that make it to heaven and the rest of us are doomed. 5) Are we denying the happiness of those with homosexual tendencies by declaring it sinful? Temporarily and in a worldly sense, yes. But in an eternal, "God is my only possible source of happiness" sense, no. The Christian life is a constant denying of one's temporary happiness to gain an infinitely greater, eternal joy. For example, it might make me temporarily happy to give the finger to someone in traffic, but eternally, such actions are killing my only chance of happiness.

I would not say that only "evangelicals" are Christians, but some of this is in the ambiguity of language. Is an "evangelical" someone who believes that everyone should know about Jesus? If yes, then I have a hard time differentiating evangelicals and Christians. But if "evangelical" is some set of American denominations or political affiliations, then it would be quite easy to be evangelical and not Christian or vice versa. I have no problem being called an "evangelical" (except for the fact that it's unclear what someone means when they say that).

I would clarify your last statement as follows: "Summarizing this main idea, the Bible/Christianity says to not do bad things, but this leads to Christianity being viewed (by non-Christians or nominal Christians) as a construction for sin management. That's because sin management feels good/concrete/natural, but there's no basis for that being a truth in life (there *is* a strong basis that it feels good/concrete/natural, but *no* basis that it works), so this helps (Christians) to shift the picture of Christianity to a broader view of the importance of ~~good intentions to live a life that glorifies God?~~ glorifying God by considering him our ultimate treasure and hope, which manifests itself as honor, love, awe, and obedience in thought and action."

**Victoria**: That explanation of worrying being a sin seems rational and congruous with the idea of sin as "self over God." I was actually just talking about this same topic with a friend a few minutes ago, when we were discussing people's proneness to worry. I think it also ties into the free will/determinism debate, since it could be a lot easier to not worry if everything were already set in stone and one didn't have the power to change it. (I suppose that could also lead one to worry about what that stone-set path was.) From my experience, I worry because I feel that I'm not doing enough to achieve whatever tasks or goals I set out to accomplish, and I don't want to feel regret (hmm, maybe regret is just post-event worry?) about not having done enough in my power to accomplish them. It also seems that sins beget other sins; for example, doing something sinful which leads one to worry about having committed that sin. I wonder what society would look like if the relative, apparent weight of those two sins (worry and homosexuality) were flipped! Maybe worrying would be less commonplace.

As to your five points, wow, those are all strong points and together makes for a persuasive—and amusing (three women in heaven!)—argument. It's probably the most judgment-free discussion I've seen with the stance of homosexuality being a sin. Commenting on 4) about the distinction between temptation and sin, does that contradict the idea of sin being motive-related? It's like one of the most quoted verses in the Bible:

> *"But I tell you that anyone who looks at a woman lustfully has already committed adultery with her in his heart."* (Mt 5:28)

Isn't temptation the motive that actually comprises sin? Less directly related: is it thought that people no longer sin in heaven because those temptations are gone?

The last part on denying present-day worldly happiness leads me to wonder how many homosexual-identifying people turned away from Christianity (whether or not they already believed) because of this sacrificing requirement. I wonder how many "true" Christians might also consider themselves homosexual. Would that have to be zero by "trueness"?

Thanks for the clarifications on that summary statement! It's consistent with my understanding on everything we've talked about so far.

When reading that *Psychology Today* article you linked, I came across a *NY Times* article[13] on the sidebar. What was interesting to me

---

[13] Joseph Carter, "The Universe Doesn't Care About Your 'Purpose,'" *The New York Times*, July 31, 2017, www.nytimes.com/2017/07/31/opinion/the-universe-doesnt-care-about-your-purpose.html. Synopsis: there is no

was the comment, "as purposeless as human evolution is, we generally benefit as a species from a belief in it." That also reminds me of the free will discussion a while ago. It doesn't do us any good to not believe in free will given our sense of direct cause and effect, but where purpose is concerned, perhaps the focus should be more on *why* to believe in something rather than *what* that purpose for that something is. In other words, shift the focus from "what is the purpose of *x*" to "what is the benefit of believing *x*."

**Steve**: Yes, sin unquestionably begets sin. The Bible often speaks of this as the hardening of one's heart:

> *"For this people's heart has grown dull, and with their ears they can barely hear, and their eyes they have closed; lest they should see with their eyes and hear with their ears and understand with their heart and turn, and I would heal them."* (Acts 28:27)

to the point that it is difficult for a person to even see their sin as a problem or see any need for God.

Your question about motives, temptations, and sin is a great one with a nuanced (and probably ambiguous answer). 1) Yes, motives matter and can be sinful. From my earlier stabbing analogy (which I now remember I got from John Piper—yikes, I just realized I plagiarized; there's more evidence of my sinful nature), we cannot judge whether something is sinful by mere actions, so it is clear that sin always has its origin *inside* of us. 2) Similarly, regarding Mt 5:28, the wording seems to imply that the problem is not in the literal eye, but in the figurative heart; the sin has already been committed in the heart (i.e., the lust has already occurred). Consider a child: he may see a piece of candy (not sin), and he may want that candy (not sin, but possibly a temptation). But the moment he says to himself, "That candy will fulfill me (even temporarily)," he has replaced God with the candy; this is where his ultimate sin originates. After he has made God inconsequential and seen his carnal desire as supreme, the external act of stealing the candy is really the second (and lesser) sin. As humans, we only get to see the second/lesser sins in people, but we know they have a greater sinful cause. 3) Given these things, I don't think that temptation and motive are the same thing, although they're both internal. In my mind, motive is the reason I do or do not respond to the presented temptation sinfully. Suppose I see someone accidentally drop $20 and walk away without noticing; I am presented with a temptation that I did not choose and may not have wanted. In fact, I would argue that I am hard-wired for deception, greed, and apathy such that my natural impulse/desire is to either pick up the money and keep it for myself or just ignore it and let

---

fundamental, underlying purpose of the universe, although we may temporarily find our own meanings in things.

"fate" decide what happens; at a minimum, I think of each of those as an option. But as long as I successfully fight those impulses in thought and action, I have committed no sin even though they existed in my mind. In other words, temptations are simply "bad options," while not yet having chosen one.

As far as the lack of sin in heaven, I'm not sure anyone knows the mechanism behind it. It most certainly could be an eradication of temptation (this is how I've heard it explained, but I believe it's only inferred from other scripture, not directly mentioned). It could also be some kind of super-ability God gives us, or that we have no desire to sin because we see the consequences clearly, or that God removes our free will so that we *cannot* choose to sin (although I'm not a big fan of that one).

Regarding Christian homosexuals, if we're talking about those with same-sex attraction who believe that dwelling in homosexual thought or performing homosexual actions are opposed to God's will and that Christ is their only hope for salvation, then I see no problem with being a homosexual and a "true" Christian at the same time.[14] I have met several of these people and sympathize with their struggle. For what it's worth, I have also met and read about former homosexuals who are now heterosexuals,[15] as corroborated by the Bible:

> *Or do you not know that wrongdoers will not inherit the kingdom of God? Do not be deceived: Neither the sexually immoral nor idolaters nor adulterers nor men who have sex with men nor thieves nor the greedy nor drunkards nor slanderers nor swindlers will inherit the kingdom of God. And that is what some of you were. But you were washed, you were sanctified, you were justified in the name of the Lord Jesus Christ and by the Spirit of our God.* (1 Cor 6:9–11)

But if we're talking about those who claim to be Christians but deny clear biblical teaching on the sinfulness of homosexuality (or even *accept* that teaching and willfully disobey it), that goes way back to conversations we were having earlier: i.e., I don't believe one can continually embrace unrepentant sin and know the God of the Bible and/or have the Holy Spirit living inside them:

> *Flee from sexual immorality. All other sins a person commits are outside the body, but whoever sins sexually, sins against their own body. Do you not know that your bodies are temples of the Holy Spirit,*

---

[14] For example, I would tend to favor the "Side B" perspective listed here: *Equip*, "Sexual Ethics & Empty Words," February 11, 2019, equipyourcommunity.org/blog/2019/2/11/sexual-ethics-amp-empty-words.

[15] Jackie Hill Perry, *Gay Girl, Good God: The Story of Who I Was, and Who God Has Always Been* (Nashville: B&H Books, 2018).

*who is in you, whom you have received from God? You are not your own; you were bought at a price. Therefore honor God with your bodies.* (1 Cor 6:18–20)

Now, nothing I've said here is particular to homosexuality. It's just as dangerous for a Christian to embrace unrepentant greed, anger, worry, etc. as "who they are:"

*Whoever conceals his transgressions will not prosper, but he who confesses and forsakes them will obtain mercy.* (Prov 28:13)

In the end, only God is able to differentiate between a repentant heart that seeks him from an unrepentant heart that seeks itself. Finally, a Christian's "identity" should not be in anything except Christ:

*Therefore, if anyone is in Christ, he is a new creation. The old has passed away; behold, the new has come.* (2 Cor 5:17)

A huge warning sign of a Christian's priorities being skewed is for them to first identify themselves by race/gender/nationality/political affiliation/sexual orientation. Those things may be facts, but they're not a Christian's *identity*:

*There is neither Jew nor Greek, there is neither slave nor free, there is no male and female, for you are all one in Christ Jesus.* (Gal 3:28)

My favorite sentence from the NY Times article you mentioned was "Purpose springs from our longing for permanence in an ever-changing universe." I completely agree! However, the author and I strongly disagree on whether such a permanence exists.

**Victoria**: That differentiation between temptation and motive was illuminating. So temptation, which is not sinful in itself, is a precursor to motive, which is potentially sinful depending on whether or not the motive acts upon the temptation.

On Christian homosexuals and "true" Christian identity, the prominent theme seems to be truth. One must be willing to see—without distortion—what the Bible says about homosexuality and must also be willing to see without distortion one's thoughts and actions in light of those teachings. I can see how this would be the case for any other sin. If you're being bad, at least don't delude yourself to think you're being good; admit your wrongdoings (is that pretty much what repentance is?) and try to be good by living a life that glorifies God.

**Steve**: Yes, and I would add that repentance is not just admission of wrong, but also desire and action to do right.

# CHAPTER 11: REFRAMING CHRISTIANITY

**Victoria**: What does it mean for a Christian to sin purposefully? Suppose it wasn't a struggle, and one chose not to resist temptation.

**Steve**: Sin is not as much "doing bad things" as "favoring things over God." In other words, God calls us to see him as ultimately supreme and worthy of our worship. When someone uses drugs, from a scientific perspective, they're taking a natural chemical (i.e., it exists in nature) and altering natural brain chemicals to feel differently. If he/she doesn't harm anyone (which is impossible to say with the drug trade, but just go with me), it would be hard to argue that they've done anything immoral. From a Christian perspective, God is the ultimate pleasure and fulfillment, so by using drugs, one has implicitly stated that God is not enough to bring us those things. (Also, God calls us have a clear mind to serve others.) So I think that for one to continually seek fulfillment in things other than God (money, sex, drugs, or even morality), one has claimed that God is not really worthy of worship, which is, in some sense, the only sin.

**Victoria**: Hmm, that's an intriguing perspective. What if God didn't bring one "ultimate pleasure and fulfillment," though? I guess that would require a paradigm shift in how one would seek that pleasure. Where does that pleasure and fulfillment come from? Serving others?

**Steve**: Yes, I think you answered your own question. It is indeed a paradigm shift. Serving others is great, but that—like morality—is more of a microcosm of God's nature. For me, it took years of examining my own life and purpose (usually unintentionally) and finally realizing that if my choices in awe/pleasure were 1) infinite God and 2) finite everything else, then he was the thing I wanted. Maybe this will help: imagine that tomorrow, you scientifically discovered all that the universe can offer (all the laws, particles, spacetime, dark energy, and dark matter), harnessed it for the good of humankind, and won all the Nobel Prizes until you died. That would probably be near the pinnacle of human existence and pleasure (OK, maybe just for a physicist), but how would your awesomeness compare to the one who created it? Or maybe you entered a life of poverty to care for orphans in a third-world country. That would be incredible, but how would it compare to the one who is the definition of good, who lost his "God privileges" to suffer as a man on our behalf? In other words, I've found everything in this universe, while often incredible, completely unworthy of worship, leaving "only" God. (And to the point of many of your other questions, I used to try to find pleasure in "not sinning," and it sucked, I sucked, and everything sucked. It doesn't work.)

**Victoria**: Okay, so we've established that if one acts in a way that favors some other thing over God, that is a sin. One can try to live more sin-free by acknowledging that God is the ultimate pleasure and fulfillment. If one has trouble acknowledging that, a paradigm shift may be needed. What would you tell someone who was at that stage? Is a strong faith in God a prerequisite? Otherwise, if someone didn't have that faith, why would they make the effort to obtain and convince themselves of that paradigm shift? More broadly speaking, does living a Christian-like life and following the teachings lead one to be Christian, or does being a Christian lead one to live such a life? I get the sense that many people are Christian because that's culturally how they grew up. If everyone in the world started on neutral ground, how might that turn out? Would Christianity still be one of the world's major religions?

Regarding "infinite God" or "finite everything else," you state that well, and I'd agree with that conclusion. There's such an impermanence to everything in human life that choosing an infinite God is almost self-evident. However, this would seem to prerequire strong faith in that infinite God (e.g., acknowledging his presence and characteristics). This point relates to my questions in the previous paragraph of whether faith is a prerequisite and what if one didn't have it.

On trying to find pleasure in "not sinning," if everything sucked and it doesn't work, but that's what you should do, then what do you do?

**Steve**: Great questions. I think that a big overarching argument I'm trying to make from the beginning is that, by definition, God is the ultimate [fill in the blank], so I wholeheartedly agree that choosing/valuing an infinite God is almost self-evident and requires very little faith. In fact, coming to God (or even recognizing what he's all about) with a strong faith is paradoxical; if one already had a strong faith, one would've already come to God. Rather, a relationship with God begins with an admission of 1) one's sinfulness and inadequacy and 2) his holiness and omni*. Those things are clear and self-evident to me, so my faith comes in areas where more evidence and experience would be necessary. In no way am I a proponent of blind, unquestioning faith, so faith to me means something like "choosing to change the way I live my life based on probable evidence or reasonable conclusions." For example, we both agree that free will cannot be proven, but we have both chosen to base our entire lives around the assumption that it does (which is pretty amazing). Or in other words, we act and live as if free will were indisputable truth because it is intellectually supportable and seems to mesh with our experiences. With Christian faith, I may have faith that 1) God has given me reasoning abilities which allow me to understand (parts of) him, 2) God cares about humans and wants to have a relationship with them, and 3) the Bible is a reliable source of truth. Those things are not proven, indisputable truth, but I have chosen to live my life based on them because of experience, lots of indirect evidence and reasoning, and a lack of viable alternatives.

I agree with you that most Christians you encounter are Christian in name only, simply because they were born in the United States. It's a part of their culture and upbringing and is the default position. As atheism and agnosticism grow in our country, I see that not as a real increase, but as people who used to call themselves Christians feeling more comfortable calling themselves what they were all along.

The last question is great, too. My perspective on sin changed because of my motivation. Earlier in my life, I thought that if I could get it all together (morality, school, job, family, happiness, possessions, being a "good Christian," etc.), then I would truly be fulfilled. It took failing in all of those areas about 50,000 times for me to see that it was going to be impossible, and that the stress and pressure would kill me. Not only that, but most of the success and goodness I had could easily be attributed to my innate intelligence or opportunities afforded by my upbringing, country, socioeconomic status, race, gender, etc., and had a lot less to do with my effort than I cared to admit. Now, I embrace my suckiness in all areas because it constantly reminds me that my pleasure is in God instead of myself, and it has removed the burden of perfection (which was a delusion anyway). As for sin, I attempt to live a good, moral life to honor God instead of doing it to gain his approval, because honestly, I don't think he's real impressed by my "goodness."

**Victoria**: When I first read your answer, I felt this unexpected sense of relief. After letting my subconscious marinate on it, I think there are several reasons why. 1) On faith not being blind and unquestioning: these have been intertwined in my mind from conversations with peers and things I've read. When someone says that at some point you have to stop asking questions and take a leap of faith, it makes me very skeptical and uncomfortable. Using probable evidence and/or reasonable conclusions *is* something I can agree with, and the example of free will is very representative. 2) As to many Christians being Christian in name only, it's strangely relieving to hear a new interpretation for the rise of agnosticism/atheism. I'm not one to jump on the bandwagon quickly, but these trends in religion had me wondering why "non-religion" was picking up speed and what that meant in terms of implications of spiritual truth. It's said that the social factors promoting atheism are financial security and education,[1] and I wonder if these factors may lead to increased confidence in one's own self and abilities, as opposed to questioning the underlying structures that position one for success. Perhaps financial security and education also lead people to be in an "outwardly successful" or similar position so as to have reduced concerns about the "how" and the "why" of human existence but instead be "trivially" focused on the concerns of day-to-day activities, personal and professional goals, etc. What do you think?

---

[1] Gabe Bullard, "The World's Newest Major Religion: No Religion," *National Geographic*, April 22, 2016, www.nationalgeographic.com/news/2016/04/160422-atheism-agnostic-secular-nones-rising-religion/.

For the last response, I really like that perspective of living life to honor God instead of doing it to gain his approval. It focuses on the "other" instead of the self. I've thought about that general idea in specific contexts such as with giving a presentation, i.e., with the goal of having others learn something versus doing it to share my results or fulfilling some academic requirement. Focusing on the other also emphasizes the means over the ends—one should focus on the intentions and processes themselves instead of being motivated by the potential outcomes.

As for suckiness leading to a reminder that your pleasure is in God, I can kind of make sense of this, but it's not super clear to me. For instance, I can imagine a scenario that goes as follows. Say something rashly out of anger → feel regret for hurting another's feelings → acknowledge that I'm a sucky, imperfect person → resolve to do better. What is an example of a flow of thought that might lead from suckiness to a removed burden of perfection and pleasure in God?

**Steve**: I think you're spot on. Christianity is not and never has been for those who (believe they) have it together. It's for those who (know they) suck:

> *"Blessed are the poor in spirit, for theirs is the kingdom of heaven. Blessed are those who mourn, for they will be comforted. Blessed are the meek, for they will inherit the earth. Blessed are those who hunger and thirst for righteousness, for they will be filled. Blessed are the merciful, for they will be shown mercy. Blessed are the pure in heart, for they will see God. Blessed are the peacemakers, for they will be called children of God. Blessed are those who are persecuted because of righteousness, for theirs is the kingdom of heaven. Blessed are you when people insult you, persecute you and falsely say all kinds of evil against you because of me."* (Mt 5:3–11)

> *And Jesus answered them, "Those who are well have no need of a physician, but those who are sick. I have not come to call the righteous but sinners to repentance."* (Lk 5:31–32)

> *To some who were confident of their own righteousness and looked down on everyone else, Jesus told this parable: "Two men went up to the temple to pray, one a Pharisee and the other a tax collector. The Pharisee stood by himself and prayed: 'God, I thank you that I am not like other people—robbers, evildoers, adulterers—or even like this tax collector. I fast twice a week and give a tenth of all I get.' But the tax collector stood at a distance. He would not even look up to heaven, but beat his breast and said, 'God, have mercy on me, a sinner.' I tell you that this man, rather than the other, went home justified before God. For all those who exalt themselves will be humbled, and those who humble themselves will be exalted."* (Lk 18:9–14)

The rich, educated, and healthy see no need for God, so it's no surprise to me that as America/Europe gets richer, more educated, and healthier, Christianity declines.

Here's a potential suckiness scenario in my own life. I say something out of anger → feel regret for hurting another's feelings → acknowledge that I'm a sucky, imperfect person → realize that this is how I've always been and will never change deep down because I've done this 800,000 times despite always "resolving to do better" → realize that God, the only one whose opinion really matters, loves me and forgave me through no effort of my own → love and praise him and begin to recall all of his other attributes and remain in awe → feel like I need to honor him → apologize to said person (i.e., God's creation), forgive myself (i.e., God's creation), ask for God's help in 1) understanding why I got angry (i.e., acknowledging his wisdom) and 2) not doing it again (i.e., acknowledging his care and concern for me) → feel more awe and love and gratitude for God because I know that I used to not be able to do this and he's changed me. This process has taken me anywhere from two minutes to ten years in the past.

**Victoria**: Hmm, interesting! Lk 5:31–32 seems a bit deceptive—for lack of a better word—at first. He says, "I have not come to call the righteous but sinners to repentance," which made me wonder what happens to the people who are righteous? But there isn't really anyone, is there? That means Jesus is calling everyone to repentance.

I can definitely identify with that scenario. It's surprising to me how much having a cat helps me to understand these topics. Mia peed on my bed the other day, which made me frustrated, but I thought about it further—about how that action didn't diminish my love for her. There are two main parts of that flow of thought (the human-only side and the human-with-God side), which relies on the central part of realizing "that God, the only one whose opinion really matters, loves me and forgave me through no effort of my own." How do you know this is true?

**Steve**: Yes! More specifically, Jesus is saying, "If you think you're good enough on your own, you're delusional and doomed. Only those who realize their need for me will be saved" (like my shark/drowning analogy from Chapter 5).

As far as the last question, that's the main theme of the Bible:

*For by grace you have been saved through faith. And this is not your own doing; it is the gift of God, not a result of works, so that no one may boast.* (Eph 2:8–9)

But perhaps you're asking a different question?

**Victoria**: Oh, I think that's all that I was asking actually. I was confused about that central part because I always thought of forgiveness of sins as something that happens at the end of a lifetime, not right after (or as) they're committed.

**Steve**: Well, since Jesus was crucified 2000 years ago, all of *our* sins were in the future, so *when* sins are forgiven is not as important as *that* they are. I often think of living in a continual state of having been forgiven.

# CHAPTER 12: A GOD OF LOVE

**Victoria**: Regarding why God cares about the relative minutiae of life, I like the cat analogy from Chapter 1. Still, have you heard any theories as to why? I suppose I don't fully follow the connection between "why would god(s) care" to "God came as Jesus." Also, how do we know God feels love? (I feel like this is tangentially related to the topic on how we know God is good but also kind of different.) I could very well do what I do for Mia without loving her, so what about people who don't feel emotions (such as those with alexithymia). Would those people have a harder time believing in God?

**Steve**: Many would say that it's just God's nature to love and be relational (which is where the Trinity comes in: the Father loves the Son loves the Spirit loves the Father loves the Spirit loves the Son). "God came as Jesus" doesn't show *why* he cares, just that he *does*. I think we could reason that the love humans experience has an ultimate higher source because it often goes against our nature. I suppose you could do what you do for Mia without loving her, but in a very real sense, the things you do for Mia show that you love her more than it shows that love makes you do good things. In other words, if love remains hidden, it's probably not love. I struggled with a lack of religious emotion for a long time, and often interpreted it as either 1) Christianity isn't real or 2) there's something wrong with me and/or my relationship with God. Now I realize that some people are just emotional and that feelings lie, so I don't worry about it (although I have become more emotional as I've gotten older, like moving from a "one" to a "three" on a scale of 1–10). I also believe that God is the creator of reason, logic, and science, so emotions may be a small part of Christianity but are by no means essential (and in fact can sometimes be harmful).

**Victoria**: Humans tend to define things within the realm of their own experiences. Why might that not apply to your statement, "Many would say that it's just God's nature to love and be relational"? From a parental standpoint, isn't it natural for a parent to love their child?

Going back to the "relative minutiae" topic, is it thought that God cares about these things because of his love, which means wanting the best for us? But the "best" for us—in accordance with our discussions about sin—means worshipping God. So, if we're supposed to live a lifestyle in which we forgo gratification and pleasure (even if it does not seem to be harming anyone/anything) in lieu of worshipping God, then—pardon my directness—does that mean God is a narcissist?

"If love remains hidden, it's probably not love." That's pretty profound.

On "religious emotion," hmm, that's interesting. That interpretation makes sense. So are you saying that instead of feeling as connected to God emotionally, you've grown to accept more of a logical connection?

**Steve:** As I sort-of mentioned earlier, if it were God's nature to love and be relational, and we only came into existence very recently, what was he doing before that? He was loving and being relational within himself: the Trinity. It doesn't help explain what the Trinity is (although I've heard it explained that there are three "whos" and one "what"), but just that it is consistent with God's nature. Anyway, the human/child relationship is lacking the power of the God/human relationship in that we feel an obligation to care for our children (maybe it's reciprocation, societal pressure, evolutionary instinct, an inherent moral compass, etc.), but from where would God get such an obligation? That's why it seems to be in his nature and not from some external moral standard to which he must adhere.

Regarding your question about God's narcissism, I think you've hit on the biggest reason why a lot of people don't like the concept of god(s); it seems to be all about it/them while we suffer. But let's assume that God is 1) truthful and 2) literally the only thing worthy of our attention and worship. Given these assumptions, if you were God, what would you tell people about where to focus their attention and worship?

Regarding your last question, yes. There are days when I "feel" like God doesn't exist, there are days when I "feel" like God doesn't care about me or anything, and there are days when I "feel" that he the most incredible, awesome, loving thing I could imagine and that he personally cares about me and has my best interest in mind. Which am I to believe? Feelings lie, so I have to examine all of my feelings in the light of scripture and (usually) emotionless reason.

**Victoria:** Hmm. I think I'm interpreting this topic differently than you. The statement being discussed is that it is God's nature to love and be relational. Assuming this is true, yes, I would think it was always true, even before human existence, which is consistent with your reply. How do we know, though, that the doings of God are motivated by love and relationality and not just objective actions that don't have a lot of love behind them, like turning on a lamp or something? What does it mean for God to be relational within himself? Google defines *relational* as "concerning the way in which two or more people or things are connected." You elaborated that God being relational is consistent with his nature, but how does that relationality manifest? My question also concerns humans. How is God relational to humans, and what might it look like if God were not relational to humans?

"Three 'whos' and one 'what.'" I don't get this. I thought it was the Trinity, not the Quadrinity.

Regarding obligation, okay, I can see that God doesn't have the same influences of obligation that humans certainly do. I just don't understand why he does what he does (the answer is love, but I don't get why this is the answer). Assuming that God is both truthful and the only thing worthy of our attention and worship, yes, of course he would tell people where to focus attention and worship. Ohhh, put into context with the discussion from Chapter 11—seeing God as the ultimate pleasure and fulfillment rather than a persnickety taskmaster—okay, that makes sense. And, as we said in the last chapter, given the self-evidence of God, this would require strong faith in him. I think I'm starting to get it.

Going back to the earlier thought that spawned this question, God cares about the minutiae because of his love for us, which means wanting the best for us, which translates into focusing attention and worship on God because perhaps he is the only thing worthy of that attention and worship?

On the last topic regarding religious emotion, that's very relatable. And, right, feelings lie. How exactly do you examine these feelings in light of scripture?

**Steve:** I am arguing that we have objective morality; that objective morality, which most often fights against every evolutionary instinct we have, must come from some external source. God would be the best/only candidate for such a thing, so "goodness" must be his nature. As far as love and relationality being "good" things, well, we've defined them that way, so we're kind of stuck there. But I suppose one could never say that a lamp "should" or "should not" be on by its nature, but we do say that love or murder "should" or "should not" happen. In other words, it's paradoxical to say that love should happen and simultaneously say that it doesn't matter if it happens. These are human definitions, but we're inferring what God is from what we as humans know and do (under the assumption that there's no way we're doing good things on our own).

"Three whos and one what" means there are three persons (personalities?) of the Trinity, but one God. I answered why a relational god must be "more than one" earlier, but in effect, maybe it's best summed up by saying that if God is love, there must be a relationship in which that love occurs: thus, the Trinity.

You said, "God cares about the minutiae because of his love for us, which means wanting the best for us, which translates into focusing attention and worship on God because perhaps he is the only thing worthy of that attention and worship?" YES! You just summed up all of Christianity (besides all of the "how")!

And as far as emotions go, emotions do play a necessary role in our relationship with God. For example, I can't help God move to a new apartment, I can't take care of his cat, I can't give him money when he has medical expenses; I can't do *any* of the things I do for people that might show them love. So it seems that a big part of my relationship with God comes through emotions like love, gratitude, and awe. However, those emotions are based on my experience and reason; i.e., emotions are post hoc rather than a priori. With relationships between people, emotions are pretty worthless. In other words, it may be true that I only act in love toward a human because I *feel* love, but the other human can't ever tell my real motivations. I mean, I do *feel* love for my wife, but that's inconsequential to her in terms of how I actually treat her.

**Victoria**: When I read your replies, it was like reading some biology textbook, where the words are comprehensible, but the overall message is enigmatic. But responding to your points out of order (esp. doing the first paragraph last) helped cleared things up for me.

I liked your sentence, "These are human definitions [of *love, good*, etc.], but we're inferring what God is from what we as humans know and do." It clarifies and emphasizes the notion that God is the reference frame for what these qualities are. My understanding feels surface level right now (it's like trying to grasp what a wave function[1] is for the first time), but rereading some of our earlier stuff should help (e.g., the earlier conversation on "how we know God isn't 'bad.'")

Thanks for the clear explanations on the Trinity and on what being relational means. This helped me to think about the paragraph above.

On my "summary of Christianity," wow, Christianity not being sin management makes way more sense this way! It's really interesting to see Christianity transform in my views from being a system of negative reinforcement ("don't do *x, y, z* because you'll go to hell") to a system of positive reinforcement ("do *a, b, c* because only God is worth it").

Regarding the part on emotions, when you put it like that, I realized that I *have* experienced post hoc emotions of the incredulity of some events—leaving me with a sense of awe and amazement about how things just happened to work out. I like the way you think about and explain concepts such as emotion in Christianity, based on experience and reason, since I feel like I don't necessarily emote on the same level that a lot of people (esp. Christians) seem to. Additionally, when I've had other conversations on these kinds of topics, I almost always reach a point when I stop questioning because I don't want the other person to feel like I'm attacking them, or because I have a repeatedly hard time grasping their meaning (especially if they answer along the lines of "you just have to believe it"). I like that you take the time to provide these thought-out answers that are digestible with reason. Also, the format helps in that I can think through these things, identify the parts that seem less clear, and formulate a careful answer.

I was amused by that description of your emotions toward your wife and toward people in general. But why would you say those emotions are worthless? I agree that other humans can't tell anyone's real motivations, but can't the emotion itself have value for the holder? For example, I'm sometimes surprised about the love I have for my cat, since

---

[1] A wave function is a quantum mechanical description of an object, usually of an atomic or subatomic particle.

I never knew what it was like to love an animal before, not having grown up with pets.

**Steve:** This conversation has been one of the best things I've ever done. I'm around Christians a lot, and we take most of these things for granted. You've forced me to seriously question everything I believe. I'll be honest about the following, too. Most of my students, even those I'm close with, disappear after graduation. You didn't, which I feel has led to a genuine friendship. As a Christian, I feel like I know/have the best news that anyone could possibly hear. As your friend, I feel compelled to tell you this really great news (aside: if you're familiar with the word "gospel," it's the Old English for "good news"), but I've tried very hard to not be pushy about it. I want to show you my own real doubts and failures and just give the news and let you decide on your own. I hope it always comes across that way.

As for your last questions, I expressed my statement above pretty poorly, but yes, I most certainly believe that emotion can have great value for the holder (and may be the *only* thing that causes one to act in a certain way). I was only referring to its practical uselessness from another's perspective.

**Victoria:** I'm glad to hear that, and I'm also glad for this (unexpected) friendship! I also very much appreciate that you aren't pushy and that you respect my freedom to shape my own beliefs. This reminds me of a conversation I had a few years ago, in which I asked why God didn't make everyone believe in him if he has the power to. The other person explained that forced love can't be genuine love, and to me there are parallels of that kind of genuineness in these interactions of people discussing ideas of truth and God and Christianity. On forcing you to question your beliefs, that's great! I've been having related conversations with other friends here. I usually avoid these debates, since I never really know what to think (or what *I* think, for that matter), but I'm now finding them as a valuable way to assess where my thoughts are and how confident I am in them.

**Steve:** Yeah, I think a lot of people are scared to question their beliefs because they're afraid of what they might find. I decided a long time ago that anything I base my life around should be able to be questioned from any angle.

# CHAPTER 13: OUR PURPOSE

**Victoria**: How has religion affected your life trajectory, your personality, etc.? Can you conjecture what that might look like without the influence of Christianity?

**Steve**: I've always been haunted by "Why?" As a scientist, that makes me do science to attempt to gain understanding. But that question is huge in my personal life as well. I might know that I should love others (objective morality), but "Why should I love others?" is just as important to me. Why should I care about my job? Why should I take care of my family? Why should I pause to look at the stars? Why should I attempt to have a positive outlook on life? Why should I let this person merge into traffic? Why should I do anything except watch TV, make money, have sex, and use drugs? So Christianity has given me the answers to "Why?", and I now live with confident meaning and purpose. When I was in my late 20s, I went through a huge crisis of faith and depression. Every day for about a year and a half, I just wanted to die. It was only an extremely tiny gleam of hope in God's goodness way in the back of my brain that kept me going, because I had pretty much decided that life was meaningless and pointless and that he didn't care about me. So I know exactly what my life would've been without that hope: I would've committed suicide, because I was already pretty close to it even with that small amount of hope present.

**Victoria**: I appreciate your openness about those raw experiences. It sounds like the apparent meaningless of life at the time was an extreme weight on your mind, the severity of which is staggering. If you don't mind my asking, why was the degree of impact so intense? Was it a gradual process into mental crisis, or was it spurred by some life-altering event?

While not to the same degree, I can somewhat relate. My life perspective has been plagued with nihilistic views over the past several years, and I've wondered about those same "why" questions. Why do anything at all? Does anything really and truly matter? When I read Jean-Paul Sartre in my philosophy course, I adopted the views that life doesn't have intrinsic meaning, and that the only sensible response is to *create* one's own purpose/meaning. Despite my agreement on the existential nihilism, I could never fully buy into Sartre's philosophy, mostly because the idea of creating one's own purpose still seems superficial to me. Why should I make the effort to pursue even that goal of creating purpose? Why do I strive to do computational chemistry for drug discovery? Yes, I want to understand nature and use that to help people, but I'm not fooling myself to think that I'll wipe out some intractable disease. Then is it just something to do to pass the time? (shrug) I see these questions as existential issues, but I don't think I deal with non-pressing issues—those that tend to be philosophical or emotional in nature—particularly well, if at all. At most, I'll contemplate it for some time, then distract myself with my day-to-day goals and responsibilities, thinking along the lines of, "I don't know where to go from there or what it means; I guess it's time to get back to analyzing those computations."

You say that Christianity has led you to live with confident meaning and purpose; what would you say those are?

**Steve**: I think it was the compounding of 1) the stress of supporting a family in grad school, 2) the types of questions you've been asking me that I didn't have answers to, 3) the seeming lack of involvement of God in my life through things like unanswered prayers (e.g., my father's death when I was 21), 4) general human suffering, 5) a lack of meaning and purpose in my attempts at being a "good" person, 6) my inability to be a "good" person, 7) my social awkwardness, which left me feeling pretty lonely even while married, 8) a little bit of hypochondria, and 9) a downward, accelerating spiral of feeling like a failure due to all of those things. Wow, that's a lot! It probably started when I was around 12 in some form and culminated around 28.

Your perspective on your own life is one very familiar to me. I hate the idea of a meaningless life so much that I would rather die than live it (even now). Even if I could be a perfect moral person (according to society's standards) and the greatest scientist ever, I would know on the inside that it was all pointless and that I was doing it for people who are also pointless. (Jesus gave an analogy of painting over tombs to make them look better while ignoring the death inside.[1] That's a great analogy for how my life used to be.) That's way too much for me to handle. I cannot and will not live that way, but I find it extremely puzzling that the rest of humanity doesn't feel the same way as me (i.e., why isn't everyone committing suicide?):

> There is but one truly serious philosophical problem, and that is suicide. Judging whether life is or is not worth living amounts to answering the fundamental question of philosophy.[2]

That's really dark, I know, but I just don't see the point of dealing with one second of frustration if life is meaningless. (After thinking about it, I suppose I believe that God must give each of us an intrinsic glimmer of hope that keeps most of us going.)

So now, I have—through great struggle—found my meaning and purpose in God alone. Nothing could ever be pointless in knowing, serving, and loving an infinite and loving thing. My job has meaning because I teach people whom God has declared have meaning. My research has meaning because I'm studying God's creation. My family

---

[1] Mt 23:27–28.
[2] Albert Camus, *The Myth of Sisyphus* (Toronto: Vintage, 1991).

has meaning because we are dedicated to serving and loving God. I spend hours per week typing in this document because I believe you, Vickie Lim, have immeasurable worth derived from God. God provides me the standard by which I live my life; I know no other possible standard. All of my happiness is ultimately derived from him. It's kind of hard to put in a grammatically correct sentence, but my life, meaning, and purpose are God alone: not in what he can do or has done for me, but directly in him because he's freaking incredible.

**Victoria**: Wow. That sounds really rough. Each of those factors in itself would be difficult to handle, and all of them together seem an unimaginably heavy burden. Did all that make you question God as to why you're going through such trials? I guess you did mention that in your list (item 3), so how do you feel that has been answered, many years later? Similarly, how have you accepted (if you have) that there exists so much suffering in the world despite God being in charge? You say that now you've found meaning and purpose in God alone. Does that mean that you also figured out the answers to those questions you had (regarding item 2)? From my experience, talking with you has brought up many questions that I didn't realize I had or questions that I otherwise wouldn't have thought of out of the blue. How did you find your answers?

That's such a strong stance you have on meaning in life! On why everyone isn't committing suicide if they don't find life to have intrinsic meaning, I think hope could be one reason as you mentioned. I also wouldn't be surprised if many people just weren't as moved by a lack of meaning. I remember having philosophical conversations in college which were really thought-provoking, but inevitably I'd stop spending time on those musings and return my attention to my specific responsibilities at the time. It's like discussing whether we are living in real life or in some simulation or dream. At some point, the conversation doesn't go anywhere, and meanwhile, there are all these tasks on the to-do list. So in addition to hope or indifference, distraction might be another reason that people get by in an apparently meaningless life. Finally, there's the more self-focused view of having to find one's own meaning and seek one's own pleasure. There could be other factors, but I would say that indifference and distraction have been the major players for me the last several years. Oddly though, thinking about finding one's own meaning, it always feels like I'm trying to *convince* myself that I need to find my own meaning in life, which I didn't realize until now. But then again, maybe wherever I direct my thoughts and however I choose to view my life will necessarily involve self-convincing.

Your last paragraph is moving! It's amazing how you have such an ardent and cohesive mentality for how you live your life. On a personal level, I don't get it, I guess. I don't know that I ever will... For example, you say that these people whom you teach have meaning declared by

God. But then earlier, you said that people only come to God by his calling. Does that mean that every person has worth, but not all are called to him? Actually, I'm not sure if this is the question I mean to ask; just feeling a sense of general blindness and incomprehension.

**Steve**: I questioned God greatly during my depression, but now I wouldn't trade it for anything, because it forced me to see and approach life in a way I never did before; Jesus was not everything to me before, but he was/is after, because he was all I had to turn to. The Bible says that we (personally and as humanity) go through hard times to 1) grow closer to God:

> But he said to me, "My grace is sufficient for you, for my power is made perfect in weakness." Therefore I will boast all the more gladly about my weaknesses, so that Christ's power may rest on me. That is why, for Christ's sake, I delight in weaknesses, in insults, in hardships, in persecutions, in difficulties. For when I am weak, then I am strong. (2 Cor 12:9–10)

> In this you rejoice, though now for a little while, if necessary, you have been grieved by various trials, so that the tested genuineness of your faith—more precious than gold that perishes though it is tested by fire—may be found to result in praise and glory and honor at the revelation of Jesus Christ. (1 Pet 1:6–7)

> I have said these things to you, that in me you may have peace. In the world you will have tribulation. But take heart; I have overcome the world." (Jn 16:33)

(C. S. Lewis said, "God whispers to us in our pleasures, speaks in our conscience, but shouts in our pains: it is His megaphone to rouse a deaf world."[3]) and 2) have opportunities to help others:

> And now, brothers and sisters, we want you to know about the grace that God has given the Macedonian churches. In the midst of a very severe trial, their overflowing joy and their extreme poverty welled up in rich generosity. For I testify that they gave as much as they were able, and even beyond their ability. Entirely on their own, they urgently pleaded with us for the privilege of sharing in this service to the Lord's people. And they exceeded our expectations: They gave themselves first of all to the Lord, and then by the will of God also to us. (2 Cor 8:1–5)

> One of them, named Agabus, stood up and through the Spirit predicted that a severe famine would spread over the entire Roman world. (This

---

[3] C. S. Lewis, *The Problem of Pain* (New York: HarperOne, 2015).

*happened during the reign of Claudius.) The disciples, as each one was able, decided to provide help for the brothers and sisters living in Judea. This they did, sending their gift to the elders by Barnabas and Saul.* (Acts 11:28–30)

But many see hard times as God's indifference or wrath and choose to not pursue him because of that. This is why the Bible is so important; it grounds us in truth that we often don't feel until much later (if ever). As far as the overall picture in my life, yes, I feel more confident than ever about my faith, but mainly because I've become less confident in myself and more confident in God. (But make no mistake: I still doubt, question, fear, and worry.)

Do you feel like you're missing something in life, or do you feel pretty satisfied (deep down apart from mundane activities)? You said you "don't get it." What do you think it would take to have an "ardent and cohesive [life] mentality?" Do you want that? Do you think it's possible? Do you think I'm delusional? Answer honestly.

**Victoria**: Hmm. So then could hard times be interpreted as tests of faith for one's connection to God? That's what came to mind when I read 1 Pet 1:6–7. I like the thought in 2 Cor 12:9–10; it's inspiring.

Those are intense questions. I do think there's something more to life that I don't get or am missing, a feeling which arises from persistent thoughts of wondering why anything at all matters. (Though they are persistent, they are far from nagging or crippling, so I don't do much to address them—not that I know how to). I keep thinking of life being a rat race, but I'm not unhappy or bored with my life.

As for what it would take to have that mentality, I don't know. I guess I don't really view it as something achievable in my own life. Do I want that mentality? I don't know that either. The answer should be yes. Wouldn't and shouldn't anyone *want* an ardent and cohesive life mentality?

Your last question made me chuckle. I honestly don't think you're delusional. Have you ever seen autostereograms? That's what this reminds me of. In high school, my geometry teacher had this book of those patterns, and almost everyone could see the 3D images, but try as I might, I never could. I didn't think there was anything wrong with my eyes, but something was defective in my brain that was supposed to process those images. So I don't think you're delusional. I just don't see what you're seeing.

**Steve**: Yes, hard times could be seen as tests of faith, but they could also be seen as random natural things that we have to respond to. I don't think we could know for sure as we go through them.

But do you agree that one or both of us *must* be delusional and/or blind in reality?

**Victoria**: It seems to be one of those things for which we'll never get concrete proof, like whether God is active, relevant, and personal today.

I suppose so, yes. If God is infinite and involved, it wouldn't make sense for him to be relevant in only a subset of people's lives. It would be contradictory of me to think, "Oh, he only applies to those people's lives," when those people are saying that he wants a relationship with every person. (Wait, so he's supposedly involved in *every single* person's life?)

**Steve**: Yes, at some level; we refer to this as common grace.[4]

---

[4] "Common grace," *Wikipedia*, en.wikipedia.org/wiki/Common_grace.

# CHAPTER 14: RELIGIOUS OR SPIRITUAL?

**Victoria**: How would you differentiate the concepts of religion and spirituality, both in general and within the lens of Christianity?

**Steve**: Honestly, I don't like either one inside or outside of Christianity. To me, religion is a set of rules and traditions that may or may not have any basis in reality. In addition, it seems set up to sustain itself; it uses emotion and/or guilt to keep people coming in so that those who benefit by it (via power, status, or money) keep benefiting by it. Spirituality, on the other hand, seems meaningless to me if it doesn't have truth in mind. Anyone can be spiritual about anything, but is it true? That doesn't seem to matter to a lot of "spiritual" people, which boggles my mind. Now, if someone asked me if I were "religious" or "spiritual," I'd say "Sure." But I'm much more concerned with finding objective truth and relating to an infinite God. That main concern is often displayed with traditional methods of worship and study one would justifiably call "religion," but that's not what I'm about.

**Victoria**: I like that answer. I like the idea of one's purpose to include "finding objective truth," which then may bring in the concepts of religiousness/spirituality, as opposed to directly searching for a religion or set of spiritual beliefs.

How do you relate to an infinite God? We've talked about this somewhat indirectly, such as via prayer and good deeds, but I'd be interested in seeing a more holistic picture. I imagine this would differ from person to person, but will the main ways of relating to God essentially be the same for all Christians?

**Steve**: I use the word "infinite" for God a lot because I don't know of a better word. Numerically infinite doesn't seem to apply, so I probably mean the following. In the same way that "infinity" encompasses all numbers, God is also "all there is." For example, he says that he is "the way and the truth and the life"[1] and that he is "love."[2] That's also weird grammar, which I've interpreted to mean that he is not only the source of those things, but the standard by which those things are measured. So those are examples of things I relate to an "infinite" God.

The Bible states clearly in two places (and in a more roundabout way in dozens of other places) what it takes to be a Christian:

*"For God so loved the world, that he gave his only Son, that whoever believes in him should not perish but have eternal life."* (Jn 3:16)

---

[1] Jn 14:6.
[2] 1 Jn 4:8.

*... because, if you confess with your mouth that Jesus is Lord and believe in your heart that God raised him from the dead, you will be saved.* (Rom 10:9)

The rest is up for debate and discussion, but we have the Bible, 2000 years of theology, and tradition to help with that. So *all* Christians, by definition, should have "done" those two verses. Of course, there are entire sets of books written on those verses and how to "do" them, but at its most basic level, that's it.

**Victoria**: That's interesting regarding 1 Jn 4:8: "Whoever does not love does not know God, because God is love." We discussed this earlier in which I wondered about people who didn't feel emotions, and you talked about religious emotion and how feelings can lie. However, there seems to be a conflict between 1) this verse claiming knowledge of God through knowing love and 2) those who have a lack of religious (or other) emotion; how can these be reconciled?

Regarding what it takes to be a Christian, that's remarkably simple. Why and how do you believe that "Jesus is Lord" and "that God raised him from the dead"?

**Steve**: A big issue here is that our language is so vague when it comes to the word "love"—in the Bible, it's often translated from a slightly better, more specific Greek or Hebrew word—so it's hard to get a good handle on what we're supposed to do. I've asked myself many times, "How do I know I believe?" and finally came to the conclusion that I know I believe because I act like I believe, even in private. In the same way, "How do I love God?" Well, if I do all of the things that love should entail, then I must love God. So emotions aren't necessary, but as mentioned earlier, they do often come about after the action rather than before (or sometimes not at all). C. S. Lewis said, "Do not waste time bothering whether you 'love' your neighbor; act as if you did. As soon as we do this we find one of the great secrets. When you are behaving as if you loved someone, you will presently come to love him."[3]

I believe that Jesus is Lord and God raised him from the dead because 1) that belief has completely changed my life for the better and 2) as referenced above, it's the entire theme of the Bible, which I believe to be true. (But maybe you're asking something else, perhaps along the lines of direct evidence?) One of my favorite preachers, John Piper, was once asked to "tweet" the essence of Christianity (i.e., sum it up in 140 characters or less). He said, "Jesus, God's Son died in the place of sinners and rose so that all who love him supremely might be forgiven all and have eternal joy in God."[4] That's it! No perfect morality, no touchy-feely

---

[3] C. S. Lewis, *Mere Christianity* (New York: HarperCollins, 2015).

[4] John Piper, "What's the Last Thing You Would Tweet?" *Desiring God*, April 10, 2017, www.desiringgod.org/interviews/whats-the-last-thing-you-would-tweet.

emotion, no impossibly absolute certainty, and no self-sufficiency! The thing is that Christianity is *hard*. You have to constantly fight your instincts. You have to believe in something you can't physically sense. You have to accept that some people will hate you. You have to care. You have to have a justification for everything you do. You have to study and pray when you're really tired and don't want to. You have to act as if everything you believe is true even though you always have an inkling that maybe you're just crazy. You don't get days off. But it's all worth it and I can't imagine life without it.

**Victoria**: I like how you reached that conclusion of how you knew you believed. It reminds me of another approach I take when I question something such as, "How do I know I like doing computational chemistry?" Then I think of what else I could be doing, or other fields I've dabbled in in the past, and then I re-realize that this is the best path for me (that I know of).

When you say, "all the things that love should entail," is that self-referential? By which I mean, God is/defines love, so when you say you love God, does that mean you act/think in a manner that is God-like yet is human-learned? I guess I'm not sure what things love should entail, aside from what I've been socialized to understand as love. Hmm, this brings to mind the "five love languages" of gift giving, quality time, words of affirmation, acts of service [devotion], and physical touch.[5]

On that C. S. Lewis quote—the idea behind it is attractive, but it seems too simple. Can't someone act like they love their neighbor, all the while hating them?

Going back to Rom 10:9, can't someone believe that God raised Jesus from the dead in the past without believing that God is involved in the present? Are those ideas somehow orthogonal? Many of these topics are converging on the idea that I don't understand "eternal joy in God," i.e., life after death. I feel as though nothing in my life and mental cultivation leads me to believe that there is life after death. The idea seems so fantastical, like the existence of Hogwarts. I'm not even sure what to ask about it.

Wow, I've never heard of Christianity described as hard before! At least in those terms. The difficulty that I usually hear relates to avoiding sin and abiding by Christian principles. Self-discipline can be hard, as applied to anything: academics, competitive sports, etc. It's reasonable that it would be so with Christianity, too. I don't get the sense from many people that Christianity is difficult, but my viewpoint is so limited. Do you think that's the case for many/most?

**Steve**: Yes, I believe love probably is self-referential in that it entails acting like God, who is love. I like the way you put that. Sure, some of that is

---

[5] Gary Chapman, *The 5 Love Languages: The Secret to Love that Lasts* (Chicago: Northfield Publishing, 2015).

learned through other humans, some by reason, some through scripture, etc., but it all ultimately points back to the Source.

As far as what it means to love God, there can and probably should be some emotional component to that as between humans, but Jesus made it very clear as to what that entails:

*"If you love me, keep my commands."* (Jn 14:15)

*Jesus replied, "Anyone who loves me will obey my teaching. My Father will love them, and we will come to them and make our home with them. Anyone who does not love me will not obey my teaching. These words you hear are not my own; they belong to the Father who sent me."* (Jn 14:23–24)

That "obedience" would include both submitting to the innate morality he's given us,

*... since what may be known about God is plain to them, because God has made it plain to them. For since the creation of the world God's invisible qualities—his eternal power and divine nature—have been clearly seen, being understood from what has been made, so that people are without excuse.* (Rom 1:19–20)

but more clearly, scripture:

*All Scripture is God-breathed and is useful for teaching, rebuking, correcting and training in righteousness, so that the servant of God may be thoroughly equipped for every good work.* (2 Tim 3:16)

"Can't someone act like they love their neighbor, all the while hating them?" Yes, of course, but Lewis is addressing those who *want* to love their neighbors but don't currently *feel* that they do. That's quite different than just acting in love while feeling hate.

"Can't someone believe that God raised Jesus from the dead in the past without believing that God is involved in the present?" If one actually believes that God raised Jesus from the dead, it would be strange to not believe in all of the other things that the Bible says about why that happened,

*He was delivered over to death for our sins and was raised to life for our justification.* (Rom 4:25)

including the eternality of it all:

*... according to his eternal purpose that he accomplished in Christ Jesus our Lord.* (Eph 3:11)

In fact, all of the New Testament was written after Jesus was resurrected, so our entire belief system is built upon the idea that what happened *then* still applies *now*:

> *For you know that it was not with perishable things such as silver or gold that you were redeemed from the empty way of life handed down to you from your ancestors, but with the precious blood of Christ, a lamb without blemish or defect. He was chosen before the creation of the world, but was revealed in these last times for your sake. Through him you believe in God, who raised him from the dead and glorified him, and so your faith and hope are in God.* (1 Pet 1:18–21)

"Many of these topics are converging on the idea that I don't understand 'eternal joy in God,' i.e., life after death. I feel as though nothing in my life and mental cultivation leads me to believe that there is life after death. The idea seems so fantastical, like the existence of Hogwarts." Ha, it does seem fantastical! So in the spirit of Hogwarts, here's something that might help that sounds like something Dumbledore might've said:

> "Good things as well as bad, you know, are caught by a kind of infection. If you want to get warm you must stand near the fire. If you want to be wet you must get into the water. If you want joy, power, peace, eternal life, you must get close to, or even into, the thing that has them. They are not a sort of prize which God could, if he chose, just hand out to anyone. They are a great fountain of energy and beauty spurting up at the very center of reality. If you are close to it, the spray will wet you; if you are not, you will remain dry."[6]

(And here's a nice commentary on that quotation.[7])

I think for many/most nominal Christians, Christianity *is* easy and, thus, probably not very fulfilling. I imagine you'll spend the rest of your life, like myself, occasionally reflecting on the difficulty of graduate school as the main reason you see satisfaction in the title "Dr. Victoria Lim." It won't be how smart people think you are or the paycheck or the research, but the fight you knew you finally won. Christianity has been easy in America for a long time because it was the majority view, and "public morality" was largely Judeo-Christian. But I think we're quickly heading to a post-Christian culture (if we're not already there). I readily welcome that, because my beliefs will be battle-tested and can no longer

---

[6] C. S. Lewis, *Mere Christianity* (New York: HarperCollins, 2015).
[7] Brad Hambrick, "C.S. Lewis on a God Infection," *Brad Hambrick*, August 13, 2012, bradhambrick.com/lewisoninfection/.

be some vague political notion or a path to popularity, nor can they lead me to some delusional comfort. Suffering, pain, exhaustion, and sadness are key ingredients to Christian joy![8]

> *You became imitators of us and of the Lord, for you welcomed the message in the midst of severe suffering with the joy given by the Holy Spirit.* (1 Thess 1:6)

> *Not only that, but we rejoice in our sufferings, knowing that suffering produces endurance, and endurance produces character, and character produces hope, and hope does not put us to shame, because God's love has been poured into our hearts through the Holy Spirit who has been given to us.* (Rom 5:3–5)

> *In all this you greatly rejoice, though now for a little while you may have had to suffer grief in all kinds of trials. These have come so that the proven genuineness of your faith—of greater worth than gold, which perishes even though refined by fire—may result in praise, glory and honor when Jesus Christ is revealed. Though you have not seen him, you love him; and even though you do not see him now, you believe in him and are filled with an inexpressible and glorious joy, for you are receiving the end result of your faith, the salvation of your souls.* (1 Pet 1:6–9)

> *But rejoice inasmuch as you participate in the sufferings of Christ, so that you may be overjoyed when his glory is revealed.* (1 Pet 4:13)

> *Now I rejoice in what I am suffering for you, and I fill up in my flesh what is still lacking in regard to Christ's afflictions, for the sake of his body, which is the church.* (Col 1:24)

They're the only things that will convince us of our complete inadequacy, thereby forcing us to God!

**Victoria**: That's pretty consistent with everything I've taken in so far. Thinking about love as obedience to God in order to act like God sounds kind of odd when taken out of context. It's like some weird Sims video game. I'm also realizing that there is a very strong emphasis on scripture which wasn't apparent to me before. Regarding 2 Tim 3:16–17 though, it brings up for me the same concern I had earlier regarding having to understand ancient Greek culture to understand the Bible. In addition, it relates back to an earlier topic about people leveraging the Bible in favor of their beliefs. There, you had said, "The Bible is made of stories and letters that have to be read that way. It's nuanced and needs to be interpreted and dealt with on a case-by-case basis." I'm glimpsing

---

[8] 2 Cor 11:16–12:9.

evidence of this here and there at IGSM[9] events; a Bible passage that seems to take only a few minutes to read and understand gets discussed for over an hour, which is surprising to me. There are so many interpretations and so much historical context to get through. It's like interpreting poetry (much of which eludes me). Also, reading in such extraordinary depth seems to indicate that it would take ages to read the Bible in full.

On God being involved in the present day, I need to think on that. This ties in closely with other topics we're discussing.

I like that Dumbledore-esque post! The snow analogy in the commentary that you referenced is illustrative. It seems that a premise of his argument is that good qualities are attributes of God, specifically things like joy, power, peace, life, and hope. I can agree that we *define* goodness and good things as God-like qualities, but the idea that you can *become* God-like from increased exposure ... well, I guess that isn't so insensible. People tend to become more like the people they spend the most time with. I like the quote, "So we are slow to accept that joy is an attribute of God and that joy does not exist apart from God." Slow acceptance is probably because of slowness to understanding.

It's definitely a fight indeed. It's interesting that you say we are heading to a post-Christian culture, because Tim Keller talks in his book[10] about both a rise and a decline of religion, that people as a whole are actually becoming more polarized.

I would say you sound battle-ready! Is there one singular event or person that/who has most challenged your beliefs?

"Suffering and pain and exhaustion and sadness are key ingredients to Christian joy!" Jeez, this parallels grad school exactly. Suffering the pre-advancement stresses, pain from practice talks that could always be better, exhaustion from not enough sleep, and sadness because projects (or at least major parts of projects) crash and burn despite how much time and energy has been invested. But then you gain knowledge and experience along the way—or something like that.

On your reference to Rom 5:3–5, I'm not sure I agree that suffering necessarily produces endurance. It seems that suffering can just wear one down, until one can handle it no more. 2 Cor 11:16–12:9 is interesting. I like the sentiment of those passages. The thing is, why? In other words, even if one is convinced of his own complete inadequacy, how does that force him to God?

**Steve**: "Also, reading in such extraordinary depth seems like it would take ages to read the Bible in full." Yes, that's what I love about it. The message is very simple, but one can spend an entire lifetime studying it.

---

[9] International Graduate Student Ministry at UC Irvine. See Chapter 15 for the beginning of this story.
[10] Timothy Keller, The Reason for God: Belief in an Age of Skepticism (New York: Dutton, 2008).

I suppose science works that way as well: I don't need to know any science to have a productive life, but I can also go unfathomably deep, which will inevitably lead to some uncertainty (well, literally with the Uncertainty Principle,[11] but that's not what I meant).

I love that you're going to IGSM!! I literally just searched for them on the web and saw pictures of you!!

"Slow acceptance is probably because of slowness to understanding." YES!! That's been my experience over and over again.

I agree with Keller that we are becoming more polarized, but that polarization is arising from a monolith of cultural/moral/political Christianity that America no longer embraces.

"Is there one singular event or person that/who has most challenged your beliefs?" My episode with depression absolutely challenged my beliefs. As far as a person goes, I don't know if you count famous people, but if so, it has to be Charles Darwin. Evolution seems so purposeless and random that it took me a very long time to reconcile it with a personal, concerned God. How about you?

"I'm not sure I agree that suffering necessarily produces endurance." I agree. I think the context of that verse is that suffering will produce endurance if viewed from the right perspective. Or to flip it around, if you *want* endurance, it will probably come through suffering. Strength in character doesn't just happen; it's created over many trials.

"In other words, even if one is convinced of his own complete inadequacy, how does that force him to God?" In the same vein as the last question, it begins with the assumption that the reader wants to feel adequate and have purpose and meaning. Those desires seem universal to humans, so the question is whether purpose and meaning actually exist. Paul is writing to people who already have some understanding and/or belief that God is inherently meaningful, purposeful, and adequate, so if he can convince them that they—apart from God—are meaningless, purposeless, and inadequate, then God himself is their only hope to fulfill their desires. Here's another way to think about it. I take pride in Americans having first landed on the moon, but that comes only via my attachment to my country. I obviously had nothing to do with the moon landings, but I *can* be indirectly awesome through my nationality. Paul is saying, "I know you want to be awesome. Everyone does. But I actually 'theologically landed on the moon' and know that I'm not awesome, so you people are definitely not awesome. However, you can be effectively awesome by associating yourself with the only thing that is awesome." I suppose I have the same goal in our conversation. I, like Paul, could claim a lot of outward awesomeness: career, academics, family, morality, nationality, health, etc. I see a lot of the same patterns of outward awesomeness in you, and my goal is to let you know how

---

[11] The Uncertainty Principle is a fundamental idea in quantum mechanics which places limits on how precisely certain quantities can be measured.

meaningless it all is on its own before you have to discover it the hard way yourself (or worse, become apathetic to it).

**Victoria**: That's definitely true regarding uncertainty! I was at a talk that discussed the interplay of science and Christianity throughout history. In the discussion afterwards, someone made a point that science seems to be more grounded and less undetermined than religion. I get how that seems true from a surface understanding (i.e., only taking science classes and consuming popular science content). But it's not until you're in the trenches that you see how messy and confusing science can be, such as with the myriad of competing hypotheses for the cause of Alzheimer's disease.

It definitely helps that IGSM is a small and welcoming group!

Depression and Darwin; I see. That reminds me of people seeking (or blaming) God during particularly trying times. I don't tend to have religion-related thoughts in difficult times, since it's never really been a part of my life (though my mom did have my siblings and me pray regularly to Buddhist figures when we were growing up. I forgot about that until now. I actually don't even know who they are, besides Buddha.) For myself, I'm not sure I have a single event/person that I can point to that has most challenged my beliefs. Apathy has always been pretty strong in this regard most of my life.

Ah, okay, I agree with the statement that endurance will likely come from suffering. Speaking of suffering, I went to a talk that discussed the idea of how suffering can exist with a good God. I've also been reading about this in Keller's book, but it didn't really make sense to me as to how they all go together. Was I supposed to view suffering as something which has underlying benefits? The "every cloud has a silver lining" idea sounds nice, but I can't imagine truly believing that in a situation in which I faced great harm or loss personally. I don't know if I could justify, for example, any worthwhile benefits from a loss of mental stability. That being said, reconciling the existence of suffering with the existence of a good God was never a concern/priority of mine since I viewed them as separate things. In other words, suffering happens because humans suck, not necessarily because God is punishing people. (I think this might reflect more of a deistic worldview?) So, "strength of character" and "Christian joy" are interesting reasons for the existence and/or benefits of suffering. Also on my mind recently is that suffering can lead to empathy for others and appreciation for what one has (e.g., experiencing the near loss of a child). Side story: Someone recently shared their experience with me of almost losing a child through a particularly trying ordeal and the positive things they took away from that event. I was musing about it in my head a few days later: "Suffering leads to enthalpy.[12] What? That doesn't sound right. Enthalpy? Oh wait, no, empathy!"

The idea of awesomeness via association makes sense. It's like passive diffusion,[13] except that the concentration gradient is always maintained because God has an infinite amount of awesomeness. I wonder what you mean by becoming apathetic to how meaningless all the outward awesomeness is. I get these phases of extreme hopelessness and apathy in everything. I just figured it's due to imbalances in my brain chemicals or something.

**Steve**: "Though my mom did make my siblings and me pray regularly to Buddhist figures..." That's an interesting concept. Buddhists do not view Buddha (or any person) as divine, correct? What is the act of praying to Buddha accomplishing?

"Apathy has always been pretty strong in this regard most of my life." Do you *want* to be apathetic? Or do you see no other way? Or you've never really even thought about it?

"Was I supposed to view suffering as something which has underlying benefits?" Yes, that is a major theme of Christianity (although the benefits might be after you die). For example, Christians believe Isaiah 53 (often entitled, "The Suffering Servant") was written 700 years before Jesus and is about Jesus. Jesus said that if people try to act like him, they should expect the same suffering:

> *It is enough for students to be like their teachers, and servants like their masters. If the head of the house has been called Beelzebul, how much more the members of his household!* (Mt 10:25)

> *Remember what I told you: 'A servant is not greater than his master.' If they persecuted me, they will persecute you also. If they obeyed my teaching, they will obey yours also.* (Jn 15:20)

But he also made it clear that many will see this hard road ahead, decide it's not worth it, and "unfollow" him (to use a social media term):

> *As they were walking along the road, a man said to him, "I will follow you wherever you go." Jesus replied, "Foxes have dens and birds have nests, but the Son of Man has no place to lay his head." He said to another man, "Follow me." But he replied, "Lord, first let me go and bury my father." Jesus said to him, "Let the dead bury their own dead, but you go and proclaim the kingdom of God." Still another said, "I will follow you, Lord; but first let me go back and say goodbye to my*

---

[12] Enthalpy is a physical quantity totaling a system's internal energy and the product of its pressure and volume. It (probably) has nothing to do with philosophy or theology.

[13] Diffusion is the movement of something from high to low concentration.

*family." Jesus replied, "No one who puts a hand to the plow and looks back is fit for service in the kingdom of God." (Lk 9:57–62)*

*"Enter through the narrow gate. For wide is the gate and broad is the road that leads to destruction, and many enter through it. But small is the gate and narrow the road that leads to life, and only a few find it." (Mt 7:13–14)*

*"Listen then to what the parable of the sower means: When anyone hears the message about the kingdom and does not understand it, the evil one comes and snatches away what was sown in their heart. This is the seed sown along the path. The seed falling on rocky ground refers to someone who hears the word and at once receives it with joy. But since they have no root, they last only a short time. When trouble or persecution comes because of the word, they quickly fall away. The seed falling among the thorns refers to someone who hears the word, but the worries of this life and the deceitfulness of wealth choke the word, making it unfruitful. But the seed falling on good soil refers to someone who hears the word and understands it. This is the one who produces a crop, yielding a hundred, sixty or thirty times what was sown." (Mt 13:18–23)*

Speaking from personal experience, I *never* want to suffer. But the depression I went through (the worst thing that ever happened to me) was the best thing that ever happened to me. It completely changed my life perspective (which I wasn't consciously aware I had) to one with daily meaning and purpose. I wouldn't trade that suffering for anything at this point. I can say the same for numerous problems with school, my job, my marriage, my kids, etc. It's very difficult to value suffering until it's over, but it can be the best thing that ever happened to you.

I honestly don't have any intellectual difficulty reconciling God and suffering, either, but it seems to be a major point of doubt and contention for a lot of people. My bigger difficulty is liking God when I suffer.

I'm sure enthalpy *and* entropy[14] can lead to empathy in a roundabout way!

"It's like passive diffusion, except that the concentration gradient is always maintained because God has an infinite amount of awesomeness." YES!!

"I wonder what you mean by becoming apathetic to how meaningless all the outward awesomeness is." Like you, I had great academic success my whole life and big dreams and ambitions to achieve. People, organizations, and grades, in one way or another,

---

[14] Entropy is a physical quantity which describes the tendency of a system to become more disordered over time.

constantly reinforced how awesome I was, and my identity become intimately tied up in just that. To keep up this identity, I had to remain perfect. I looked for perfect grades, perfect research, a perfect job, a perfect wife, perfect kids, and perfect morality. If any of those things showed cracks, it was a sign that everyone was wrong about me (at least in my mind), and then ... who was I? I had no other way to identify what I was about. Grad school can absolutely murder one's perceived awesomeness, and I don't think I have to explain that one to you. As I neared completion of my PhD, the burden of the stress and anxiety and (delusional) perfectionism all came crashing down at once, and I had no real answers for why I was doing what I was doing. I thought to myself, "I've gone through all of this to become absolutely miserable?! What the heck?!" Then the depression deepened further and further until finally, God slowly changed my perspective. However, I went through all that because *I've always really cared* about finding meaning and purpose and just didn't know what I was missing. To address your question then, I've seen many people go the opposite way that I did: complete apathy toward whether life does or can have meaning in the face of everything "going well." I sense that the fact that everyone thinks you're awesome doesn't mean a lot to you deep down; it never did to me, either, because we know better. But I think the "apathy" route is much more dangerous than the "despair" route because (especially as an American) it can lead to just enough satisfaction in money, things, prestige, sex, approval, entertainment, comfort, etc., that one never dares to step back and do difficult and painful things like give money until it hurts, show kindness to people who treat you poorly, or awkwardly step into a friend's life with enough love to tell her she's lost and desperately needs Jesus. Apathy is a self-fulfilling prophecy: "Life and people don't really matter, so I won't do anything that really matters, which makes what I do not really matter, which confirms what I already thought." I've been there!

"I just figured it's due to imbalances in my brain chemicals or something." Yes, but you decided to make it that way;[15] now fix it!

**Victoria**: I'm not sure if "prayer" is the right word for it, but we would light some incense, get on our knees, and say a silent message of supplication or thanksgiving to each of the three figures. This only really happened during times of trial (on a childhood scale, that meant an upcoming test or swim meet), on certain days of the year (like Chinese New Year), or after the death of a family member. I actually don't know that much about Buddhism. I probably know more about Christianity than Buddhism at this point. I think people must believe that these figures have some sort of divine power; else, why pray?

I certainly don't want to be apathetic. I think I was for a huge part of my life, and when I found out that I was really into chemistry (freshman

---

[15] "Neuroplasticity," *Wikipedia*, en.wikipedia.org/wiki/Neuroplasticity.

year, thanks to Dr. Stace[16]), it surprised and delighted me. Then gradually everything leveled out again. In a sense, I don't experience the higher highs and lower lows, but even the flat-line apathy feels a lot emptier, too. I guess I just see it as a part of who I am.

I have two different thoughts on suffering as Jesus did: 1) It sort of makes sense given that people are created to be God-like and strive to act God-like. But suffering came from The Fall[17] (right?), which makes me wonder: 2) On expecting the same suffering, there's no way anyone can experience the same magnitude of suffering that Jesus did, right? It's crazy to think about the scale of sin (magnitude of evilness, let's say), and I'm continually astounded by the terrible things that people do. It seems that the scale of sinfulness extends toward infinity, or at least toward the asymptote of Jesus-scale suffering.

I would agree that there is value in suffering, which can be hard to see or appreciate in the moment. Sometimes I fear that I won't come out on the other side to realize those gains.

That was an eloquently accurate discussion on identity, especially on apathy. A lifetime of that self-fulfilling prophecy would be misery.

Fixing in progress, I hope.

**Steve**: "On expecting the same suffering, there's no way anyone can experience the same magnitude of suffering that Jesus did, right?" That's a great question which I've pondered much myself. From one perspective, yes; from another, no. Jesus lived 30-some years, but his ministry (which included some major opposition) only lasted three. I'm sure that was hard, but it probably wasn't harder than being a Christian in North Korea.[18] He was arrested and underwent an excruciating, humiliating, brutal crucifixion, but that all took place within a day.[19] There are people with decades-long psychological and physical problems that I would argue have suffered worse (in total) than being crucified. But from another point-of-view, the important point isn't how much suffering Jesus went through, but what his suffering was about. If a perfect, omni* God became a human, then in that sense, the drop from God to human is infinitely greater than the drop from human to suffering human, so maybe one could view that as suffering. Also, it's hard to pinpoint his emotional, mental, and spiritual states, but I would argue that bearing the burden of the sins of the entire world counts as pretty substantial suffering as well (and that to which we can't relate).

---

[16] Dr. Justin Stace, a chemistry professor at Belmont University. He's Victoria's former teacher, Steve's friend, and an all-around great guy.

[17] Gen 3.

[18] "World Watch List," *Open Doors USA*, www.opendoorsusa.org/christian-persecution/world-watch-list/.

[19] Jn 18–19.

"Sometimes I fear that I won't come out on the other side to realize those gains." Me, too. But I've realized that if I never make it about me to begin with, it doesn't really matter.

# CHAPTER 15: THE AFTERLIFE

**Victoria**: So, a weird thing happened to me today. This morning, I left my apartment about half an hour later than usual (because I spontaneously decided to make pancakes), and about halfway through my walk to the office, some random guy stopped me and asked if I was a graduate student. That was a bit surprising in itself since people often think I'm an undergrad. Anyway, I said that I was, and he invited me to this graduate student welcome dinner hosted by the International Graduate Student Ministry (IGSM). I assured him I was neither international nor an incoming graduate student, but he encouraged me to go regardless. I did end up going (free food is a powerful lure), not expecting the hour-long message about Christianity beforehand. I didn't realize IGSM was a Christian group. The message was given by a chemistry professor, who talked about the National Institutes of Health in Bethesda, MD, and related that to the Pool of Bethesda[1] with its healing capabilities. He also talked about the idea of life being a series of rat races and questioned why we run those races (I've wondered this myself plenty of times). During dinner afterwards, I chatted with this woman named Virginia, who was part of the IGSM chapter at Berkeley[2] and was helping to start up IGSM in Irvine.[3] (The chemistry professor who gave the message is starting a sabbatical at UCI also for that reason.) Virginia and I were talking about general life and Christianity, which brought up the same topic that we're currently discussing—how we know whether or not God is relevant in the present-day and on a personal level. In her answer, she referred to souls and the afterlife, but I don't really understand/believe in either, so it was hard for me to follow. I think they're related topics; i.e., if I believed in an afterlife, I'd have to believe in the existence of souls. She seemed to be of the mindset that if I didn't believe in life after death, none of this Christianity stuff would matter. I've never thought about these things in conjunction. Do you have comments on that, and would you agree?

All this seemed so coincidental because I wouldn't have known about this event had I left at my usual time. Also, it was this guy's last flyer. Furthermore, I most likely would not have gone if we hadn't already been discussing these philosophical and faith-related topics. Our conversation has led me to be more open about seeking my own

---

[1] Jn 5:1–15.
[2] The University of California, Berkeley.
[3] The University of California, Irvine.

answers for truth in the universe. Additionally, I got a new book at this event! It's called *The Reason for God* by Timothy Keller.[4]

**Steve**: That's quite brave of you to go to such a thing! I love it! Yes, I agree that if there is no life after death, none of this matters:

> *If only for this life we have hope in Christ, we are of all people most to be pitied.* (1 Cor 15:19)

I suppose that's because my definition of "matters" includes some form of eternality, and I don't see how it couldn't.

I love that you're reading Tim Keller. He's a great thinker, and I think you'll enjoy his book.

**Victoria**: I've finished the first chapter, and I really like it so far. It sometimes quotes my thoughts and doubts verbatim, even some that I haven't realized or articulated for myself. Related to what we're talking about, Keller mentioned that our worldview/"narrative identity" is determined by our deep-seated beliefs in the purpose of human life. I wonder if one's stance on the purpose of human life causes, is caused by, or is correlated with one's stance on life after death. Did you ever question the existence of life after death, or was that something you always took to be true?

**Steve**: I've questioned and doubted and disbelieved literally every part of my faith I can think of at some point, so that certainly includes the afterlife. My current belief in the afterlife is simply a conclusion I draw from the whole of scripture (it's frequently mentioned[5]) and a reasoned-out faith (why would Jesus have gone to all that trouble for just the normal human lifespan?). But, like Paul, I would consider myself a delusional fool if there is no afterlife.

**Victoria**: Wouldn't you have to already be inclined to believe in the afterlife before deciding to believe what the Bible says on the afterlife? Is there anything outside the Bible that points toward the existence or nonexistence of the afterlife? I know there's a possibility that any one thing I believe may not be true, but if I start from an open-minded standpoint of not believing in the afterlife, I don't know if I could rationally switch conclusions based on a single source.

**Steve**: "Wouldn't you have to already be inclined to believe in the afterlife before deciding to believe what the Bible says on the afterlife?" I don't know why anyone would believe in the afterlife apart from the Bible (or another religious text), so it would be strange to me to think of someone needing to believe in it before they believed what the Bible said about it. Rather, I think you'd have to be inclined to believe the Bible (and post

---

[4] Timothy Keller, The Reason for God: Belief in an Age of Skepticism (New York: Dutton, 2008).

[5] www.biblegateway.com/quicksearch/
?qs_version=NIV&quicksearch=heaven&begin=47&end=73

hoc reasoning) to believe what the Bible says on the afterlife. In other words, in the following order, I 1) recognize my own sinfulness and need for help, 2) see Christianity as a solution, 3) see the Bible as the detailed description of that solution, and as a result, 4) believe what the Bible says about the afterlife.

"Is there anything outside of the Bible that points toward the existence or not of the afterlife?" There are plenty of stories of near-death experiences,[6] but I'm very skeptical of them. More importantly, there's plenty of belief in the afterlife throughout human history.[7] Along those lines...

> "Creatures are not born with desires unless satisfaction for those desires exists. A baby feels hunger: well, there is such a thing as food. A duckling wants to swim: well, there is such a thing as water. Men feel sexual desire: well, there is such a thing as sex. If I find in myself a desire which no experience in this world can satisfy, the most probable explanation is that I was made for another world. If none of my earthly pleasures satisfy it, that does not prove that the universe is a fraud. Probably earthly pleasures were never meant to satisfy it, but only to arouse it, to suggest the real thing. If that is so, I must take care, on the one hand, never to despise, or to be unthankful for, these earthly blessings, and on the other, never to mistake them for the something else of which they are only a kind of copy, or echo, or mirage. I must keep alive in myself the desire for my true country [heaven], which I shall not find till after death; I must never let it get snowed under or turned aside; I must make it the main object of life to press on to that country and to help others to do the same."[8]

Victoria: For some reason I have the sense that there are people who are not religious yet do believe in an afterlife. I suppose that would be insensible. It seems kind of circular, though. Doesn't your flow of thought implicitly rely on the fact that there's an afterlife? In other words, if one didn't believe in the afterlife, one might not realize a need for help regarding sinfulness, which would not lead to Christianity as the solution.

"Creatures are not born with desires unless satisfaction for those desires exists." This can't be proved, though, can it?

"If I find in myself a desire which no experience in this world can satisfy, the most probable explanation is that I was made for another

---

[6] "Near-death experience," *Wikipedia*, en.wikipedia.org/wiki/Near-death_experience.

[7] "Afterlife," *Wikipedia*, en.wikipedia.org/wiki/Afterlife.

[8] C. S. Lewis, *Mere Christianity* (New York: HarperCollins, 2015).

world." What is that desire, specifically? If one doesn't have that desire, then one simply doesn't believe?

"If none of my earthly pleasures satisfy it, that does not prove that the universe is a fraud." One can never actually experience *everything*, so how can one say that absolutely no pleasures will satisfy that desire?

I remember having difficulty reading C. S. Lewis, wanting to question almost every other line he wrote. Anyway, I guess the fact that many people believe in the afterlife isn't compelling in itself to me, but maybe it shouldn't be outside of a foundational belief of religion.

**Steve**: "Doesn't your flow of thought implicitly rely on the fact that there's an afterlife? In other words, if one didn't believe in the afterlife, one might not realize a need for help regarding sinfulness which would not lead to Christianity as the solution." Wow, great question! I haven't thought of it like that before. I think 1) my sinfulness, 2) God's holiness, and 3) my potential to have a relationship with him have nothing to do with an afterlife. But 1) my need for a savior, 2) my hope for a future, and 3) every meaning I attach to anything have everything to do with an afterlife. So the answer isn't black-and-white in those terms, but the lack of an afterlife would certainly change Christianity at its core. In a hypothetical universe with Christianity but no afterlife, I would probably not be a Christian. Sure, I could have a temporary relationship with God and pull from his wisdom to become successful and happy before I die, but why would that matter? I'm not even sure I would like to worship an infinitely great but temporary thing (in fact, I believe that would be an oxymoron). What would be the point? So I guess you're right at some level: I do have some a priori belief in the afterlife/eternality for which Christianity provides a solution. But I would argue that I have very good, non-Christian reasons to believe in an eternal god who wishes to have a relationship with me (e.g., the beginning of our discussion), and that belief naturally unfolds into a belief in the afterlife. So maybe a more accurate cause/effect train for me would be

1) Nature points to an eternal, omniscient, omnipotent creator.
2) I have inexplicable feelings of consciousness, morality, design, purpose, eternality, etc., which imply that this creator is personal.
3) It logically follows that this personal eternal god would want to remain personal and eternal (i.e., in the afterlife) because he/she/it cannot change (as we discussed).
4) I know that I have seriously screwed up that ingrained morality/design/purpose (i.e., even by my own flawed standards: I know I said earlier that I'm not absolutely sure of *anything*, but this could be an exception) and have thus damaged/severed my relationship with that creator.
5) I see Christianity as a solution.
6) I see the Bible as the particular description of that solution.
7) I believe the details about the afterlife given in the Bible.

"'Creatures are not born with desires unless satisfaction for those desires exists.' This can't be proved though, can it?" No, probably not. I would not say he's proving anything here, just making an argument that the idea of the afterlife is not illogical.

"'If I find in myself a desire which no experience in this world can satisfy, the most probable explanation is that I was made for another world.' What is that desire, specifically? If one doesn't have that desire, then one simply doesn't believe?" He's talking about *any* desire and is making the general argument that nothing in this world ultimately satisfies us: i.e., *we always want more and better no matter how much have.* I agree with that sentiment 100% after many decades of living. So his question is really, "Why do we have unquenchable desires in this life?" and his answer is "Because they point to an ultimate fulfillment in God in eternity."

"'If none of my earthly pleasures satisfy it, that does not prove that the universe is a fraud.' One can never actually experience everything, so how can one say that absolutely no pleasures will satisfy that desire?" No one has ever *proven* that I can't flap my arms really fast and fly, so how can you say that I can't? No one has ever *proven* that there aren't dragons that fly around and become invisible every time we look at them (maybe like the Flying Spaghetti Monster or something). But I'm sure you agree that this is not how science and logic work: we start with the preponderance of evidence or lack thereof, and proving/disproving and/or completeness are impossible and unnecessary. Lewis' argument (and mine) is that in the whole history of humanity, there is no evidence that any human has been completely fulfilled, and we (all humans I've met) certainly don't feel it in our own lives; therefore, we (Christians) don't believe it's possible and see earthly unfulfillment as consistent with (not necessarily positive evidence for) an afterlife.

**Victoria**: "In a hypothetical universe with Christianity but no afterlife, I would probably not be a Christian. Sure, I could have a temporary relationship with God and pull from his wisdom to become successful/ happy before I die, but why would that matter?" I think this is sort of where my mental stance is. It's not the past I have doubts with, but the present and future. That is to say, it is generally undisputed that Jesus existed, and I'm on board with this, but I'm still processing the message and implication of his ministry, which is maybe limited by the fact that I don't believe in an afterlife. It would probably change how I think about things if I allowed for the possibility that an afterlife exists (or that *the* afterlife exists). I'm not sure which is harder for me to believe: that there is a loving and just God who is both personal and relevant, or that there is life after death.

I follow this new cause/effect train better! Point 3 here, as a result of 1 and 2, addresses the concern of having to have a priori views of an afterlife because, tautologically, an eternal god is infinite in time. It seems that one must include personal experience for belief in God, the afterlife, etc. (e.g., point 2). Tangentially, this reminds me of a recent conversation I had with my advisor, who said he didn't grow up Christian, but then believed in the Bible after he'd read it. It seemed strikingly simple.

"We always want more and better no matter how much have." This is intriguing to think about in the lens of religion. I usually think about desires in life as striving up the pyramid toward self-actualization.[9] Religion seems to focus on what "self-actualization" may—or should—look like, i.e., what it means to realize "personal potential, self-fulfillment, seeking personal growth and peak experiences."[10] So the top of the pyramid in a Christian viewpoint might be "ultimate fulfillment in God in eternity." The zenith of this pyramid can't fully be attained in the present life, but it's like an asymptote that people strive for, knowingly or not. Thoughts?

"So his question is really, 'Why do we have unquenchable desires in this life?' and his answer is 'Because they point to an ultimate fulfillment in God in eternity.'" This is interesting! Sometimes I think about hedonic adaptation (also referred to as the hedonic treadmill[11]) in the context of impending or imagined life events. It is always possible to strive for more, despite any advancements gained in life, such as in one's net worth, power, or status. It's hard to be satisfied with all that you have when you're looking at what others have or what level comes next. I always saw the natural response to the hedonic treadmill as being to find satisfaction and gratitude no matter where you are in life, but it seems that C. S. Lewis is saying that the hedonic treadmill may actually be revealing a desire to relate with God.

Your clarification makes sense regarding how a lack of complete fulfillment in this life is consistent with an afterlife. A part of me is a bit dissatisfied (maybe irrationally) that there isn't any widely accepted positive evidence for the afterlife outside of the Bible. Then again, I mentioned earlier that even if I had witnessed Jesus and his works directly, I might not be as convinced as I think I would/should be. So evidence for or against an afterlife might not mean as much as I think it would.

**Steve**: "It seems that one must include personal experience for belief in God, the afterlife, etc. (e.g., point 2)." When I said, "I have inexplicable feelings of consciousness, morality, design, purpose, eternality, etc., which imply that this creator is personal," that wasn't meant to be "Steve's personal experience." *You* have inexplicable feelings of consciousness. *You* have inexplicable feelings of morality. *You* have inexplicable feelings of

[9] "Maslow's hierarchy of needs," *Wikipedia*, en.wikipedia.org/wiki/Maslow's_hierarchy_of_needs.

[10] Saul McLeod, "Maslow's Hierarchy of Needs," *SimplyPsychology*, 2018, www.simplypsychology.org/maslow.html.

[11] "Hedonic treadmill," *Wikipedia*, en.wikipedia.org/wiki/Hedonic_treadmill.

purpose (or you wouldn't do anything at all). Granted, maybe you're lacking feelings of design and eternality, but you can certainly run with the idea that almost everything you do and feel every single second of your life is governed by completely unscientific ideas. Is it plausible (I'm not asking for provable, just plausible) that these things come from an external source? Is it plausible, given your belief in God, that God is that external source, thereby making him personal? Belief is not a yes-or-no, black-or-white answer to a question (or even lots of questions) but acting in accordance with the preponderance of evidence and reason. Wouldn't it be strange for a god to create a well-ordered universe with absolutely no intention?

As for the self-actualization pyramid, yes, I can get on board with that (with the small caveat that Christian self-actualization means finding self-fulfillment in something that's not yourself—to the point that one must forget oneself).

Yes, I also like the asymptotic approach toward fulfillment in eternity. Geeky examples are the best.

"A part of me is a bit dissatisfied (maybe irrationally) that there isn't any widely accepted positive evidence for the afterlife outside of the Bible." Me, too. That would completely change everything about humanity, wouldn't it? Maybe God likes humanity this way: wrestling with doubt. I'm convinced that no matter what incredible miraculous thing I witnessed, I could explain it away, so doubt is hard to avoid.

# Chapter 16: Following the Intellectuals

**Victoria:** While reading *The Reason for God*,[1] I've noticed that Keller mentions Richard Dawkins a few times here and there. Sometimes I wonder how convincible I am; i.e., if I am convinced by some of Keller's arguments, maybe I would also be swayed by Dawkins' arguments. This makes me curious: when you were in your "doubting phase," did you consider many viewpoints in the argument for and against Christianity? Have you read/questioned any of Dawkins' work?

**Steve:** I'm still in my doubting phase, and I hope I never leave it. I'm a huge skeptic of every worldview that claims to know The Truth (which seems to be all of them, including my own). I love reading dissent and disagreement with Christianity, because it makes me question and investigate everything I believe. So far, such investigations have only strengthened my faith and made it feel more grounded in reason and history than feelings. I've read a lot of what Dawkins has written (though admittedly none of his full-length books) and listened to a lot of what he's said. I find his arguments to be more anti-religion than pro-atheism, which is strange to me (although I suppose that the word "atheism" itself implies that's what atheists do). I think he uses weak argumentation that tends to just ridicule and react to religious beliefs without providing justification:[2]

> "Without God, the universe could not have come into existence." If that's what you think, go away and learn some physics.[3]

> Racism? No. Religion is not race. You can't renounce your race. You can, and should, renounce your stupid religion.[4]

Moreover, he constantly appeals to evolution and the Big Bang to support his arguments, but I already fully believe in those, so what am *I* supposed to do with them? Although I find his arguments weak, I do fully support his fight against postmodernism:

---

[1] Timothy Keller, The Reason for God: Belief in an Age of Skepticism (New York: Dutton, 2008).

[2] William Lane Craig, "Richard Dawkins' Argument for Atheism in The God Delusion," *Reasonable Faith*, April 23, 2007, www.reasonablefaith.org/writings/question-answer/richard-dawkins-argument-for-atheism-in-the-god-delusion.

[3] Richard Dawkins, *Twitter*, October 11, 2017, twitter.com/RichardDawkins/status/918078459569737729.

[4] Richard Dawkins, Twitter, September 19, 2017, twitter.com/RichardDawkins/status/918078459569737729.

All humanity should be proud of Newton & the precision of eclipse forecasting (oh but surely an eclipse is only a social construct?).[5]

Excellent article by Michael Shermer.[6] He doesn't say this but it's arguable that campus idiocy helped elect Trump.[7]

This is something atheists and scientists and Christians should be fighting against together. As an aside, I feel the same way about Neil deGrasse Tyson and Carl Sagan. They're average scientists (that's not an insult; I'll gladly leave the option that they're better than me) who seem to have an agenda that betrays their own beliefs (i.e., if there is no God, then why does it matter so much to them that I believe in him?). I have much more respect for non-theists like Nietzsche, Darwin, Freud, Skinner, Einstein, and Hawking, who've made huge contributions to their fields and more consistently present arguments *for* atheism by letting their work speak for itself.

**Victoria**: When someone feels the need to incorporate ridicule, name-calling, etc. into any kind of argument, it makes the arguer lose credibility. So I see your point with Dawkins.

"If there is no God, then why does it matter so much to them that I believe in him?" I never thought about it like this before, but that's curious. If one is convinced that there is a God and that God is personal and has omni* characteristics, it makes sense to share that with others because of the potential gain of a relationship with God. But what would a critic gain from trying to convince someone out of belief? I suppose someone might say more critically thinking individuals and fewer blind followers in society. And maybe that would be true for some people, but a critical evaluation of the facts can apparently lead one to the opposite conclusion presented by the critic.[8]

I'm surprised by your statement regarding those scientists who present arguments for atheism through their work. What do you mean by that?

**Steve**: Each of those guys have presented very strong challenges to Christianity in my mind. In brief: Nietzsche says we seem to be doing fine without God, Darwin says nature seems to do fine without God,

[5] Richard Dawkins, *Twitter*, August 21, 2017, twitter.com/RichardDawkins/status/899708854338019329.

[6] Michael Shermer, "The Unfortunate Fallout of Campus Postmodernism," *Scientific American*, September 1, 2017, www.scientificamerican.com/article/the-unfortunate-fallout-of-campus-postmodernism/.

[7] Richard Dawkins, *Twitter*, August 16, 2017, twitter.com/RichardDawkins/status/897973055095541760.

[8] Lee Strobel, *The Case for Christ: The Case for Christ: A Journalist's Personal Investigation of the Evidence for Jesus* (Grand Rapids, MI: Zondervan, 2016).

Freud says God only exists in our minds because we *want/need* him to, Skinner says our ability to choose God is an illusion, Einstein says that if even space and time aren't fixed, how can we be sure of anything else?, and Hawking says maybe the multiverse will explain our improbable existence. Those are huge obstacles to overcome for belief (much bigger than Richard Dawkins ranting that religion ruins society). Generally, I think a lot of people have to overcome the fact that some (but certainly not all[9]) of the smartest and most prolific contributors to society throughout history have seen no evidence or need for God. But that's actually consistent with what the Bible already says: Christianity is not made for the "best" or "smartest" people:

> *Do not deceive yourselves. If any of you think you are wise by the standards of this age, you should become "fools" so that you may become wise. For the wisdom of this world is foolishness in God's sight. As it is written: "He catches the wise in their craftiness;" and again, "The Lord knows that the thoughts of the wise are futile."* (1 Cor 3:18–20)

> *Here is a trustworthy saying that deserves full acceptance: Christ Jesus came into the world to save sinners—of whom I am the worst.* (1 Tim 1:15)

> *Moses said to the LORD, "Pardon your servant, Lord. I have never been eloquent, neither in the past nor since you have spoken to your servant. I am slow of speech and tongue." The LORD said to him, "Who gave human beings their mouths? Who makes them deaf or mute? Who gives them sight or makes them blind? Is it not I, the LORD? Now go; I will help you speak and will teach you what to say."* (Ex 4:10–12)

> *But the LORD said to Samuel, "Do not consider his appearance or his height, for I have rejected him. The LORD does not look at the things people look at. People look at the outward appearance, but the LORD looks at the heart."* (1 Sam 16:7)

> *Philip found Nathanael and told him, "We have found the one Moses wrote about in the Law, and about whom the prophets also wrote—Jesus of Nazareth, the son of Joseph." "Nazareth! Can anything good come from there?" Nathanael asked. "Come and see," said Philip.* (Jn 1:45–46)

> *"There was a rich man who was dressed in purple and fine linen and lived in luxury every day. At his gate was laid a beggar named*

---

[9] "List of Christian Nobel laureates," *Wikipedia*, en.wikipedia.org/wiki/List_of_Christian_Nobel_laureates.

*Lazarus, covered with sores and longing to eat what fell from the rich man's table. Even the dogs came and licked his sores. "The time came when the beggar died and the angels carried him to Abraham's side. The rich man also died and was buried. In Hades, where he was in torment, he looked up and saw Abraham far away, with Lazarus by his side. So he called to him, 'Father Abraham, have pity on me and send Lazarus to dip the tip of his finger in water and cool my tongue, because I am in agony in this fire.' "But Abraham replied, 'Son, remember that in your lifetime you received your good things, while Lazarus received bad things, but now he is comforted here and you are in agony. And besides all this, between us and you a great chasm has been set in place, so that those who want to go from here to you cannot, nor can anyone cross over from there to us.' "He answered, 'Then I beg you, father, send Lazarus to my family, for I have five brothers. Let him warn them, so that they will not also come to this place of torment.' "Abraham replied, 'They have Moses and the Prophets; let them listen to them.' "'No, father Abraham,' he said, 'but if someone from the dead goes to them, they will repent.' "He said to him, 'If they do not listen to Moses and the Prophets, they will not be convinced even if someone rises from the dead.'"* (Lk 16:19–31)

*On hearing this, Jesus said to them, "It is not the healthy who need a doctor, but the sick. I have not come to call the righteous, but sinners."* (Mk 2:17)

*When pride comes, then comes disgrace, but with humility comes wisdom.* (Prov 11:2)

*And he said: "Truly I tell you, unless you change and become like little children, you will never enter the kingdom of heaven."* (Mt 18:3)

*"The greatest among you will be your servant. For those who exalt themselves will be humbled, and those who humble themselves will be exalted."* (Mt 23:11–12)

# CHAPTER 17: FINDING MEANING IN MONOTONY

**Victoria**: Do you ever feel like life is just going through the "daily grind"? Or do you have a stronger sense of meaning in life brought about by strong Christian faith? Does it waver? Before "advancement (to candidacy) season," grad school was starting to feel like a boring treadmill: research, eat, sleep, repeat. Though preparing for my advancement this past month was intense, it was refreshing as it afforded me a break from my own research (as we have to design and defend our own original research proposal). It was a time I could learn a new subfield to my heart's content without stressing about expectations of delivering research results. With that over, I'm transitioning back into research life, but I hope to stave off the "daily grind" feeling. I can't imagine what this would feel like in more of a "real-world" job that would be more structured (and more indefinite in duration) compared to graduate school.

**Steve**: "Do you ever feel like life is just going through the "daily grind?" Yes, of course. In fact, if one more student asks a question that I just answered because they were staring at their phone, I might snap! And I've been teaching the same material for many years to numbers of sometimes apathetic, whiny, or hostile students (although the large majority of my students are great). That can get old pretty quick. Apart from my job, even though I love them dearly, there are times I feel it with my kids, wife, church, and family (and I'm sure they feel it with me). I feel it with the never-ending stupidity of American politics and the fear of an inevitable war with someone. I feel it when I'm in traffic or when I don't have "enough" money. I feel it when I'm sick or bored or tired. But mostly I feel it when I criticize myself for not getting better in so many ways.

"Or do you have a stronger sense of meaning in life brought about by strong Christian faith?" Yes, that's literally all that keeps me going. My personality is naturally very unforgiving, perfectionist, and standoffish, so I get very frustrated having to deal with people (students, colleagues, family, everyone). I have to fight that with every fiber of my being, because I know it's sinful. I dealt with a situation recently in which I decided to compliment someone I have very little respect for (I have strong evidence that they lack motivation and character). My theology teaches me that that person has value given by God, and that I should show that through my actions rather than deepening a rift. Even more, there are times when I must admit that I seriously lack motivation and character, or, like my students, fall into patterns of apathy, whining, and complaining. The only way for me to make sense of myself and other people is to live for the glory of God. I respond kindly to the kid on his phone because God loves him and has shown me great mercy; I know of no better way to show what God is about than to act like him. I love to teach because I'm helping people who have worth given by God. I do research to learn about God's creation. I sit in traffic because I'm providing food for a family whom God wants to keep alive. It's the only way I know to go about life, and it turns my natural inclinations of frustration to joy, purpose, and meaning.

Yes, I waver, but my wavering is all the more a reminder of my complete and utter dependence on and need for God. I've recently trained myself to recognize my own negative emotions and turn them into statements about myself and God. It's been very helpful in creating joy.

# CHAPTER 18: BIBLE STUDY IN JOHN

**Steve**: Here's my idea for our remote Bible study. If you're OK with going through John, you'll read a certain passage of scripture from that book, post which verses you read and then your thoughts, comments, and questions. I'll then read the same passage and give you my thoughts. This can go back and forth until you feel like it's time to move on (or quit!), and then we'll repeat (or not!). You'll see in your Bible that the sections are divided up in a logical fashion with headings (i.e., John 1:1–18 says "The Word Became Flesh" in my Bible), so that might be a good way to decide what to read next. I'll start with the first one, but you can lead after that. If you're OK with all that, here goes.

**Victoria**: Sounds like a good plan. Do you mind if we go through several sections simultaneously? Inertia makes it easier for me to keep going rather than to start. If you think it could hinder discussion though, I'm fine with one at a time.

**Steve**: Yeah, that's fine if you're OK with waiting a little more for me to catch up.

**Victoria**: No problem. Also, do you have suggestions on how to read the Bible? While going through the study Bible, I found myself getting bogged down reading all the footnotes and the extra stuff in the margins, so I switched to a non-study Bible. I occasionally refer back to the study Bible for background information.

**Steve**: We had these little cards passed out recently at church that give some helpful general guidelines.[1] The first is for reading (with the acronym REAP), the second for praying (with the acronym (PRAY). It's better to spend a little more time dissecting a small passage than trying to swallow a large passage.

### Read the Word: 2 Tim 3:16

- **Read**. Humbly ask the Holy Spirit to open your eyes, enlighten your mind, and satisfy your heart. Read the passage.
- **Examine**. What is happening? Key words, phrases, ideas. What do you learn about God? Man? Sin? Jesus and our need for redemption?
- **Apply**. What sin is there to confess? What truth to believe? Is there an example to follow? Command to obey? Knowledge to obtain?
- **Pray**. Spend time praying through the passage and your application. Ask God to continue to change your heart, mind, and relationships.

---

[1] Courtesy of Steele Wright, former Minister of Young Adults at First Baptist Church Joelton; originally created by David Platt.

## Pray the Word: Mt 6:9–13

- **Praise**. Worship God for who He is and what He has done. Recite truths about God and why you are thankful for them.
- **Repent**. Confess your sins to God. Allow the Holy Spirit to convict you, and then acknowledge your need for Jesus. Receive His forgiveness.
- **Ask**. What are some particular needs in your life right now? What about the lives of those around you? Your family? Your church? The world?
- **Yield**. Surrender your life to Jesus. Humble yourself, and allow Him to conform you more into His image.

[To the reader: In the following chapters, we suggest reading through each section of John before reading through our discussion.]

# CHAPTER 19: JOHN 1

## JOHN 1:1-18

**Steve**: This chapter starts the same way that the entire Bible starts:

*In the beginning God created the heavens and the earth.* (Gen 1:1)

It's as if John—the author, and one of Jesus' closest disciples[1]—is saying to the reader (most likely a first-century Jew very familiar with the Old Testament), "Hey, this is big; pay attention!" The whole "Word" thing is confusing until you read that the "Word" was God in human form who, in the context of verses 14 and 17, is clearly Jesus in John's mind. This means that John saw and heard enough during his time with and after Jesus to posit a potentially blasphemous idea: Jesus is God in human form. John risked everything in making this claim: earthly and eternal death. Anyway, John claims that Jesus made everything and everything is about him. Although Jesus was a human, he has existed forever, but it was (unsurprisingly) difficult for most of the Jews to see this. John also claims that Jesus is our hope to become God's children and is the way that God has made himself known to humans. Verses 6–9, which reference "John," are not about the author; they are about a guy we usually call "John the Baptist;" his story comes later. (In fact, every reference to "John" in the book of John is about "John the Baptist." The author John refers to himself as "the disciple whom Jesus loved."[2]) The book starts like a journal article abstract: the huge claim is made at the beginning, and the rest of the book sets out to provide evidence for that claim.

**Victoria**: That was a good explanation. I read the footnotes (there are so many of them), and your clarifications helped. It's cool to think about this introduction in terms of an abstract of a journal article. Thoughts I had: 1) the "children of God" concept is bizarre to me. There is a footnote that talks about how "the believer becomes God's 'child,' but only Jesus is God's 'son.'" But it also says that believers are sons by adoption. There's no similar concept to this in human life, is there? 2) Verse 14 has a short description mentioning incarnation. This took me by surprise, until I realized that the literal definition of incarnation is not necessarily the same as its connotation. 3) A footnote on verse 10 says, "people are morally responsible to the Word because the Word made them." This is interesting to me. I never thought of people being born with this specific moral responsibility to God.

---

[1] Lk 6:13–16.
[2] "Who was the disciple whom Jesus loved?" *Got Questions*, www.gotquestions.org/disciple-whom-Jesus-loved.html.

**Steve**: 1) "Children of God" can be confusing. Every mention of it in the New Testament[3] means "Christians." But in general society, people often say that all humans are "children of God." I think this is meant in a rhetorical sense (even by those who may not have a specific belief in God) to say that we are all equal. To make matters worse, though, the Bible says that all humans are made in the image of God,

> Then God said, "Let us make man in our image, after our likeness. And let them have dominion over the fish of the sea and over the birds of the heavens and over the livestock and over all the earth and over every creeping thing that creeps on the earth." (Gen 1:26)

which does have children-like connotations, but I think more likely refers to the things that humans and God possess that animals do not: reason, love, morality, etc. In the "it means Christians" sense, you are correct in your understanding that being a Christian means being brought into God's family,

> For those who are led by the Spirit of God are the children of God. The Spirit you received does not make you slaves, so that you live in fear again; rather, the Spirit you received brought about your adoption to sonship. And by him we cry, "Abba, Father." The Spirit himself testifies with our spirit that we are God's children. Now if we are children, then we are heirs—heirs of God and co-heirs with Christ, if indeed we share in his sufferings in order that we may also share in his glory. (Rom 8:14–17)

which he already set up with the Father/Son language:

> ... and behold, a voice from heaven said, "This is my beloved Son, with whom I am well pleased." (Mt 3:17)

> "Abba, Father," he said, "everything is possible for you. Take this cup from me. Yet not what I will, but what you will." (Mk 14:36)

Still, yes, Jesus is God's son, too, making us brothers and sisters of him as well (only in a familial way, not in an equal-on-the-hierarchy way):

> For those whom he foreknew he also predestined to be conformed to the image of his Son, in order that he might be the firstborn among many brothers. (Rom 8:29)

---

[3] *Bible Gateway*, www.biblegateway.com/quicksearch/ ?quicksearch="children+of+god"&qs_version=NIV.

You made me realize how confusing this can be if you didn't grow up with this language. Here's a different way of saying it: Jesus is The Son, eternal and equal to God, and possibly called that because it gave us some way to understand his earthly subordination to The Father:

*"Father, if you are willing, take this cup from me; yet not my will, but yours be done." (Lk 22:42)*

A Christian is also son or daughter, but only in some kind of figurative sense. (Aside: Mormons believe this more in a literal sense, but let's please not talk about that now!) So, weirdly, I don't think either "Son of God" or "children of God" are to be taken as literal phrases at face value. Maybe you said it best: this is the best poor analogy we have. 2) Can you explain what you mean? 3) Yes, this is a subset of an overarching theme of Christianity: we believe we are ultimately accountable to God and owe him everything. By the way, the word translated "Word" is the Greek word Λόγος (Logos),[4] which in other parts of the New Testament is translated into words like "statement," "story," "message," "news," "report," "speech," "reason," "account," "matter," "speaker," and "teaching."[5] (It also becomes the suffix for English words such as biology, theology, sociology, etc.) This is huge! John is saying that Jesus is the visible message of a hidden God, just like me typing this sentence is the visible message of my hidden thoughts. In fact, that's what a "word" is!

**Victoria**: 1) Although this is still confusing, it's now less confusing. I'll settle with that idea of the subordinate yet sort-of-equal relationships of God/Jesus and Jesus/Christians. 2) The term incarnation makes me think about *reincarnation*, the cycle of rebirth, but in this case there's no "re," just the singular flesh-forming process. Tangent: if Jesus comes back to Earth again, that's not reincarnation, is it? 3) That's unexpectedly deep!

**Steve**: 2) Argh! Your questions are hard! In the literal sense of the word "reincarnation," yes, I suppose it would be (although many Christians believe he never lost his bodily form, so the "re" part might not be valid). The Bible does say that we will ultimately be raised from the dead one day like Jesus was:[6] i.e., into bodily form, not floaty spirits. But Christians avoid the word "reincarnation" like the plague because of its more popular—but different—usage in eastern religions. The Christian belief is more or less that you will remain what makes you you, rather than undergoing a karmic, fundamental change.

**Victoria**: Ha ha, you seem to answer them well enough! On your answer, that's what I would have guessed, so I'm okay to move on.

---

[4] "John 1:1," *Bible Hub*, biblehub.com/interlinear/john/1-1.htm.
[5] "Strong's Greek: 3056. λόγος (logos)," *Bible Hub*, biblehub.com/greek/strongs_3056.htm.
[6] 1 Cor 15.

## JOHN 1:19–28

**Victoria**: It seemed like the Jewish leaders *wanted* to believe that John the Baptist was a VIP. Or rather, a very important person of one of the three mentioned. Why is that? The Pharisees are usually portrayed as super righteous but are ultimately the antagonists. Are they really that bad, or is that exaggerated? It seems like the Pharisees are just trying to follow what's right. Reading the footnote on verse 24, it says the Pharisees were "religious leaders who were extremely scrupulous about attaining righteousness and keeping God's favor by observing every minute detail of his law as they understood it and by establishing an oral tradition about how to observe it." As someone who tends to think very literally, it seems reasonable to me that they would try to observe the details of keeping the law, provided the motives were good.

**Steve**: John the Baptist was a crazy guy[7] living in the desert[8] (and also Jesus' cousin: Jesus' mother Mary and John the Baptist's mother Elizabeth were related[9]) who claimed that parts of the Old Testament were about him.[10] That was a pretty big deal in and of itself. But then he also insulted the Jewish leaders[11] and was baptizing people in a way that was a little different than what had been done before: a representation of inward cleanliness…

> … and they were baptized by him in the river Jordan, confessing their sins. (Mt 3:6)

rather than a ritual thing.[12] So, all of those things put together made people pay attention (even if they didn't believe his message).

Regarding the Pharisees, there are certain examples of guys who seemed to be doing the right thing:

> Now there was a man of the Pharisees named Nicodemus, a ruler of the Jews. This man came to Jesus by night and said to him, "Rabbi, we know that you are a teacher come from God, for no one can do these signs that you do unless God is with him." (Jn 3:1–2)

> Now there was a man named Joseph, from the Jewish town of Arimathea. He was a member of the council [thus, he was a religious leader; it's unclear if he was a Pharisee], a good and righteous man,

---

[7] Mt 3:4.

[8] Mt 3:1.

[9] Lk 1:36,57,60.

[10] Jn 1:23, Is 40:3.

[11] Mt 3:7–10.

[12] "The Jewish Roots Of Baptism," *One for Israel*, www.oneforisrael.org/bible-based-teaching-from-israel/was-baptism-originally-jewish/.

*who had not consented to their decision and action; and he was looking for the kingdom of God. This man went to Pilate and asked for the body of Jesus. Then he took it down and wrapped it in a linen shroud and laid him in a tomb cut in stone, where no one had ever yet been laid. It was the day of Preparation, and the Sabbath was beginning. The women who had come with him from Galilee followed and saw the tomb and how his body was laid. Then they returned and prepared spices and ointments. On the Sabbath they rested according to the commandment.* (Lk 23:50–56)

*When they heard this, they* [the Sanhedrin] *were furious and wanted to put them* [the apostles] *to death. But a Pharisee named Gamaliel, a teacher of the law, who was honored by all the people, stood up in the Sanhedrin and ordered that the men be put outside for a little while. Then he addressed the Sanhedrin: "Men of Israel, consider carefully what you intend to do to these men. Some time ago Theudas appeared, claiming to be somebody, and about four hundred men rallied to him. He was killed, all his followers were dispersed, and it all came to nothing. After him, Judas the Galilean appeared in the days of the census and led a band of people in revolt. He too was killed, and all his followers were scattered. Therefore, in the present case I advise you: Leave these men alone! Let them go! For if their purpose or activity is of human origin, it will fail. But if it is from God, you will not be able to stop these men; you will only find yourselves fighting against God." His speech persuaded them. They called the apostles in and had them flogged. Then they ordered them not to speak in the name of Jesus, and let them go.* (Acts 5:33–40)

In general, the Pharisees were extremely dedicated to their cause and refused to follow the practices of the Romans (and were killed for it[13]). They also had rivals, the Sadducees,[14] who were Jewish leaders who compromised their faith, catered to the authorities, and thus became rich and powerful. So the Pharisees were actually popular with the common people at that time. That being said, Jesus had some unbelievably harsh words for them.[15] Essentially, they used religion to 1) manipulate and guilt people and 2) bolster their own status by extolling their own righteousness. (Jesus also wasn't a fan of the Sadducees,[16] but I think he picked on the Pharisees so much more because the Sadducees were so obviously corrupt that they didn't need

---

[13] "Pharisees: The Roman period," *Wikipedia*, en.wikipedia.org/wiki/Pharisees#The_Roman_period.

[14] "What are the differences between the Sadducees and Pharisees?" *Got Questions*, www.gotquestions.org/Sadducees-Pharisees.html.

[15] Mt 23, Mt 15:1–14.

[16] Mt 16:5–12.

to be addressed. Mt 16:5–12 is one of the funniest passages of scripture to me. The disciples were clueless! If you feel that way—like I often do—know that you're in good company.) I think we still speak of the Pharisees so much because their example is the easiest trap that a well-meaning, dedicated Christian can fall into. It is so easy to convince yourself that God is on your side because you believe you're a good, moral person while judging, condemning, and complaining about everyone around you:

> The heart is deceitful above all things and beyond cure. Who can understand it? (Jer 17:9)

We see this type of behavior everywhere in politics and with many "Christians"[17] but also more subtly in the prosperity gospel.[18] At some level, it should be a reminder to all Christians that even our seemingly righteous deeds—in and of themselves—are ultimately worthless in God's eyes...

> All of us have become like one who is unclean, and all our righteous acts are like filthy rags; we all shrivel up like a leaf, and like the wind our sins sweep us away. (Is 64:6)

and that he alone is our righteousness:

> But whatever were gains to me I now consider loss for the sake of Christ. What is more, I consider everything a loss because of the surpassing worth of knowing Christ Jesus my Lord, for whose sake I have lost all things. I consider them garbage, that I may gain Christ and be found in him, not having a righteousness of my own that comes from the law, but that which is through faith in Christ—the righteousness that comes from God on the basis of faith. (Phil 3:7–9)

(Ironically, going around calling people Pharisees can be just at pharisaical.)

In summary, I don't think God would've been displeased with a Jew during that time who attempted to follow every minute detail of the law but humbly recognized his/her failures in doing so and dependence on God in becoming righteous. However, the Pharisees were usually nothing like that.

---

17 "Westboro Baptist Church," *Wikipedia*, en.wikipedia.org/wiki/Westboro_Baptist_Church.
18 "Prosperity theology," *Wikipedia*, en.wikipedia.org/wiki/Prosperity_theology.

**Victoria**: Locusts and wild honey, ew. If John the Baptist was a crazy guy who insulted the Jewish leaders, why wouldn't he have been persecuted by them instead of being asked if he was the Messiah?

If even the good things that people try to do are worthless, what's the point of doing them?

Mt 16:5–12 is amusing regarding the interpretation of "yeast." Why does Jesus seem to speak in so many analogies, since they sometimes make things more confusing?

**Steve**: "Why wouldn't he have been persecuted by them instead of being asked if he was the Messiah?" This probably would have happened eventually, but his ministry was cut short because he was killed by King Herod for saying that he shouldn't have taken his brother's wife (the nerve!).[19] That being said, Jesus was much more confrontational in terms of his theology and his "blasphemous" claims about himself (basically the whole book of John). So at some level, I think people were content letting John the Baptist be a crazy guy in the desert, while Jesus didn't afford them that opportunity.

What's the point of doing good things? 1) They're still "good" in that they reflect the character of God and thus should still be done because everything is about him. But they're not "good" in the sense that they outweigh our sinfulness in some kind of "God now thinks I'm a good person because I helped an old lady across the street" sort of way. He sees the rotten inside of us (both in ultimate motivations and in good/bad comparisons). 2) They are an outward example to others regarding what Christ has done for us, showing that our internal faith is real,

> *What good is it, my brothers and sisters, if someone claims to have faith but has no deeds? Can such faith save them? Suppose a brother or a sister is without clothes and daily food. If one of you says to them, "Go in peace; keep warm and well fed," but does nothing about their physical needs, what good is it? In the same way, faith by itself, if it is not accompanied by action, is dead. But someone will say, "You have faith; I have deeds." Show me your faith without deeds, and I will show you my faith by my deeds. You believe that there is one God. Good! Even the demons believe that—and shudder. You foolish person, do you want evidence that faith without deeds is useless? Was not our father Abraham considered righteous for what he did when he offered his son Isaac on the altar? You see that his faith and his actions were working together, and his faith was made complete by what he did. And the scripture was fulfilled that says, "Abraham believed God, and it was credited to him as righteousness," and he was called God's friend. You see that a person is considered righteous by what they do and not by faith alone. In the same way, was not even Rahab the prostitute considered righteous for what she did when she gave*

---

[19] Mt 14:3–12.

*lodging to the spies and sent them off in a different direction? As the body without the spirit is dead, so faith without deeds is dead. (Jas 2:14–26)*

sort of like the "Word" analogy earlier. In other words, they are less "I will now choose to do this good thing because it makes me feel good, makes other people like me, etc." and more "This is what Jesus was about, so that's what I'm going to do." It's helpful to think this way, because you no longer wait for feelings to occur before you act. 3) Most importantly, a Christian's entire purpose is to glorify and honor God. Good deeds do that. This works in two ways. First, they're done to serve someone or something God has created and deemed worthy, so we are implicitly showing God's value through good service. Second, they are done simply out of gratitude to Jesus and/or trying to be like Jesus. Trying to copy what Jesus has done is a great compliment to him.

"Why does Jesus seem to speak in so many analogies?" He was asked the same question:

*Then the disciples came and said to him, "Why do you speak to them in parables?" And he answered them, "To you it has been given to know the secrets of the kingdom of heaven, but to them it has not been given. For to the one who has, more will be given, and he will have an abundance, but from the one who has not, even what he has will be taken away. This is why I speak to them in parables, because seeing they do not see, and hearing they do not hear, nor do they understand. Indeed, in their case the prophecy of Isaiah is fulfilled that says: "'You will indeed hear but never understand, and you will indeed see but never perceive." For this people's heart has grown dull, and with their ears they can barely hear, and their eyes they have closed, lest they should see with their eyes and hear with their ears and understand with their heart and turn, and I would heal them.' But blessed are your eyes, for they see, and your ears, for they hear. For truly, I say to you, many prophets and righteous people longed to see what you see, and did not see it, and to hear what you hear, and did not hear it." (Mt 13:10–17)*

I like this answer[20] a lot, especially the bottom paragraph:

Our Lord Jesus understood that truth is not sweet music to all ears. Simply put, there are those who have neither interest in nor regard for the deep things of God. So why, then, did He speak in parables? To those with a genuine hunger for God, the parable is both an effective and memorable vehicle for the conveyance of divine truths.

---

[20] "Why did Jesus teach in parables?" *Got Questions*, www.gotquestions.org/Jesus-parables.html.

Our Lord's parables contain great volumes of truth in very few words—and His parables, rich in imagery, are not easily forgotten. So, then, the parable is a blessing to those with willing ears. But to those with dull hearts and ears that are slow to hear, the parable is also an instrument of both judgment and mercy.

Here's another way to think about it. If you want God, you have to seek him,

> *"Ask, and it will be given to you; seek, and you will find; knock, and it will be opened to you."* (Mt 7:7)

because Christianity isn't just intellectual assent to ideas; it's a whole mind, body, spirit, emotion, and lifestyle transformation.

> *Therefore, if anyone is in Christ, he is a new creation. The old has passed away; behold, the new has come.* (2 Cor 5:17)

I think if Jesus just laid out everything clearly and exactly in some book, 1) the book would be too big and its content too unyielding (the same could be said for a science book that attempted the same feat), so that it would be overwhelming and useless to us, and 2) we would worship the book instead of him. So, instead, he chose stories (very common in his culture) that make the point concisely and impactfully and force the listener and/or reader to dig deeper (i.e., into him). There's also something to be said about this verse:

> *"Do not give dogs what is sacred; do not throw your pearls to pigs. If you do, they may trample them under their feet, and turn and tear you to pieces."* (Mt 7:6)

You and I have told each other things about ourselves that have left us vulnerable to each other in a beautiful way. I've told a few people about my depression, anxiety, and worry struggles, and while I'm not really ashamed of it at this point, it would be a little unsettling if you wrote an op-ed in *The New York Times* making fun of me (but I am laughing at that thought!). In other words, those "pearls" were for you (and ultimately God), and it would be a shame to see them "trampled on" by others; they mean a lot to me. Jesus' teachings were certainly pearls, and he spoke in a way (often through parables) that couldn't easily be "trampled on" (e.g., endlessly debated, mocked, etc.) by the people in front of him. It was like, "take it or leave it." Or to put it another way, Jesus was an incredible teacher but an intentionally lousy information-giver.

**Victoria**: Hmm, it's hard for me to reconcile "good" and "worthless." It seems to reflect the act of always striving, but never achieving.

I don't understand what is meant in the first reference you posted, especially Mt 13:12. Is Jesus trying to say that he's being purposely vague since they're not going to understand either way ("because seeing they do not see")? The second link from *Got Questions* clears it up some, but what does it mean that "to those with dull hearts and ears that are slow to hear, the parable is also an instrument of both judgment and mercy?" Who is judging? The teller of the parable? Who's showing mercy? How does mercy come about from that? The main idea/explanation is clear, though, with the second reference and with your explanation.

I'm glad that you're a good information-giver at least. I would be so lost otherwise.

**Steve**: "Hmm, it's hard for me to reconcile 'good' and 'worthless.' It seems to reflect the act of always striving, but never achieving." No, I don't think it's a Sisyphean task. Let me try a different angle. God is the ultimate meaning and purpose of everything in the universe. Therefore, everything derives its worth and goodness from him alone. Therefore, it is an oxymoron to say that a thing is good apart from its ultimate connection to God. So if I say that the thing I do is righteous in and of itself (effectively supposing that there is some higher moral order above God), God says that that kind of thinking is worthless and means nothing to him, although the same act done out of honor toward him and recognition of his goodness has actual meaning and worth. Or to put it another way, suppose God didn't exist but every human suddenly became perfectly moral in a way that maximally benefited everyone and created some kind of intergalactic utopia. When we all eventually died in the entropic heat death of the universe,[21] what meaning did any of that have? What good did our righteous deeds accomplish? What was the purpose of any of that? It was all simultaneously "good" and worthless. But God is saying that good × worthless = worthless, sort of like $10^{100} \times 0 = 0$. Jesus summed it up in an incredibly unsettling way:

> Then they said to him, "What must we do, to be doing the works of God?" Jesus answered them, "This is the work of God, that you believe in him whom he has sent." (Jn 6:28–29)

Paul said the same:

> For we hold that one is justified by faith apart from works of the law. (Rom 3:28)

All we have to do is believe?! I honestly hate that, because it destroys every notion of goodness and hard work I want to believe about myself,

---

[21] "Heat death of the universe," *Wikipedia*, en.wikipedia.org/wiki/Heat_death_of_the_universe.

but after decades of thinking about it, I see no other way, and it's become the best news I've ever heard. That news makes me want to then do good things to honor the creator of the news.

You know the feeling as a scientist when the universe seems incomprehensible, unclear, or hidden (maybe even "purposely vague") and you want to understand it? What do you do? You pursue answers through research, and sometimes along the way, you find answers and understanding you never planned to find. I think Jesus is like that in a lot of ways. The way he presents himself always leaves me wanting more in a way that forces me to pursue and develop a relationship with him; that wouldn't exist if he were just an information-giver. (I do suppose that it might be inevitable for finite beings to view an infinite being as incomprehensible, however. In other words, *could* Jesus have explained everything to us? I doubt it.) I think Jesus shows us that those who want to follow him through faith will be given more and more of him (like the universe and scientists), while those who don't want to follow him will be given nothing (like flat-earthers):

> For the message of the cross is foolishness to those who are perishing, but to us who are being saved it is the power of God. For it is written: "I will destroy the wisdom of the wise; the intelligence of the intelligent I will frustrate." Where is the wise person? Where is the teacher of the law? Where is the philosopher of this age? Has not God made foolish the wisdom of the world? For since in the wisdom of God the world through its wisdom did not know him, God was pleased through the foolishness of what was preached to save those who believe. Jews demand signs and Greeks look for wisdom, but we preach Christ crucified: a stumbling block to Jews and foolishness to Gentiles, but to those whom God has called, both Jews and Greeks, Christ the power of God and the wisdom of God. For the foolishness of God is wiser than human wisdom, and the weakness of God is stronger than human strength. (1 Cor 1:18–25)

I think that sentence you're asking about ("judgment and mercy") is referring to the fact that we're *all* dull and slow to learn about these things. That can be an instrument of judgment (from God) when we never learn them (i.e., choose to reject him):

> "But I will show you whom you should fear: Fear him who, after your body has been killed, has authority to throw you into hell. Yes, I tell you, fear him." (Lk 12:5)

But in God's mercy, he looks on our dumbness with compassion and still chooses to save us:

*When he saw the crowds, he had compassion on them, because they were harassed and helpless, like sheep without a shepherd.* (Mt 9:36)

**Victoria**: It basically boils down to true intentions? Something can be *either* good or worthless based on why the act was done. Based upon how you're defining "good," the intergalactic utopia example couldn't actually have *simultaneous* goodness and worthlessness then, which is what you're saying with that equation.

**Steve**: Yes, it can be thought of as true intentions, but our intentions are hard to decipher, so that might not be helpful. I prefer to think about it as having your cause and effect in the right order. Are you doing good to become righteous? That's the wrong/impossible way. Or did God make you righteous through faith, and now you do good to honor him? That's the Christian way; everything is backward from the way we normally think:

*The greatest among you shall be your servant.* (Mt 23:11)

*... and said to them, "Whoever receives this child in my name receives me, and whoever receives me receives him who sent me. For he who is least among you all is the one who is great."* (Lk 9:48)

*But God chose what is foolish in the world to shame the wise; God chose what is weak in the world to shame the strong; God chose what is low and despised in the world, even things that are not, to bring to nothing things that are, so that no human being might boast in the presence of God. And because of him you are in Christ Jesus, who became to us wisdom from God, righteousness and sanctification and redemption, so that, as it is written, "Let the one who boasts, boast in the Lord."* (1 Cor 1:27–31)

Yes, regarding the intergalactic utopia. (That's one of my favorite sentences I've ever typed.)

Finally, I wouldn't call it "hard to get..."

*"Ask and it will be given to you; seek and you will find; knock and the door will be opened to you."* (Mt 7:7)

as much as "hard to follow:"

*Then Jesus told his disciples, "If anyone would come after me, let him deny himself and take up his cross and follow me. For whoever would save his life will lose it, but whoever loses his life for my sake will find it. For what will it profit a man if he gains the whole world and forfeits his soul? Or what shall a man give in return for his soul?"* (Mt 16:24–26)

**Victoria**: The cause and effect explanation was helpful.

# CHAPTER 20: JOHN 2

## JOHN 2:1–12

**Victoria**: This text was covered at one of the first Bible studies I attended with IGSM, so I don't have much to ask about here. Although we discussed this part, it's still odd to me that Jesus addresses his mother (or should I say "mother?") as "woman."

**Steve**: Mary was definitely Jesus' mother,

> ... to be registered with Mary, his betrothed, who was with child. And while they were there, the time came for her to give birth. And she gave birth to her firstborn son and wrapped him in swaddling cloths and laid him in a manger, because there was no place for them in the inn. (Lk 2:5–7)

but Joseph was only his "father:"

> This is how the birth of Jesus the Messiah came about: His mother Mary was pledged to be married to Joseph, but before they came together, she was found to be pregnant through the Holy Spirit. (Mt 1:18)

Anyway, my footnote Jn 2:4 says, "The Greek for *Woman* does not denote any disrespect." This[1] seems to concur. Still, Jesus does not seem to make his family a priority over anyone else,

> While he was still speaking to the people, behold, his mother and his brothers stood outside, asking to speak to him. But he replied to the man who told him, "Who is my mother, and who are my brothers?" And stretching out his hand toward his disciples, he said, "Here are my mother and my brothers! For whoever does the will of my Father in heaven is my brother and sister and mother." (Mt 12:46–50)

which was pretty amazing in that family-centered culture (e.g., married sons would just build extra rooms onto their parents' houses[2]). I do find it interesting/funny that 30ish-year-old Jesus basically didn't want to perform this miracle, but his mom passive-aggressively made him. It seems that she knew he was "special" and was prodding him on to greatness: so mom-like!

---

[1] "Was Jesus being rude to Mary when He referred to her as "woman" in John 2:4?" *Got Questions*, www.gotquestions.org/Jesus-Mary-woman.html.
[2] Jn 14:2.

**Victoria**: That's intriguing, regarding Jesus as God but man. Did he have Mary's DNA, then? Where would the Y chromosome have come from? Did Jesus ever get sick, and, if so, would he heal himself? Were his immune, metabolic, physiological, etc. systems normal? These are more rhetorical questions; I'm just musing aloud.

How do you draw the conclusion that he didn't want to perform the miracle? Based on his response, it seemed that he wasn't opposed but was rather biding his time.

**Steve**: "Did he have Mary's DNA then?" My completely uninformed guess: yes. "Where would the Y chromosome have come from?" I have no clue; I've wondered about that myself. "Did Jesus ever get sick, and, if so, would he heal himself? Were his immune, metabolic, physiological, etc. systems normal?" Given statements like this...

> For we do not have a high priest who is unable to sympathize with our weaknesses, but one who in every respect has been tempted as we are, yet without sin. (Heb 4:15)

and the fact that he allowed himself to be killed on a cross, the standard view is that Jesus was just a normal guy in terms of his humanness. He probably got sick and sad...

> Jesus wept. (Jn 11:35)

and accidentally hit his thumb with a hammer:

> Isn't this the carpenter? Isn't this Mary's son and the brother of James, Joseph, Judas and Simon? Aren't his sisters here with us?" And they took offense at him. (Mk 6:3)

Regarding the miracle, yes, that's what I meant.

**Victoria**: Heb 4:15 makes Jesus sound like not a normal human. How can someone not sin? Doesn't it mean they're actually better than the rest of us (superhuman?). Regarding Mk 6:3, I looked around neighboring passages but didn't see any mention of a hammer.

**Steve**: Regarding Heb 4:15, what I mean by "normal guy" is in terms of his physical nature. He looked like a normal guy...

> For he grew up before him like a young plant, and like a root out of dry ground; he had no form or majesty that we should look at him, and no beauty that we should desire him. (Is 53:2)

and was thirsty...

> After this, Jesus, knowing that all was now finished, said (to fulfill the Scripture), "I thirst." (Jn 19:28)

and bled...

> *But one of the soldiers pierced his side with a spear, and at once there came out blood and water.* (Jn 19:34)

and died...

> *When Jesus had received the sour wine, he said, "It is finished," and he bowed his head and gave up his spirit.* (Jn 19:30)

like a normal guy. There are also certain times when he says he doesn't know things:

> *"But concerning that day and hour no one knows, not even the angels of heaven, nor the Son, but the Father only."* (Mt 24:36)

With regard to Mark 6:3, I was just referring to the fact that Jesus' occupation was a carpenter (or some kind of craftsman), so he probably hit his thumb with a hammer at some point; the Bible doesn't say he hit his thumb with a hammer!

All of that being said, Christians certainly don't believe that Jesus was "just" a normal guy. He performed dozens of miracles,[3] claimed to be God,[4] glowed,

> *There he was transfigured before them. His face shone like the sun, and his clothes became as white as the light.* (Mt 17:2)

didn't sin,

> *God made him who had no sin to be sin for us, so that in him we might become the righteousness of God.* (2 Cor 5:21)

and had some kind of special communication with God:

> *As soon as Jesus was baptized, he went up out of the water. At that moment heaven was opened, and he saw the Spirit of God descending like a dove and alighting on him. And a voice from heaven said, "This is my Son, whom I love; with him I am well pleased."* (Mt 3:16–17)

---

[3] "Miracles of Jesus: From Healing the Sick to Turning Water Into Wine," *Learn Religions*, www.learnreligions.com/miracles-of-jesus-700158.

[4] Hank Hanegraaff, "Did Jesus Claim to Be God?" *Oneplace*, www.oneplace.com/ministries/bible-answer-man/read/articles/did-jesus-claim-to-be-god-8825.html.

The whole thing about Jesus being a man and God at the same time is known as the hypostatic union,[5] and no one really understands how it works, just that it is.

**Victoria**: I'll go over the links more in depth and move onto the next section tomorrow. Thanks for the email,[6] Dr. Robinson. While I was reading it, it felt like you were following/preempting my train of thought. There's a lot I don't understand about my life and how I'm living it.

The bit on Jesus not knowing the day and hour (of the end times?) is intriguing. How does one know something while not knowing?

**Steve**: I'm not sure this analogy works for someone like Jesus, but for you and I, we can say things like "I know that I will die with absolute certainty" but not have any clue what the details are. Perhaps he knew the inevitability of what he was saying but not the details. (There is a line of theology—open theism[7]—in which the future doesn't actually exist, so God doesn't "know" it in that sense, but being all-powerful, he can will whatever he wants into existence, so he "knows" that it will happen. I'm not really sure how I feel about that.) Perhaps Jesus' knowledge was limited because omniscience can't fit into a squishy human brain made of neurons, so the Father chose to reveal only certain things to him?

**Victoria**: Hmm, but if God doesn't actually know the future, then doesn't that argue against his omniscience? On the other hand, the squishy brain theory (ha ha) sounds more plausible.

**Steve**: If you're referring to Jesus being God and not knowing the future, another solution is that he knew everything, but most of it subconsciously.[8] An analogy might be that you know most of the elements on the periodic table, but they are not a part of your current conscious state; you have to recall them from your subconscious memory or experience some trigger to bring them out. I'm OK with that or—given the clear fact that he lowered himself to become a man[9]—that he decided to temporarily not know everything (although I could probably become convinced that the latter perspective is too extreme in that it too easily brushes aside Jesus' God nature).

On the other hand, if you're referring to open theism discounting God's omniscience, an open theist would probably say that God still perfectly knows the future because he's going to will it to happen, not because it already exists. It's a different sort of omniscience. An

---

[5] David Mathis, "What Is the Hypostatic Union?" *Desiring God*, December 19, 2007, www.desiringgod.org/articles/what-is-the-hypostatic-union.

[6] See Appendix.

[7] "Open theism," *Wikipedia*, en.wikipedia.org/wiki/Open_theism.

[8] William Lane Craig, "#410 Incarnation and Omniscience," *Reasonable Faith*, February 22, 2015, www.reasonablefaith.org/writings/question-answer/incarnation-and-omniscience/.

[9] Phil 2:7.

(admittedly insufficient) analogy might be that I "know" I'm going to finish typing this sentence because I'm going to make sure it happens, but I still don't have the ability to see the future.

## JOHN 2:13–26

**Victoria**: In the commentary in my Bible for verses 19–22, it says Jesus is the new temple. We had talked earlier on how Jesus represented a different way of doing things (such as not having animal sacrifices anymore), but what was the point of doing away with temples? Were these distinct from churches?

**Steve**: There was only one temple at that time,[10] and it was the earthly center of the Jewish faith. Through the priests and sacrifices, the Jews were connected with God. Jesus was essentially saying that 1) through him, we can have direct access to God[11] and 2) animals sacrifices were no longer needed,[12] so the temple would no longer be necessary. Another important consequence of this is that connection to God would no longer be associated with a certain group of people (the Israelites), but would be for all people:

> *There is neither Jew nor Gentile, neither slave nor free, nor is there male and female, for you are all one in Christ Jesus.* (Gal 3:28)

The Jewish analogy to churches would be synagogues,[13] which came around between the Old and New Testament. Jesus was known to teach in synagogues.:

> *… but he said to them, "I must preach the good news of the kingdom of God to the other towns as well; for I was sent for this purpose." And he was preaching in the synagogues of Judea.* (Lk 4:43–44)

**Victoria**: Ah, okay. Tangential question regarding Eph 2:11–22: what does circumcision have to do with it?

**Steve**: Circumcision was performed on male Jews as a sign of their covenant with God and being set apart from the surrounding people:

> *On the eighth day the boy is to be circumcised.* (Lev 12:3)

Paul was making the point that being circumcised used to be a sign that one was a believer (i.e., by being a Jew), but now it has nothing to do with outward appearances or ethnicity. It's all about an internal decision to follow Christ:

---

[10] "Second Temple," *Wikipedia*, en.wikipedia.org/wiki/Second_Temple.

[11] Eph 2:11–22.

[12] Heb 10:1–18.

[13] Synagogue, *Wikipedia*, en.wikipedia.org/wiki/Synagogue.

*But a Jew is one inwardly, and circumcision is a matter of the heart, by the Spirit, not by the letter. His praise is not from man but from God.* (Rom 2:29)

# CHAPTER 21: JOHN 3

## JOHN 3:1-21

**Victoria**: My commentary on verse 6 stands out to me: "Like generates like. Humans physically produce more (spiritually dead) humans. Only God's Spirit can produce spiritual life."

On verse 7, should Nicodemus have not been surprised due to something in the Old Testament that says new birth is a must?

Is verse 16 one of the most quoted verses in the Bible? I've heard this so many times.

**Steve**: I love that explanation of verse 6. I feel that way in my own life: when I keep doing and thinking the same things, the same things keep happening (duh!).

I've never really thought too much about verses 7 and 11 in the context of "What should the Jewish leaders have known?" I found a couple of resources.[1,2] I think they (and Jesus) are saying that the Old Testament is very clear in terms of how to follow God (repentance, faith, obedience, worship), and it's really not different in basic principles (God alone making us new) than it is in the New Testament; just different in practice and seeing through a different lens (i.e., Jesus vs. law).

Yes, John 3:16 is undoubtedly the most famous verse in the Bible. Why do you think that is?

**Victoria**: In the first reference, the author says, "I think it is a bit of a stretch to attempt to find explicit reference to the new birth in any one Old Testament passage." Given that and your statement of difference in practice, I can see how it might be hard to come up with—or trace—the idea of rebirth as Jesus is teaching to Nicodemus. Maybe it's like a scientific theory which was true yet unpopular, so it never made it to the forefront of biblical teachings.

On John 3:16, is this essentially the thesis sentence of Christianity?

**Steve**: Yes, I think you're right. God set up the Old Testament laws as a means to being transformed on the inside. But many Jews saw the law as the end in itself never experienced that "new birth." (Maybe you've picked up on it, but this chapter is where the popular (and often pejorative) phrase "born-again Christian" comes from. It usually means

---

[1] Michael Patton, "Is the New Birth in the Old Testament? or Why Was Christ So Hard on Nicodemus in John 3:10?" *Credo House*, January 13, 2011, credohouse.org/blog/is-the-new-birth-in-the-old-testament-or-why-was-christ-so-hard-on-nicodemus-in-john-310.

[2] William Barrick, "What Nicodemus Should Have Known: Rediscovering the New Birth in the Old Testament," *Shepherds' Conference*, March 2014, drbarrick.org/files/papers/other/New_Birth_in_the_OT_SC.pdf.

that the person believes they have some kind of personal relationship with God instead of being a merely "cultural" Christian.)

Yes, you're right again. This statement makes Christianity easily accessible to anyone, but has so much theology in it as well: 1) God exists, 2) God is loving, 3) God has a son, 4) God loved sacrificially, 5) our "default" state is perishing, 6) God doesn't want us to perish, 7) we can live forever, 8) we only have to believe, and 9) this is for everyone. Are these not the main issues we've been discussing for months?!

**Victoria**: Now that you mention it, I do hear "born-again Christian" used pejoratively. I suppose people will mock or criticize anything.

That's a lot more to unpack than it initially seems! It's an elegant and compact statement.

### JOHN 3:22-26

**Victoria**: This one is pretty cryptic. In verses 25–26, if John is testifying in support of Jesus, why are his disciples so envious of Jesus' popularity?

In verse 29, if Jesus is the bridegroom, who is the bride? It's kind of amusing to see the note about how John the Baptist is the "ancient equivalent of a 'best man'" to Jesus.

Verses 33–34 are interesting; can you expound on these?

**Steve**: For verses 25–26, I think being a couple of degrees removed causes problems like this. In other words, John the Baptist was all about Jesus, but his disciples seemed to be all about him. Paul warned against this type of thinking:

> *I appeal to you, brothers and sisters, in the name of our Lord Jesus Christ, that all of you agree with one another in what you say and that there be no divisions among you, but that you be perfectly united in mind and thought. My brothers and sisters, some from Chloe's household have informed me that there are quarrels among you. What I mean is this: One of you says, "I follow Paul"; another, "I follow Apollos"; another, "I follow Cephas"; still another, "I follow Christ." Is Christ divided? Was Paul crucified for you? Were you baptized in the name of Paul?* (1 Cor 1:10–13)

In other words, the further we are removed from the source, the more likely it is that divisions occur. This is why Christianity is split into Catholic, Protestant, and Orthodox traditions, and each of those has further divisions. It's not good because Jesus prayed for our unity:

> *"I have given them the glory that you gave me, that they may be one as we are one—I in them and you in me—so that they may be brought to complete unity. Then the world will know that you sent me and have loved them even as you have loved me."* (Jn 17:22–23)

But it's not hopeless, either; we "officially" agree on the important things: the deity of Christ and his death and resurrection for the salvation of sinners. My personal take is to forget all the tradition, fancy churches, chanting, and prescribed prayers and simplify it as much as possible: live a life to honor and glorify God alone with belief and service.

On verse 29, "the church" (meaning the entirety of Christian believers) is the bride:

> Husbands, love your wives, just as Christ loved the church and gave himself up for her to make her holy, cleansing her by the washing with water through the word, and to present her to himself as a radiant church, without stain or wrinkle or any other blemish, but holy and blameless. (Eph 5:25–27)

> I am jealous for you with a godly jealousy. I promised you to one husband, to Christ, so that I might present you as a pure virgin to him. (2 Cor 11:2)

The picture comes from the practice at that time of a husband literally paying a price to be able to marry his wife;[3] Jesus paid a figurative price (his life) to have us, so he referred to himself as the bridegroom:[4]

> And Jesus said to them, "Can the wedding guests fast while the bridegroom is with them? As long as they have the bridegroom with them, they cannot fast. The days will come when the bridegroom is taken away from them, and then they will fast in that day. (Mk 2:19–20)

On verses 33–34, a theme that is repeated over and over in this book by both Jesus and John (the author) is that the God who the Jews knew and worshipped sent Jesus as his authoritative voice; in verse 34, "the one whom God has sent" is Jesus. Whatever Jesus said was God's message to them (an analogy: Jesus is the White House press secretary, and God the Father is the President; yikes, hopefully that's the last time I make that analogy). So the basic idea is that if you believe what Jesus is saying, then you're believing the correct things about God, too:

> Jesus answered: "Don't you know me, Philip, even after I have been among you such a long time? Anyone who has seen me has seen the Father. How can you say, 'Show us the Father?'" (Jn 14:9)

---

[3] Hayyim Schauss, "Ancient Jewish Marriage," *My Jewish Learning*, www.myjewishlearning.com/article/ancient-jewish-marriage/.
[4] Mt 25:1–13.

It may seem weird to us that he would even say this, but Jesus' main audience was Jewish, so he repeatedly reiterated this point because it was a huge paradigm shift for them. Maybe think of it this way. If you talk to your parents on the phone, how do you know it's really them? Well, the phone company displays their number which you have verified, and the person on the other end may say things that only your parent could know. In the same way, every time Jesus performs a miracle, it's a direct sign from God that he is who he says he is; it's not so much about the person benefiting from the miracle. This is why most believe that we no longer see the same types of huge, verifiable miracles today that are present in the Bible: we have what we need to believe (the Bible, nature, and reason). God's main concern isn't "fixing" everything or healing everyone all the time, especially with the perspective that death is a good thing:

*For to me to live is Christ, and to die is gain.* (Phil 1:21)

Ultimately, all of this is huge; the deity of Christ is the hinge on which all of Christianity turns, so John says it in one form or another a whole lot.

**Victoria**: Great explanations; I don't have anything else on this section.

# CHAPTER 22: JOHN 4

### JOHN 4:1-26

**Victoria**: I've studied this before with IGSM. On a second pass, I have a question regarding "living water" in verse 10. According to the footnote, the living water that Jesus says he gives refers to "'the gift of God,' the eternally satisfying life that Jesus provides through the Spirit, who produces spiritual life." The water analogy seems odd to me. Instead of saying that he would give the woman living water, why wouldn't he just say he would have given her eternal or spiritual life? Is there something significant about water over other elements like earth or fire?

**Steve**: The simple answer is that they were standing next to a well, so water was the easiest analogy. But I think there's a lot more to it than that. 1) Jacob's well is in a summer desert,[1] so you can imagine that water was the number one thing that people cared about; it was absolutely vital and couldn't be taken for granted. Jesus is saying the same thing of himself. He also called himself the bread of life:

> Then Jesus declared, "I am the bread of life. Whoever comes to me will never go hungry, and whoever believes in me will never be thirsty." (Jn 6:35)

2) We also have:

> Jesus answered, "It is written: 'Man shall not live on bread alone, but on every word that comes from the mouth of God.'" (Mt 4:4)

I think about it more and more the older I get: I'm going to be dead one day. Literally dead, not breathing, talking, teaching, or anything. It's crazy to think about. I won't need water or food then because they'll no longer do their job of keeping me alive. Neither will money, degrees, a job, friends, family, or marriage. Apparently, then, all of the things that keep me alive now aren't as great or important as I think they are. So isn't it strange that they're all we tend to think about? Jesus is saying that what we consider to be so important now really doesn't mean much, and if we want to have fulfillment, it's in him:

> For our light and momentary troubles are achieving for us an eternal glory that far outweighs them all. So we fix our eyes not on what is seen, but on what is unseen, since what is seen is temporary, but what is unseen is eternal. (2 Cor 4:17-18)

---

[1] "Nablus," *Wikipedia*, en.wikipedia.org/wiki/Nablus#Climate.

The eternal mindset is so different than this "I need water" mindset we go through a million times in our lives. Think about the four most important things in the world: air, water, food, and shelter. The vast majority of humanity has those four things, and all of humanity has the first one. The state of the world should tell you that having all of the most important things that life can offer is not fulfilling! Think about that! Isn't it weird/crazy/insane?! We keep getting thirsty over and over again, no matter how much water we drink. Our standard of living keeps getting higher, and we still want more. People assure us they love us, but it takes just a few seconds to feel lonely. This woman at the well was looking for companionship and sex to fulfill her, but it was clear from her life that infinite men would not do. The Robinson Translation of verse 14 is, "Are you tired of always wanting or achieving more? Here I am. With me, you won't (and can't) want more."

So how does this work in the Christian mindset? Water, companionships, and sex are not things that fulfill us; they are great gifts from the one who can. I can turn water into an object of gratefulness toward God (gratefulness *is* fulfilling), which glorifies God (properly valuing things *is* fulfilling) and leads me to eternal life (which *is* fulfilling). When I die and water is no longer necessary, my life will have been all about seeing God as the center of everything anyway, so dying isn't such a big deal. An atheist may be thankful for water, but to whom? Does it even mean anything to be thankful to nothing (or to an equally meaningless water company)? The happiest, wealthiest, most moral atheist in the world can only be delusionally fulfilled because all of his/her possessions and effort ultimately point nowhere. But this isn't just about atheists or water. It's about what we're all guilty of: valuing temporal things above eternal things.

But wait, there's more! This woman was a Samaritan,[2] someone despised by the Jews in Jesus' time because of their twisting of Judaism. Jesus was a Jew, but didn't offer her his religion; he offered her himself. In the same way, Christianity is not supposed to be a religion (a specified pattern of doing things), but a following of Christ with a new mindset and general way of life. For example, the New Testament doesn't say a lot about exactly what we need to do in our daily lives, but it tells me how to treat everything as a whole:

*So, whether you eat or drink, or whatever you do, do all to the glory of God.* (1 Cor 10:31)

*And whatever you do, in word or deed, do everything in the name of the Lord Jesus, giving thanks to God the Father through him.* (Col 3:17)

---

[2] "Samaritans," *Wikipedia*, en.wikipedia.org/wiki/Samaritans.

It's beautiful that way, because it's a life of freedom instead of just rules:

*"So if the Son sets you free, you will be free indeed."* (Jn 8:36)

Finally, Jesus does say things like "living earth" with agricultural examples...[3]

*Even now the one who reaps draws a wage and harvests a crop for eternal life, so that the sower and the reaper may be glad together.* (Jn 4:36)

and "living fire" when speaking of his ability to change/purify things:

*... for our "God is a consuming fire."* (Heb 12:29)

*In all this you greatly rejoice, though now for a little while you may have had to suffer grief in all kinds of trials. These have come so that the proven genuineness of your faith—of greater worth than gold, which perishes even though refined by fire—may result in praise, glory and honor when Jesus Christ is revealed.* (1 Pet 1:6–7)

*They saw what seemed to be tongues of fire that separated and came to rest on each of them. All of them were filled with the Holy Spirit and began to speak in other tongues as the Spirit enabled them.* (Acts 2:3–4)

In fact, he calls himself many things[4] to give us glimpses as to what he is like. He does such a good job of using the things the (often illiterate) people knew and understood to explain himself. It would be like if he was giving a lecture on a whiteboard and said, "I am the dry erase marker that writes eternal words on your blank soul" or something. It cuts deeper than, "Hey, y'all, I'm awesome, so listen up."

**Victoria**: I agree with your statement, "We keep getting thirsty over and over again, no matter how much water we drink." I think it's true regardless of one's religious beliefs. On how it all works in the Christian mindset, you raise an interesting question of where one's possessions and efforts will ultimately point, whether it's to temporal delusions or an eternal God. It's a convincing point, though it seems that a prerequisite belief is the existence of a personally involving afterlife.

I like that Robinson Translation. I wholly agree with the statement that "having all of the most important things that life can offer is not fulfilling."

---

[3] Mt 13:1–43.

[4] "The Names Jesus Calls Himself," *Help Me with Bible Study*, helpmewithbiblestudy.org/2JesusChrist/NamesJesusCallsHimself.aspx.

What does it mean to be "thankful to nothing"? I've seen a lot of resources say that practicing gratitude is beneficial for mental health.[5] Maybe it's delusional fulfillment if gratefulness isn't ultimately directed towards God, but there is value that comes out of it.

The dry erase marker metaphor is a good one.

**Steve:** Keep hanging in there with the afterlife thing. If Jesus and the Bible are convincing, the afterlife will be, too. If they aren't, not so much.

Yes, gratitude is huge for happiness and mental health, even if God doesn't exist. But I think we generally don't grasp the meaning of gratitude. It's not feeling happy or glad for things or because things are going well; that's happiness. Gratitude involves giving thanks to someone or something; to whom does an atheist give thanks or feel thankful toward? If it's to another equally meaningless person, I don't see the point of that. (Besides that, people can't "feel" our gratitude like I imagine God can, so it's hard to transfer gratitude to people anyway.)

**Victoria:** Hmm, I'll try.

"If [the target of gratitude is] to another equally meaningless person, I don't see the point of that."—I think this statement could be asserted by both atheists (*A*) and Christians (*C*) to each other. *A* would believe that both *A*'s target of gratitude and *C*'s target of gratitude are nonexistent. However, *A* could acknowledge that there might not be an external, objective point of thanking a nonexistent entity yet continue to do so for reasons of mental/emotional well-being. On the other hand, *C* would believe that only *A*'s target is nonexistent and not see the point of *A* being grateful to something not there.

**Steve:** Yes, of course. I suppose my point is that *A*'s gratitude and *C*'s gratitude are fundamentally different things. There have been times when I've thanked God for awful things happening in my life. I'm thankful to an actual person who I love and want to receive glory and honor. It certainly doesn't prove that atheists are delusional, but it's another form of the continual line of thought that makes me very skeptical of atheism, being that *atheists believe there is no meaning, but they act like there is.* Many of them are good, thoughtful, caring, grateful people, but I've never heard a convincing argument from any of them on why they are so and why I should also be so.

**Victoria:** Thanking God for awful things happening in your life ... because of how it opened other doors? Or led to new realizations? My friend had this interesting perspective that he usually heard people claiming that it "was God's doing" or "part of God's plan" for bad things that happen. I feel like someone like yourself would disagree, so I didn't know what to make of that.

---

[5] "Practicing Gratitude can be Good for Mental Health and Well-Being," *American Psychiatric Association*, April 4, 2017, www.psychiatry.org/news-room/apa-blogs/apa-blog/2017/08/practicing-gratitude-can-be-good-for-mental-health-and-well-being

**Steve**: Yes, I can look back on bad things in my life and see how they've changed me for the better. For example, my bout with depression made me less judgmental and more sympathetic to other people's struggles. Also, my own doubts and skepticism have forced me to seriously examine my own faith and made it stronger and more meaningful.

You're right, I'm not a big fan of people making blanket statements about "God's plan." I've heard people say things like "Hurricane X is a sign of God's wrath on City Y." That makes me cringe. I don't discount that possibility, but how on earth could someone know that for sure? We *all* deserve God's wrath, so all I know is that Jesus' death was *the* sign of God's wrath on humanity. Yes, God has ultimate control over everything, but he doesn't always get what he wants:

> *This is good, and pleases God our Savior, who wants all people to be saved and to come to a knowledge of the truth.* (1 Tim 2:3–4)

This is all why the following is so important:

> *And we know that in all things God works for the good of those who love him, who have been called according to his purpose.* (Rom 8:28)

We can't possibly see or understand everything about God's interaction with the world, but we can trust him that it works out for good in the end.

**Victoria**: Weird. I never thought about it before, but I always subconsciously believed that if God is omni*, then of course he always gets what he wants. I suppose that doesn't account for human free will.

### JOHN 4:27–38

**Victoria**: In reading verse 37, it seems like Jesus is the sower since he is doing God's will, and it's through him that people can eventually be saved. But then verse 38 and the footnote indicate otherwise, saying that "others" are the sowers (which includes John the Baptist). Who's sowing what for whom?

**Steve**: Jesus is definitely the Ultimate Sower (that's a good wrestling name), but that doesn't exclude others from sowing as well. In that context, sowing would be doing anything that eventually leads someone to be a Christian doing Christian things:

> *He also said, "This is what the kingdom of God is like. A man scatters seed on the ground. Night and day, whether he sleeps or gets up, the seed sprouts and grows, though he does not know how. All by itself the soil produces grain—first the stalk, then the head, then the full kernel in the head. As soon as the grain is ripe, he puts the sickle to it, because the harvest has come."* (Mk 4:26–29)

Jesus later states that once he was gone, it was the disciples' job to do good works and make more followers of him:

> "Therefore go and make disciples of all nations, baptizing them in the name of the Father and of the Son and of the Holy Spirit, and teaching them to obey everything I have commanded you. And surely I am with you always, to the very end of the age." (Mt 28:19–20)

> "But you will receive power when the Holy Spirit comes on you; and you will be my witnesses in Jerusalem, and in all Judea and Samaria, and to the ends of the earth." (Acts 1:8)

Humans can do some of the external work, but only God can do the internal work needed for salvation. Using his farming analogy, notice that both the one who does the work (the sower: God or humans) and the one who receives the benefit (the harvester/reaper: humans) both get joy out of it. That's ideal Christianity: we get happiness for ourselves when we serve God and others:

> If you keep my commands, you will remain in my love, just as I have kept my Father's commands and remain in his love. I have told you this so that my joy may be in you and that your joy may be complete. My command is this: Love each other as I have loved you. (Jn 15:10–12)

**Victoria**: Then reaping is benefiting from God's love? One of the notes says that "John the Baptist ... sowed but did not live long enough to reap." I thought Jesus died for people in the past, too.

**Steve**: It's not one single answer.[6] Maybe a general way of saying it is that Christianity takes a lot of work on the front end to see benefits on the back end. The workers and those who benefit (in this world) may or may not be the same people. The benefits could be spiritual, mental, emotional, or physical. I think in the context of those verses, I would write the Robinson translation as follows. "Hey, stop worrying so much about who's talking to whom and whether you're well fed and things like that. We have a lot of work to do. I'm doing it. Others are doing it. Join with me and let's start working. There are a lot of people out there that can benefit from our work, and time is short, so come on!"

**Victoria**: The thing is, we mortals never really know if one reaps in kind what one sows; e.g., those with good lives and bad works or those with bad lives and good works. I'm not arguing against sowing and reaping, but I feel the same arguments that apply to convince one of Christianity can easily be applied in the other direction.

---

[6] "What does the Bible say about sowing and reaping?" *Got Questions*, www.gotquestions.org/sowing-and-reaping.html.

Dr. Robinson, can you just modernize the Bible and write a Robinson translation for the whole thing? :)

**Steve**: You're exactly right—in this world. Things in this life will not work out according to who the "good/bad" people are:

> *But I tell you, love your enemies and pray for those who persecute you, that you may be children of your Father in heaven. He causes his sun to rise on the evil and the good, and sends rain on the righteous and the unrighteous.* (Mt 5:44–45)

let alone the Bible's claim that there are no good people:

> *Everyone has turned away, all have become corrupt; there is no one who does good, not even one.* (Ps 53:3)

Most of the disciples died horrific deaths.[7] John the Baptist was beheaded:

> *So he immediately sent an executioner with orders to bring John's head. The man went, beheaded John in the prison, and brought back his head on a platter. He presented it to the girl, and she gave it to her mother.* (Mk 6:27–28)

It was the same fate for many others:

> *Women received back their dead, raised to life again. There were others who were tortured, refusing to be released so that they might gain an even better resurrection. Some faced jeers and flogging, and even chains and imprisonment. They were put to death by stoning; they were sawed in two; they were killed by the sword. They went about in sheepskins and goatskins, destitute, persecuted and mistreated— the world was not worthy of them. They wandered in deserts and mountains, living in caves and in holes in the ground. These were all commended for their faith, yet none of them received what had been promised, since God had planned something better for us so that only together with us would they be made perfect.* (Heb 11:35–40)

The Christian life is never ever about, "If I do good things, good things will happen to me (or even happen in general)." I agree with you that things aren't always so clear, and that the fact that awful things happened to God's most faithful followers is not the most compelling argument for Christianity. But it is extremely compelling to me that

---

[7] "Does the Bible record the death of the apostles?" *Got Questions*, www.gotquestions.org/apostles-die.html.

these people jumped right into the fire, knowing what they were getting into. They're either completely crazy, or they saw something amazing with their own eyes. I have a really hard time believing the former when I see life- and society-changing verses like these:

> *"You have heard that it was said, 'Eye for eye, and tooth for tooth.' But I tell you, do not resist an evil person. If anyone slaps you on the right cheek, turn to them the other cheek also. And if anyone wants to sue you and take your shirt, hand over your coat as well. If anyone forces you to go one mile, go with them two miles. Give to the one who asks you, and do not turn away from the one who wants to borrow from you. "You have heard that it was said, 'Love your neighbor and hate your enemy.' But I tell you, love your enemies and pray for those who persecute you, that you may be children of your Father in heaven. He causes his sun to rise on the evil and the good, and sends rain on the righteous and the unrighteous. If you love those who love you, what reward will you get? Are not even the tax collectors doing that? And if you greet only your own people, what are you doing more than others? Do not even pagans do that? Be perfect, therefore, as your heavenly Father is perfect.* (Mt 5:38–48)

Jesus doesn't seem like a crazy person to me.

I'm scared to death of the Robinson translation. I want the Bible to change me, not reinforce everything I already think.

**Victoria**: Yeah... With these discussions, the Keller book, Keller book discussions, and IGSM stuff, I'm hearing these concepts over and over. I don't know what impact it's making.

**Steve**: It's interesting that you say that. What would you expect to see and/ or feel if it were making an impact?

**Victoria**: Something. Anything. I think my heart must be closed.

**Steve**: If I can read between the lines here, you feel like you're trying to know and understand God, and the process that you've been going through should've created some kind of feeling of satisfaction or understanding that believers seem to have? That if all this is real, there should be some kind of emotional confirmation?

1. No. We all have different temperaments and personalities. There are some that seem to only "feel" God and haven't had an ounce of logic or reason ever get within 50 yards of them. I have serious questions about them. Don't think that's a lofty goal; it's not yours.

2. I'm pretty sure that if I were an atheist, I would feel a lot more satisfied and content with my daily life. So many questions and difficulties would have simple, straightforward answers (but none of the biggest and most important). Christianity leaves me with a vague, unresolvable dissatisfaction with the world, because things aren't the way they should be. That's normal.

3. You can't "feel" your way into faith. To me, faith is acting on a set of disputable facts because they make the most sense or have the weightiest evidence. Feelings aren't involved.

4. Feelings lie. We don't use them in science for that reason. Don't use them to discern truth about Christianity either.

5. For me, feelings are the end benefit of faith, not the foundation of it. When I read Jn 3:16, I do have feelings of love and gratitude and awe, but only in the context that I have gone through the cold, hard process of weighing and debating evidence in my mind. And sometimes I don't have feelings of love and gratitude and awe. Sometimes I just read it and whine about myself.

6. Feelings usually don't come as much when I'm alone as when I'm with other Christians. I know you've said that you've gone to IGSM, and that type of thing in addition to making church friends can go a long way. I'd invite you to church, but the 2,000-mile trip may be inconvenient for you.

7. You need one feeling: a desire for God. The fact that you feel bad that you don't have feelings indicates that you do have a desire for God! Otherwise, why would you care? That one feeling takes care of everything else and will guide you where you want to go if you stoke it.

**Victoria**: That's the thing, Dr. Robinson. I don't feel like I have that desire. I'm actually at an IGSM retreat in the mountains now (we have a bit of down time at the moment). I wasn't planning on it originally since my boyfriend and I were supposed to celebrate both of our birthdays this weekend. One of the leaders called me and convinced me to go; I agreed, figuring that I might learn a thing or two. But I can't shake the apathy; I can't seem to care. "Whoever does not know love does not know God,"[8] and I don't know if I know love, even. I don't know if I want to keep going with all this. My advisor has invited me to church with him and his family before, but I don't know about that either.

**Steve**: Fair enough. The last thing I want to do is drag you along to somewhere you don't want to go.[9] I care about you too much to do that. Let's give this thing a rest; you sound weary. If you want to resume it at some point, send me an email and I'd be happy to pick it back up again. If you never want to mention it again, that's fine, too. You're the best student I've ever had, so I'm 100% confident that you'll think through these things with intelligence and come to an informed decision. (Possible) parting words: God loves you and you matter.

**Victoria**: How do you know? I guess that's part of the reason I wanted to learn the Bible. How do you know God cares, and why does God care? (Because "God is love", but that's more of an intellectual understanding that I find hard to grasp.)

---

[8] 1 Jn 4:8.
[9] Jn 21:18.

**Steve**: Well, I suppose that's what we're trying to figure out, isn't it? It's much the same way I know anything: through a system of checks and balances that take lots of perspectives (empirical, societal, logical, emotional, etc.) into account. For example, for me to even trust a physics textbook, I need lots of non-scientific corroboration. I need to know that humans are trustworthy, because a human wrote it. I need to be able to relay my own experience of seeing the arc of a thrown ball to the equations for projectile motion to see if they mesh. I need to see a chain of reasoning that makes sense. Or maybe another way to put it is, "Is this the best whole explanation for all of these different things I'm asking about?" In place of an impossible certainty, I think that's what Christianity gives.

**Victoria**: Can you clarify "all of these different things" (e.g., why are we, the collective we, here)? That last sentence is what is sometimes referred to as taking a "leap of faith," right? I used to interpret the concept of the leap of faith as, "There are some questions that can never be answered so just shut up and believe" (kind of like not trying to understand quantum physics: "shut up and calculate"[10]). I like the perspective and the nuance that you bring up though, of faith being an active, not passive, process.

**Steve**: By "all of these different things," I mean meaning, purpose, coherence, morality, rationality, etc.: essentially all of the questions we've been wrestling with. And, yes, of course, why are we here? (The answer is to glorify God—to reveal his worth—but that takes a lot of explaining, hence the many words so far.)

I suppose I'm trying to convince you that Christianity is not a leap of faith but rather—as a whole—the most reasonable and complete answer to a world of questions. I'm not saying it answers every question to my satisfaction, so if you want to call it a leap of faith that I believe certain things about God without understanding them, I'm fine with that. But from my perspective, that's no more a leap of faith than a physicist saying he believes that physics (i.e., the laws of nature, not the study thereof) perfectly explains black holes without understanding how. Both the Christian and the physicist would have foundational reasons for making such claims. For example, the Trinity makes no sense to me; I can't comprehend it at all. But if I understand for all kinds of other justified reasons (e.g., biblical, personal, societal, etc.) that God is relational, then the Trinity actually seems to be a logical (yet bizarre) conclusion. Similarly, we can't seem to make complete sense of black holes with our current laws of physics, but in the context of the overwhelming success of physics over the last 500 years, it would be ridiculous to then say that black holes must have some magical, non-physical element to them or that physics just doesn't work.

---

[10] David Mermin, "Could Feynman Have Said This?" *Physics Today* **57** (5), 10 (2004).

## JOHN 4:39–42

**Victoria:** I don't have comments here.

**Steve:** Testimony from women was generally ignored or discredited in that culture.[11] You can see the disciples' surprise that Jesus was even talking to a woman in verse 27. There are two big things to get out of this. 1) Jesus wasn't very concerned with social norms. 2) Suppose that none of the stories of Jesus actually happened, and John (the author) had some devious or malicious intent in trying to convince his first-century reader that they did. He never would've included testimony from a woman, because that would've pretty much negated his credibility. (It would be similar to me trying to convince you that dragons are real because my three-year-old nephew said he saw one.) Therefore, there's a high probability that John is simply recording what he knows to be true. The same line of reasoning can be applied to the resurrection: the first witnesses were women.[12]

**Victoria:** Ha ha, right. I've often seen, read, or heard about the same ideas on women being the first witnesses despite their lack of social status. I like that present-day kid example.

## JOHN 4:43–54

**Victoria:** Given Jesus' statement in verse 48 and the "superficial welcome" in verse 45, I'm kind of surprised Jesus went ahead and healed the man's son.

**Steve:** I'm with you. I really can't discern any pattern of where, when, and on whom Jesus decided to perform miracles. I think that's because the miracles were about himself and not the recipient. Sickness and disease were ways of life at that time,[13] so Jesus often displayed his authority and power with healing. I'm not sure he would do the same types of things if he were around today.

**Victoria:** That's a fascinating thought. What are some things you think he might do if he were around today?

**Steve:** I was hoping you wouldn't ask that—and I left it vague on purpose—because I have no clue. He has a pattern of never really acting the way I want him to act, and everything I thought of in response to your question were things I would want him to do. But I do feel confident in the following: 1) He would do things that made his authority quite clear and 2) he would constantly remind us that our priorities were way out of whack.

---

[11] "Testimony in Jewish law: Ineligible witnesses," *Wikipedia*, en.wikipedia.org/wiki/Testimony_in_Jewish_law#Ineligible_witnesses.

[12] Mt 28:1–10.

[13] "Life expectancy: Variation over time," *Wikipedia*, en.wikipedia.org/wiki/Life_expectancy#Variation_over_time.

**Victoria**: Is it really unexpected for our priorities to be way out of whack when we respond to practically immediate feedback?

**Steve**: No, of course not. But "expected" is not the same as "right." I've expected my kids to be the same selfish, deceitful people that I am since they were born, but I would be remiss to not correct them. I "expect" heavier objects to always fall faster based on my experience and immediate feedback, but I needed to be corrected.

**Victoria**: That's a fair point.

# CHAPTER 23: JOHN 5

### JOHN 5:1–15

**Victoria**: I have the same general thoughts I had on Jn 4:43–54. Also this invalid throws Jesus under the bus, so that doesn't seem cool. Does this healing combined with the fact that the healed man continues to sin imply that Jesus only fixed people physically, but not mentally?

**Steve**: Good question. It's difficult to pinpoint what it means to "fix someone mentally." For example, my wife and I have different temperaments and personalities in a lot of ways, and that can be frustrating for both of us, but those opposites provide checks and balances and can be complementary as well. I'm sure she would like to "fix me mentally" sometimes, but I would disagree that that's the best thing. Now, if you mean to say that Jesus' healing should've or could've included making the guy a better moral person or making him stop sinning completely, that's a different issue. 1) Human free will in making choices (or at least perceived free will) seems to be extremely important to God. I believe it's the only logical conclusion under the assumption of an omni* God coinciding with the existence of evil. I believe it's because the benefits of choosing to love God—rather than being forced to—outweigh the negative consequences of inevitable sin. 2) Personally, I'd love to stop sinning, but I've found that my sin continually drives me back to God. I often don't recognize his greatness until I recognize my own inadequacy. It's not that we need to continually sin to know God,

> *What shall we say, then? Shall we go on sinning so that grace may increase? By no means! We are those who have died to sin; how can we live in it any longer?* (Rom 6:1–2)

but I do think that God can use bad things for his own purposes.[1,2] There are dozens of stories in the Bible like that, including the crucifixion.

**Victoria**: That's funny. Yes, I meant to say "fixing" in terms of making someone a better moral person. Your response regarding free will sounds reasonable.

From your first John Piper reference: "[Paul] is saying that for Christians—the called, those whose hearts have been brought from enmity to love for God—all things work for good all the time." What if someone has a terrible life, which didn't plainly end for good? How

---

[1] John Piper, "All Things for Good: Part 1," *Desiring God*, June 9, 2002, www.desiringgod.org/messages/all-things-for-good-part-1.

[2] John Piper, "All Things for Good: Part 2," Desiring God, June 16, 2002, www.desiringgod.org/messages/all-things-for-good-part-2.

could anyone know that Paul's statement is true? In the same reference, the section entitled "What the Love of God Is" is so ... emotional.

Anyway, it seems the second Piper reference is getting more at what you're saying about how bad things can be utilized for good: "No, just as Joseph's brothers meant it (purposed it, designed it) for evil, so also God meant it (purposed it, designed it) for good." This would necessarily hold true for things like the Holocaust (probably the most cited extreme example ever), but I would never dare assert the "utility for good" of the Holocaust.

**Steve**: This might sound like a cop-out, but "end for good" might not mean "before you die." It might mean in eternity. That's God's promise to us: temporary suffering, eternal joy.

> *Consider it pure joy, my brothers and sisters, whenever you face trials of many kinds, ...* (Jas 1:2)

Remember that Paul is not just making statements out of the blue, but is basing his authority on his encounter with Christ, his theological training, and reason.[3] I think he's using all three here: it's illogical to think that God would've died on a cross, and then think that things wouldn't work out in the end:

> *He who did not spare his own Son, but gave him up for us all—how will he not also, along with him, graciously give us all things?* (Rom 8:32)

Regarding the Holocaust, Paul is certainly not saying that all things can be twisted and interpreted in such a way that we could say, "The Holocaust was actually a good thing." But I believe he is saying that 1) God can bring good out of any bad thing (e.g., the atrocities of World War II have affected our consciences thus far to prevent World War III), and 2) for *each individual believer*, God's goodness finally wins in his/her life: maybe after they die, but eventually.

**Victoria**: Hm. Okay.

**Steve**: You're not inspiring confidence in my responses; ha ha!

**Victoria**: Ah, no, they're fine! It's the "it's not you, it's me" concept. I feel like I'm waning (as touched on above).

### John 5:16–30

**Victoria**: On the footnote for verse 19, it says that "it is impossible for the Son to act independently," yet he is "much more than an agent." Where does the "much more" part come in? I don't have much more on this section, except that in a higher view, everything focuses on the Son as being of, with, and from the Father. Why is there no (or very little)

---

[3] Gal 1.

mention of the Holy Spirit? If anything, it's hard to see that that exists (and what it/he is).

**Steve**: I believe your footnote is referring to the fact that there were many "agents" of God in the past: Abraham, Moses, Isaiah, John the Baptist, etc. Jesus was also that, but also claimed divinity, putting him on a different level.

The Holy Spirit is generally positioned to do the work when Jesus leaves:

> *But very truly I tell you, it is for your good that I am going away. Unless I go away, the Advocate will not come to you; but if I go, I will send him to you.* (Jn 16:7)

Besides that, Jesus' audience was having a hard enough time with him alone,

> *On hearing it, many of his disciples said, "This is a hard teaching. Who can accept it?"* (Jn 6:60)

so maybe it wasn't the best time to introduce more new theology.

One of my favorite verses is 24. Note that Jesus does not say that we cross from bad to good, but from death to life.[4]

**Victoria**: "Unless I go away, the Advocate will not come to you." Why not? Also—why not bring in the Holy Spirit before Jesus?

From your reference: "Faith is a gift." Hm, okay.

**Steve**: This is a Trinity question, to which I almost never know the answer. All I can say is that they have different roles and do different things.

It's not true that the Holy Spirit was absent before Jesus,[5] but that Christians just have a different (more developed?) understanding.

Yeah, the Bible is pretty clear that this whole thing (including faith) is dependent on God, not on us. The perception that Christianity is "believing real hard" is wrong. I suck real bad at believing; I'm a huge skeptic about everything. So I don't base my assurance that I'm a Christian on how much I believe. Rather, I examine my life from two angles. 1) What do I simply acknowledge to be true based on reason, evidence, and emotion? If I internally acknowledge the fundamentals of Christianity,

> *... because, if you confess with your mouth that Jesus is Lord and believe in your heart that God raised him from the dead, you will be saved.* (Rom 10:9)

---

[4] John Piper, "Stop Living a Half-Life with God," *Desiring God*, March 23, 2016, www.desiringgod.org/interviews/stop-living-a-half-life-with-god.

[5] "The Holy Spirit in the Old Testament," *Thomas Nelson Bibles*, February 21, 2017, www.thomasnelsonbibles.com/the-holy-spirit-in-the-old-testament/.

then I must be a Christian, and that must be evidence of God's work in my life to produce faith:

> *Therefore I want you to understand that no one speaking in the Spirit of God ever says "Jesus is accursed!" and no one can say "Jesus is Lord" except in the Holy Spirit.* (1 Cor 12:3)

2) Does my external life reflect the life of someone who has internal belief?

> *But the fruit of the Spirit is love, joy, peace, patience, kindness, goodness, faithfulness, gentleness, self-control; against such things there is no law.* (Gal 5:22–23)

If so, I must be a believer:

> *By this my Father is glorified, that you bear much fruit and so prove to be my disciples.* (Jn 15:8)

**Victoria**: I guess I'll just have to continue reading and find out more about the Trinity in due time.

What does it mean to suck real bad at believing? Do you ever have doubt in your own faith?

**Steve**: *I never stop doubting my faith.* Never ever ever, not for one second. I'm too flawed and finite to have it all together. I've tried my hardest but have never succeeded in conjuring up faith on my own. If there is one single alternate possibility to anything I believe (which is true for every single thing I believe), I absorb, consider, and live with it. I wish it weren't this way; I'd love to have 100% assurance in Christianity. But here's the amazing thing about all that: my shortcomings in that regard only increase the evidence that I am absolutely helpless:

> *"I am the vine; you are the branches. If you remain in me and I in you, you will bear much fruit; apart from me you can do nothing."* (Jn 15:5)

and desperately need Christ:

> *... and a woman was there who had been crippled by a spirit for eighteen years. She was bent over and could not straighten up at all. When Jesus saw her, he called her forward and said to her, "Woman, you are set free from your infirmity." Then he put his hands on her, and immediately she straightened up and praised God.* (Lk 13:11–13)

because I'm not even good at believing things. That strengthens my faith. More than that, the Bible says that even faith itself comes from God, not us:

> Now to each one the manifestation of the Spirit is given for the common good. To one there is given through the Spirit a message of wisdom, to another a message of knowledge by means of the same Spirit, to another faith by the same Spirit, to another gifts of healing by that one Spirit, ... (1 Cor 12:7–9)

Still, I can live the Christian life with a 99% assurance that God exists. I can worship Jesus when I feel 90% confident that he was actually resurrected. Heck, I'm only 80% sure that quantum mechanics is the proper description of physical reality, but I can still base my entire career and research on it. This is what I want you to hear: Absolutely nothing is certain,[6] but we can use our minds to discern what's likely and live based on that. If it seems quite likely that the Bible and its depiction of Jesus are true based on the evidence and your knowledge of yourself, then do what he said; love him and your neighbor:

> Jesus replied: "'Love the Lord your God with all your heart and with all your soul and with all your mind.' This is the first and greatest commandment. And the second is like it: 'Love your neighbor as yourself.'" (Mt 22:37–39)

That makes you a Christian. If it's not convincing, live your life to the fullest and do your best to enjoy the next 60 years:

> We have this one life, let's enjoy it, let's live it to the full ... Don't identify yourself so passionately with this business called religion.[7]

### JOHN 5:31–47

**Victoria**: I wonder if those who doubted Jesus and led him to his death considered the possibility that they were very wrong.

**Steve**: Based on the conversations I've had over the past few years with dozens of people, they absolutely considered that they might be wrong; we all doubt, despite outward appearances. But I think that—in their minds—they had too much to lose to follow him. In that vein, it's more about potentially losing everything to follow the only thing that matters than being a super-confident believer.[8]

---

[6] "Cogito, ergo sum," *Wikipedia*, en.wikipedia.org/wiki/Cogito,_ergo_sum.

[7] Richard Dawkins, *Negus Media International*, March 7, 2010, www.negusmedia.com.au/interviews/interview135.html.

[8] Phil 3:1–14.

# CHAPTER 24: JOHN 6

### JOHN 6:1-15

**Victoria:** What's the big issue with Jesus being king? Why did he have to go away?

**Steve:** The Jews had the correct idea that the Messiah would be a king. But their conception was that he would be an earthly king,[1] throw off Roman oppression, and make their lives better. He wanted no part in politics,

> Later they sent some of the Pharisees and Herodians to Jesus to catch him in his words. They came to him and said, "Teacher, we know that you are a man of integrity. You aren't swayed by others, because you pay no attention to who they are; but you teach the way of God in accordance with the truth. Is it right to pay the imperial tax to Caesar or not? Should we pay or shouldn't we?" But Jesus knew their hypocrisy. "Why are you trying to trap me?" he asked. "Bring me a denarius and let me look at it." They brought the coin, and he asked them, "Whose image is this? And whose inscription?" "Caesar's," they replied. Then Jesus said to them, "Give back to Caesar what is Caesar's and to God what is God's." And they were amazed at him. (Mk 12:13–17)

because his kingdom was infinitely bigger and could affect us from the inside out rather than the other way around. Ironically, he was crucified under a sign claiming his kingship:

> And over his head they put the charge against him, which read, "This is Jesus, the King of the Jews." (Mt 27:37)

### JOHN 6:16-24

**Victoria:** This is probably one of the most referenced acts of the Bible, at least in secular conversation.

**Steve:** Yes, and this version[2] contains the story of Peter.

### JOHN 6:25-59

**Victoria:** I don't have comments here.

**Steve:** I love the mundaneness of all of this. Jesus is basically saying, "I'm the most important thing there is," and the people are like, "Um, you look pretty ordinary to us." That sort of sums up the main contention with

---

[1] "The Messiah's Misunderstood Mission," *Beyond Today*, www.ucg.org/bible-study-tools/booklets/jesus-christ-the-real-story/the-messiahs-misunderstood-mission.

[2] Mt 14:22–33.

Christianity in general, no? The fact that Christians claim a relationship with a supernatural being but seem so ordinary (and flawed) themselves makes believing hard. In many ways, Christianity is so internal in terms of how it can change one's thoughts and attitudes that it's hard for others to see. That's a big reason why, even though Christianity is based on internal faith,

> *This righteousness is given through faith in Jesus Christ to all who believe. There is no difference between Jew and Gentile, ...* (Rom 3:22)

doing external things is still critical:

> *In the same way, faith by itself, if it is not accompanied by action, is dead.* (Jas 2:17)

**Victoria**: Are they exhibiting the sin of pride, then? Assuming that some didn't believe because they felt older, wiser, and like they had more life experience.

I think the mention of external things is worthwhile since I don't hear that emphasized as much as internal belief. I guess it's because general society talks about doing the external things a lot, so those who discuss God and the Bible focus on the internal.

**Steve**: Every sin is the sin of pride. Sin is a statement that my way and my thinking are better than God's way and his thinking.

I think you're right about internal/external. With Christianity, our focus is on Jesus, which can only be an internal thing. For example, suppose an atheist and I each give $100 to a charity. On the surface, these appear to equivalent acts (i.e., my money doesn't go to Jesus). The difference is in the motivation. If God is real, it's infinitely more important that I internally worship him in the act of giving than that I give. At the most basic material level, that $100 will help some collection of atoms perform a different function, and that doesn't seem meaningful to me.

**Victoria**: *Every* sin is the sin of pride? So all sins fall under the pride umbrella? Would you say there is a hierarchy of sins?

**Steve**: Ultimately, yes, every sin is the sin of pride:

> In the end, there are only two kinds of people in the world: those who say to God, "Thy will be done," and those who in the end God says to them, "Thy will be done."[3]

As for a hierarchy of sins: 1) No:

---

[3] C. S. Lewis, *The Great Divorce* (New York: HarperOne, 2015).

> *For whoever keeps the whole law and yet stumbles at just one point is guilty of breaking all of it.* (Jas 2:10)

> *... for all have sinned and fall short of the glory of God, ...* (Rom 3:23)

These are in the sense of "everybody's guilty, so it doesn't matter if there's a hierarchy of sin." 2) Yes:

> *Truly I tell you, people can be forgiven all their sins and every slander they utter, but whoever blasphemes against the Holy Spirit will never be forgiven; they are guilty of an eternal sin.* (Mk 3:28–29)

Jesus is effectively saying that anyone can be forgiven of anything except an ultimate rejection of God (which, of course, might be evidenced by a complete callousness to sin). 3) Maybe. Considering the various punishments listed in the Old Testaments for different sins, they were clearly considered "different." That falls into the ceremonial vs. civil vs. moral law debate [To the reader: this is addressed in Chapter 25]. So in short, it depends on what you mean by hierarchy.

**Victoria**: Jas 2:10 sounds extreme.

**Steve**: If sin comes from a list of right and wrong, you're correct. If sin is an act of rebellion against the most valuable thing in existence, James makes sense.

### JOHN 6:60–70

**Victoria**: I don't have comments here.

**Steve**: This, along with the previous verses, is yet more evidence to me that the Bible isn't made up. Who would, if they wanted to start a made-up religion using a fictional historical narrative, create plausible criticisms of that religion that show a mass rejection of its teachings? I would love to say that Jesus is so awesome that those who followed him couldn't turn back. But they did. They left him in droves. So in actuality, he was so awesome that most people couldn't handle him. It's also a reminder that easy, prosperous, American Jesus doesn't exist and never has. He calls us to suffer...

> *Then Jesus said to his disciples, "Whoever wants to be my disciple must deny themselves and take up their cross and follow me."* (Mt 16:24)

and be weird:

> *Do not conform to the pattern of this world, but be transformed by the renewing of your mind. Then you will be able to test and approve what God's will is—his good, pleasing and perfect will.* (Rom 12:2)

**Victoria**: What exactly are the plausible criticisms here? Ha ha, I like the statements on Jesus being so awesome and calling us to (suffer and) be weird. What is meant by the renewing of the mind? Reading the Bible? Going to church? Also how do you keep pulling out all these verses? It's like you have the Bible memorized.

**Steve**: 1) You're standing right in front of us and don't seem that special. You should probably be glowing or something if you're God.[4] 2) If you're the Messiah, you should be overthrowing the Roman rule over us, and you're not doing that.[5] 3) If you're the Messiah, you should be from Bethlehem, not Galilee.[6] 4) We know your family. Your dad was just a carpenter. You're just a carpenter.[7] You're too ordinary to back up the claims of being a descendant of David, who was a king.[8] 5) You're not solving our problems like the Messiah is supposed to. You just keep talking about how awesome you are.[9] 6) You don't seem to be taking God's commands very seriously, such as not working on the Sabbath.[10] 7) You keep speaking in metaphors, and we have no idea what you're talking about.[11]

The Greek word μετανοέω (metanoeó)[12] is often translated as "repent" in the New Testament. It literally means to "change one's mind." The word that we translate "repent" in the Old Testament (שׁוּב: shub[13]) literally means "to turn around." That's how I view this renewing of the mind (the Greek word μεταμορφοῦσθε ≈ "metamorphosis"[14]). Praying, reading, and attending church might be evidence that such a transformation has occurred, but they aren't the transformation. Let's take this verse as an example:

> *From that time on Jesus began to preach, "Repent, for the kingdom of heaven has come near." (Mt 4:17)*

I don't think our English word "repent" does it justice. Most modern readers would take this verse to say: "From that time on Jesus began to

---

[4] Jn 6:30.

[5] Jn 6:15.

[6] Jn 7:52.

[7] Jn 6:42.

[8] Mt 1:1.

[9] Jn 6:41.

[10] Jn 5:18.

[11] Mt 13:10.

[12] "Strong's Greek: 3340. μετανοέω (metanoeó)," *Bible Hub*, biblehub.com/greek/strongs_3340.htm.

[13] "Strong's Hebrew: 7725. שׁוּב (shub)," *Bible Hub*, biblehub.com/hebrew/strongs_7725.htm.

[14] "Strong's Greek: 3339. μεταμορφόω (metamorphoó)," *Bible Hub*, biblehub.com/greek/strongs_3339.htm.

preach, 'Stop sinning, and promise God you'll never do it again, for the kingdom of heaven has come near.'" But the verse literally says, "From that time on Jesus began to preach, 'Change your minds, for the kingdom of heaven has come near." So what does that mean? Considering that he's talking to a primarily Jewish audience, I take his words to refer to changing their minds about—in the context of the "kingdom of heaven"—1) what a kingdom looks like and 2) what heaven is about. In other words, his intention was to completely redirect their focus from the things of this world to the things of God...

*Set your minds on things above, not on earthly things.* (Col 3:2)

and to switch from a mindset of "I'm good because I obey most of these external laws" to "I suck and only God can help me." This "renewing of the mind" then just becomes a new way of thinking about everything. "Kim Jong-un is a monster who must be destroyed" vs. "Kim Jong-un is a sinner who must be prayed for." "I'm tired of dealing with all of these whiny students" vs. "God loves these students and put me in a place to serve them." "My goal is to become rich and famous" vs. "My goal is to use whatever wealth and status God gives me for his glory." It literally changes your motivation, mood, demeanor, goals, and purposes.

For most of the Bible verses I reference, I don't have a specific verse reference in mind like, "That's Colossians 3:2." Instead, after decades of reading, studying, and attending church, I know what the Bible says in general, and then I just have to find it specifically. For example, these were my steps for that last Bible verse. 1) I know the Bible talks about thinking according to God's ways, not the world's. 2) So I searched Google for "bible things of this world." 3) The results were not what I had in mind, but I know that Paul wrote about it. 4) So I searched Google for "bible things of this world paul." 5) Boom, there's exactly the verse I had in the back of my mind as the second result. It's sort of like knowing that NaCl is an ionic bond but needing to look up its properties in a table to do chemistry with it (and confirm that I didn't just make stuff up).

**Victoria**: On the list of criticisms against Jesus and his teachings, I'm not sure I would see 1) or 7) as valid points against him. Was 2) prophesied? And why would 3) be valid if he or someone in his family could just vouch that he was born in Bethlehem. And on 5), didn't he solve problems like healing people? But I can see the weight of reasons 4) and 6).

Hmm, your explanation on the word "repent" makes that verse a lot more understandable. Those are illustrative examples of how one's mindset changes through transformative repentance. The idea of changing or renewing one's mind reminds me of a recent conversation I had with my advisor in which I was wondering if everyone in heaven would be essentially the same person because everyone is good.

I like the walkthrough of your thought process! Good analogy.

**Steve**: 2) Here's a good reference in which the Messiah was described as a king:

> *Rejoice greatly, Daughter Zion! Shout, Daughter Jerusalem! See, your king comes to you, righteous and victorious, lowly and riding on a donkey, on a colt, the foal of a donkey. I will take away the chariots from Ephraim and the warhorses from Jerusalem, and the battle bow will be broken. He will proclaim peace to the nations. His rule will extend from sea to sea and from the River to the ends of the earth.* (Zech 9:9–10)

There aren't prophecies about specifically overthrowing Roman rule (except maybe this[15]), but the implication is that this entire-earth-ruling king couldn't exist at the same time as Caesar. So most Jews at that time were expecting him to physically rule:

> *Jesus, knowing that they intended to come and make him king by force, withdrew again to a mountain by himself.* (Jn 6:15)

3) Sure, that's possible, but not easily done 2000 years ago (especially while speaking to a crowd). 5) Yes, but not everyone was healed, and not everyone witnessed the healings. Put yourself into the shoes of a random person shopping in Jerusalem when one day a guy starts preaching that you should eat his flesh and drink his blood: not a convincing message in my mind.

What conclusion did you come to in that conversation?

**Victoria**: But he/God will physically rule in the afterlife? I would think it should be easier when speaking to a crowd because you can tell more people at once, but Jesus never seemed to try to defend himself in response to accusations.

Basically, the answer was no, not everyone would be the same person because the qualities that distinguish us today can also be present in the good versions of people. His example was that someone could be extremely recalcitrant in one setting but extremely devoted in another setting. In both cases, that person consistently demonstrates tenacity.

**Steve**: One of my biggest fears is being misunderstood, so I'm continually amazed that it didn't seem to bother Jesus very much. He seems confident beyond human possibility to me sometimes.

---

15 "Four kingdoms of Daniel," *Wikipedia*, en.wikipedia.org/wiki/ Four_kingdoms_of_Daniel.

Yes, the afterlife seems to be physical, not entirely ethereal.[16]

---

[16] Matt Perman, "Will the Resurrection of the Body Be a Physical Resurrection from the Dead?" *Desiring God*, January 23, 2006, www.desiringgod.org/articles/will-the-resurrection-of-the-body-be-a-physical-resurrection-from-the-dead.

# CHAPTER 25: JOHN 7

## JOHN 7:1–13

**Victoria**: I don't know if I would agree with verse 7, i.e., that "the world cannot hate you, but it hates [Jesus]."

**Steve**: This is a condemnation of his brothers in the context of verse 5. His brothers were "of the world" in the following sense:

> *Do not love the world or anything in the world. If anyone loves the world, love for the Father is not in them.* (1 Jn 2:15)

The world does not hate itself,[1] so his brothers would not be hated either; see also:

> *If a kingdom is divided against itself, that kingdom cannot stand.* (Mk 3:24)

**Victoria**: Part of that sounds like it could come from a Buddhist text about not holding onto worldly desires or possessions. What do you mean when you say the world does not hate itself, and what does that have to do with the Academy Awards? Isn't there plenty of conflict within this world, even between people of the same country, ethnicity, and beliefs? I'm still confused by verse 7.

**Steve**: There are definitely some parallels in Christian and Buddhist teaching.[2]

From a Christian perspective, people are divided into two camps: Christians and "the world." By "the world," we mean those whose beliefs, actions, and teachings do not line up with Christianity. Even though the world is certainly divided up into fighting factions, Christian teaching would say that all of these divided kingdoms are ultimately fighting against Christ...

> *"Whoever is not with me is against me, and whoever does not gather with me scatters."* (Mt 12:30)

and that, ultimately, people, no matter who they are, are not our problem:

---

[1] "Academy Awards," *Wikipedia*, en.wikipedia.org/wiki/Academy_Awards.

[2] "Jesus and Buddha: The Parallel Sayings," *Beliefnet*, www.beliefnet.com/faiths/2000/02/jesus-and-buddha-the-parallel-sayings.aspx.

*For our struggle is not against flesh and blood, but against the rulers, against the authorities, against the powers of this dark world and against the spiritual forces of evil in the heavenly realms.* (Eph 6:12)

When he says that the world does not hate itself, he's saying that, in the end, all non-Christians support all other non-Christians' battle against Christ, whether they're consciously doing this or not. I know this sounds weird, but it's being approached from a spiritual, eternal perspective rather than a physical, temporal perspective. (I mentioned the Academy Awards as an example of how the world loves itself. The richest and most famous people in the world gather annually to tell each other how great they are.)

So here's the Robinson translation of verses 5–7. "Jesus' brothers didn't believe that he was the Messiah or son of God. Therefore, they were part of the world which fights against Christ. That part of the world was already mad at Jesus, because he condemned their beliefs and actions. So when his brothers asked him to go to a festival in which people would be angry if he showed up, he said, 'Go on ahead. They'll try to kill me, but you'll be fine, because you're one of them.'" It was a pretty strong indictment. Eventually, they did believe:

*They all joined together constantly in prayer, along with the women and Mary the mother of Jesus, and with his brothers.* (Acts 1:14)

In addition, his brother James is traditionally believed to have written the biblical book of James. This is more evidence to me that something overwhelmingly convincing must've happened to them (because there's no way I would believe that one of my brothers is the Messiah).

**Victoria**: That's an interesting use of the word "support." Your translation made a lot more sense. In none of those sentences are you using "brother" literally, are you? I'd assumed not, but now I'm questioning.

**Steve**: Yes, I mean literal brothers (technically, half-brothers). After the virgin birth,

*"How will this be," Mary asked the angel, "since I am a virgin?"* (Lk 1:34)

Jesus' parents, Mary and Joseph,

*This is how the birth of Jesus the Messiah came about: His mother Mary was pledged to be married to Joseph, but before they came together, she was found to be pregnant through the Holy Spirit.* (Mt 1:18)

had more children...

*"Isn't this the carpenter's son? Isn't his mother's name Mary, and aren't his brothers James, Joseph, Simon and Judas? Aren't all his sisters with us? Where then did this man get all these things?"* (Mt 13:55–56)

and he had a normal family:

*Then Jesus' mother and brothers arrived. Standing outside, they sent someone in to call him. A crowd was sitting around him, and they told him, "Your mother and brothers are outside looking for you." "Who are my mother and my brothers?" he asked. Then he looked at those seated in a circle around him and said, "Here are my mother and my brothers! Whoever does God's will is my brother and sister and mother."* (Mk 3:31–35)

(It seems that Joseph died at a young age, because he's not really mentioned much after the beginning of the gospels.) This was undoubtedly another thing that made people think he was just a normal guy.

**Victoria**: Mk 3:35 makes me question if anyone is a literal relation.

**Steve**: In that verse, Jesus is trying to make a distinction between his spiritual family and literal family, implying that he had a literal family. He's also saying that his mission can't be slowed, redirected, or stopped by anyone, including his immediate family.

### JOHN 7:14–24

**Victoria**: On verses 22–23, my comment isn't so much about the point Jesus is making but about his reference to keeping the law. I couldn't help but think that there are so many laws; do circumcise boys, don't work on the Sabbath, etc. It doesn't make sense to me why all these laws even exist.

**Steve**: There are 613 commandments in Jewish law.[3] Christians generally think of them in three categories.

The first is *civil law*, which pertains to the fact that the Israelites were actually a nation and needed governmental regulation. These laws often seem strange (and inappropriate) to us because they reflect an ancient middle eastern culture. Here are some examples:

*"Anyone who curses their father or mother is to be put to death."* (Ex 21:17)

*For instance, a man may go into the forest with his neighbor to cut wood, and as he swings his ax to fell a tree, the head may fly off and*

---

3 "613 commandments," *Wikipedia*, en.wikipedia.org/wiki/ 613_commandments.

*hit his neighbor and kill him. That man may flee to one of these cities and save his life.* (Deut 19:5)

*If a man happens to meet a virgin who is not pledged to be married and rapes her and they are discovered, he shall pay her father fifty shekels of silver. He must marry the young woman, for he has violated her. He can never divorce her as long as he lives.* (Deut 22:28–29)

The second is *ceremonial law.* These laws were created to prepare people for the worship of God and to set them apart from the surrounding culture. (Much like the Genesis account of creation, many of these laws seem to have been written as a response to the practices of those living nearby.[4]) The general theme is "God is holy; take him seriously in thought and action but also in outward cleanliness (as a symbol)." Here are some examples:

*And the pig, though it has a divided hoof, does not chew the cud; it is unclean for you.* (Lev 11:7)

*"Whoever touches the man who has a discharge must wash their clothes and bathe with water, and they will be unclean till evening."* (Lev 15:7)

*"Do not cut the hair at the sides of your head or clip off the edges of your beard."* (Lev 19:27)

Finally, there are the *moral laws*, which point toward the breaking of some kind of standard of goodness and rightness in God's eyes. Here are some examples:

*"You shall not murder."* (Ex 20:13)

*"You shall not steal."* (Ex 20:15)

*"If a man has sex with an animal, he must be put to death, and the animal must be killed."* (Lev 20:15)

Now, to a first-century Jew, there was absolutely no distinction between these laws. They were all to be obeyed, not categorized or questioned. Jesus himself revered these laws:

---

[4] Dennis Bratcher, "Israel's Codes of Conduct Compared to Surrounding Nations," *The Voice*, www.crivoice.org/lawcodes.html.

*For truly I tell you, until heaven and earth disappear, not the smallest letter, not the least stroke of a pen, will by any means disappear from the Law until everything is accomplished.* (Mt 5:18)

But another thing is happening at the same time. As must happen in our own court system, sometimes one must decide which law has priority over another (or other considerations). For example, if my child cut off his finger, is it OK for me to drive one mile per hour over the speed limit to get him to the emergency room? I think/hope every judge in America would say that it was acceptable for me to break the law in that manner in that specific case. So in these verses, we have a case where two ceremonial laws conflict. A Jewish boy should be circumcised:

*On the eighth day the boy is to be circumcised.* (Lev 12:3)

But no one is to work on the Sabbath (Saturday):

*... but the seventh day is a sabbath to the LORD your God. On it you shall not do any work, neither you, nor your son or daughter, nor your male or female servant, nor your animals, nor any foreigner residing in your towns.* (Ex 20:10)

Does he have to wait for the Sabbath to be over to obey the law? Well, the experts in the law apparently made a provision for something like that and justified their decision in their minds. (Over many years, hundreds of interpretations of these types of nuances became sort of a law unto themselves.[5]) But then they give Jesus no wiggle room when *he* performs a miracle on the Sabbath,

*Therefore the Jews started persecuting Jesus, because he was doing such things on the sabbath.* (Jn 5:16)

and he calls out their hypocrisy. (You might recall that they had bigger issues as well...

*For this reason the Jews were seeking all the more to kill him, because he was not only breaking the sabbath, but was also calling God his own Father, thereby making himself equal to God.* (Jn 5:18)

and were trying to justify their dislike of Jesus with scripture.) This is a microcosm of Jesus' ministry. He was all about the law, but only in the context that it was written to show God's value and holiness (via our obedience),

---

[5] "The Rules of the Pharisees," *PursueGOD*, www.pursuegod.org/rules-pharisees/.

*For by works of the law no human being will be justified in his sight, since through the law comes knowledge of sin.* (Rom 3:20)

not be an end in itself.

It was in that context that early Christianity began to distinguish between the civil, ceremonial, and moral law. Do pigs have some physical trait by which moral uncleanness is transferred that cows do not have? No, that's nonsense. Therefore, God's command to not eat pigs must be a part of ceremonial Jewish law, not some objective moral standard. As Christianity is not owned by any particular race or nation as Judaism was, it would be impossible for it to spread if the first Jewish Christians told the first Gentile Christians that they couldn't be around pigs or idols. It would be equally impossible for those living under the Roman Empire's rule to follow the Jewish civil law instead of the Roman civil law. In some cases, these laws (or prevailing attitudes) were explicitly repealed. Here are some examples:

*About noon the following day as they were on their journey and approaching the city, Peter went up on the roof to pray. He became hungry and wanted something to eat, and while the meal was being prepared, he fell into a trance. He saw heaven opened and something like a large sheet being let down to earth by its four corners. It contained all kinds of four-footed animals, as well as reptiles and birds. Then a voice told him, "Get up, Peter. Kill and eat." "Surely not, Lord!" Peter replied. "I have never eaten anything impure or unclean." The voice spoke to him a second time, "Do not call anything impure that God has made clean." This happened three times, and immediately the sheet was taken back to heaven.* (Acts 10:9–16)

*"You have heard that it was said, 'Love your neighbor and hate your enemy.' But I tell you, love your enemies and pray for those who persecute you, ..."* (Mt 5:43–44)

*... you also, like living stones, are being built into a spiritual house to be a holy priesthood, offering spiritual sacrifices acceptable to God through Jesus Christ.* (1 Pet 2:5)

(The last one dismantles the Old Testament system of priests.) However, as the Jews saw no distinction between the laws, categorizing them is not necessarily an exact science. In uncertain cases, it takes a lot of study of things like Jewish customs and asking questions of whether the New Testament continues to support an idea or squashes it. As a modern example, progressive Christians would argue that the Old Testament's condemnation of homosexuality in Lev 18 and 20 is 1) just as invalid to the modern Christian as the Old Testament's condemnation of wearing clothes made of different materials in Leviticus 19 and 2) in a book of instructions for priests and thus not pertinent to the average person. Conservative Christians would argue that 1) the surrounding verses in Lev 18 and 20 are all immoral acts even by modern sensibilities, so homosexuality would be no exception, and 2) the New Testament is very clear in corroborating the Old Testament command,

> *Because of this, God gave them over to shameful lusts. Even their women exchanged natural sexual relations for unnatural ones. In the same way the men also abandoned natural relations with women and were inflamed with lust for one another. Men committed shameful acts with other men, and received in themselves the due penalty for their error.* (Rom 1:26–27)

> *Or do you not know that wrongdoers will not inherit the kingdom of God? Do not be deceived: Neither the sexually immoral nor idolaters nor adulterers nor men who have sex with men nor thieves nor the greedy nor drunkards nor slanderers nor swindlers will inherit the kingdom of God.* (1 Cor 6:9–10)

> *We also know that the law is made not for the righteous but for lawbreakers and rebels, the ungodly and sinful, the unholy and irreligious, for those who kill their fathers or mothers, for murderers, for the sexually immoral, for those practicing homosexuality, for slave traders and liars and perjurers—and for whatever else is contrary to the sound doctrine that conforms to the gospel concerning the glory of the blessed God, which he entrusted to me.* (1 Tim 1:9–11)

at least with regard to homosexual *acts*. This gets more complicated by the fact that while a conservative Christian might support the Levitical *moral* condemnation of homosexuality, they would not support the *civil* penalty of death.

All of this really brings home the idea that we are *all* guilty of sin...

> *Has not Moses given you the law? Yet not one of you keeps the law. Why are you trying to kill me?"* (Jn 7:19)

and desperately in need of grace:

> *For it is by grace you have been saved, through faith—and this is not from yourselves, it is the gift of God—* (Eph 2:8)

Here's what I mean (and I want you to answer this question): Suppose you died and met a holy and perfect God. He then decides to forget all of his laws momentarily and instead judges you only by your own personal standard of morality for yourself and others. Would you be judged as righteous and blameless? If not (i.e., you can't even meet your *own* standard of morality) then it's sort of pointless to argue about which things are sins and which aren't until after we've come to understand Jesus' main points: 1) stop thinking of yourself as good,

> *"Why do you call me good?" Jesus answered. "No one is good—except God alone."* (Lk 18:19)

and 2) start recognizing him as our only hope:

> *Praise be to the God and Father of our Lord Jesus Christ! In his great mercy he has given us new birth into a living hope through the resurrection of Jesus Christ from the dead, ...* (1 Pet 1:3)

And there's the answer to your question (that wasn't a question); the law exists to convince us of both of those things:

> *Therefore no one will be declared righteous in God's sight by the works of the law; rather, through the law we become conscious of our sin. But now apart from the law the righteousness of God has been made known, to which the Law and the Prophets testify. This righteousness is given through faith in Jesus Christ to all who believe. There is no difference between Jew and Gentile,* (Rom 3:20–22)

**Victoria**: The categorization of the commandments makes it easier to think about. The explicit repealing of the laws is intriguing; was this basically to "update" God's commands based on how society had progressed? If so, that brings up an older question I had about why the Bible is (now) a static text that hasn't been changed or added to. Not all parts of the Bible can be interpreted literally, so why is there not another section saying, "this was the law then but now you should do this"?

"Would you be judged as righteous and blameless?" No.

On Lk 18:19, I don't see why Jesus would deny being good if he was also sort of God.

So you're basically saying laws exist to convince people of those two main points (that we humans are not good and that God is our only hope), but it doesn't really matter what the laws themselves are?

**Steve**: It wasn't so much to "update the laws" as society progressed as to usher in a new covenant (sort of an agreement between God and us regarding how we would relate to each other):

> *And no one pours new wine into old wineskins. Otherwise, the wine will burst the skins, and both the wine and the wineskins will be ruined. No, they pour new wine into new wineskins."* (Mk 2:22)

1) The moral laws never change, even if they're not crystal clear to us or may have a different cultural context (For example, immodesty is always wrong, but it may be culturally dependent.) Moral goodness is an inherent part of God's essence. 2) Jesus became everything the temple sacrifice used to be,

> *The next day John saw Jesus coming toward him and said, "Look, the Lamb of God, who takes away the sin of the world!" (Jn 1:29)*

so ceremonial laws became useless:

> *"If the offering is a burnt offering from the flock, from either the sheep or the goats, you are to offer a male without defect. You are to slaughter it at the north side of the altar before the LORD, and Aaron's sons the priests shall splash its blood against the sides of the altar."* (Lev 1:10–11)

3) Christianity is not attached to a nation, so civil laws became irrelevant.

The Bible doesn't have a clear, static list of dos and don'ts because 1) it can't possibly list them all, and 2) so much is gray and not black-and-white, especially in modernity. Is it wrong to use an adblocker? Is it wrong to invest in stocks of companies that improve people's lives but harm the environment? For these types of things, one has to use one's best judgment to honor Christ. Paul himself allowed for a lot of freedom in choosing to do this or that thing that others might consider sinful:[6] that freedom is necessary to keep a group of very different people (e.g., a church) from tearing each other to pieces. 3) It's not clear now who would make such a list. The Bible relies on the testimonies of those close to the events, so any modern person would be unqualified to make such additions. We're also still making tons of scientific and archaeological findings that help us read and interpret the Bible, so even though a static text is probably necessary, static interpretations are probably impossible.

The moral laws matter in that they reflect the character of God, which is the point of being a Christian. But as mentioned, they're sometimes incomplete and fuzzy. However, I would wholeheartedly agree that the details of the laws are much less important than the lawgiver. Otherwise, the lawgiver himself would be subject to them (and not be God), rather than being the source of them. In other words, is God *really* concerned that a collection of atoms named Vickie lied that one time (tsk, tsk)? I don't see how that could be possible. But is God *really* concerned that he was not valued properly, as evidenced by Vickie's lying? Yes, because 1) he is the source of truth and Vickie fought against

---

[6] 1 Cor 8, Rom 14.

his nature, and 2) as the most valuable thing in existence, he *should* (moral statement there) be valued above Vickie's desire to lie. (Gosh, what did you say? Rumors are flying everywhere around here.)

Jesus wasn't denying that he was good. It was a rhetorical question aimed at making us think that if he is good, he must be God.

**Victoria**: Of the examples you listed on some laws being repealed, what about...

> *"You have heard that it was said, 'Love your neighbor and hate your enemy.' But I tell you, love your enemies and pray for those who persecute you, ..."* (Mt 5:43–44)

Would that fall into the category of moral law?

What do wine and wineskins have to do with the new covenant? You referenced...

> *Do not destroy the work of God for the sake of food.* (Rom 14:20a)

Isn't everything supposed to be the work of God?

"The Bible relies on the testimonies of those close to the events, so any modern person would be unqualified to make such additions." Why doesn't God appear to people anymore?

"The details of the laws are much less important than the lawgiver." This statement is consistent with how you've previously defined sin (prioritizing oneself over God). Given this context, it makes sense that the laws may help people avoid sin.

Uh... Who said I said what?

**Steve**: Mt 5:43–44 is a subset of Jesus' attempt to simplify the moral commandments:

> *Jesus replied: "'Love the Lord your God with all your heart and with all your soul and with all your mind.' This is the first and greatest commandment. And the second is like it: 'Love your neighbor as yourself.' All the Law and the Prophets hang on these two commandments."* (Mt 22:37–40)

Those are the two things God asks of us, and I'm convinced that in cases of unclarity, he honors our attempts at doing what we think is best in that context. (We can use clearer cases to guide us, sort of like Supreme Court decisions using legal precedent.)

With the wineskins, Jesus is saying that it would be a mistake to try to force his new ways into the old structure (i.e., civil and ceremonial laws based on nationality and legalism).

In Rom 14, Paul is saying that if Christians become angry at each other over *secondary* matters, they've all violated God's *primary* command of loving each other.

"Why doesn't God appear to people anymore?" 1) How do you know he doesn't? 2) Clear instances of God's appearing were pretty rare, even in the Bible. Remember that it was written over a period of about 1500 years. Life was pretty mundane for the vast majority of people during that time period. 3) Immediately before Jesus died on the cross, he said:

*When he had received the drink, Jesus said, "It is finished." With that, he bowed his head and gave up his spirit.* (Jn 19:30)

In other words, everything he came to accomplish on the cross was done. After he was resurrected, the last thing he said to the disciples before he left was to tell people what they saw:

*But you will receive power when the Holy Spirit comes on you; and you will be my witnesses in Jerusalem, and in all Judea and Samaria, and to the ends of the earth." After he said this, he was taken up before their very eyes, and a cloud hid him from their sight.* (Acts 1:8–9)

They did, as attested in the later books of the New Testament. Given those things, there doesn't seem to be any new message we need to receive:

*But even if we or an angel from heaven should preach a gospel other than the one we preached to you, let them be under God's curse!* (Gal 1:8)

"Who said I said what?" Ha ha, I completely made all of that up! I was just using you and a hypothetical lie you told to help explain how God views our sin. I'm sure you're more moral than I am, so it was not meant as an indictment!

**Victoria**: Comparing the law of "love your neighbor and hate your enemy" to the law of "love your enemies and pray for those who persecute you," I don't see how the latter is a simplification of the former. They seem like completely different messages.

Regarding Romans 14, I'm confused. Is he not talking about literal eating?

Regarding your answers to why God doesn't appear to people, 1) I don't know. I would think that if God did appear to people it would be bigger news. 2) That's reasonable. 3) Kind of a segue here, but the idea of Jesus departing in a cloud is strange. If Jesus is human, then he would also need oxygen wherever he goes, right? But does that limit God's omnipotence? (But maybe he doesn't have basic human limitations. Then is he human?)

Oh! Ha ha, okay.

**Steve:** "Hate your enemy" is not in the Old Testament. Jesus was referring to a common ethic of the time[7] (and one that is readily apparent today across all cultures). So in that particular case, you are correct; Jesus was preaching a completely different message. But he was doing it in a way that simplified all of ethics into "love God and people."

Yes, Paul is talking about literal eating. Meat-eaters, vegetarians, and vegans should all be welcome in church and in God's kingdom. But if the vegans start condemning the vegetarians, or the meat eaters judge the vegans, then everyone has lost sight of what's really important. A more common example in the modern church would be different views over baptism. Some churches belief you must be baptized to be saved. Some churches believe that baptism is simply an outward expression of faith. Some churches believe you should be sprinkled on the head. Some churches believe your whole body should go under the water. Some churches believe that babies can be baptized. Some churches think that babies shouldn't be baptized. Right or wrong, everyone has some justification for believing such things. These differences are understandable, but when we start saying that *these* Christians are heretics and *those* Christians are not saved, Paul is saying to us: "Stop! It's all about Jesus! These are secondary issues that are tearing you apart internally and making you look foolish externally!"

As to God appearing, 1) Maybe. If Christianity is correct, then when God showed up as Jesus, he was known to only a very tiny percentage of the world and was hated and killed. 3) Yeah, it is strange. It also seems that if he could've shot up into the sky, he also could've gone through the ground, which means he would have had to have been hovering on the ground in a way that made it look like he was walking around like normal. Ha ha! It seems that his time on Earth was a normal human physical experience except when it wasn't: i.e., in miracles and his resurrection and ascension. Remember that these things were also pretty rare for him; there were only 40 or so miracles in 30-some years.[8]

As far as God's omni* in the human form of Jesus, he does appear limited sometimes. He was clearly not omnipresent. He also claims to not know some things:

*"But about that day or hour no one knows, not even the angels in heaven, nor the Son, but only the Father."* (Mt 24:36)

*At once Jesus realized that power had gone out from him. He turned around in the crowd and asked, "Who touched my clothes?"* (Mk 5:30)

---

[7] "The Community Rule," *ibiblio*, www.ibiblio.org/expo/deadsea.scrolls.exhibit/Library/commrule.html.

[8] Mary Fairchild, "Miracles of Jesus: From Healing the Sick to Turning Water Into Wine," *Learn Religions*, April 17, 2019, www.learnreligions.com/miracles-of-jesus-700158.

(Maybe omniscience just can't fit in our hundred billion neurons.) But then he also does some omniscient-sounding things, too:

> *Immediately Jesus knew in his spirit that this was what they were thinking in their hearts, and he said to them, "Why are you thinking these things?"* (Mk 2:8)

> *"Now we can see that you know all things and that you do not even need to have anyone ask you questions. This makes us believe that you came from God."* (Jn 16:30)

I think this is important because a major tenet of Christianity is that Jesus became human to relate to us:

> *For this reason he had to be made like them, fully human in every way, in order that he might become a merciful and faithful high priest in service to God, and that he might make atonement for the sins of the people. Because he himself suffered when he was tempted, he is able to help those who are being tempted.* (Heb 2:17–18)

But at the same time, we believe he was divine and had the characteristics of God:

> *The Son is the image of the invisible God, the firstborn over all creation. For in him all things were created: things in heaven and on earth, visible and invisible, whether thrones or powers or rulers or authorities; all things have been created through him and for him. He is before all things, and in him all things hold together.* (Col 1:15–17)

The short answer is that, like the Trinity, no one understands this, even the writers of the Bible. The longer answer is that he had two distinct natures, but they are not mutually exclusive. And perhaps when we read things that give opposite perspectives, we should try to interpret them as applying to different things. For example, we each have a mind and a body (unless one comes from a completely naturalistic worldview). They are distinct, but not contradictory, and having one does not make you lose the other. In fact, they complement each other in a way that makes you *more* of a person when you have both, not less. When I say, "Vickie is smart," I am clearly referring to your mind and not your body, although they are *both* (and each) you. When I say, "Vickie is sitting," I am clearly referring to your body and not your mind, even though they are *both* (and each) you. There are some words that could go either way, though. If I said, "Vickie is able," I could be referring to mind, body, or both. Perhaps sometimes the words we read about Jesus are applying to one or the other or both of the aspects of his dual nature. Or maybe he retained only some divine characteristics as a human and regained them after his ascension. Some think he retained his essence and equality with God but lost some of his "divine privileges."[9] Back to the short answer: no one understands this.

**Victoria**: Regarding "hating your enemy," after the priority of God, there are things that are sins. So then why would they have to stop fighting for what they believe is right—assuming they understood what the priority was?

1) Oh, wow. I always thought he was much more widely known, but I think that's colored by my present-day assumptions. 3) That averages to about more than one miracle a year, and probably more so given that he didn't start as a child (although I don't actually know that). So not that rare? That's more of a rhetorical question for argument's sake.

"But about that day or hour no one knows..." Is this the resurrection? Or the end times?

"Who touched my clothes?" We talked about the surrounding passage of this verse in a Bible study awhile back. I'm inclined to believe that he really did know who touched his clothes but was just asking publicly to have her come forward of her own accord.

Overall, I guess if no one understands it, then no one understands it. The mind/body analogy is a helpful analogy. I feel a bit uncomfortable that God, in the form of Jesus, is not very comprehensible, but this uncomfortableness is also bemusing given that I wholeheartedly believe in science when there's a lot we don't understand in science.

**Steve**: 1) The only sin is prioritizing yourself over God, so there really aren't other sins. 2) This is why denominations exist. People with strong beliefs about a topic can form a smaller group in which the adherents follow those beliefs. I think the Bible offers us that freedom (to keep fighting for what we believe is right, both individually and in small groups), but it doesn't offer us the freedom to hate or belittle those who disagree with us. Granted, everyone has a different idea regarding what is worth dividing over and what isn't, so it's a complicated issue. For some issues, the Bible acts more like a flexible tether than a solid rock.

3) Jesus' ministry was only about three years,[10] so you're right that his miracles were more condensed (about a dozen per year). There may have been more:

*Jesus did many other things as well. If every one of them were written down, I suppose that even the whole world would not have room for the books that would be written.* (Jn 21:25)

[9] John Piper, "Did Jesus Diminish His Divine Power to Become Human?" *Desiring God*, December 18, 2017, www.desiringgod.org/interviews/did-jesus-diminish-his-divine-power-to-become-human.

[10] "How long was Jesus' ministry?" *Got Questions*, www.gotquestions.org/length-Jesus-ministry.html.

But his ministry was certainly not limited to just amazing things:

*But Jesus often withdrew to lonely places and prayed.* (Lk 5:16)

Regarding "Who touched my clothes?" you're quite possibly right. But that interpretation presupposes that he was omniscient (which I'm OK with), rather than allowing the text to speak for itself.

I agree with your discomfort over the incomprehensibility of Christ's dual nature. But think of it this way: if the biblical God is real, *should* we be able to understand him?

*"For my thoughts are not your thoughts, neither are your ways my ways," declares the* LORD. *"As the heavens are higher than the earth, so are my ways higher than your ways and my thoughts than your thoughts."* (Is 55:8–9)

These gods[11] make sense to me; they're just like us, so they were probably invented by us. This God[12] is impossible to understand, so he seems less like the product of human invention.

**Victoria:** Maybe we shouldn't be able to understand the Trinity fully, but why couldn't we at least understand one-third of it? How are people expected to follow something they barely understand? At least in science, we know that it's possible to build our knowledge in areas that we don't understand, and often we know how to go about building that knowledge. There is a lot that science has yet to explain about the natural world, but I fully believe that with ongoing time and resources (financial, human, technological, etc.), we will continue to progress in our scientific understanding. I don't see that as true for knowing God. Am I wrong?

**Steve:** "Why couldn't we at least understand one-third of it?" I think we do understand each one-third of the Trinity. I also think we understand the concept of God as a singular being. We just don't understand how a thing can be one thing and multiple things at once. However, we also have no clue how one photon can go through two slits.[13] I think it would be unfair to assume that we can possibly understand the latter but never the former. On what grounds could one make such an assertion? We've made almost no progress in answering the metaphysical questions

---

[11] "List of Greek mythological figures," *Wikipedia*, en.wikipedia.org/wiki/List_of_Greek_mythological_figures.

[12] "Trinity," *Wikipedia*, en.wikipedia.org/wiki/Trinity.

[13] Scott Bonham, "Quantum Reflections," *God and Nature*, 2018, godandnature.asa3.org/bonham-quantum-reflections.html.

posed by quantum field theory[14] and general relativity[15] 100 years ago. We still don't even know what a measurement is,[16] our theories of the multiverse are probably untestable,[17] and even the best scientific data still needs human interpretation.

"How are people expected to follow something they barely understand?" That's every single part of our existence! Every step you take follows laws of gravity that no one *completely* understands. You understand very well how to *respond* to gravity, but you have no clue how to *understand* gravity. Every weather pattern involves turbulence; we don't have a complete understanding of turbulence, but we still plan our weekends based on weather forecasts. Most of us drive cars which contain dozens of components that we've never even thought about, let alone understood, but cars work and we trust them. In effect, the set of "what we know we don't know" is growing faster than "what we know." Your assumption of us being able to figure everything out is not borne out by history, which is why I love science; it gives you questions along with your answers. Our ignorance of science increases as we learn more science, but people have survived and done OK throughout history with almost zero scientific knowledge. We simply don't need a complete understanding of science to survive and thrive. In the same way, our ignorance of God increases as we learn more about him, and we don't need a complete understanding of him to follow him and thrive under him.

"Am I wrong?" No, of course not. We will absolutely continue to progress in science. But I think it's a stretch to say that we are progressing toward some finite goal in which our understanding will be (or even could be) final or complete. Rather, while we progress, we become more ignorant.

**Victoria**: "We just don't understand how a thing can be one thing and multiple things at once." I would add, at least for myself, not understanding how the three things relate to each other interpersonally and not understanding how each of the three relate to humans. As you said, maybe it is unfair to assume that we'll eventually understand quantum mechanics but never the holistic concept of the Trinity. In science there are seminal discoveries that mark progress in understanding, and there is clear evidence of research in progress by people all over the world. Is there such a thing for understanding God?

---

[14] Quantum field theory is our current understanding of fundamental particles and their interactions.

[15] General relativity is our current understanding of gravity, space, and time.

[16] "Measurement in quantum mechanics," *Wikipedia*, en.wikipedia.org/wiki/Measurement_in_quantum_mechanics.

[17] "Multiverse: Arguments against multiverse theories," *Wikipedia*, en.wikipedia.org/wiki/Multiverse#Arguments_against_multiverse_theories.

It seems this is a more personal journey in terms of marking progress in one's understanding, but what about Christianity-wide?

Living a life passively in accordance with some beliefs is different than actively devoting one's life to those beliefs. One may not understand gravity, weather, or cars, but we can trust that someone out there knows these things to a greater extent. We can find resources to learn more about those things ourselves, or we can just apply that existing knowledge to plan events and travel. On the other hand, if you choose to change your life to have a completely new sense of focus, knowing that that life won't be easier but may even be harder, you'd want to know a lot more about that new direction of focus. And you'd probably want to know about that more than knowing how the weather works. For our lack of understanding in quantum mechanics, we just "shut up and calculate," but for our lack of understanding of who God is, "shut up and believe" doesn't seem right. Despite all that, maybe you're right: "We simply don't need a complete understanding of science to survive and thrive. In the same way, our ignorance of God increases as we learn more about him, and we don't need a complete understanding of him to follow him and thrive under him."

I've always thought, perhaps too optimistically, that if humans survived long enough, we'll get to the point in which what we know (collectively) surpasses what we know we don't know. Though I'm not aware of any evidence that favors that thought.

**Steve**: Yes, absolutely (for progress in understanding God)! Think about what happened historically. Jesus lived for 30-some years and then physically left. He didn't leave anything he had written and rarely[18] gave us "Hey, here's what I meant when I said that" explanations. It appears that he specially appointed his disciples and Paul to lay out the foundations of Christian theology throughout the rest of the New Testament. Over the next 1900+ years, numerous theologians[19] have greatly helped us understand the nature of God through reason and philosophy (and more recently, science[20,21]). Two of my favorite expositors who are alive today are John Piper[22] and William Lane Craig.[23] My understanding of God is probably 80% theology and 20% personal experience.

---

[18] Mk 4:10–20.

[19] Trevin Wax, "Christianity's 5 Most Important Theologians," *The Gospel Coalition*, May 27, 2014, www.thegospelcoalition.org/blogs/trevin-wax/christianitys-5-most-important-theologians/.

[20] *American Scientific Affiliation*, network.asa3.org/.

[21] *BioLogos*, biologos.org/.

[22] "John Piper (theologian)," *Wikipedia*, en.wikipedia.org/wiki/John_Piper_(theologian).

[23] "William Lane Craig," *Wikipedia*, en.wikipedia.org/wiki/William_Lane_Craig.

"Shut up and believe." Ha ha! I agree wholeheartedly, it doesn't have the same ring to it as "Shut up and calculate." I *never* want anyone to accept or live according to Christian principles on blind faith alone. That's just a dumb way to go about it. Maybe trying to explain my own reasoning pattern will help.

1. I can't know *anything* with 100% certainty, so I'm forced to live my life according to my experience and the most probable interpretations and expectations of past and future events. Thus, I weigh evidence.

2. *Something* exists rather than nothing, and I can't figure out a way for that to be true without some ultimate source. Therefore, a creator probably exists, and by just about any definition, we call that thing god(s).

3. I am conscious.
   a. I can't figure out a way for that to be true unless it were bestowed on me by some outside source of consciousness. Therefore, a personal creator probably exists, which we call God.
   b. If my consciousness is an illusion, I have no control over my thoughts and reasoning abilities.
   c. So the fact that I believe I can reason between these options forces me to consider a) to be the more probable option. (Side note: I know of no better argument against atheism than to show that, if atheism is true, then we have no a priori reason to believe atheists' arguments.)

4. So now there's probably a personal God, which makes me think he would have revealed himself to humanity in some kind of coherent way: enter religion.

5. So what is the most probable religion (if God actually created it)? To me, it would be one in which
   a. a God very different than me exists (otherwise, we probably invented it).
   b. it is based in historical reality and not someone's mind (otherwise, it seems too arbitrary).
   c. it provides answers to life's biggest questions (a personal God would be able to do that).
   d. it gives me a purpose (a personal God would *want* to do that).
   e. God seems to be involved in the lives of humans (otherwise, what's the point?).
   f. it affirms the equality of humans (science says we're equal).
   g. the founder(s) did not materially gain from it (otherwise, it's probably a scam).
   h. Christianity seems to fit the bill in all those regards.

6. So, if Christianity is the most probable, coherent worldview, then I should live according to it.

At no point did I "shut up and believe" in any of those steps any more than I "shut up and believe" that an electron is a wave and a particle at the same time.[24] Rather, I look at the data, and, sometimes in discomfort, find the most probable interpretation and act accordingly. I will grant you that science provides repeatability and quantitative insight that faith cannot and will not. But I posit that none of life works that way beyond science. For example, suppose I emailed you and said, "Hey, my family will be in Irvine this weekend. We'd love to meet you and take you out for dinner!" Assuming you were free, (I hope) you would join us. Now, when you showed up at the restaurant, think of how many unfounded assumptions you already made: 1) that I was the one who actually sent the email, 2) that I will actually be there and it wasn't a mean joke, 3) that I haven't become a serial killer, etc. You would have had zero evidence beforehand that any of these things were true. So why would you show up? Because of a trust relationship you've built with me, email, society, etc. But at no point could you be sure like you can be sure with science. And yet 90% of your day is filled with those kinds of interactions.

Christianity is the same thing. Do I know for certain that it's true? Nope, that's impossible. But do the historical facts and the reasoning behind it make it probable enough for me to go "visit it at a restaurant?" especially if there's the possibility that it would be the greatest meal of my life? And especially if someone I trust recommended that restaurant to me and can't stop talking about it? Yeah, definitely; that doesn't seem unreasonable at all. It seems that it would be foolish *not* to go. And while I might not be certain about that first visit, the next one thousand would solidify in my mind that it was the right decision all along (or perhaps prove my naïveté, in which case I would visit a different restaurant).

**Victoria**: It almost seems that Jesus doesn't want everyone to be saved:

> ... so that, "they may be ever seeing but never perceiving, and ever hearing but never understanding; otherwise they might turn and be forgiven!" (Mk 4:12)

Why not?

I can see how Jesus was a big step forward in understanding God, but I don't know enough theology to understand the contributions of theologians in context and magnitude. In science, there are events such as the invention of a vaccine or the discovery of the Higgs boson that seem to inarguably advance science as a whole. Could the same be said about the works of those theologians? Does it depend on what branch of Christianity one might fall in?

---

[24] "Wave–particle duality," *Wikipedia*, en.wikipedia.org/wiki/Wave-particle_duality.

I think points 2) and 3a) would be absent or most contentious from the perspective of an atheist. Personally, I am inclined to believe that something exists rather than nothing, but at the same time, I can't deny that our collective existence isn't a game of highly improbable odds. I really like that side note on trust in consciousness/reason as an argument against atheism. This was more fleshed out in *The Reason for God*, and it was eye-opening.

Point 5a) doesn't seem well-substantiated. After all, aren't humans made in the image of God?

On point 5c), do you mean "would not"?

Just curious, have you investigated to see if other religions could also fit the same bill?

"Science provides repeatability and quantitative insight that faith cannot and will not. But I posit that none of life works that way beyond science." Yes, but going through life this way (e.g., the trust/email scenario) is more of the passive, default route, whereas following a religion is an overturning of how one considers everything in life and devoting one's life to a whole new focus. So one might not need repeatability and quantitative insight to decide to meet at a restaurant because the stakes are low. However, if you emailed me and said you were going to give me a house in Hawaii because of a windfall you gained, I would certainly be a lot more probing of how believable that is before I spend a bunch of money to fly out there, change my career/family plans, etc.

**Steve**: Here's a not-bad explanation of Mk 4:12.[25] We see Jesus using sarcasm elsewhere, too.[26] It would be the equivalent of me saying, "I'm glad physics is hard. Otherwise, my students might pass!"

The theologians in the link I gave you definitely made big contributions toward our understanding of God. But this is a little different when comparing it to scientific progress. 1) Christianity is simple enough for children,

> *And he said: "Truly I tell you, unless you change and become like little children, you will never enter the kingdom of heaven." (Mt 18:3)*

> *Jesus said, "Let the little children come to me, and do not hinder them, for the kingdom of heaven belongs to such as these." (Mt 19:14)*

so we don't "need" theologians to understand Christianity (they're just bonuses for the curious and hard-to-please like myself). On the

---

[25] "Lest They Return, and I Should Heal Them," *The Expository Files*, www.bible.ca/ef/expository-mark-4-10-12.htm.

[26] Rachel Dawson, "Yes, Jesus was Sarcastic ... and it Worked," *Crosswalk*, May 5, 2017, www.crosswalk.com/blogs/christian-trends/yes-jesus-was-sarcastic-and-it-worked.html.

contrary, quantum field theory and general relativity are not simple enough for children, and we need trained scientists to explain them. 2) Theology is debatable; empirical science, not so much. So while there can be branches of Christianity which disagree, that's not really a thing in science.

"I think points 2) and 3a) would be absent or most contentious from the perspective of an atheist." Yeah, of course. But atheists have no explanation for either one, and I'll take *an* explanation over *no* explanation.

I also "can't deny that our collective existence isn't a game of highly improbable odds." That's exactly why I think a creator is more probable.

If you don't like my 5a), let me put it another way. 1) Yes, God created us in his image, but I interpret that to mean in our capabilities (reason, accountability, etc.), not our actions. 2) If God is just like us,[27] I don't want to worship him, because we suck.[28]

"On point 5c), do you mean 'would not'?" No, I mean "would," and by "personal God," I mean one who relates to me, not one who is like a person.

Yes, although not completely, I have investigated other religions to the best of my time and ability; I encourage you to do the same.

Great rebuttal on the restaurant thing; Jesus agrees with you:

> *"The kingdom of heaven is like treasure hidden in a field. When a man found it, he hid it again, and then in his joy went and sold all he had and bought that field. Again, the kingdom of heaven is like a merchant looking for fine pearls. When he found one of great value, he went away and sold everything he had and bought it."* (Mt 13:44–46)

If you're thinking about Christianity as an option (and I honestly have no idea if you are or aren't), it will never happen unless you view it as a treasure:

> *You, God, are my God, earnestly I seek you; I thirst for you, my whole being longs for you, in a dry and parched land where there is no water.* (Ps 63:1)

And that won't happen unless you view yourself and humanity as having an otherwise unsolvable problem:

> *... for all have sinned and fall short of the glory of God, ...* (Rom 3:23)

---

[27] "Are the ancient Greek or Roman gods analogies for human emotions?" *Quora*, www.quora.com/Are-the-ancient-greek-or-roman-gods-analogies-for-human-emotions.

[28] "World War II," *Wikipedia*, en.wikipedia.org/wiki/World_War_II.

But if it does happen, nothing else matters:

> *What is more, I consider everything a loss because of the surpassing worth of knowing Christ Jesus my Lord, for whose sake I have lost all things. I consider them garbage, that I may gain Christ ...* (Phil 3:8)

**Victoria**: Huh, so God has sarcastic qualities in him; that's interesting.

I guess I don't fully understand what your 5c) means. You were saying that the most probable religion would provide answers to life's biggest questions, and Christianity fits because God is a personal God. Does that mean the answer to life is to develop a personal relationship with God and all the other related things (spreading the word, etc.)?

While I do believe that humans suck, including myself, I can't also say that I have a longing for God like I would long for water in a dry and parched land.

**Steve**: 5c): Um, more like: When I think of what a religion should provide, one of those things would be answers to big questions. Now, while we would expect to receive such answers from a personal God, we would have no such expectation from an impersonal god (e.g., if god were "the forces of nature"). Christianity "provides" such a personal God.

If you were in the desert, you would long for water because you would realize there's a big problem without it. Surely you see human sinfulness as a bigger problem than being really thirsty?

**Victoria**: What are the answers that this personal God provides? Is it the stuff we've been discussing all along?

Sinfulness certainly is a bigger problem than being thirsty. The solution to the thirsty problem is straightforward. The solution to the sin problem ... I don't know.

**Steve**: Yeah, not just a bunch of facts, but providing guidance on how to live and what our purpose is.

Yeah, I get the issue in relating it to thirst. Do you know of other solutions for sin? Or think maybe there isn't a solution?

**Victoria**: I've never thought of sin having a solution. People can go to counseling or anger management or do whatever to try to reduce various sins, but it's an ad hoc band-aid type of approach.

**Steve**: Yeah, great point. Christianity does not make one stop sinning. Rather, in that context, it provides a solution for our accountability before a sinless God.

## JOHN 7:25–44

**Victoria**: I don't have comments.

**Steve**: Wow, again, the Bible is its own worst critic. This chapter continues to lay out arguments against Jesus' validity, and I haven't quite picked up on that before. The disciples must've had a legitimate reason to believe. And although I think it addresses these questions like verse 42 elsewhere,

> *After Jesus was born in Bethlehem in Judea, during the time of King*
> *Herod, Magi from the east came to Jerusalem ...* (Mt 2:1)

it becomes clearer that Jesus isn't only asking people to intellectually assent to a set of ideas[29] (although that is part of it). He's asking them to recognize who he is. He was a freaking lunatic if he wasn't God. This—one of my all-time favorite quotes—sums it up quite nicely:

> The message of Christ is not Christianity. The message of Christ is Christ.[30]

He wasn't real concerned with (metaphorically) whipping out his birth certificate to satisfy them, which is amazing to me. (This paragraph was more for me than you. I'm just transferring thoughts to the keyboard: ha ha!)

**Victoria:** Being someone who isn't a quick follower (e.g., of clothing trends, new technology, etc.), I feel like it would be hard to be one of the first followers. Did they ever doubt Jesus?

Is faith-doubt a sin?

**Steve:** All of Jesus' disciples left him when he was arrested:

> *Then everyone deserted him and fled.* (Mk 14:50)

This is yet more evidence of the veracity of the gospels. Matthew and John (and possibly Mark) were some of Jesus' closest followers and admitted that they failed the biggest test of their lives.

Faith is neither 100% certainty nor believing unwarranted ideas. It is a time-tested, evidence-based, what-is-the-most-probable-explanation-of-all-of-this way-of-living. There has never been one moment of my life when I have been absolutely certain of anything (unless I was arrogantly mistaken), so that kind of unwavering faith is an impossible standard. Lacking it is normal, not sinful. But when one has decided to believe and commit one's life to Christ, the sinful part would come in not trusting the things he's said...

> *"For I know the plans I have for you," declares the LORD, "plans to*
> *prosper you and not to harm you, plans to give you hope and a future."*
> (Jer 29:11)

---

[29] "Noble Eightfold Path," *Wikipedia*, en.wikipedia.org/wiki/Noble_Eightfold_Path.

[30] Gary Amirault, "Quotes About Jesus Christ," *Tentmaker*, www.tentmaker.org/Quotes/jesus-christ.htm.

> *And we know that in all things God works for the good of those who love him, who have been called according to his purpose.* (Rom 8:28)

or flat-out denying the basic tenets of Christianity:

> *For what I received I passed on to you as of first importance: that Christ died for our sins according to the Scriptures, that he was buried, that he was raised on the third day according to the Scriptures, and that he appeared to Cephas, and then to the Twelve. After that, he appeared to more than five hundred of the brothers and sisters at the same time, most of whom are still living, though some have fallen asleep. Then he appeared to James, then to all the apostles, and last of all he appeared to me also, as to one abnormally born.* (1 Cor 15:3–8)

If you're wondering how you know you believe, your actions (fruits) will testify that your thoughts and beliefs are real:

> *Thus, by their fruit you will recognize them.* (Mt 7:20)

**Victoria**: The distinction between not having certainty and not trusting in some aspects of what he said is a blurry line to me. Can you give some examples of what fruits lead you to believe that your thoughts and beliefs are real?

**Steve**: Listing my good deeds makes me nauseous:[31]

> *... not by works, so that no one can boast.* (Eph 2:9)

> *May I never boast except in the cross of our Lord Jesus Christ, through which the world has been crucified to me, and I to the world.* (Gal 6:14)

To honor your question, however, I will do just that, but I want it to be clear that I am absolutely convinced that 1) these things do not make me good; only Jesus does, 2) I do not have the capacity to do them on my own; only God's work in me can produce good things in a sinner like myself,[32] and 3) this list would be 1000 times longer if you asked me to list my sins (please don't). In the following list, there might be some people who would do these things without believing. That's great for them, but I would probably stop most of them (because I would see no point to continue them), thereby providing evidence to me that I believe.

1. I pray regularly, including daily prayer with my family regarding international missions.
2. I read the Bible regularly and try to follow its guidance.

---

[31] Mt 6:1–18, Phil 3, Mt 23.
[32] Phil 1:1–11.

3. I give a good chunk of my income to Christian ministry.
4. I spend hours per week in preparation for and in a Bible study with Belmont students.
5. I spend hours per week helping lead a weekly meeting of college students at my church.
6. I spend hours per month in preparation for teaching Sunday school at my church.
7. I spend hours per month visiting church visitors and sick members.
8. I spend hours per week typing in this document.
9. I have forgiven everyone who has ever wronged me. I hold no grudges and hate no one. I have gone out of my way to specifically love two people in the last year who have intentionally and clearly insulted me to my face.
10. I attend church four times a week to worship and gain instruction.
11. I am generally in continuing conversation/counseling with Belmont students regarding deep personal issues.
12. I lead my family in Bible study.
13. I constantly wrestle with stressful theologies in my mind (when atheism would provide so much more ease).
14. I recognize Jesus as the solution to my and the world's problems and use the Bible to try to solve both to the best of my influence. Politics are generally irrelevant to me.
15. I talk with and attempt to show love to people even when every introvert bone in my body wants to run away.
16. I regularly perform acts of service with and outside of my church (e.g., yard cleanup, serving the homeless, counting pills for missionaries, meal delivery, etc.).
17. I have remained physically and emotionally faithful to my wife for over two decades despite temptations and possible opportunities to be unfaithful.
18. I attempt to honor God with what I choose to consume and not consume (physically and mentally).
19. I continually listen to preaching, apologetics, and worship music to keep me sharp.
20. I love the teachings of Jesus. They make me go "Wow, I love him!"
21. I legitimately care whether those I know know God and where they spend eternity.
22. Rarely an hour goes by in which I do not think about God and whether my thoughts and actions are pleasing to him.
23. I feel guilt for and wrestle with my sins and try not to excuse or justify them.

Maybe there's more. I don't know or care. This was terrible. Add it to my list of sins.

**Victoria**: That seemed painful for you (sorry!!). I was curious in how you realized your beliefs were working, so to speak, and so I see that list as your explaining and not your boasting. Number 9 is interesting to me. I think this would be really, really hard for me. They say to "forgive and forget," but usually what happens is I forget before I forgive. There isn't anyone I hate, but I tend to remember when someone has wronged me, so that I might not get burned again in the future. How can you love someone who has intentionally and clearly insulted you to your face? What does it mean to love them? Do they know you love them? Number 15 would be hard for me too. Number 22 is surprising to me.

**Steve**: I don't think there's a way for you to know whether I am explaining or boasting. Only I can know and be held accountable for that. I know my beliefs are working because I don't naturally *want* to do any of these things (in the short term). I *want* to be angry and watch TV all day. My beliefs tell me there's an eternal purpose behind each of those things, even though they often make me tired, uncomfortable, and/or sad.

I can only love and forgive people because I realize how much I've been forgiven:

> *"Therefore, I tell you, her many sins have been forgiven—as her great love has shown. But whoever has been forgiven little loves little."* (Lk 7:47)

That's it. I think that to love someone means to want and strive for the best for them. My belief is that the best for everyone is Jesus. So if someone insults me, their best isn't my wrath. Their best is my decision to turn the other cheek,

> *"You have heard that it was said, 'Eye for eye, and tooth for tooth.' But I tell you, do not resist an evil person. If anyone slaps you on the right cheek, turn to them the other cheek also. And if anyone wants to sue you and take your shirt, hand over your coat as well. If anyone forces you to go one mile, go with them two miles. Give to the one who asks you, and do not turn away from the one who wants to borrow from you."* (Mt 5:38–42)

and let them see Jesus. Besides my family, I do sometimes tell people I love them (not the two people I mentioned because I don't think they would receive it well), but actions speak louder than words.

As for number 22, it's sort of like this. Those who have grown up as Americans have American culture so ingrained in them that when they do things like shake someone's hand, apply for a job, attend a funeral, etc., they don't think, "I'm doing this this way because I'm an American." Rather, it just is. Christ is everything to me...

> *Here there is no Gentile or Jew, circumcised or uncircumcised, barbarian, Scythian, slave or free, but Christ is all, and is in all.* (Col 3:11)

and I have another citizenship ingrained in me:

> *But our citizenship is in heaven. And we eagerly await a Savior from there, the Lord Jesus Christ, ...* (Phil 3:20)

But this was not an overnight thing; it took decades to become like this.

**Victoria**: You're right that I could never know, but I just want to add that I've never perceived you as a boastful kind of person.

Forgiveness goes back to the personal relationship thing, doesn't it? To forgive or be forgiven by a friend for some wrongdoing is a relatable concept. Without a personal feeling of connectedness to God, could one realize the same weight of forgiveness?

Regarding the citizenship analogy, hmm. American culture is so ingrained in Americans that we don't think about it. But if you say the God-kingdom-citizenship is ingrained in you, then wouldn't the analogy follow that you wouldn't think about it every hour?

**Steve**: I'm glad you perceive me that way on the outside. But I'm also well aware of my internal desire to have people think I'm great. That's a constant battle I have to face.

For me, it's not a personal feeling of connectedness as much as an evidence-based understanding that we are connected. But yes, the idea that God personally did something for me for which I cannot repay him is huge. Forgiving friends but not enemies is the way we humans like to think, but God did something drastically different:

> *For if, while we were God's enemies, we were reconciled to him through the death of his Son, how much more, having been reconciled, shall we be saved through his life!* (Rom 5:10)

> *"If you love those who love you, what credit is that to you? Even sinners love those who love them. And if you do good to those who are good to you, what credit is that to you? Even sinners do that. And if you lend to those from whom you expect repayment, what credit is that to you? Even sinners lend to sinners, expecting to be repaid in full. But love your enemies, do good to them, and lend to them without expecting to get anything back. Then your reward will be great, and you will be children of the Most High, because he is kind to the ungrateful and wicked."* (Lk 6:32–35)

On the last thing, good point. Let me try again. Thinking about God is so ingrained in me that I don't have to try to think about him; rather, it's second nature.

## JOHN 7:45–52

**Victoria**: I don't have any comments.

**Steve**: They're still referring to an Old Testament prophecy,

*"But you, Bethlehem Ephrathah, though you are small among the clans of Judah, out of you will come for me one who will be ruler over Israel, whose origins are from of old, from ancient times."* (Mic 5:2)

that the Messiah would come from Bethlehem, not Galilee.[33] Jesus' hometown was Nazareth...

*He went to Nazareth, where he had been brought up, and on the Sabbath day he went into the synagogue, as was his custom. He stood up to read, ...* (Lk 4:16)

in Galilee but he was born in Bethlehem (which they were possibly unaware of), so they were interpreting the prophecy differently.

**Victoria**: Why wouldn't he just say he was born in Bethlehem, then?

**Steve**: 1) It doesn't appear that he was around for that conversation in either verse 42 or 52. 2) A more general theme is that Jesus doesn't just go around answering people's questions or solving their problems,

*Someone in the crowd said to him, "Teacher, tell my brother to divide the inheritance with me." Jesus replied, "Man, who appointed me a judge or an arbiter between you?" Then he said to them, "Watch out! Be on your guard against all kinds of greed; life does not consist in an abundance of possessions."* (Lk 12:13–15)

because he always has some bigger message to convey:

*"You are a king, then!" said Pilate. Jesus answered, "You say that I am a king. In fact, the reason I was born and came into the world is to testify to the truth. Everyone on the side of truth listens to me."* (Jn 18:37)

Do I personally find that frustrating? Yes, quite, but it's also a conviction of my own small-mindedness.

**Victoria**: Huh, yeah, this has come up a few times recently. I wonder if Jesus had to struggle to be patient with people, especially with their missing the point all the time. Though maybe being patient wasn't an issue if he's the sort of God who is love.

**Steve**: Yes, he often seems impatient when dealing with people,

*He sighed deeply and said, "Why does this generation ask for a sign? Truly I tell you, no sign will be given to it."* (Mk 8:12)

---

[33] "Map of Israel in the New Testament," *Bible History Online*, www.bible-history.com/maps/Map-Israel-New-Testament-Times-color9.jpg.

*"Are you still so dull?" Jesus asked them.* (Mt 15:16)

*He said to them, "How foolish you are, and how slow to believe all that the prophets have spoken!"* (Lk 24:25)

*"You unbelieving and perverse generation," Jesus replied, "how long shall I stay with you? How long shall I put up with you? Bring the boy here to me."* (Mt 17:17)

*"Do you still not understand? Don't you remember the five loaves for the five thousand, and how many basketfuls you gathered?"* (Mt 16:9)

but his long-term patience with us is probably an indication that he's being more corrective than impatient.[34]

**Victoria**: He definitely sounds irked and impatient in Mt 17:17.

I think I may have asked this earlier, but why wouldn't Jesus speak clearly and not in parables to have more people be saved? Why be exclusionary?

**Steve**: Jesus definitely got irked:

*When it was almost time for the Jewish Passover, Jesus went up to Jerusalem. In the temple courts he found people selling cattle, sheep and doves, and others sitting at tables exchanging money. So he made a whip out of cords, and drove all from the temple courts, both sheep and cattle; he scattered the coins of the money changers and overturned their tables. To those who sold doves he said, "Get these out of here! Stop turning my Father's house into a market!" His disciples remembered that it is written: "Zeal for your house will consume me."* (Jn 2:13–17)

Sometimes we need to be rebuked,

*But when Jesus turned and looked at his disciples, he rebuked Peter. "Get behind me, Satan!" he said. "You do not have in mind the concerns of God, but merely human concerns."* (Mk 8:33)

and he has every right to do so:

*Then Jesus came to them and said, "All authority in heaven and on earth has been given to me."* (Mt 28:18)

---

[34] David Mathis, "Perfect Patience with the Worst of Sinners," *Desiring God*, July 6, 2016, www.desiringgod.org/articles/perfect-patience-with-the-worst-of-sinners.

Great question about speaking in parables. 1) I think Jesus demands that we seek him to find him, which requires an examination of his words. It's sort of like in a romantic human relationship, where both people have to pursue each other for it to work. 2) It's impossible to lay everything out. There's too much overlap between questions and he'd eventually have to preach the Theory of Everything[35] and our brains would explode. 3) It was (and still is) a common way[36] for wise people to speak in the Middle (and Far) East. It's a way of forcing introspection that stating facts doesn't do.

**Victoria:** I suppose love doesn't necessarily entail infinite patience.

Ha ha: preaching the Theory of Everything. Jesus and science don't go together in my mind. Not that I see them as incompatible, just not associated.

**Steve:** Yes, I agree. For example, have infinite patience with a drug addict in one's family would be the opposite of love.

Yeah, we don't normally think of Jesus as a science guy, but Paul did:

*The Son is the image of the invisible God, the firstborn over all creation. For in him all things were created: things in heaven and on earth, visible and invisible, whether thrones or powers or rulers or authorities; all things have been created through him and for him.* (Col 1:15–16)

**Victoria:** Col 1:15 almost sounds self-contradictory; i.e., for something to be the image of something invisible.

**Steve:** More Trinity weirdness.

---

[35] "Theory of everything," *Wikipedia*, en.wikipedia.org/wiki/Theory_of_everything.

[36] Richard Feloni, "A top LinkedIn exec says the Dalai Lama parable CEO Jeff Weiner told him at their first meeting changed his management style," *Business Insider*, April 2, 2017, www.businessinsider.com.au/management-advice-linkedin-jeff-weiner-2017-3.

# CHAPTER 26: JOHN 8

### JOHN 8:1–11

**Victoria**: First, a meta-comment: why was this passage not originally included in the earliest manuscripts (as it says in my Bible)? Second, on the text itself: I like how it seems to say that the judgment of man is of no importance (relatively), since each one of us has sin. It reminds me of this…

> *Why do you see the speck that is in your brother's eye, but do not notice the log that is in your own eye?* (Mt 7:3)

At the same time, however, would that woman eventually have to face judgment for her actions? How does Jesus just forgive her like that, and what if she didn't have a change of heart?

**Steve**: As far as the canonicity of this passage, we now have the ability like none other throughout history to be able to examine thousands of early manuscripts and see how they stack up against our modern Bible. These 11 verses aren't in most of the earliest manuscripts at all, and when they are, they end up in different places. Since we don't have any of the original texts, every early manuscript we do have (in conjunction with their mutual agreement) is our best guess at what the original said. In addition, the fact that there is very little early commentary on such a profound passage of scripture means that it probably wasn't even known about by most early church leaders and theologians.[1] Thus, the logical conclusion is that it wasn't in the earliest manuscripts simply because John didn't write it. However, the text we read in the Bible was almost certainly transmitted orally to begin with (in reflection of that culture, with reasonably high accuracy),[2] so it's quite possible that this story really happened but wasn't written down until later. One reason it's included in most Bibles still is just that it's been there for a very long time. Besides that, it seems to fit Jesus' character (although one could reasonably argue that that's circular reasoning) and doesn't alter the main message that scripture teaches. There are lots of other contemporary texts that we don't include in the Bible (e.g., the Gospel of Thomas[3]) because they don't seem to have been accepted by the early Christians; their rejection/ignorance of such texts carries significant weight.

---

[1] Don Carson, *The Gospel According to John* (Downers Grove, IL: InterVarsity Press, 1991).

[2] John Walton and Brent Sandy, *The Lost World of Scripture* (Downers Grove, IL: InterVarsity Press, 2013).

[3] "Gospel of Thomas," *Wikipedia*, en.wikipedia.org/wiki/Gospel_of_Thomas.

As far as the text itself, I think there are several things going on. First, as you mentioned, this is clearly a story about the self-righteousness of humans vs. the actual righteousness of God. I just read a great book[4] about the psychology of human self-righteousness, how we're all self-obsessed, and how Jesus came to give us hope in the midst of all of it. This woman (and the conspicuously absent man she was with) knew adultery was wrong, so the Pharisees weren't teaching her anything by threatening her. In their minds, they were on the good team and she was on the bad team, and it was necessary in their minds to let everyone know that. (This is the foundation of modern politics and social media as well.) If you had asked the Pharisees why they were doing it, they probably would've given a mixed reply of "This is what God told us to do" and "We can't have everyone going around committing adultery; think of the consequences!" I think those are both well-intentioned, correct, and even noble thoughts. In fact, I think Jesus' actions showed that he agreed with both of those sentiments. However, the amazing thing is that he dealt with it in a completely different way. In his mind, God is on the good team and we're all on the bad team, but in the words of Ravi Zacharias, "Jesus Christ didn't come into the world to make bad people good. He came into the world to make dead people live." [5] [To the reader: ironically, well after this was written, Ravi Zacharias has now also been publicly shamed like this woman, only posthumously.[6]] In other words, he didn't lecture her on the evils of adultery to make her stop doing it; as a Jewish woman, she already knew about it. Instead, he was showing her a new way in following him. If she followed him, the adultery issue would take care of itself. But it doesn't work in reverse like the Pharisees hoped: stopping adultery doesn't automatically make one follow God.

Second, Jesus was showing that he was unleashing an entirely new way of thinking:

*He told them this parable: "No one tears a piece out of a new garment to patch an old one. Otherwise, they will have torn the new garment, and the patch from the new will not match the old. And no one pours new wine into old wineskins. Otherwise, the new wine will burst the skins; the wine will run out and the wineskins will be ruined. No, new wine must be poured into new wineskins. And no one after drinking old wine wants the new, for they say, 'The old is better.'"* (Lk 5:36–39)

---

[4] Brant Hansen, *The Truth about Us* (Ada, MI: Baker Books, 2020).

[5] Ravi Zacharias, *Twitter*, November 20, 2013, twitter.com/ravizacharias/status/403333034134364161.

[6] Joe Carter, "Report: Ravi Zacharias Engaged in Sexual Abuse," *The Gospel Coalition*, February 12, 2021, www.thegospelcoalition.org/article/report-ravi-zacharias-sexual-abuse/.

In fact, some people think that he was writing the names of the Pharisees in the dust as an Old Testament reference to their fleeting lives and worldview:

> LORD, you are the hope of Israel; all who forsake you will be put to shame. Those who turn away from you will be written in the dust because they have forsaken the LORD, the spring of living water. (Jer 17:13)

Third, with regard to your last questions, it brings a verse we read earlier back into mind:

> The man who was healed had no idea who it was, for Jesus had slipped away into the crowd that was there. Later Jesus found him at the temple and said to him, "See, you are well again. Stop sinning or something worse may happen to you." (Jn 5:13–14)

Here again, Jesus is not declaring that sin doesn't matter or doesn't exist. In fact, it's the reason he died a bloody death for us. Rather, he is showing that he has the authority to forgive sins and restore us to a right relationship with God:

> Which is easier: to say, 'Your sins are forgiven,' or to say, 'Get up and walk'? But I want you to know that the Son of Man has authority on earth to forgive sins." So he said to the paralyzed man, "Get up, take your mat and go home." (Mt 9:5–6)

Now, if the woman had just run out of there and continued sleeping around, effectively trampling on Jesus' offer of forgiveness, yes, I think she would've eventually faced judgment. See, he can simultaneously easily forgive sins like this because what is adultery to an infinite God, and also take sin very seriously because one's choice to follow one's one way instead of his is a direct affront to his worthiness. I'm convinced that God is not concerned with our sinfulness except that it directly interferes with his holiness and our ability to have a right relationship with him (and this is why the argument "As long as it's not hurting anyone else…" doesn't work).

**Victoria:** Ah okay, we've discussed what gets considered canon before. I think I saw you mention that Brant Hansen book before; it's something I've been meaning to read once life calms down a bit. I probably don't realize my own extent of self-obsession.

I like the Ravi Zacharias quote. It reminds me of something I read on thinking about some of the current events in the right perspective—along the lines of, "It's too bad that George Floyd died, but protestors shouldn't be looting" versus "It's too bad about stores being looted, but George Floyd shouldn't have had to die that way." It can be easy to be caught up in the little details of earthly life—be good, don't sin, etc.—without remembering the bigger picture of following God.

On the "as long as it's not hurting anyone else" argument for what's considered moral or at least what's not immoral, I've heard and have personally subscribed to this idea before. A counterargument is you might not see the ripple effects from an action that doesn't appear to hurt anyone else. But I can see as you said how our actions can have the weight of sinfulness even if not directly affecting others because it reflects one's attitude and stance toward God.

## JOHN 8:12-20

**Victoria**: I found the continual focus on the specific hour intriguing: how it's so definite. Then again, I suppose the end of the world would also be definite and not declared upon a whim. Could Trump end up in heaven? I guess so, based on our Nazi/Hitler discussion.

**Steve**: I think "hour" is probably best thought of as a general time frame (as a number of translations attest[7]). Remember that the Greeks and Jews had idioms just like we do (e.g., "kicked the bucket"), and translators have to find a balance between directly translating a word like "hour" and conveying the actual meaning of "it wasn't his time." You can see the various definitions of the word ὥρα here.[8]

"Could Trump end up in heaven?" Ha ha, I'm not sure which part of the passage this is in reference to, but my answer is: Yes, anyone can end up in heaven. But if he does end up in heaven, he will forever be known as Worst President Ever in Heaven. (Kidding.)

**Victoria**: That kind of phrasing—even as a general time frame—makes it sound like life is deterministic.

**Steve**: That again touches on the Calvinism vs. Arminianism debate. (I've recently found some satisfaction in Molinism,[9] which is a compromise between the two.[10]) But I still wouldn't equate the foreknowledge of an event with it being predetermined. In other words, I believe God can know the future without forcing the future.

**Victoria**: That last nuance is clarifying.

## JOHN 8:21-30

**Victoria**: I don't have comments.

**Steve**: "Son of man" is a reference to an Old Testament prophecy:

[7] "Jn 8:20," *Bible Gateway*, www.biblegateway.com/verse/en/John%208:20.

[8] "5610. hóra," *Bible Hub*, biblehub.com/greek/5610.htm.

[9] "Molinism," *Wikipedia*, en.wikipedia.org/wiki/Molinism.

[10] Eli Ayala, "What is Molinism? Middle Knowledge? Eli Ayala Explains." *YouTube*, www.youtube.com/watch?v=jSVo5BKnaiI; William Lane Craig, "What Is Molinism?" *YouTube*, www.youtube.com/watch?v=1urPYaB0JGs.

*"In my vision at night I looked, and there before me was one like a son of man, coming with the clouds of heaven. He approached the Ancient of Days and was led into his presence. He was given authority, glory and sovereign power; all nations and peoples of every language worshiped him. His dominion is an everlasting dominion that will not pass away, and his kingdom is one that will never be destroyed."* (Dan 7:13–14)

By calling himself this, Jesus is claiming to be both the Messiah and human + God wrapped into one. It's one of the most amazing and potentially blasphemous things he could've said about himself (besides verse 58).

**Victoria**: What did "son of man" mean when it was said in Daniel?

**Steve**: The phrase we translate as "son of man" was the Aramaic כבר אנש: "kibar 'anash," which literally means "like a man." In the Septuagint—the Greek translation of the Old Testament[11]—it reads ὡς υἱὸς ἀνθρώπου, which is literally "like a son of man." But to a native speaker, these phrases are idioms meaning "human being."[12] So Daniel, a Jew, is prophesying hundreds of years before Jesus that one day a human would arrive who would be all-powerful, eternal, and worshipped regardless of nationality. That's a completely insane thing for a faithful Jew[13] to write. 1) A central tenet of Judaism is the Shema,[14] a prayer which explicitly mentions God's "oneness." Jesus himself mentions the Shema...

*One of the teachers of the law came and heard them debating. Noticing that Jesus had given them a good answer, he asked him, "Of all the commandments, which is the most important?" "The most important one," answered Jesus, "is this: 'Hear, O Israel: The Lord our God, the Lord is one. Love the Lord your God with all your heart and with all your soul and with all your mind and with all your strength.' The second is this: 'Love your neighbor as yourself.' There is no commandment greater than these." "Well said, teacher," the man replied. "You are right in saying that God is one and there is no other but him. To love him with all your heart, with all your understanding and with all your strength, and to love your neighbor as yourself is more important than all burnt offerings and sacrifices."* (Mk 12:28–33)

in his teaching, affirming God's oneness, and this is why it was so hard for Jews to recognize this man as also God. (This is why Christians claim

---

[11] "Septuagint," *Wikipedia*, en.wikipedia.org/wiki/Septuagint.

[12] "Son of man," *Wikipedia*, en.wikipedia.org/wiki/Son_of_man.

[13] Dan 6:10.

[14] "Shema," *Judaism 101*, www.jewfaq.org/shemaref.htm.

belief in one God as well, but in three parts.) 2) God alone is to rule the earth,

> *The LORD will be king over the whole earth. On that day there will be one LORD, and his name the only name.* (Zech 14:9)

so saying that a person would do the same is crazy (and makes the Old Testament contradict itself if Jesus is not God).

Regarding prophecy and its fulfillment, the following facts are indisputable (i.e., you can read them yourself or virtually all scholars agree—there are many more than these,[15] but they're representative):

1. An exemplary Jew (Daniel[16]) predicted that a man would reign over the earth and be worshiped:

> *"In my vision at night I looked, and there before me was one like a son of man, coming with the clouds of heaven. He approached the Ancient of Days and was led into his presence. He was given authority, glory and sovereign power; all nations and peoples of every language worshiped him. His dominion is an everlasting dominion that will not pass away, and his kingdom is one that will never be destroyed."* (Dan 7:13–14)

which is against fundamental Jewish teaching:

> *"You shall have no other gods before me."* (Ex 20:3)

2. Another exemplary Jew (Isaiah[17]) predicted that a man would be killed (literally pierced) for people's sins:

> *But he was pierced for our transgressions, he was crushed for our iniquities; the punishment that brought us peace was on him, and by his wounds we are healed.* (Is 53:5)

3. Another exemplary Jew (Micah[18]) predicted that the Messiah would come from Bethlehem:

> *"But you, Bethlehem Ephrathah, though you are small among the clans of Judah, out of you will come for me one who will be ruler over Israel, whose origins are from of old, from ancient times."* (Mic 5:2)

---

[15] "Top 40 Most Helpful Messianic Prophecies," *Jews for Jesus*, January 15, 2015, jewsforjesus.org/answers/top-40-most-helpful-messianic-prophecies/.
[16] "Daniel (biblical figure)," *Wikipedia*, en.wikipedia.org/wiki/Daniel_(biblical_figure).
[17] "Isaiah," *Wikipedia*, en.wikipedia.org/wiki/Isaiah.
[18] "Micah (prophet)," *Wikipedia*, en.wikipedia.org/wiki/Micah_(prophet).

4. A Jew named Jesus was crucified.[19]
5. His first followers were willing to die for him.[20]

The following claims are disputable (i.e., we have no extrabiblical evidence that he said or did these things):

1. Jesus claimed to be God (the reason he was eventually killed):

   *"Very truly I tell you," Jesus answered, "before Abraham was born, I am!" At this, they picked up stones to stone him, but Jesus hid himself, slipping away from the temple grounds.* (Jn 8:58–59)

2. Jesus claimed to be that son of man from Daniel:

   *"I am," said Jesus. "And you will see the Son of Man sitting at the right hand of the Mighty One and coming on the clouds of heaven."* (Mk 14:62)

3. Jesus claimed to be the Messiah:

   *The woman said, "I know that Messiah" (called Christ) "is coming. When he comes, he will explain everything to us." Then Jesus declared, "I, the one speaking to you—I am he."* (Jn 4:25–26)

4. The purpose of Jesus' mission was to die for people's sins:

   *The next day John saw Jesus coming toward him and said, "Look, the Lamb of God, who takes away the sin of the world!"* (Jn 1:29)

5. Jesus was born in Bethlehem:

   *After Jesus was born in Bethlehem in Judea, during the time of King Herod, Magi from the east came to Jerusalem ...* (Mt 2:1)

6. Jesus was raised from the dead.[21]

   *The angel said to the women, "Do not be afraid, for I know that you are looking for Jesus, who was crucified. He is not here; he has risen, just as he said. Come and see the place where he lay. Then go quickly and tell his disciples: 'He has risen from the dead and is going ahead*

---

[19] "Historicity of Jesus," *Wikipedia*, en.wikipedia.org/wiki/Historicity_of_Jesus.
[20] "Persecution of Christians in the Roman Empire," *Wikipedia*, en.wikipedia.org/wiki/Persecution_of_Christians_in_the_Roman_Empire.
[21] Matt Perman, "Historical Evidence for the Resurrection," *Desiring God*, September 12, 2007, www.desiringgod.org/articles/historical-evidence-for-the-resurrection.

*of you into Galilee. There you will see him.' Now I have told you."* (Mt 28:5–7)

I choose to be a Christian, insofar as I can choose,

*Therefore I want you to know that no one who is speaking by the Spirit of God says, "Jesus be cursed," and no one can say, "Jesus is Lord," except by the Holy Spirit.* (1 Cor 12:3)

because the disputable claims provide the most probable explanation of the indisputable facts. I'd love to hear your broad perspective on these paragraphs. Am I crazy?

**Victoria**: Aren't all physicists at least a bit of crazy?

I'm surprised some of the things you listed as disputable aren't actually indisputable. If Jesus caused as much of a stir as he did, why wouldn't there have been extrabiblical evidence that he claimed to be God, the Messiah, etc.?

How far in advance was Jesus prophesied? For those who believe in the truth of the Old Testament but do not believe Jesus was who he said he was, how do they explain these prophecies?

No, I don't think you're crazy. And I don't believe these claims are wrong, else I'd probably devote my life to investigating this history, which many others have done. I can get on board with these claims from an intellectual standpoint, but as you said earlier, "Christianity isn't just intellectual assent to ideas; it's a whole mind, body, spirit, emotion, and lifestyle transformation."

**Steve**: Yes.[22]

*I'm* reasonably certain of those claims, but they're not things that are universally accepted as true. There is plenty of extrabiblical evidence[23] that his first followers believed him to be God, but none that he himself said it. But if he never said it, 1) it would require a mass self-destructive delusion of his first followers, the likes of which we've never seen before or since, and 2) the writers of the New Testament would have invented a literary genre (i.e., historical fiction) 1600 years before we think it existed.[24] In addition, it may be unfair for us (as a society) to expect extrabiblical sources for Jesus when we generally validate

---

[22] "Project Orion (nuclear propulsion)," *Wikipedia*, en.wikipedia.org/wiki/Project_Orion_(nuclear_propulsion).

[23] Michael Gleghorn, "Ancient Evidence for Jesus from Non-Christian Sources," *Be Thinking*, www.bethinking.org/jesus/ancient-evidence-for-jesus-from-non-christian-sources.

[24] William Eggington, *The Man Who Invented Fiction* (New York: Bloomsbury, 2016).

primary secular sources.[25,26] (That is, every book of the New Testament was traditionally written by a witness or interviewer of witnesses.[27]) But I get it; this stuff isn't normal.

The last book in the Old Testament was written 400 years before Jesus arrived on the scene. So prophecies were written between 400 and 1500 years prior. Non-believers either say the whole Bible is nonsense/coincidence:

> Bookstore put Bible on Fiction shelf: bit.ly/17Jfqjh Er, yes? So? (I once saw a bookshop shelf labelled "Religion and UFOs")[28]

or that we're interpreting it wrong.[29]

Wait, are you saying that you (intellectually) believe the historical claims of Christianity (especially that Jesus died and was raised from the dead)?!

**Victoria**: Ha ha, your comment on the invention of historical fiction reminds me of the movie *The Invention of Lying*. That's a good point regarding expectations of various sources. Differences probably arise in large part because the stakes are a lot higher.

What about people who aren't full non-believers of the Bible (i.e., they believe in the truth of the Old Testament but not in Jesus); what would they say? I guess my question is about what a Jewish person would say about these apparent references about Jesus from the Old Testament. Coincidence, I suppose.

Yeah. If the evidence points toward that, I can't deny it unless I take the time to find convincing evidence otherwise.

**Steve**: Apparently, I saw that movie (because I rated it), but I don't remember much about it. I can never remember what happened in movies or books, just that I saw/read them. That doesn't seem normal.

I think most Jews would say that the references we believe to be about Jesus were actually to someone else yet to come (i.e., the real Messiah) and that we're reading the text wrong (e.g., literally vs. metaphorically). If one's perspective is that the Messiah would/will save Israel in a cultural, racial, or national way, then I agree that Jesus failed that test. But if one's perspective is that Jesus would save Israel in a redeeming-the-individuals-within-Israel way, then that's the Christian

---

[25] "Recorded history," *Wikipedia*, en.wikipedia.org/wiki/Recorded_history.

[26] "Primary source," Wikipedia, en.wikipedia.org/wiki/Primary_source.

[27] "The New Testament Authors," *God is For Us*, godisforus.com/information/bible/ntdocs/authors.htm.

[28] Richard Dawkins, *Twitter*, November 20, 2013, twitter.com/richarddawkins/status/403281940947554304.

[29] "Judaism's view of Jesus," *Wikipedia*, en.wikipedia.org/wiki/Judaism's_view_of_Jesus.

idea.[30] Keeping in mind that the few examples I gave are just the tip of the iceberg,[31] I think the evidence points toward Jesus fulfilling the messianic predictions.

OK, that's mind-blowing to me! I'm having a hard time processing it. If someone were raised from the dead, wouldn't that change everything? Wouldn't that be something that would lead you to believe that Christ was who he said he was, which would make you a Christian? (I'm not at all being critical or trying to be pushy; I'm genuinely curious about what I see as a disconnect between your stated beliefs and your stated doubts. Please help me understand!)

**Victoria:** Ha ha! Not enough brain space for those memories.

I don't know. I don't think he's a liar or a lunatic.[32] I suppose relevance is a big factor in the disconnect. Relevance in both the temporal and personal aspects (i.e., "that was then, this is now").

**Steve:** Is the Big Bang temporally and personally relevant to you?

**Victoria:** No, it isn't...

**Steve:** Hmm, it is to me; it created me and everything I interact with. In fact, the Big Bang is still happening.[33] So what kind of things would say are temporally and personally relevant to you?

**Victoria:** The Big Bang is something I would consider important, but I don't have any care for it one way or the other. It's there, it's happening, and I contribute little to no mental energy on it, because what would be the point? Things that are temporally and personally relevant to me are in my everyday life—family and friends, health, my research, etc.

**Steve:** I see. Do you think that someone who raised himself from the dead might have some important things to say about how you should interact with those things?

**Victoria:** Probably. I mean, just based on the Bible study here so far, there's been a lot of important things said about how one should live and advice given that's generalizable enough to apply to the entire human race. But I don't know about the specific, personal impact about those things.

**Steve:** So are you sort of in the "The Bible speaks generally to everyone but not personally to me" camp?

**Victoria:** I suppose so. There are certainly parables and passages that I relate to because I am a human who has to deal with my own sins.

**Steve:** OK, That's interesting. What would it take for you to adhere to a religion?

**Victoria:** That's a challenging question. I'm not sure I know the full answer, but maybe it's conviction. The opposite of apathy. The interest, enthusiasm, and concern to understand that my life is drastically

---

[30] Rom 9.

[31] "Old Testament Prophecies of Jesus," *Learn Religions*, www.learnreligions.com/prophecies-of-jesus-fulfilled-700159.

[32] "Lewis's trilemma," *Wikipedia*, en.wikipedia.org/wiki/Lewis's_trilemma.

[33] "Dark energy," *Wikipedia*, en.wikipedia.org/wiki/Dark_energy.

missing something which is addressed by religion. That brings to my mind the people whose lives become turned around by religion. I have a friend whose uncle struggled with alcoholism but turned his life around and became a devout Christian. From the way my friend talks about his uncle's situation, I think he (my friend) sees Christianity as a crutch for the weak, not necessary for those who can handle life. I can relate to that. Why adhere to anything unless you deliberately need or want it?

**Steve**: Yep, you nailed it. And Jesus agrees with you and your friend:

> *On hearing this, Jesus said to them, "It is not the healthy who need a doctor, but the sick. I have not come to call the righteous, but sinners."* (Mk 2:17)

**Victoria**: If Christianity or religion in general are a crutch for the weak, does that mean those who are "fortunate" in life (in terms of resources, family, etc.) are just going to hell? I suppose one could argue that every person is a sinner and thus has to realize his or her own need to be saved, but you'd have to believe there's something to be saved from beforehand.

**Steve**: No, I think it has almost nothing to do with external circumstances (e.g., wealth, nationality, health, intelligence, etc.). Rather, Jesus is making a statement about how we view him and ourselves. Those who view themselves as desperately in need of God will seek and find him:

> *"Ask and it will be given to you; seek and you will find; knock and the door will be opened to you. For everyone who asks receives; the one who seeks finds; and to the one who knocks, the door will be opened."* (Mt 7:7–8)

Those who believe themselves to be self-sufficient and good will see no need for God, will not seek him, and will not find him.[34] In other words, Jesus is not talking about whether people are *actually* weak/sick or strong/healthy (because he thinks we're all weak),

> *"I am the vine; you are the branches. If you remain in me and I in you, you will bear much fruit; apart from me you can do nothing."* (Jn 15:5)

but whether people *recognize* that they are weak…

> *If anyone thinks they are something when they are not, they deceive themselves.* (Gal 6:3)

---

[34] Is 2:10–22.

and follow him. (And even that's not so much about "hey, you better recognize!" as it is just the truth. It's sort of like rebellious toddlers; they're dependent on their parents whether they acknowledge it or not, but they can make their life easier or harder by acknowledging or denying that truth.)

Regarding hell or being "saved from something," if heaven is just being with God forever,

> No longer will there be any curse. The throne of God and of the Lamb will be in the city, and his servants will serve him. They will see his face, and his name will be on their foreheads. There will be no more night. They will not need the light of a lamp or the light of the sun, for the Lord God will give them light. And they will reign for ever and ever. (Rev 22:3–5)

then it follows that those who don't want God now (i.e., those who say "I am enough") definitely won't want him forever, so heaven would be torture for them. Heaven is all about Christ,

> We know also that the Son of God has come and has given us understanding, so that we may know him who is true. And we are in him who is true by being in his Son Jesus Christ. He is the true God and eternal life. (1 Jn 5:20)

so if we're being saved from anything, it's being saved from ourselves and the perspective that we are good, self-sufficient creatures who don't need God. The Bible calls this a destructive perspective...

> When pride comes, then comes disgrace, but with humility comes wisdom. (Prov 11:2)

that's been repeated throughout history, sometimes loudly[35] and sometimes quietly.[36]

## JOHN 8:31–47

**Victoria**: On verse 44, I thought sin came about because of not prioritizing God. Or is it actually influenced by the devil? Does the devil actually exist? If so, what is the purpose of his existence?

---

[35] "Joseph Stalin," *Wikipedia*, en.wikipedia.org/wiki/Joseph_Stalin.

[36] Steve Robinson, Ph.D., *Belmont University*, www.belmont.edu/chemphys/faculty_staff/steverobinson.html.

**Steve**: Here are short[37] and long[38] answers. Here's an analogy. Suppose I'm a mob boss and you're one of the members of my family. If I tell you to murder my rival and you do it, we're both responsible and will be held accountable. In addition, both you and I would not have properly valued the law, which was the reason we committed our crime. I'm the devil/Satan, you're you, and the law is God.

The Bible supports the idea that Satan exists,[39] but certainly not as a cartoon with horns and a pitchfork. I think that imagery came from Dante's *Inferno*.[40]

Here's why Satan exists.[41] Here's more.[42] My personal understanding is that he was an angel who had been given free will (like us) and chose to rebel against God:

> *How you have fallen from heaven, morning star, son of the dawn! You have been cast down to the earth, you who once laid low the nations! You said in your heart, "I will ascend to the heavens; I will raise my throne above the stars of God; I will sit enthroned on the mount of assembly, on the utmost heights of Mount Zaphon. I will ascend above the tops of the clouds; I will make myself like the Most High." But you are brought down to the realm of the dead, to the depths of the pit.* (Is 14:12–15)

> *He replied, "I saw Satan fall like lightning from heaven."* (Lk 10:18).

**Victoria**: From that excerpt, Is 14:13 reminds me of the typical movie trope of rejecting or going beyond authority, like by the pupil of some kung fu master. I watched *Doctor Strange* recently, and it's in there too.

One of the common reasons listed for Satan's existence is that it brings more glory to God. While I can get that light is emphasized when there is darkness, it's curious to me that a non-Satanic-existence level of glory and praise isn't "enough."

**Steve**: Ha ha, I love the idea of God as a kung fu master and Satan as a rebellious and outcast student!

---

[37] Billy Graham, "Answers," *Billy Graham Evangelistic Association*, June 1, 2004, billygraham.org/answer/when-we-sin-who-is-responsible-us-or-the-devil/.

[38] "Is the devil to blame for our sin and suffering?" *Bible.org*, bible.org/question/devil-blame-our-sin-and-suffering.

[39] "Satan," *OpenBible*, www.openbible.info/topics/satan.

[40] Dante Alighieri and John Ciardi, *The Divine Comedy* (New York: Berkley, 2003).

[41] John Piper, "Why Does God Allow Satan to Live?" *Desiring God*, November 26, 2008, www.desiringgod.org/interviews/why-does-god-allow-satan-to-live.

[42] Bob Bevington, "Why Satan Exists," January 13, 2016, www.desiringgod.org/articles/why-satan-exists.

I suppose I see it the following way. If I drugged my wife every day to convince her that she loved me, it wouldn't mean as much to me as if she chose to love me by her own free will. The *ability* to choose good or bad makes the *choice* of good better and the *choice* of bad worse. Satan is believed to have both that ability to choose and be an influence over others' choices.

**Victoria**: Right, but why would Satan's absence reduce our free will? Won't we still have temptations, won't we still have pride, and won't sin still lead us astray? To extend your analogy, your wife has the free will to love you and does so, but still you decide to hire a constant stream of men to try and capture her attention. Why would her untempted love not be enough?

**Steve**: That's probably the funniest analogy I've ever heard! I love it!

This whole thing is related to God's sovereignty again. I'm not of the mindset that God said to himself, "I will create a being who will betray me, causing people to have more choices, thereby giving me more glory." Rather, I would say that God said to himself, "The best possible reality is one in which beings can freely choose me, even if that means that some (including Satan) will not. So I will create such beings." I imagine that we would still have temptations and sin if Satan weren't around, but I like to think of humans and Satan under the umbrella of "free will," and with him being an influencer rather than a causer. So using your analogy, no, I would not hire a stream of men to tempt my wife to make her love me more or prove that our love was genuine. But I honestly do value the fact that—according to her—there have been many men who have attempted to woo her, and she has rejected them. I appreciate the fact that those men, by their own free will, attempted to sin, and were, by my wife's own free will, rejected. Our marriage has been strengthened in that process, even to the point that I do not wish to live in a universe in which other men have *not* hit on my wife. In the same way, I don't believe that God tempts us directly—

> *When tempted, no one should say, "God is tempting me." For God cannot be tempted by evil, nor does he tempt anyone; but each person is tempted when they are dragged away by their own evil desire and enticed."* (Jas 1:13–14)

—although he may put us in situations in which temptations are strong—

> *No temptation has overtaken you except what is common to mankind. And God is faithful; he will not let you be tempted beyond what you can bear. But when you are tempted, he will also provide a way out so that you can endure it.* (1 Cor 10:13)

but rather allows Satan to live and influence in what he considers to be the best possible reality.

As an aside, it's hard to imagine "enough" being God's goal. Thus, a common fallback position for questions of theodicy is that this is the *best possible* creation, even though there are bad parts. I think this is justified due to 1) our understanding of God in other areas (i.e., his omni*) and 2) the fact that goodness is fraught with badness and difficulty seems to be true in many other areas as well.[43,44,45,46]

**Victoria**: I suppose that is a more amenable perspective. Satan's existence leading to strengthening faith makes it seem that his (maybe unintentional) role is to separate the wheat from the chaff in terms of faith.

That's a good point regarding "enough." If you're omni* and you are also love itself, then no amount of mortal devotion could be enough. I'm not sure if I can see how other areas having good and bad justifies that necessarily, but I can see how it might help to understand it.

### JOHN 8:48–58

**Victoria**: I don't have comments.

**Steve**: In verse 58, Jesus said of himself, "I am," which is how God refers to himself:

> God said to Moses, "I am who I am. This is what you are to say to the Israelites: 'I am has sent me to you.'" (Ex 3:14)

This was the final straw for the Pharisees, and they tried to kill him. Jesus does not allow us the option of just thinking he was a good teacher or prophet. Think of major characters in world religion and politics: Moses, Buddha, Gandhi, Muhammad, Jefferson, Hitler, Martin Luther King, Jr., etc. Few of them claimed deity (e.g., Alexander the Great, Caesars), but even they didn't claim to be the only God there is (well,

---

[43] Collin Barras, "The real reasons why childbirth is so painful and difficult," *BBC*, December 22, 2016, www.bbc.com/earth/story/20161221-the-real-reasons-why-childbirth-is-so-painful-and-dangerous.

[44] Edward Abramson, "Why Is It So Hard to Exercise?" *Psychology Today*, December 17, 2017, www.psychologytoday.com/us/blog/its-not-just-baby-fat/201712/why-is-it-so-hard-exercise.

[45] Alex Lickerman, "Why Raising Children Is So Hard," *Psychology Today*, January 15, 2012, www.psychologytoday.com/us/blog/happiness-in-world/201201/why-raising-children-is-so-hard.

[46] Wolfgang Pauli, *Quote Fancy*, quotefancy.com/quote/1571949/Wolfgang-Pauli-Physics-is-very-muddled-again-at-the-moment-it-is-much-too-hard-for-me.

except maybe the Kim family[47]). I mean, Jesus puts us all in an awkward spot here and forces our hand:

*"But what about you?" he asked. "Who do you say I am?"* (Mt 16:15)

Is he nuts? Are we nuts? That's why Christianity is an all-or-nothing, risky proposition:

*Large crowds were traveling with Jesus, and turning to them he said: "If anyone comes to me and does not hate father and mother, wife and children, brothers and sisters—yes, even their own life—such a person cannot be my disciple. And whoever does not carry their cross and follow me cannot be my disciple. Suppose one of you wants to build a tower. Won't you first sit down and estimate the cost to see if you have enough money to complete it? For if you lay the foundation and are not able to finish it, everyone who sees it will ridicule you, saying, 'This person began to build and wasn't able to finish.' Or suppose a king is about to go to war against another king. Won't he first sit down and consider whether he is able with ten thousand men to oppose the one coming against him with twenty thousand? If he is not able, he will send a delegation while the other is still a long way off and will ask for terms of peace. In the same way, those of you who do not give up everything you have cannot be my disciples.* (Lk 14:25–33)

**Victoria:** Have you met anyone who has literally given up everything they had for Christianity (Lk 14:33)? And Lk 14:26 doesn't make sense to me: "If anyone comes to me and does not hate father and mother, wife and children, brothers and sisters—yes, even their own life—such a person cannot be my disciple." Isn't God about love and not about hate?

**Steve:** No, I have not personally known anyone to give up "literally everything," although I believe those people do exist[48] and my American experience is simply not typical. Keep in mind, though, that Lk 14:33 is probably more of a statement like, "In the same way, those of you who do not give up everything you [cling to, worship, value above God, etc.] cannot be my disciples." I know this because 1) the Bible commands us to give...

*Each of you should give what you have decided in your heart to give, not reluctantly or under compulsion, for God loves a cheerful giver.* (2 Cor 9:7)

---

[47] "North Korean cult of personality," *Wikipedia*, en.wikipedia.org/wiki/North_Korean_cult_of_personality.
[48] "World Watch List," *Open Doors USA*, www.opendoorsusa.org/christian-persecution/world-watch-list/.

and that would be impossible if we had literally nothing (except once, I suppose) and 2) Jesus had rich friends:

> *Six days before the Passover, Jesus came to Bethany, where Lazarus lived, whom Jesus had raised from the dead. Here a dinner was given in Jesus' honor. Martha served, while Lazarus was among those reclining at the table with him. Then Mary took about a pint of pure nard, an expensive perfume; she poured it on Jesus' feet and wiped his feet with her hair. And the house was filled with the fragrance of the perfume. But one of his disciples, Judas Iscariot, who was later to betray him, objected, "Why wasn't this perfume sold and the money given to the poor? It was worth a year's wages." He did not say this because he cared about the poor but because he was a thief; as keeper of the money bag, he used to help himself to what was put into it. "Leave her alone," Jesus replied. "It was intended that she should save this perfume for the day of my burial. You will always have the poor among you, but you will not always have me." (Jn 12:1–8)*

It's the same idea for Lk 14:26: based on dozens of other references, Jesus must be using hyperbole, which he likes to do:

> *"Again I tell you, it is easier for a camel to go through the eye of a needle than for someone who is rich to enter the kingdom of God."* (Mt 19:24)

So the general thought is this: "If you choose to follow me, many/most/all of your friends and family will disown/abandon/hate you [especially true for his audience at that time]. If you don't love me so much more than them [in hyperbolic comparison, it could be called "hate,"] that you're willing to let that happen, you can't [also probably saying that you *won't*] be my disciple."

**Victoria**: So that's basically saying all true Christians are (or should be) willing to give up every single thing in their lives, including their lives, for God? But how does one know what's given up for God and what's done by oneself? If Joe Schmoe was fired from work, is that God's calling or Joe's mediocrity? I suppose it's case-dependent, but how does one parse the possible different causes?

As for the latter verse, I guess I'm okay with that. It would definitely be a stretch for me to come to that interpretation a priori.

**Steve**: Yes. Only you can know whether you do something for God. For example, I decided at the end of graduate school that 1) life at a Research I[49] school would make my God-given duties as a father and husband too difficult for me, and 2) working at a smaller Christian school would

---

[49] "Research I university," *Wikipedia*, en.wikipedia.org/wiki/Research_I_university.

allow me to minister to students in a way I wouldn't be able to otherwise. So I gave up a lot of money to do what I thought God wanted me to do (assuming someone would've hired me at a Research I school, ha ha!). But 1) that decision is different for everyone and 2) I never heard some heavenly voice telling me specifically what to do. Rather, I believe that God mainly speaks to me through the Bible, and it led me to that decision. If you're fired from your job because you hold Christian beliefs,[50] that's clear cut. But if you're just fired, it may be because you're a jerk.[51]

> *If you suffer, it should not be as a murderer or thief or any other kind of criminal, or even as a meddler.* (1 Peter 4:15)

Rarely do we get to know what's behind past/present/future events and specifically how God was/is/will be involved. But that's OK, because it lines up perfectly with God giving us the freedom to choose our own destiny, and I don't have to worry about being in lockstep with some strict yet ambiguous plan he has for me. I talk with students all the time about "God's will." They want to know what career God wants them to have, who they should marry, where they should live, etc. I'm absolutely convinced that God's will is for us to be happy,

> *Rejoice always, pray continually, give thanks in all circumstances; for this is God's will for you in Christ Jesus.* (1 Thess 5:16–18)

and all those other things are choices we *get* to make within that context.

I completely agree with you about Lk 14:26. Some of the hard sayings of the Bible need to be interpreted in the context of what the vast majority of it is saying for us to understand them. Suppose I went home today, and my wife said, "I'm leaving." I would not immediately interpret that as "I want a divorce." I would probably think it was "I'm going to the store" or something. That's because we have a strong, healthy marriage, and I interpret ambiguous statements in that light. It's the same with the Bible.

**Victoria:** Ha ha! Is *The Babylon Bee* the new *The Onion*?

There's so much that involves the concept of free will. Its role in actual love, the existence/influence of Satan, consideration of God's involvement, etc. I've never heard it explicitly said that God's will is for

---

[50] Tom Strode, "Judge Challenges Atlanta Policy Used to Fire Christian Fire Chief over Devotional," *Christianity Today*, December 20, 2017, www.christianitytoday.com/news/2017/december/atlanta-christian-fire-chief-kelvin-cochran-in-court.html.

[51] "Man Unsure If He's Persecuted Because He's A Christian Or Because He's A Massive Jerk," *Babylon Bee*, January 30, 2017, babylonbee.com/news/man-unsure-hes-persecuted-hes-christian-hes-massive-jerk/.

us to be happy. Is that reiterated throughout the Bible? I think if that were indeed true and one were able to believe it, that would reduce a lot of anxiety about how to live a life to fulfill "God's will."

**Steve**: *The Babylon Bee* is *The Onion* for Christians and/or conservatives. It makes fun of pretty much everything, though.

Yes, I believe that concept of happiness and/or joy is reiterated throughout the Bible.[52] It's laid out especially well in *Desiring God*.[53] In fact, that book changed my perspective about Christianity more than anything else I've encountered; here's a short summary.[54] Unfortunately, many Christians view Christianity as trying to find a balance between competing interests: God's glory and one's own happiness, which results in neither happening. In reality, they are the same thing.

**Victoria**: John Piper's "rose story" is a good analogy for understanding that. If God's glory and one's own happiness are the same thing, what explains the happiness one might feel from doing something that is outside of God's glory?

**Steve**: All good things originate from God:

> *Every good and perfect gift is from above, coming down from the Father of the heavenly lights, who does not change like shifting shadows.* (Jas 1:17)

But they may just be a glimpse of his goodness used in the wrong way. Suppose I solicit a prostitute for a night and have a good time. I'm partaking in a good thing that God created (sex), and my enjoyment of that night ultimately points to the creator of that good thing. Therefore, God is glorified in that respect. However, the wake of destruction I would leave for myself, the prostitute, my family, and society, would all create a huge imbalance in badness (self-glorification) that heavily outweighed the goodness (God-glorification). So good feelings still glorify God even if they result from sin. (For example, nuclear weapons are bad, but Einstein can still be glorified by them.) I suppose I could apply that to any sin: my good feeling when I murder my enemy comes from a sense of security and accomplishment. These are good, God-given feelings, but they are placed on the wrong object; my security and accomplishment should come directly from and point directly to Christ. Even things which don't have a sin component glorify God: an atheist giving his atheist girlfriend flowers is a legitimately good thing, and God

---

[52] "Joy," *Open Bible*, www.openbible.info/topics/joy.

[53] John Piper, *Desiring God: Meditations of a Christian Hedonist* (Sisters, OR: Multnomah Publishers, 2003).

[54] John Piper, "How to Explain Christian Hedonism over Lunch," *Desiring God*, June 4, 2014, www.desiringgod.org/interviews/how-to-explain-christian-hedonism-over-lunch.

is glorified in his kindness, because God gave him the ability to be kind whether he acknowledges it or not.

There's one more side to this, though. Since this is all ultimately about God, then although good deeds glorify God apart from the person doing them, the person him/herself cannot glorify God without faith…

> *But whoever has doubts is condemned if they eat, because their eating is not from faith; and everything that does not come from faith is sin.* (Rom 14:23)

(where I'm using "faith" here as the intention of doing some good thing to please God rather than just doing it). Maybe here's a good summary: rocks glorify God by their mere existence,

> *"I tell you," he replied, "if they keep quiet, the stones will cry out."* (Lk 19:40)

but rocks don't go to heaven. God will be glorified regardless of whether we partake in it.

**Victoria**: Rom 14:23 is interesting: "everything that does not come from faith is sin," yet God can still be glorified by sin?

**Steve**: God set up a universe that maximizes his glory. Besides all of the good things, it includes sin, Satan, pain, destruction, and entropy. But the Bible directly condemns the line of thinking in which we purposely sin to make God look better:

> *What shall we say, then? Shall we go on sinning so that grace may increase? By no means! We are those who have died to sin; how can we live in it any longer?* (Rom 6:1–2)

That leads to our own destruction, which is not what God wants at all.

**Victoria**: That's profound. I can see that concept reflected in human-scale stuff like self-victimizing. Romans seems to be a heavily referenced book, at least in this general conversation. Is that because you know it better, or is it more relevant?

**Steve**: Matthew, Mark, Luke, John, and Acts basically show what Jesus and his first disciples said and did. Then Paul in Romans describes what it all means:[55,56] (That's why it's important/relevant and I like it. It's the book that my Belmont Bible study is going through, so a lot of it is on my mind.) Then he and some other disciples write letters to new churches and believers around the Mediterranean: 1 Corinthians to Jude. Then

---

[55] *BibleProject*, "Overview: Romans Ch. 1-4," *YouTube*, October 18, 2016, youtu.be/ej_6dVdJSIU.

[56] *BibleProject*, "Overview: Romans Ch. 5-16," *YouTube*, October 18, 2016, youtu.be/0SVTl4Xa5fY.

John (the same guy who wrote the book we're in) wrote Revelation, summarizing how it all goes down:[57,58].

**Victoria**: Paul: that's who you say is one of the greatest Christians, right? Was Revelation written to a specific group like some of the other writings? A question I had while watching the first BibleProject video you referenced: Is Jesus literally related to Abraham? Or is it one of those "all Christians are brothers and sisters" kind of relation?

From the second video, the "grafted on" thing is *weird*.

I watched the videos on Revelation and, I don't know, this seems more fairy tale to me than anything else I've come across so far.

**Steve**: Yes, I believe Paul was one of the greatest Christians ever because of his self-sacrificial, God-exalting life and his laying down the foundations of Christian theology.

Revelation was written to seven churches in Asia Minor[59] but seems to contain general messages for all of time and space.[60]

Jesus, like all ethnic Jews, was a literal descendant of Abraham.[61]

In the sense that fairy tales use symbolism to convey important truth and life lessons, yes, I agree. The difference here is that John is using this symbolism to tell us about how the rest of time plays out, not just tell us how to live. I imagine that would be hard to do in such a condensed way without symbolism. Christians argue about Revelation more than any other book because it seems to have been left intentionally vague, probably for this reason:

> He said to them: "It is not for you to know the times or dates the Father has set by his own authority." (Acts 1:7)

**Victoria**: Knowing the times or dates is not the same thing as knowing what goes down, though.

**Steve**: I just meant more like, "It's not for us to know." I imagine our priorities would be different or wrong if we had specific certainty about the future.

---

[57] *BibleProject*, "Overview: Revelation Ch. 1-11," *YouTube*, December 14, 2016, youtu.be/5nvVVcYD-0w.

[58] *BibleProject*, "Overview: Revelation Ch. 12-22," *YouTube*, December 14, 2016, youtu.be/QpnIrbq2bKo.

[59] Rev 1:11.

[60] Rev 21:1.

[61] Mt 1:1–17.

# CHAPTER 27: JOHN 9

### JOHN 9:1–12

**Victoria**: Verse 3: why that man? Why anyone? That might be more of a rhetorical question.

**Steve**: "Why that man?" I have no clue. "Why anyone?" I also have no clue. Even Paul was perplexed as to why God would do any of this:

> *You see, at just the right time, when we were still powerless, Christ died for the ungodly. Very rarely will anyone die for a righteous person, though for a good person someone might possibly dare to die. But God demonstrates his own love for us in this: While we were still sinners, Christ died for us.* (Rom 5:6–8)

> *When you read this, you can perceive my insight into the mystery of Christ, ...* (Eph 3:4)

> *For the message of the cross is foolishness to those who are perishing, but to us who are being saved it is the power of God.* (1 Cor 1:18)

That's why it's described as a gift:

> *For the wages of sin is death, but the gift of God is eternal life in Christ Jesus our Lord.* (Rom 6:23)

There's not a logical reason for it (except to throw a blanket statement of "that's God's nature" on it).

I love this story, though. Although there are parallels between Christianity and other religions, this is not one of them. Christianity is anti-karma in so many ways:

> *"Neither this man nor his parents sinned," said Jesus, "but this happened so that the works of God might be displayed in him."* (Jn 9:3)

> *"... that you may be children of your Father in heaven. He causes his sun to rise on the evil and the good, and sends rain on the righteous and the unrighteous."* (Mt 5:45)

> *There is something else meaningless that occurs on earth: the righteous who get what the wicked deserve, and the wicked who get what the righteous deserve. This too, I say, is meaningless.* (Eccles 8:14)

*In fact, everyone who wants to live a godly life in Christ Jesus will be persecuted, ...* (2 Tim 3:12)

**Victoria**: That makes sense with real life being anti-karma. That reminds me, a friend told me I should read Ecclesiastes because, given that life doesn't follow the $x \rightarrow y$ mindset (e.g., do good things $\rightarrow$ have good things happen to you), I don't find that there is intrinsic meaning in life.

**Steve**: Yes, I agree with your friend. It was traditionally written by Solomon[1] (or someone writing from the perspective of Solomon[2]) who had everything anyone could hope for and ultimately found all of it meaningless. In the end, he came to this conclusion (spoiler alert):

*Now all has been heard; here is the conclusion of the matter: Fear God and keep his commandments, for this is the duty of all mankind.* (Eccles 12:13)

It's perhaps the most relatable book in the Bible to me.

Perhaps you can convince yourself to write "I don't find that there is intrinsic meaning in life," but your actions convince me otherwise. You're too diligent and too friendly for me to believe you; sorry!

**Victoria**: I really identified with it when I read it. Though it was hard for me to make the connection between "everything is meaningless" to "fear God and keep his commandments." My advisor sent me a video[3] on it, which helped somewhat.

I was thinking about your response the past few days—about how my words and actions don't always seem to line up. I don't know if my actions speak that strongly for themselves. I try to do the best I can because I want to grow intellectually, personally, etc. Is that my purpose, then? There's not meaning in that purpose, however, since I'm finite. Most days I don't think about purpose; inertia is what keeps things going. Otherwise, when I'm in a grayer mood, fear (of failure) keeps things going.

**Steve**: That video was incredible! I love *BibleProject*! I even felt a little convicted watching it myself. Yikes!

It's hard to think about purpose at your age because it feels like you're just trying to catch your breath and get started. But here's where I'm coming from: 1) You inexplicably act like you have purpose when you believe you don't. 2) Finite and temporary purpose and meaning don't exist, and you know it. 3) Therefore, there's something eternal in you that you haven't (yet) recognized.

---

[1] "Solomon," *Wikipedia*, en.wikipedia.org/wiki/Solomon.
[2] John Walton, "Who Wrote Ecclesiastes and What Does It Mean?" *Zondervan Academic Blog*, October 21, 2017, zondervanacademic.com/blog/who-wrote-ecclesiastes-and-what-does-it-mean.
[3] "Overview: Ecclesiastes," *YouTube*, June 10, 2106, youtu.be/lrsQ1tc-2wk.

**Victoria**: Ha ha! I like its lighter message of enjoying the simple things in life, too.

I'm not sure I see anything metaphysical about it. While I don't believe that life has meaning intrinsically, I acknowledge that there are factors that lead me to live purposefully. In addition to self-growth, there are also bills to pay, mouths to feed, and experiences to be had.

**Steve**: I suppose this is a point on which we currently have an irreconcilable difference. Your viewpoint turned into a nightmare existence for me when I subscribed to it.

### JOHN 9:13-34

**Victoria**: Verse 25: "I was blind but now I see." That's more than just literal seeing, isn't it?

**Steve**: We Christians would love to make that a figurative statement, and perhaps it was. But I sort of hope it wasn't, and the context of that verse leads me to believe that my hope is confirmed. 1) It sounds like a police interrogation, in which the Pharisees were only looking for facts, not opinions or theological musings. 2) The man himself gets frustrated when the Pharisees dispute his testimony (i.e., he's upset that they won't believe his story rather than it seeming like a theological argument). 3) Even though the man says that Jesus was a prophet (which is understandable considering what happened), he isn't sure whether Jesus is a "sinner" or not (verse 25, although he reasons with the Pharisees later in 31–33), so he's not willing to opine about his status too much until pushed. Again, I think that if the writer of the story (John) were trying to falsely convince me that Jesus was the sinless son of God, he would've left no doubt in my mind that everyone else was immediately convinced of that. But here, the religious experts and even a man he healed weren't sure (at least at first). However, if John were simply writing down what he saw, the story would have the same open-endedness and uncertainty we all experience every day. So I interpret his words literally.

### JOHN 9:35-41

**Victoria**: I don't have comments.

**Steve**: Because of their claims of being righteous disciples of God, Jesus is holding the Pharisees the most accountable. It's clear that he placed absolutely no value in righteous appearances or knowledge:[4]

> *But the other criminal rebuked him. "Don't you fear God," he said, "since you are under the same sentence? We are punished justly, for we are getting what our deeds deserve. But this man has done nothing wrong." Then he said, "Jesus, remember me when you come into your*

---

[4] Lk 7:36–50, Lk 18:9–17, Jn 8:1–11.

*kingdom." Jesus answered him, "Truly I tell you, today you will be with me in paradise." (Lk 23:40–43)*

*But the Pharisees and the teachers of the law muttered, "This man welcomes sinners and eats with them." (Lk 15:2)*

Rather, humility ≈ righteousness in his economy:

*For all those who exalt themselves will be humbled, and those who humble themselves will be exalted." (Lk 14:11)*

**Victoria**: That's consistent with everything I've heard so far about Jesus, and therefore also about God, I guess. Do the three members of the Trinity have different personalities? I assume what one says would be consistent with what the other two believe, so that they're never in conflict. But something sets them apart, right? Is it a physical something or personality, too?

From Lk 18:9–17: "anyone who will not receive the kingdom of God like a little child will never enter it." How is one supposed to receive the kingdom like a little child? How can you undo all that you know and have experienced?

I got confused when rereading this section at verse 39. If air quotes were a thing then, would that go here? Something like: "For judgment I have come into this world, so that the blind will see and those 'who see' will become blind."

**Steve**: Here's a good summary of the Trinity,[5] but again, it probably won't be satisfying. This[6] is pretty good, too.

Regarding children, it goes back to this verse:

*Be warned, my son, of anything in addition to them. Of making many books there is no end, and much study wearies the body. (Eccles 12:12)*

Intellectual knowledge isn't what matters:

*For the wisdom of this world is foolishness in God's sight. As it is written: "He catches the wise in their craftiness;" (1 Cor 3:19)*

Rather, God asks us to trust him like a child trusts his parents:

*"Which of you fathers, if your son asks for a fish, will give him a snake instead? Or if he asks for an egg, will give him a scorpion? If you then,*

---

[5] Matt Perman, "What Is the Doctrine of the Trinity?" *Desiring God*, January 23, 2006, www.desiringgod.org/articles/what-is-the-doctrine-of-the-trinity.

[6] "Holy Spirit," *BibleProject*, bibleproject.com/explore/holy-spirit/.

> *though you are evil, know how to give good gifts to your children, how much more will your Father in heaven give the Holy Spirit to those who ask him!"* (Lk 11:11–13)

This is why the Bible uses such personal language for God:

> *"Abba, Father," he said, "everything is possible for you. Take this cup from me. Yet not what I will, but what you will."* (Mk 14:36)

I can state from personal experience that my desire to *understand* God has sometimes detracted from my willingness to *trust* him, and that I have a lot of work to do in that regard. Keep in mind that this isn't "blind faith" anymore than your cat trusting in you to feed her daily; she has a good reason to trust you even though she can't fully comprehend you.

Regarding verse 39, yes, this is where Jesus makes the transition from literal to figurative; otherwise, it wouldn't make any sense. I would take it a step further: "For judgment I have come into this world, so that the 'blind' will 'see' and those who 'see' will become 'blind.'" I love the mental picture of Jesus air quoting, by the way.

**Victoria**: From the first reference, I find it intriguing when he says, "The Trinity has a very significant application to prayer. The general pattern of prayer in the Bible is to pray to the Father through the Son and in the Holy Spirit." What does that mean in practice?

Regarding Eccles 12:12 and 1 Cor 3:19, I feel like they can be twisted to denounce those who are scholars, but that doesn't seem right.

So you're saying the quest to understand can undermine the quest to trust, so go about it with the quest to trust, and then understanding (might) come later?

**Steve**: Praying through the Son and in the Holy Spirit means to recognize that the Holy Spirit leads you to speak with God…

> *In the same way, the Spirit helps us in our weakness. We do not know what we ought to pray for, but the Spirit himself intercedes for us through wordless groans.* (Rom 8:26)

through the door that Jesus opened. It may or may not change the specific words that I would say in a prayer, but it would change my attitude in prayer by keeping my focus on what my faith is about.

Regarding childlike faith, I'm saying that from my experience, *learning* about God is easy, comfortable, and objective; it *feels* righteous and was the modus operandi of the Pharisees. *Trusting* God is hard, uncomfortable, and subjective—and actually *is* righteous. That was the modus operandi of Jesus. Neither the Bible nor I am denouncing scholars, but if that understanding doesn't produce trust, it's worthless. I believe Jesus values the simple trust of a five-year-old than these hundreds of pages we're writing. Or to put it another way, my wife would value my love, honor, and trust in our marriage infinitely more than if I read hundreds of books about women and marriage and became an expert in both. Ideally, both understanding and trust reinforce and build on each other.

# CHAPTER 28: JOHN 10

### JOHN 10:1-21

**Victoria:** Lots of sheep analogies. This time Jesus isn't the baby sheep[1] but is the gate and the shepherd.

**Steve:** Yeah, his listeners (shepherds, farmers, etc.) would have picked up immediately on the fact that Jesus was saying they were "dumb, directionless, and defenseless,"[2] and that he's their only spiritual protection against themselves and other threats.

Verses 19–21 show that many/most people thought Jesus was crazy, which is understandable, I suppose. But believers like myself can't reconcile "crazy" with the totality of things he said and did.

**Victoria:** Taking the analogy further, sheep can't have always been that dumb, directionless, defenseless. How would they have survived? Isn't it due to humans' domestication of them that made them that way? So, what makes us that way?

I don't get the sense that people today really think he's crazy.

**Steve:** I obviously don't mean to say that sheep can't survive on their own. (Some people think they're smart.[3]) But think about why Jesus says we're sheep...

> *When he saw the crowds, he had compassion on them, because they were harassed and helpless, like sheep without a shepherd.* (Mt 9:36)

when our culture says we're supposed to think of ourselves as tigers.[4]

**Victoria:** Okay, I shouldn't carry the analogy too far. Basically, we're sheep because we're dumb, directionless, and defenseless, but not because we were evolved to be. (I love that last reference.)

**Steve:** Yes, it's a spiritual, not physical, analogy.

### JOHN 10:22-42

**Victoria:** Jn 10:29: do people not fall out of faith? Jn 10:34–36: this is confusing even with the footnote.

**Steve:** Verse 29 is a verse that Calvinists like a lot. They say that since Christians have no real part in choosing God (because humans are so depraved), they also cannot lose their faith when it's solidly in Christ

---

[1] Jn 1:36.

[2] Tim Challies, "Dumb, Directionless, Defenseless," *Challies*, August 26, 2013, www.challies.com/christian-living/dumb-directionless-defenseless/.

[3] Harriet Constable, "Sheep are not stupid, and they are not helpless either," *BBC*, April 19, 2017, www.bbc.com/earth/story/20170418-sheep-are-not-stupid-and-they-are-not-helpless-either.

[4] Katy Perry, "Roar," *YouTube*, September 5, 2013, youtu.be/CevxZvSJLk8.

(and that people who "lose their faith" merely had the internal and external *appearances* of genuine faith). I take a more moderate approach to this verse, thinking it just means that a solid faith in Christ won't be upended (i.e., that there's nothing to upend it), and that that firmness of faith comes only through Christ's help. An analogy would be holding a ball, letting it go, and saying "Nothing will stop the law of gravity from acting on this ball." A huge gust of wind could make it *appear* otherwise, but ultimately, gravity will still be doing its thing.

For verses 34–36, this reference[5] points out that "gods" is used to refer to humans in authority. Does that help?

**Victoria**: Both of those responses help.

---

[5] "What does the Bible mean by 'you are gods' / 'ye are gods' in Psalm 82:6 and John 10:34?" *Got Questions*, www.gotquestions.org/you-are-gods.html.

# CHAPTER 29: JOHN 11

### JOHN 11:1-16

**Victoria:** Jn 11:15: I'm amused by Jesus sounding snarky.

**Steve:** I've never really interpreted that with snarkiness, but it certainly could've been. Couldn't God have given us a movie instead of a book? :)

Notice Thomas here in verse 16, ready to die for Jesus. Later on, he refuses to believe without sensory evidence:

> *Now Thomas (also known as Didymus), one of the Twelve, was not with the disciples when Jesus came. So the other disciples told him, "We have seen the Lord!" But he said to them, "Unless I see the nail marks in his hands and put my finger where the nails were, and put my hand into his side, I will not believe." (Jn 20:24–25)*

Then we have Peter, who vowed to follow Jesus no matter what:

> *Peter asked, "Lord, why can't I follow you now? I will lay down my life for you." (Jn 13:37)*

A little later, he claims to having nothing to do with Jesus:

> *Then the servant girl who kept the door said to Peter, "You are not also one of this Man's disciples, are you?" He said, "I am not." (Jn 18:17)*

These disciples are the "heroes" of the Christian faith, but look how wishy-washy they are. It's more evidence that Christianity is not about being good and trying really hard.

**Victoria:** Thomas' response of requesting sensory evidence sounds like something I would say in that setting. Did all the disciples fail Jesus at some point or another? Did Jesus like the ones who failed him less?

**Steve:** They all (and we all) failed at some point. But that's the beauty of the gospel; it's not about our failure (becomes it's common to all of us), it's about his grace. In fact, if he chooses favorites at all, it's not those who fail the least; rather, it's those who are humble enough to see themselves as having no moral standing before him:

> *While Jesus was having dinner at Levi's house, many tax collectors and sinners were eating with him and his disciples, for there were many who followed him. When the teachers of the law who were Pharisees saw him eating with the sinners and tax collectors, they asked his disciples: "Why does he eat with tax collectors and sinners?" On hearing this, Jesus said to them, "It is not the healthy who need a*

*doctor, but the sick. I have not come to call the righteous, but sinners."*
(Mk 2:15–17)

*To some who were confident of their own righteousness and looked down on everyone else, Jesus told this parable: "Two men went up to the temple to pray, one a Pharisee and the other a tax collector. The Pharisee stood by himself and prayed: 'God, I thank you that I am not like other people—robbers, evildoers, adulterers—or even like this tax collector. I fast twice a week and give a tenth of all I get.' "But the tax collector stood at a distance. He would not even look up to heaven, but beat his breast and said, 'God, have mercy on me, a sinner.' "I tell you that this man, rather than the other, went home justified before God. For all those who exalt themselves will be humbled, and those who humble themselves will be exalted." (Lk 18:9–14)*

*"The teachers of the law and the Pharisees sit in Moses' seat. So you must be careful to do everything they tell you. But do not do what they do, for they do not practice what they preach." (Mt 23:2–3)*

## JOHN 11:17–37

**Victoria**: I don't have comments. I heard this passage (and surrounding parts) discussed in the Easter service I went to.

**Steve**: Bible trivia: Jn 11:35 is the second shortest verse in the Bible. This is the shortest:

*He said: (Job 3:2)*

I love the realness of verse 37. Jesus shows compassion, and instead of being moved by it, people say, "Why didn't he just not let him die in the first place?" This is me in a nutshell. Also notice the possibility of simultaneous belief ("he healed the blind guy" and "he could've healed Lazarus") and doubt ("why doesn't he do things the way I think they should be done?"): also me in a nutshell.

You went to an Easter service? Where? With whom? What did you think about it?

**Victoria**: That's interesting! "He said:" seems incomplete, though.

Is the people's response in verse 37 improper? Was Jesus trying to prove a point?

Yes, I was invited by my advisor who goes to Berean Community Church.[1] I thought it was okay overall. The person giving the message made some blanket statements that I didn't really agree with. For example, he said something about how Christians are kinder, more generous, etc. than most people.

---

[1] Berean Community Church, bereancc.com.

**Steve:** No, their response was completely valid in verse 37. But yeah, Jesus had a bigger plan in mind. Analogy: I teach my kid to ride a bike, let go, and they crash. The kid could legitimately say, "Couldn't dad have held on and kept me from crashing?" Yep, but that wouldn't be the point. Which leads to a bigger issue (possibly the biggest issue for many people): Can't God just stop all bad things from happening? Yep, but that's not his goal, so he won't. His bigger goal is to redeem us through those bad things.

I agree that that blanket statement is a little too vague to hold water, the main issue being how we define Christian (a discussion we've had before). If "Christian" means someone who fits some cultural definition of religious adherence, forget it. But if "Christian" means someone who embraces and lives by texts like these,

*Give to everyone who asks you, and if anyone takes what belongs to you, do not demand it back.* (Lk 6:30)

*But the fruit of the Spirit is love, joy, peace, forbearance, kindness, goodness, faithfulness, gentleness and self-control. Against such things there is no law.* (Gal 5:22–23)

then it would be true by definition.

**Victoria:** That's a good analogy. I would say that I (and I think people in general) tend to be shortsighted when it comes to understanding why things happen the way they do. On the other hand, it's easy to see patterns or a story in events, even when there's not (apparently there's a word for it: apophenia[2]).

This is not related to the current topic, but if someone who didn't believe in Christianity were hypnotized to believe it, would that person be considered Christian?

**Steve:** Yes, Christians are some of the worst when it comes to apophenia,[3] especially with regard to their interpretations of the book of Revelation;[4] it's embarrassing.

I would argue that being hypnotized to believe something doesn't really count as believing it because there was no choice made. But it does bring up related fuzziness in terms of who can/will be held accountable for their beliefs (e.g., small children, the mentally disabled,

---

[2] Apophenia, *Wikipedia*, en.wikipedia.org/wiki/Apophenia.

[3] "Perceptions of religious imagery in natural phenomena," *Wikipedia*, en.wikipedia.org/wiki/
Perceptions_of_religious_imagery_in_natural_phenomena.

[4] "Barack Obama religion conspiracy theories: Claim that Obama is the Antichrist," *Wikipedia*, en.wikipedia.org/wiki/
Barack_Obama_religion_conspiracy_theories#Claim_that_Obama_is_the_Antichrist.

those with traumatic brain injuries, etc.) Some have tried to clarify these issues,[5] but they remain hard to deal with. Jesus seems to say, "Let me worry about it, not you:"

> *But the one who does not know and does things deserving punishment will be beaten with few blows. From everyone who has been given much, much will be demanded; and from the one who has been entrusted with much, much more will be asked.* (Lk 12:48)

**Victoria**: The thought of Obama being the Antichrist is laughable. When you speak of fuzziness and people trying to clarify those issues, are you referring to different stances and interpretations within Christianity? I can't remember the contexts in which we talked about it. It makes sense for humans not to worry about it; after all, we're not the judge.

**Steve**: Yeah, the whole "who gets to go to heaven in outlier circumstances" is a big problem for a lot of people. It bothers me a little, too, but I think that's more of my own "I want to know everything" attitude than a theological problem. But yes, some have tried to solve this problem with interpretations of how we are saved. If it's only God's prerogative, then it makes God look unfair. If it's human choice, then it becomes unclear what constitutes a choice. This is another reason why I think the truth lies somewhere in between.

**Victoria**: Why shouldn't it only be God's prerogative though? How does that make him look unfair?

**Steve**: Of course it is God's prerogative,

> *Then the LORD spoke to Job out of the storm: "Brace yourself like a man; I will question you, and you shall answer me. "Would you discredit my justice? Would you condemn me to justify yourself?* (Job 40:6–8)

> *Therefore God has mercy on whom he wants to have mercy, and he hardens whom he wants to harden. One of you will say to me: "Then why does God still blame us? For who is able to resist his will?" But who are you, a human being, to talk back to God? "Shall what is formed say to the one who formed it, 'Why did you make me like this?'" Does not the potter have the right to make out of the same lump of clay some pottery for special purposes and some for common use?* (Rom 9:18–21)

and many are comfortable with the fact that we are merely creatures whose creator may do with us whatever he pleases (I'm personally OK with that theology). However, the difficulty comes when trying to

---

[5] John MacArthur, "The 'Age of Accountability,'" *Grace to You*, www.gty.org/library/articles/A264/the-age-of-accountability.

balance that with other scripture that hints that God treats everyone equally:

> *"... that you may be children of your Father in heaven. He causes his sun to rise on the evil and the good, and sends rain on the righteous and the unrighteous."* (Mt 5:45)

> *For God does not show favoritism.* (Rom 2:11)

> *Then Peter began to speak: "I now realize how true it is that God does not show favoritism ...* (Acts 10:34)

So suppose a guy on a remote island lives and dies without possibly having access to knowledge of Jesus. There are two different ways that one might think of what happens to him. The first is the recognition that he is a sinner...

> *... for all have sinned and fall short of the glory of God, ...* (Rom 3:23)

and will receive God's wrath...

> *Put to death, therefore, whatever belongs to your earthly nature: sexual immorality, impurity, lust, evil desires and greed, which is idolatry. Because of these, the wrath of God is coming.* (Col 3:5–6)

as a just punishment; that is, God would clearly be justified in sending him to hell because he did not follow Christ:

> *Jesus answered, "I am the way and the truth and the life. No one comes to the Father except through me."* (Jn 14:6)

However, it would seem that God was unfair to that man in not giving him the same access to the saving gospel that I have. The second way to think of this hypothetical man is that even though he didn't have the ability to follow Christ to escape judgment, he could've had the ability to repent of his sinfulness in the context of an apparent creator and an innate moral compass:

> *For since the creation of the world God's invisible qualities—his eternal power and divine nature—have been clearly seen, being understood from what has been made, so that people are without excuse.* (Rom 1:20)

Thus, given God's mercy...

> *If we confess our sins, he is faithful and just and will forgive us our sins and purify us from all unrighteousness.* (1 Jn 1:9)

and fairness,

> *But the one who does not know and does things deserving punishment will be beaten with few blows. From everyone who has been given much, much will be demanded; and from the one who has been entrusted with much, much more will be asked.* (Lk 12:48)

God could allow him to enter heaven based on the fact that he did not outright reject him.

After writing all of that, I think I see for the first time what the debate is really about. Do we enter heaven because we accept Christ, or do we enter because we do not reject him? (And to be clear, rejecting him would include apathy…

> *Never be lacking in zeal, but keep your spiritual fervor, serving the Lord.* (Rom 12:11)

and denying his clear teachings of exclusivity,

> *Jesus answered, "I am the way and the truth and the life. No one comes to the Father except through me."* (Jn 14:6)

so it wouldn't let people with possible knowledge of him off the hook.) There are some verses that could lead to either interpretation:

> *Who is the liar? It is whoever denies that Jesus is the Christ. Such a person is the antichrist—denying the Father and the Son. No one who denies the Son has the Father; whoever acknowledges the Son has the Father also.* (1 Jn 2:22–23)

> *Whoever believes in the Son has eternal life, but whoever rejects the Son will not see life, for God's wrath remains on them.* (Jn 3:36)

I do wrestle with what the "correct" answer to that dilemma is. However, for me, it is infinitely more important that I *was* given access to the gospel—so what am I going to do with it?

**Victoria**: I see what you mean. Earlier when you said that his sole prerogative makes him look unfair, I had thought that it would be more fair than having multiple judges or a judge who wasn't omniscient, because that would mean his judgment is not uniform (like human judges' sentencing[6]).

So to the debate you raised, if rejection includes apathy and denying the teachings of exclusivity, is the question more so whether people enter heaven because they have accepted Christ or because they did not *knowingly* reject him? Related to your last sentence, it reminds me of the philosophical question of whether we're living in a computer simulation. Either way we can't do anything about it; we can only work with what we have.

**Steve**: Yes, I like your clarifying statement.

Yes, we can't do anything about it, but not in a defeatist sort of way. From my perspective, it's more like this is a better-than-you-could've-done-or-imagined sort of way.

### John 11:38–44

**Victoria**: I'm sure that must've been a pleasant sight.

**Steve**: This passage is great because the King James Version says, "he stinketh."

Verse 42 clears up a little about God's dealings with us. He didn't *need* to do most of the stuff he did, but he did it for our benefit. I think it can even relate to things like pain: we don't *need* it like we need food, but we get it for our own benefit:

> Not only so, but we also glory in our sufferings, because we know that suffering produces perseverance; perseverance, character; and character, hope. (Rom 5:3–4)

**Victoria**: That's funny!

Regarding our benefit from suffering, is that true only in mortal life? In other words, in hell, suffering would just be for suffering, and in heaven, one doesn't need suffering for perseverance, character, or hope?

**Steve**: Yes. (However, I wouldn't characterize hell as suffering for the sake of suffering. The suffering of hell is the result of willfully rejecting God.)

### John 11:45–57

**Victoria**: In John 11:51–52, the double meaning here is interesting.

**Steve**: Yes, the Bible is full of double prophecies like this.[7]

**Victoria**: Typological prophecy. That's a fancy phrase. Do you also study theology texts?

---

[6] Ben Bryant, "Judges are more lenient after taking a break, study finds," *The Guardian*, April 11, 2011, www.theguardian.com/law/2011/apr/11/judges-lenient-break.

[7] Hank Hanegraaff, "Typological Fulfillment: The Key to Messianic Prophecy," *Christian Research Journal*, **34** (4), 2011, www.equip.org/PDF/JAF1344.pdf.

**Steve**: Yes, but mostly as an amateur when I need help; I don't read too much in academic journals or anything. But the funny thing is that even though I don't know Greek vocabulary, learning the Greek alphabet through physics has allowed me to read/pronounce Greek, so I've taken an interest in looking at the untranslated New Testament. For example, this week I found out that the word "witnesses" here...

> *But you will receive power when the Holy Spirit comes on you; and you will be my witnesses in Jerusalem, and in all Judea and Samaria, and to the ends of the earth."* (Acts 1:8)

is actually μάρτυρες (martyres) from which we get our word "martyrs." The word is correctly translated as "witnesses," but it helped me to realize that the first-century Christians must have synonymized being a witness and being a martyr, which really changes how I view what Jesus was asking his disciples—and therefore, us—to do:

> *Then he said to them all: "Whoever wants to be my disciple must deny themselves and take up their cross daily and follow me."* (Lk 9:23)

> *They will put you out of the synagogue; in fact, the time is coming when anyone who kills you will think they are offering a service to God.* (Jn 16:2)

**Victoria**: That deeper level of understanding is neat.

# CHAPTER 30: JOHN 12

### JOHN 12:1-11

**Victoria**: This passage is also familiar to me from elsewhere. Did Lazarus end up getting killed?

**Steve**: We don't have any evidence that Lazarus was killed, but eventually dying twice was surely a strange experience.

Notice in verse 8 that Jesus sounds like a jerk. But it points again to the fact that Jesus' main message was not for us to be good, moral people, but rather to be worshipers of him (which, of course, should be evidenced through good deeds). Not understanding this is what has made Christianity judgmental and political in the minds of so many people (both Christians and non-Christians).

**Victoria**: Yeah, he does kind of sound like a jerk. I think that could be misinterpreted out of context to not care for the poor or to believe that Jesus is selfish. Is he saying that one should care for the poor because of, not instead of, caring about Jesus?

**Steve**: Well, it would be a huge mistake for us to say that we shouldn't help people because we're so busy worshiping Jesus or something like that. That idea is clearly condemned:[1]

> *Jesus replied, "And why do you break the command of God for the sake of your tradition? For God said, 'Honor your father and mother' and 'Anyone who curses their father or mother is to be put to death.' But you say that if anyone declares that what might have been used to help their father or mother is 'devoted to God,' they are not to 'honor their father or mother' with it. Thus you nullify the word of God for the sake of your tradition. You hypocrites! Isaiah was right when he prophesied about you: 'These people honor me with their lips, but their hearts are far from me. They worship me in vain; their teachings are merely human rules.'"* (Mt 15:3-9)

I think the difference is that as Jesus does not have a physical presence with us now, our worship consists of our thoughts, speech, and actions (such as helping the poor). But when he was physically present with them, performing a kind physical act toward him was the right thing to do.

**Victoria**: That seems a bit ambiguous regarding knowing what the right thing was at the time.

**Steve**: The right thing is always to worship Christ. But when he's not physically present, it doesn't make sense for me to physically bow down to him or anything, so worship must consist of other things.

---

[1] Lk 10:25-37.

## JOHN 12:12-19

**Victoria**: I don't have comments.

**Steve**: There's some good prophecy, history, and culture stuff in these verses explained here.[2] Essentially, Jesus came to bring peace, not war.

Also, this was only days before Jesus was crucified. Notice how many people followed him at this point. But most left when 1) the leaders finally and formally turned against him, and 2) it became apparent that he would not rule as an earthly king.

**Victoria**: Is he supposed to return again? Is that to rule as an earthly (universal?) king?

**Steve**: Yes, in a new/restored creation:

> Then I saw "a new heaven and a new earth," for the first heaven and the first earth had passed away, and there was no longer any sea. (Rev 21:1)

**Victoria**: There's no more sea?!

**Steve**: Ha ha, maybe. I wouldn't take it as a literal description, though. For example, this verse...

> The wall was built of jasper, and the city was made of pure gold, clear as crystal. (Rev 21:18)

talks about pure gold being clear, which is obviously not right (and was also obvious to people 2000 years ago). John's point isn't a literal description, but a big-picture understanding of a new place using metaphors for which we can gain few specifics.

## JOHN 12:20-36

**Victoria**: I'm not sure why verse 24 is worded the way it is; isn't death inevitable to man, anyway?

Verse 25 is quoted a lot.

Verse 28: What it must be like to be in that crowd and hear that...

**Steve**: Verse 24: Sure, everyone dies, but not everyone is a "kernel of wheat" capable of producing a crop. Some of us die producing nothing, or even worse, destruction.

Verse 25 is central to Christian belief. Jesus is claiming that if 80 years of comfort is our goal, we're in for a rude awakening, because it ultimately amounts to nothing.

Verse 28: Yeah, it's strange to me that not everyone heard the same thing. A similar thing happens here:

---

[2] "Why would a king ride a donkey instead of a warhorse (Zechariah 9:9-10)?" *Got Questions*, www.gotquestions.org/king-ride-donkey.html.

> *The men traveling with Saul stood there speechless; they heard the sound but did not see anyone.* (Acts 9:7)

Maybe it's some kind of metaphor for this verse we discussed earlier:

> *He said, "Go and tell this people: 'Be ever hearing, but never understanding; be ever seeing, but never perceiving.' Make the heart of this people calloused; make their ears dull and close their eyes. Otherwise they might see with their eyes, hear with their ears, understand with their hearts, and turn and be healed."* (Is 6:9–10)

**Victoria**: What does it mean to be a kernel of wheat in this context, then? Surely even those who produce good things in this life aren't literally dying to produce them?

With everyone not hearing the same thing, does that mean that some (those who heard) are more amenable to belief than others, perhaps because of the Holy Spirit?

**Steve**: Yes, not everyone is literally dying to further God's kingdom, but a "dying to self" is necessary.[3]

As to your last question, yeah, possibly. I've taken a real interest in this recently. I'm having weekly face-to-face discussions with an atheist friend of mine and have also listened to dozens of debates between Christians and atheists; it just seems that there's some kind of gap that's hard to overcome for the two sides to agree. It almost feels like it's a *willingness* (or lack thereof) more than a clear logical process. Could the Holy Spirit be a part of that? Sure.

**Victoria**: It makes a lot more sense when the meaning is not literally dying. I've heard that verse (verse 24) two other times this past week: at an IGSM thing and while reading *The Brothers Karamazov*.[4] It only now makes sense.

I agree that there must be willingness involved and not just logic. Ah! It's like that book you lent me.[5] Francis Collins was talking about miracles in terms of Bayes' theorem.[6] Anyone who has a prior probability of zero will certainly have a posterior probability of zero. So even if the chain of logic is laid out, it can be disregarded, interpreted differently, etc. But the willingness can certainly be nudged by human influences.

---

[3] "Dying to Self," *Open Bible*, www.openbible.info/topics/dying_to_self.

[4] Fyodor Dostoevsky, *The Brothers Karamazov* (New York: Farrar, Straus and Giroux, 2002).

[5] Francis Collins, *The Language of God* (New York: Free Press, 2007).

[6] "Bayes' theorem," *Wikipedia*, en.wikipedia.org/wiki/Bayes'_theorem. Bayes's theorem predicts the probability of an event based on prior knowledge.

**Steve**: Well said! This whole thing is such a strange mixture of reason, logic, emotion, science, subjective experience, and human will, and the latter is summed up here:

> *"Ask and it will be given to you; seek and you will find; knock and the door will be opened to you."* (Mt 7:7)

That is, if you don't look for it, you won't see it. Of course, the atheist response is that that leads to the problem of seeing things that aren't there,[7] but I see the reason/logic side of Christianity as balancing that out.

### JOHN 12:37-50

**Victoria**: Verse 42: Does that mean the Pharisee leaders who *did* believe in him would still be saved?

**Steve**: Yes, although this verse complicates it:

> *Whoever is ashamed of me and my words, the Son of Man will be ashamed of them when he comes in his glory and in the glory of the Father and of the holy angels.* (Lk 9:26)

This is the importance of baptism, for example: it's a public display of one's faith, because real faith should not be hidden:

> *"You are the light of the world. A town built on a hill cannot be hidden. Neither do people light a lamp and put it under a bowl. Instead they put it on its stand, and it gives light to everyone in the house. In the same way, let your light shine before others, that they may see your good deeds and glorify your Father in heaven.* (Mt 5:14–16)

So while these verses are saying that it's troubling that some believers would not go public, I don't think it's saying they weren't saved, especially given the story of Peter a few days later;[8] he was clearly saved:

> *And I tell you that you are Peter, and on this rock I will build my church, and the gates of Hades will not overcome it.* (Mt 16:18)

**Victoria**: Okay, that's good to know. So hiding faith is not good, but the outcome is the same anyway (in being saved), even though the finer details of the outcome will differ?

**Steve**: Yes.

---

[7] "Pareidolia," *Wikipedia*, en.wikipedia.org/wiki/Pareidolia.
[8] Lk 22:54–62.

**Victoria**: So then if one's goal is just to be saved, but at like a passing grade and not being top of the class, then what's to prevent that person to just live for himself?

**Steve**: I would argue that if one's goal is just to be saved and/or live for oneself, one may not be saved at all. Christianity is entirely Christ-centered, so it's sort of a contradiction in terms to be a Christian and have oneself at the center. However, there's still a difference between "living for yourself" and, for example, being too timid, anxious, or uncertain to share the gospel with anyone else or make your faith public. There's a lot of room for continuous personal failure in Christianity, but not of the proud, stubborn, or self-centered variety.

# CHAPTER 31: JOHN 13

### JOHN 13:1-17

**Victoria**: The way verse 2 is worded almost makes me sympathetic toward Judas since he was a victim of the devil's prompting. It seems that any of the other disciples could have been Jesus' betrayer. Did Jesus originally invite Judas into his discipleship knowing that he was going to be betrayed in such a manner?

I found this in verse 8 interesting: "Unless I wash you, you have no part with me."

**Steve**: You just hit on two of the most debated topics in Christianity: 1) How responsible are we for our own sin, given all of the other factors at play (e.g., environment, upbringing, incomplete knowledge, genetics, God, Satan, etc.)? 2) What did Jesus know as a man? The "good enough" answers that we get by with are 1) it's obviously complicated, but our willingness to commit sin at all makes us responsible, and 2) we can only guess based on the things he said and did in the same way we do for anyone. In short, we have no clue. That being said, I would argue that since this was God's plan all along,

> *All inhabitants of the earth will worship the beast—all whose names have not been written in the Lamb's book of life, the Lamb who was slain from the creation of the world.* (Rev 13:8)

none of this was just happenstance, but that God in his sovereignty laid things out in conjunction with Judas' free will to choose:

> *And he is not served by human hands, as if he needed anything. Rather, he himself gives everyone life and breath and everything else. From one man he made all the nations, that they should inhabit the whole earth; and he marked out their appointed times in history and the boundaries of their lands. God did this so that they would seek him and perhaps reach out for him and find him, though he is not far from any one of us.* (Acts 17:25-27)

I understand your sympathy, but that's a slippery slope to go down, even from a secular point of view, because I imagine we could excuse any behavior by focusing on external causes.

As far as the washing part, yes, it is a very interesting statement. Jesus is speaking to those who believe themselves to be unworthy of him and saying that it's just as bad as believing that we are *too* worthy of him. In other words, he just calls us to accept what he did for us with no strings attached.

### JOHN 13:18-30

**Victoria**: Why wouldn't Judas just cancel his plans once he was publicly revealed by Jesus?

**Steve**: This is human nature. The same could be said for any number of things we do that hurt ourselves or others that could've been nipped in the bud like adultery, drug abuse, etc. This is the focus of Rev 16 as well (lots of metaphors) in which God continually sends judgment, and instead of it making people turn back to him, it makes them hate and rebel against him even more.

### JOHN 13:31-38

**Victoria**: Verses 31-32 are worded confusingly.

**Steve**: I agree; here's a better "plain English" translation:

> When he had left, Jesus said, "Now the Son of Man is seen for who he is, and God seen for who he is in him. The moment God is seen in him, God's glory will be on display. In glorifying him, he himself is glorified—glory all around! (Jn 13:31–32, MSG)

It was just a way of saying, "Here we go; it's time for all this to come to its climax and purpose."

**Victoria**: Verse 34: Why wasn't "love one another" a command before Jesus came?

**Steve**: It was:

> "Do not seek revenge or bear a grudge against anyone among your people, but love your neighbor as yourself. I am the LORD." (Lev 19:18)

> The foreigner residing among you must be treated as your native-born. Love them as yourself, for you were foreigners in Egypt. I am the LORD your God. (Lev 19:34)

However, in the Old Testament, God's followers were bound to each other already by a common race, heritage, ethnicity, history, and law. In the New Testament, you have people who have little to no commonality (and often hostility)...

> Utterly amazed, they asked: "Aren't all these who are speaking Galileans? Then how is it that each of us hears them in our native language? Parthians, Medes and Elamites; residents of Mesopotamia, Judea and Cappadocia, Pontus and Asia, Phrygia and Pamphylia, Egypt and the parts of Libya near Cyrene; visitors from Rome (both Jews and converts to Judaism); Cretans and Arabs—we hear them declaring the wonders of God in our own tongues!" (Acts 2:7–11)

having to get along with each other; the main Christian interpersonal ethic then becomes love rather than externalities.

[To the reader from Steve: You may have picked up on the fact that the last couple of chapters have been terser than usual. The busyness of life, work, and school caught up with us, and we were both feeling burned out. Thus, our Bible study was put on hiatus here for a considerable time. In that period, however, Victoria made the decision to follow Christ, which was completely unexpected to me. I had not felt that I was very successful in convincing her of much, so I was overjoyed to hear this news. (It's also strong evidence that human arguments can only go so far in leading someone to Jesus.) There was much celebration outside of this text.[1] Victoria has humbly requested that she not be the focus of this book, but this was unbelievably great news to me.]

---

[1] Lk 15:10.

# CHAPTER 32: JOHN 14

## JOHN 14:1–14

**Victoria**: I've heard verse 2 often. There are many rooms. I guess this might mean "unlimited" rooms, since God is infinite? Also, what is he needing to prepare? Does God actually need to prepare things, or is this a figure of speech?

Verse 12: I understand the first half, but how would one do "greater works than [Jesus]" given that he is one with the most-high God?

Verse 14: This is where prayer comes in? Though when I read things like this, I'm skeptical since not everything asked for in God's name will be granted (not that it should be, but the phrasing of "anything" implies it would be).

**Steve**: This reminds me of Hilbert's paradox,[1] but it's mostly a reference to Jewish wedding customs. In congruence with other Jesus/church wedding analogies,[2] Jesus is referring to the common practice of a son building an extra room onto his father's house for he and his bride and eventual family to live in rather than moving away. This required him to leave his fiancée for a little while to do the construction. So he's saying that he's going to disappear but won't forget about us. Literally, he's pointing to his death, resurrection, and ascension, and our eternal life with and through him. I mean, he was a craftsman, so maybe he's just been up there building rooms this whole time, ha ha! But yes, it's a figure of speech.

Inserting a little here, we did talk about it some earlier, but when Jesus says in verse 6 that he is "the way and the truth and the life," it reminds me of the strange grammar that is sometimes used to convey a really important point, such as:

> For to me, to live is Christ and to die is gain. (Phil 1:21)

> We know also that the Son of God has come and has given us understanding, so that we may know him who is true. And we are in him who is true by being in his Son Jesus Christ. He is the true God and eternal life. (1 Jn 5:20)

When we're trying to talk someone up, we say that they *have* certain positive traits, not that they *are* those positive traits. I just love that Jesus ramps it up a notch in this way. For example, instead of just telling the truth, he *is* the truth, the standard by which all things are measured.

---

[1] "Hilbert's paradox of the Grand Hotel," *Wikipedia*, en.wikipedia.org/wiki/Hilbert%27s_paradox_of_the_Grand_Hotel.
[2] Mk 2:19, Rev 19:7–9, Mt 25:1–13, Eph 5:22–25.

And instead of running after a great, promising life that Jesus offers, I'm running after *him*. These are completely different concepts from our traditional way of viewing God. Beautiful.

I love that you asked about verse 12, because I just heard a great explanation of it recently (but I don't remember who said it). Out of all the miracles (including creation itself) that Jesus performed, there is not a greater miracle than the transformation of a free, rebellious heart into a God-seeking one. When a person does that (of course, with God's sovereign direction), he or she is doing something far greater and more impossible than turning water into wine. On a more practical note, I've also heard this verse explained in terms of the small numbers of people that Jesus brought to himself while on earth vs. the large numbers that his followers have led to him since then, and that he was basically foreshadowing Christian evangelism:

> But you will receive power when the Holy Spirit comes on you; and you will be my witnesses in Jerusalem, and in all Judea and Samaria, and to the ends of the earth." (Acts 1:8)

In verse 14, that "in my name" phrase can be tricky. I grew up ending all of my prayers with "In Jesus' name I pray. Amen." A few years ago, I realized it was just a thing I said without any meaning behind it, so I stopped (and had a guy yell at me for not saying it after I prayed for him). In fact, I felt I was taking God's name in vain:

> "You shall not misuse the name of the LORD your God, for the LORD will not hold anyone guiltless who misuses his name." (Ex 20:7)

So I absolutely do not think that praying in God's name is akin to some magic formula that gets you whatever you want. Rather, it's a way of saying that God and I are on the same page and are walking alongside each other in agreement. It's like this verse:

> Take delight in the LORD, and he will give you the desires of your heart.
> (Ps 37:4)

It's a self-fulfilling prophecy, because if you take delight in God, then you have already gotten the desire of your heart: contentment, meaning, purpose, and joy. A Lamborghini just isn't going to do the job. So the point is that if you ask for something in Jesus' name, you will be doing it 1) in hope of the best overall eternal outcome, and 2) in the knowledge that he is king and that however he answers your prayer is going to be the best way, thereby giving you what you asked for. In other words, it's not a prayer to make things happen a certain way, but rather a prayer of humble submission to his better way, whence we find real joy.

**Victoria**: Your point about verse 6 reminds me about Plato's concept of Forms (we discussed this some in Chapter 5). For example, quoting Wikipedia on platonic idealism, "A Tree is the ideal that each of us holds that allows us to identify the imperfect reflections of trees all around us."[3] So while people can exemplify goodness or truthfulness, we're imperfect reflections of Jesus, who *is* goodness and truth.

On verse 12, why is "the transformation of a free, rebellious heart into a God-seeking one" the greatest miracle? It seems almost ordinary. Does it relate to how humans have free will, so God doesn't force us to believe, whereas he can make other things happen?

Regarding verse 14, that's a good interpretation. With the right priorities, you already have what you ultimately want. I heard a message recently on why God doesn't answer prayers, and one response was that the prayers may reflect idols of the heart. When you want something really, really badly, you can lose sight of everything else. Recently, for me, that was career advancement. I was desperate to land a job and leave grad school. The day before my (one and only) job interview, I was tense and high-strung. But I came to accept that if I didn't get the job, I would still be okay, and I could only try and follow where God leads me. This realization gave me peace and contentment, and, well, it worked out in the end.

**Steve**: Regarding the miraculousness of transforming a person's heart, water does not have a will to resist being transformed into wine. Leprosy does not have a will to resist being healed. (I mean, *Mycobacterium leprae* are working to stay alive in some sense, but it would be a stretch to say they *want* to stay alive.) This is in complete contrast to what the Bible says about us:

> *All have turned away, all have become corrupt; there is no one who does good, not even one.* (Ps 14:3)

So, yes, there are two going-in-opposite-directions intentions here that get reconciled: the love of God and the free will of humans. (Of course, the Calvinist perspective is that God manipulates the will of humans with the same ease in which he turned water into wine. I don't disagree that he *can*, but I disagree that he *does*; I see it more as a leading rather than a pushing.)

Your last paragraph is beautiful. Dallas Willard defines joy as "a pervasive and constant sense of wellbeing,"[4] and that's what you chose to have instead of living in tension. And wow, what a change I see in you from the beginning of our discussion! Think about this: by believing in the Son, the Holy Spirit led you to live in the trust of the Father in the

---

[3] "Platonic idealism," *Wikipedia*, en.wikipedia.org/wiki/Platonic_idealism.

[4] "Willard Words," *Dallas Willard*, old.dwillard.org/resources/WillardWords.asp.

face of a nebulous future. That turned into a real chemical reaction in your brain that made you feel better and gain a different perspective, irrespective of your external circumstances. That positive reinforcement plan (to be clear: even if you had not gotten the job) is the incredible work of God to get you to understand what he's about, and it's only the beginning.

**Victoria:** ☺

### JOHN 14:15–31

**Victoria:** Verse 21: How is Jesus showing himself to those who keep his commands? Maybe related to his response to Judas' question (verse 22). Is he saying that they are coming not physically, but in spirit?

Verse 26: How does the Holy Spirit remind people of the teachings? I feel like these reminders are external, from reading the Bible, attending church services, etc.

Verse 27: That's comforting. The world is crazy.

Verse 30: I'm wondering about the word choice here. The NIV (New International Version) says that "the prince of this world is coming," but that's confusing, since isn't prince below king, and wouldn't God be the king? The ESV (English Standard Version) says that "the ruler of this world is coming," which makes more sense to me.

**Steve:** First, notice that Jesus says that we will receive this "advocate" to help us, be with us, live with us, be in us, adopt us, teach us, and remind us of his words. Think about why someone would say those types of things to anyone; both Jesus and the disciples must have felt that the latter needed help, spiritual fulfillment, companionship, teaching, and reminders. (Some of the most repeated phrases in the Bible are "Do not fear" and "I am with you," so God must know that we are constantly in fear and feeling like he's not around.) Now, if those are roles of the Holy Spirit, I need them to work in my mind, not just in my body or the external world. For example, suppose you had two options for the rest of your life: joy + disease vs. depression + health. Maybe I'm alone in this, but I'd much rather have the first, in that I believe I *am* my mind more than I *am* my body (e.g., I could lose a leg and still be the same "me," although of course I will have a body in eternity,[5] and it and the external world are present checks on my mind to make sure it's conforming with reality). Or consider whether you would rather have a country where everyone's mind was right (i.e., rational, moral, compassionate, etc.) or whether all the laws and penalties were right. That's a no-brainer, right? (I guess that's ironic, given that we would choose the brain option.) Now suppose you're a disciple and you follow this guy Jesus around for three years, everything's great (at least in terms of purpose), and then he's gone. Do you want to just continue in his external system (e.g., preaching, miracles, relationships, etc.), or do

---

[5] 1 Cor 15.

you want what he had *in his mind and heart* for yourself? It's clearly the latter: enter the Holy Spirit.

So in verse 21, the continuation of Jesus takes the form of an inward presence of God in the believer, and it is the Holy Spirit's influence in our lives that allows us to be like Jesus at all. From a naturalistic perspective, we are just the most highly evolved beasts, and there's plenty of evidence that we tend to act that way. But if I obey a command of Jesus (e.g., love my enemy), I am moving off the naturalistic path onto a spiritual one, and I am getting a glimpse of what it's like to be Jesus (i.e., he is showing himself to me).

In verse 26, my unsatisfactory (and only) answer is that God must be able to work in us in subtle, undetectable ways. Now, it doesn't *always* have to be that way, such as in the case where we started this discussion, you were invited to a Bible study, and you began having discussions with your Christian advisor all at the same time. There are too many coincidences going on there to claim any kind of subtlety. But if God wants to (sometimes slowly) reveal himself in one's life through seemingly mundane processes like Bible reading, attending church, rational thinking, etc., that seems to be in complete congruence with his supernatural creation of a very natural world. I imagine that if I put a mouse in my house and my cat later killed it, my cat would think that something completely natural just happened, because my cat doesn't understand my will or intentionality. Besides that, there are too many impossible-to-answer questions to claim that there are no supernatural forces acting in my life. Would I have started reading the Bible on my own? Would I have gone to church on my own? Would I have begun asking myself deep questions on my own? We just don't have enough information to definitively state one way or the other. An atheist would generally use Occam's Razor[6] to say that the natural, godless explanation is a simpler—and thus, more favorable—explanation, and it just might be for any given event. But that type of thinking creates at the onset far more uncertainty and complexity just in terms of how an atheist with no free will—and thus, no alternative-choosing ability— could even use Occam's Razor. And to counter an obvious argument, our belief that the Holy Spirit uses seemingly natural processes to remind us of Jesus' teachings is not a leap of faith, but rather a consequence of the more established fact that most people aren't following Jesus' teaching by default; i.e., when we do follow them, we must have been reminded of them. This has been a long, rambling way of saying I need to have enough humility to believe that an infinite God doesn't have to conform to my ideas of how forthright he should be.

As for verse 27, this is still related to the Holy Spirit. When Jesus said this,

---

[6] In essence, Occam's Razor says that given many explanatory alternatives, the simplest is preferred.

*Blessed are the peacemakers, for they will be called children of God.* (Mt 5:9)

it was predicated on this:

*The mind governed by the flesh is death, but the mind governed by the Spirit is life and peace.* (Rom 8:6)

That is, just like one can't give money unless one has money, one can't make peace unless one has peace. Peace treaties and pacts and marches are only as good as the people who create them, and that's a very low bar considering the Bible's opinion of human goodness. What we lack from our current leaders and the leaders of all kinds of movements is the inner peace that has actually produced positive change in the past:

"In the midst of outer dangers, I have felt an inner calm and known resources of strength that only God could give. In many instances I have felt the power of God transforming the fatigue of despair into the buoyancy of hope."[7]

Regarding verse 30, Paul later goes farther than "prince:"

*The god of this age has blinded the minds of unbelievers, so that they cannot see the light of the gospel that displays the glory of Christ, who is the image of God.* (2 Cor 4:4)

The most common thought is that these types of descriptions are simply referring to Satan having significant influence in the world. There are other passages in which idols and even humans (as discussed briefly earlier regarding Jn 10:34) are called gods in the same manner (as simply a way of expressing real or perceived authority):

*"You shall have no other gods before me."* (Ex 20:3)

*"I said, 'You are "gods"; you are all sons of the Most High.'"* (Ps 82:6)

The unequivocal conclusion of the rest of scripture is that God is the only real king/ruler/god, without equal or chance of being overthrown. Some take the heretical positions of saying that Satan "is a spirit son of

---

[7] Martin Luther King and James M. Washington, *A Testament of Hope: The Essential Writings and Speeches* (New York: HarperOne, 2003).

God,"[8] and "Jesus was Lucifer's older brother."[9] I don't use the word "heretical" lightly, and believe that equating Jesus, the creator of all things,

> *The Son is the image of the invisible God, the firstborn over all creation. For in him all things were created: things in heaven and on earth, visible and invisible, whether thrones or powers or rulers or authorities; all things have been created through him and for him.* (Col 1:15–16)

> *So then, about eating food sacrificed to idols: We know that "An idol is nothing at all in the world" and that "There is no God but one." For even if there are so-called gods, whether in heaven or on earth (as indeed there are many "gods" and many "lords"), yet for us there is but one God, the Father, from whom all things came and for whom we live; and there is but one Lord, Jesus Christ, through whom all things came and through whom we live.* (1 Cor 8:4–6)

with Satan (by inference a created being), is enough to disqualify one from calling oneself a Christian. The divinity and supremacy of Christ are non-negotiable tenets of Christianity. (In the latter passage, Paul is most likely referring to the polytheism or Caesar cult[10] of his time.)

**Victoria**: It's encouraging how often the Bible repeats "Do not fear" and "I am with you." To use your statement of moving off a naturalistic path and onto a spiritual one, I think even trusting in the Holy Spirit is moving toward the spiritual path, given the strong internal concept we have of "seeing is believing." Otherwise, if we fed into our fears that God isn't around, then it would feel as if our prayers were going off into the void unheard, leading to fewer prayers and less trust in God, tendencies toward atheism/deism, etc.

Regarding verse 26, maybe the Holy Spirit also has influence on one's conscience and sense of morality? I agree with your last sentence about God working in ways beyond human understanding. On your point about Occam's Razor, can't said atheist still have free will?

On verse 30, wow, I did not grasp this at all before. 2 Cor 4:4 which you referenced also seems appropriate for the distractions of modern

---

[8] "Satan," *The Church of Jesus Christ of Latter-day Saints*, www.churchofjesuschrist.org/study/manual/gospel-topics/satan?lang=eng.
[9] "How can Jesus and Lucifer be spirit brothers when their characters and purposes are so utterly opposed?" *The Church of Jesus Christ of Latter-day Saints*, www.churchofjesuschrist.org/study/ensign/1986/06/i-have-a-question/how-can-jesus-and-lucifer-be-spirit-brothers-when-their-characters-and-purposes-are-so-utterly-opposed?lang=eng.
[10] "Imperial cult of ancient Rome," *Wikipedia*, en.wikipedia.org/wiki/Imperial_cult_of_ancient_Rome.

times (e.g., social media, Netflix) making the gospel seem unnecessary or irrelevant. With the understanding that this "prince" refers to Satan, why is verse 31 worded the way it is? In other words, why is Satan's presence meant to show the world that Jesus loves and obeys the Father? Also, wasn't Satan already around?

**Steve**: Yes, the Holy Spirit definitely interacts with our conscience and sense of morality, but I wouldn't say that's detectable in any way except in perhaps one's own reflection on how they might otherwise have chosen before. So again, it falls into the category of intimate personal experience that is hard to prove to anyone.

Yes, I believe that atheists have free will just like everyone else. The problem is that there is no naturalistic explanation—and probably no *possible* naturalistic explanation—that allows for such a thing. Hence, freely chosen arguments for atheism must borrow from supernaturalism.[11] Or to put it another way, for an atheist to choose the simpler alternative of atheism, he/she must reject atheism. (This does assume that atheism and naturalism go hand-in-hand. I *have* heard some atheists claim to be Platonists instead of naturalists to allow for things like objective morality, but that makes very little sense to me.)

As for verse 31, it falls into the category of "God lets bad things happen for a greater good":

> "You intended to harm me, but God intended it for good to accomplish what is now being done, the saving of many lives." (Gen 50:20)

Satan is mentioned explicitly by Paul as actually helping him and others out in the long-term:

> Therefore, in order to keep me from becoming conceited, I was given a thorn in my flesh, a messenger of Satan, to torment me. (2 Cor 12:7)

> ... hand this man over to Satan for the destruction of the flesh, so that his spirit may be saved on the day of the Lord. (1 Cor 5:5)

It's also abundantly clear that Satan played a huge role in the fall of humans,

> Then the LORD God said to the woman, "What is this you have done?" The woman said, "The serpent[12] deceived me, and I ate." (Gen 3:13)

which necessitated the crucifixion of Christ, which Satan also played a role in:

---

[11] Frank Turek, *Stealing from God: Why Atheists Need God to Make Their Case* (Colorado Springs, CO: NavPress, 2015).
[12] Rev 12:9, 20:2.

*As soon as Judas took the bread, Satan entered into him. So Jesus told him, "What you are about to do, do quickly." (Jn 13:27)*

Thus, in the end, Satan's curse on us ended up being our blessing, much like what is seen in the book of Job. So there's some kind of strange thing going on in which Satan is simultaneously destroying the world and being used by God for God's better purposes. He's like a tragic, pitiful Shakespearean character or something.

Given all of that, yes, Satan did a great job of revealing the character and commitment of Jesus (which we can see explicitly in his temptations in the desert in Mt 4:1–11). And, yes, he's been doing that for a long, long time.

In fact, I don't think I ever told you this, but I experienced a pretty scary thing once that's related to this discussion. When I was going through the severe depression I told you about earlier, I had frequent panic attacks: heart-pounding, nerve-tingling, sweat-inducing panic attacks several times a week. On one particular day, I had another, but I had gotten so used to them that I knew how to deal with them: I went outside near my lab and laid in the grass, closed my eyes, and tried to relax. On that day, no one was within 200 yards of me except some birds, so it was very quiet. After a minute or so, I heard an audible, distinct, clear-as-day voice say, "It's time to die." It was a male American accent with the contraction in a normal conversational tone, just like that. I shot up, expecting to see either an ax murderer or someone playing a trick on me, but there was no one: just the birds again. I ran inside and tried to process what just happened. It seemed unlikely that I was going crazy, because I had been able, before and after, to externally carry on with my normal grad school duties and family and church life, and I had never before or after heard such a thing. So, I reasoned that I must've heard some supernatural voice. Now, it was and is the scariest thing that ever happened to me; it was in no way a comfort. It felt very demonic and still does. But over the years, I've put it in the context of what Jesus said:

*Very truly I tell you, unless a kernel of wheat falls to the ground and dies, it remains only a single seed. But if it dies, it produces many seeds. (Jn 12:24)*

*For whoever would save his life will lose it, but whoever loses his life for my sake will find it. (Mt 16:25)*

Looking back at that moment, it was absolute rock-bottom for me, but Jesus was getting ready to change me in so many ways even up to the moment I write these words. It *was* time for me to die, and so much of me has died since then for the glory of God. I know all of this sounds completely bonkers, and no one is more skeptical of it than me. But it happened, and I believe God used Satan to change me for the better.

**Victoria**: Ah, the free will concept goes back to one of the original topics of this whole conversation.

With Satan's role in "original sin," it seems that if he never existed, none of this would have to occur: God using (repurposing?) Satan's works for the greater good, the inherent sin of humans, and Jesus being crucified. From that thought, it seems like the world could have gone very differently in which humans were never separated from God. That seems preferable. But I suppose if our current reality was "all part of the plan," it better fits with the idea that "God lets bad things happen for a greater good"; however, that assumes that the net good of this life is greater than the net good if humans were never separated from God. That inequality for me is hard to believe from just my own perspective of what is good, but I suppose I could see it hold in light of what we talked about in the discussion for Jn 14:1–14 (about there being no greater miracle than repentance and the transformation of the heart).

That sounds like a terrifying experience! What doesn't kill you makes you stronger ... literally. I'm intrigued by some of the unanswerable questions surrounding that experience, like how close you may have come to death. That reminds me, doesn't the Bible say something about God not giving you more than you can handle? Maybe that incident had just the right amount of influence to leave a mark on and change your life?

**Steve**: If we start with the assumption that God is omnibenevolent (and I do think we have some good experiential and scriptural reasons to believe so), then we have to come to the conclusion that this world is the best of all possible worlds. That is, despite all the evil, tragedy, and despair we experience and see around us, there is something about God and us freely choosing each other through the suffering—especially in the context of him having entered the suffering with us—that represents the pinnacle of what life can be. I think there are three possible worlds: 1) the one we live in, in which sin and suffering are real but purposeful, 2) the one you mentioned in which sin and suffering (and by extension, free will) were eliminated, and 3) one in which suffering is real but has no purpose. As for World 2, I can't claim to have suffered as much as many others, but I can say that I would rather knowingly suffer, reflect on it, and come out for the better (either here or in eternity) than be something like an animal which doesn't really have the ability to process such a thing. In other words, it's not hard for me to see that bad things can lead to better things, whether by human choice, natural consequence, or Satan's influence. Admittedly, that "better world" is sometimes hidden in a still-terrible world. For example, the inhumanity of the fighting in World War I led to, in some respects, more humane fighting in World War II (e.g., no chemical warfare), even though World War II was one of the worst events in human history. As for World 3, it's simply an alternative explanation we have in our heads for what we see around us, and we have to decide if we embrace it or not.

> His interest quickened when, in a more emphatic tone, the preacher said that there were some things we could grasp as touching God, and others we could not. There was no doubt as to the existence of good and evil and, as a rule, it was easy to see the difference between them. The difficulty began when we looked into the nature of evil, and among things evil he included human suffering. Thus we had apparently needful pain, and apparently needless pain; we had Don Juan cast into hell, and a child's death. For while it is right that a libertine should be struck down, we see no reason for a child's suffering. And, truth to tell, nothing was more important on earth than a child's suffering, the horror it inspires in us, and the reason we must find to account for it. In other manifestations of life God made things easy for us and, thus far, our religion had no merit. But in this respect He put us, so to speak, with our backs to the wall. Indeed, we all were up against the wall that plague had built around us, and in its lethal shadow we must work out our salvation. He, Father Paneloux, refused to have recourse to simple devices enabling him to scale that wall. Thus he might easily have assured them that the child's sufferings would be compensated for by an eternity of bliss awaiting him. But how could he give that assurance when, to tell the truth, he knew nothing about it? For who would dare to assert that eternal happiness can compensate for a single moment's human suffering? He who asserted that would not be a true Christian, a follower of the Master who knew all the pangs of suffering in his body and his soul. No, he, Father Paneloux, would keep faith with that great symbol of all suffering, the tortured body on the Cross; he would stand fast, his back to the wall and face honestly the terrible problem of a child's agony. And he would boldly say to those who listened to his words today: "My brother, a time of testing has come for us all. We must believe everything or deny everything. And who among you, I ask, would dare to deny everything?"[13]

In other words, Camus is putting this choice before us: will we see this world as a net good ("believe everything") or not ("deny everything")? I think one's answer to that question determines a lot about one's entire worldview. In practical terms, Camus, an atheist, believed that for the Christian to fight against suffering was to fight against God, because God has willed for suffering to be. But I believe the Christian perspective is quite different than that: this is the best of all possible worlds because God has given us the ability to fight suffering along with him. It allows

---

[13] Albert Camus, *The Plague* (New York: Vintage, 1991).

us to live in a dynamic, relational, purposeful world that wouldn't exist if we were sinless automatons. And even heaven will not be a static, meaningless world, because it will be filled with people who have chosen God through the messiness of this one. We will forever understand the wonderful love of God through the terrible cross of Christ.

Yes, the Bible says the following (where "temptation" and "tempted" can also be translated as "testing" and "tested"):

> *No temptation has overtaken you except what is common to mankind. And God is faithful; he will not let you be tempted beyond what you can bear. But when you are tempted, he will also provide a way out so that you can endure it.* (1 Cor 10:13)

That's always been an ambiguous verse to me, because I'm not sure what the alternative would look like (i.e., how I could be tempted beyond my endurance?). But in the context of what we've been talking about, if there really is a spiritual battle of good and evil going on outside of our normal senses, I suppose it's reasonable to think that God is somehow holding back the evil out to get me.

**Victoria:** Why does World 2 have to lack free will? Is there not a possible world in which we have free will *and* no sin? While humans have free will to do good or bad things, I thought free will was a separate concept from sin. Or are you saying that with free will, sin inevitably results (but also, what if Satan never existed)?

Thinking about Camus' question, to deny everything seems more delusional and, well, in denial. So if to fight suffering with God leads to greater net good in the World 1 that we live in, then that seems generally preferable.

**Steve:** Yes, free will is a separate concept from sin, so I do mean the latter: namely, that free will inevitably begets sin in this life. Many would say that Satan himself was caught in the same trap as us, in that he freely chose to rebel against God. I'm not one to blame Satan for all my problems, so I'm not going to say that it's all his fault that I'm messed up. In fact, "satan" is just the Hebrew noun שָׂטָן, which means "accuser" or "adversary" and doesn't have to apply to a specific being we call Satan.[14] (This makes some people believe that Satan doesn't exist as an individual but that the word rather refers to some sort of general opposition to believers. I disagree with that stance because of the way Jesus and others refer to him.[15]) In our case, the evolutionary instinct for selfishness (and sin in general) seems hardwired (not in the sense that it can't be overcome, just that it's our default behavior). I do think free will remains in a sinless heaven/new earth, but it works because

---

[14] "Satan," *Wikipedia*, en.wikipedia.org/wiki/Satan.
[15] Lk 10:18, Lk 22:31, Job 1:6–2:7.

we are able to finally see the outcomes of our choices. Right now, sin often seems like the better option, but one day we will see more clearly:

> *For now we see only a reflection as in a mirror; then we shall see face to face. Now I know in part; then I shall know fully, even as I am fully known.* (1 Cor 13:12)

**Victoria**: So to summarize, we live in a world in which sin and suffering exist purposefully (or so we choose to believe). Lack of sin and suffering would also mean lack of free will (in this world), but it is achievable beyond this world once we realize the weight of what we do. I suppose that means the full realization leads to our rewiring of sorts so that we don't default to sin anymore.

**Steve**: Yes, as long as we acknowledge that the word "purposefully" leads to tomes on God's sovereignty and interaction with the world.

**Victoria**: Ha!

# CHAPTER 33: JOHN 15

### JOHN 15:1-17

**Victoria:** I like the general message of this passage, and it seems to be one of the more commonly known/discussed parts of the Bible. In verse 2, what does it mean practically to be a vine which has been cut off? Does verse 4 point to the necessity of the church community? Regarding verses 9, 10, and 12: someone asked me recently what it meant to follow God, and I think these verses address it well. In verse 16, is Jesus saying this to them specifically, or is he saying that none of his followers choose him? This is similar to our discussion earlier on how people come to realize God.

**Steve:** Looking back through John, Jesus first establishes his authority with teaching and miracles. Then, once his disciples are firmly on board, he pulls back the curtain as to what's going on inside them before moving more toward daily Christian living. That's where we are now. This fruit analogy is great because it gives us the ability to have assurance and confidence in a couple of ways. 1) How do I *know* I'm in fellowship with Jesus? By the fruit I produce. Paul makes the distinction clear:

> *The acts of the flesh are obvious: sexual immorality, impurity and debauchery; idolatry and witchcraft; hatred, discord, jealousy, fits of rage, selfish ambition, dissensions, factions and envy; drunkenness, orgies, and the like. I warn you, as I did before, that those who live like this will not inherit the kingdom of God. But the fruit of the Spirit is love, joy, peace, forbearance, kindness, goodness, faithfulness, gentleness and self-control. Against such things there is no law.* (Gal 5:19–23)

In this perspective, there are three things expected from a vine: deadly fruit,[1] no fruit, or succulent fruit. Jesus is saying that good grapes don't just happen; they come from a vine, and he's that vine. Is it possible for a grape to exist apart from the vine (e.g., is it possible for a non-Christian to be kind)? Yes, of course, but this is more a statement to Christians on how to continue to produce good fruit: stay with the vine. When our continual walk with the Spirit produces both positive inner feelings and outward actions, it is direct evidence of a healthy relationship with Jesus. 2) The vine delivers the nutrients to the branches and fruit, so the pressure is on the former, not the latter. One of the beautiful teachings of Jesus is the idea of giving us rest (i.e., taking our burdens upon himself):

---

[1] 2 Kings 4:39–40.

*"Come to me, all you who are weary and burdened, and I will give you rest. Take my yoke upon you and learn from me, for I am gentle and humble in heart, and you will find rest for your souls. For my yoke is easy and my burden is light."* (Mt 11:28–30)

So I can either virtue signal to Twitter mobs, or I can rest in the fact that my moral failings have been taken care of. I can either live in angst over the latest news story which I will have forgotten by tomorrow, or I can live in the comfort of God's sovereignty. I can either post a political rant on Facebook about "those people," or I can actually love the person in front of me. When I finally realize that God is in charge of me and this world (and I have to "finally realize" things just about daily)—that he is the vine—then the pressure is off me, and I feel free to make a real difference in the world. For example, think of the tangible difference you can make in someone's life by saying, "I'm a sinner, but here's how God has shaped my life for the better, and I'd like to talk to you about it" (an effective "I need God" perspective) instead of "I want you to change all of your opinions and morals to match mine" (an ineffective "I am God" perspective). In some ways, I feel like Jesus is saying, "If you want to be and feel useful, stay with me." And, of course, this is in the context that some grapes need to be squished to be useful.

So in verse 2, being cut off from the vine probably applies in a couple of different ways. The most obvious is with regard to salvation. Those branches which want nothing to do with the vine don't make it (verse 6). But I think there's also the idea here of—as you mentioned—a church community (local or global). Sometimes we need to be pruned so that someone else can be grafted in:

*Consider therefore the kindness and sternness of God: sternness to those who fell, but kindness to you, provided that you continue in his kindness. Otherwise, you also will be cut off. And if they do not persist in unbelief, they will be grafted in, for God is able to graft them in again.* (Rom 11:22–23)

In other words, for a time, it might be best for the vine and other branches that I get set aside for a little while, possibly as a rebuke, but possibly because someone else needs to step in. I think it's a mistake to think that every pruned branch is done for. For example, in 1910, Asians and Africans comprised 6.6% of the world's Christians. One hundred years later, they made up 37.3%,[2] and I'm sure the number is even higher now.

Yes, I think you're spot on with verses 9–12.

---

[2] "Global Christianity – A Report on the Size and Distribution of the World's Christian Population," *Pew Research Center*, December 19, 2011, www.pewforum.org/2011/12/19/global-christianity-exec/.

As for verse 16, I think he's speaking to all believers:

*"No one can come to me unless the Father who sent me draws them, and I will raise them up at the last day."* (Jn 6:44)

That is, without God's enabling, we could not freely choose him. I think it's interesting to see here also that Jesus not only says we are saved *so that* we might bear fruit, but also points out a definitive cause and effect: salvation leads to works, but works do not lead to salvation. In other words, he could have said, "Because you are all bearing fruit, I have chosen you," but that's clearly not his message.

**Victoria**: That's a clear and descriptive explanation of the fruit analogy, especially with context from Galatians. To clarify, people are the branches and not the fruit, right? The verses describe it that way, but some of your response refer to people as the fruit (kind non-Christians; being squished). So then the point that some grapes need to be squished to be useful would refer to verse 15:2 of some branches needing to be pruned (which may be a painful experience).

If we as people are branches which produce fruit which can be either deadly or succulent, how can no fruit be an option? The fruit can be of the flesh or of the Spirit, but it's generally not the case that we are doing absolutely nothing (unless that's like newborn babies or coma patients?).

Related to my question in the first paragraph, all humans—regardless of whether or not they are Christian—are the branches, then? This makes the "cut off from salvation" meaning make more sense. I initially thought only Christians were the branches so I was uncertain on whether it could mean that an unfruitful Christian gets cut off from salvation.

It is interesting to see that order of the conditional statement. Not only that there's nothing that we can do to earn salvation, but also that one who is saved *will* bear good fruit and not just no fruit or deadly fruit … though we can still stray after getting saved?

**Steve**: Yes, he is saying that people are branches, and what they do is their fruit (e.g., kindness). I am by no means a horticulturist, but I imagine that on a grapevine, you would prune branches based almost entirely on whether they produce fruit, not just on their own appearance. In that sense, the fruit and branches are pretty intertwined in terms of their status. As far as the squishing of grapes, I read a lot of stories about persecuted Christians, and I think about Chinese pastors who are put in prison.[3] They're some of the most courageous people I know, but when they are put in prison, their ability to serve their congregations (i.e., their fruit) is "squished." But, ironically, it's their very willingness to

---

[3] "Help Chinese Christians Amid Intense Attacks," *Voice of the Martyrs,* www.persecution.com/china2020/.

have their lives cut off (either literally or practically) that has inspired so many people around the world to be bold for the gospel. So to make what I'm saying as clear as possible, the fruit of Christians may come easily or painfully depending on your external circumstances and the people around you, but if it's done through the nourishment of the vine, it's always good. The pruning, however, is done by God himself, and may either be a permanent cutting off or a temporary, loving form of discipline. I'm sorry if my take is a little confusing, but this sums it up: Stay with Jesus, and things will be good.

As far as no fruit, I think this refers to people who believe that Christianity is an entirely personal or even political way of living. Such people might have gone to church their whole lives or prayed a "saving" prayer when they were seven but don't live lives for Jesus. Their main concerns are personal status or political gain, which Jesus cared nothing about:

> Jesus said, "My kingdom is not of this world. If it were, my servants would fight to prevent my arrest by the Jewish leaders. But now my kingdom is from another place." (Jn 18:36)

It's a worldwide reality that one can be of Religion X because that's just one's culture, but the teachings of that religion haven't really caused any transformation. That type of thinking allowed slavery to exist in the Bible Belt. (That's clearly bad fruit, but there was a lot of indifference to it as well.) In our day, this video[4] sums it up the idea of "no fruit" as well as any I know.

I do think Jesus is mainly talking to his followers here and giving them a warning about staying with him. But I suppose the analogy is big enough to handle an interpretation of all humans being made in the image of God and either remaining with him or being cut off from him. As far as unfruitful Christians being cut off from salvation, I'll try to say this carefully, because none of us is in a perfect position to look at someone's fruit and decide whether he/she is a Christian. A Christian cannot be cut off for lack of fruit,

> For it is by grace you have been saved, through faith—and this is not from yourselves, it is the gift of God—not by works, so that no one can boast. (Eph 2:8–9)

but a lack of fruit may be evidence (especially self-evidence) that one is not a Christian:

---

[4] *Desiring God*, "You Have One Life, Don't Waste It – John Piper", *YouTube*, youtu.be/mfpmbmsvu3A.

*In the same way, faith by itself, if it is not accompanied by action, is dead.* (Jas 2:17)

Suppose I say I love baseball but never play it, watch it, read about it, or talk about it. No one would then say I am not *allowed* to love baseball. Rather, they would say that I simply *don't* love baseball. Same with Jesus. I think this is also the proper Christian response to all kinds of besetting sins we see in other people (*after* we've properly understood our own): we should never say that someone is excluded from salvation because of their behavior, but we might reasonably say that someone's behavior is (undoubtedly incomplete) evidence of their exclusion from salvation. Then, the unequivocally appropriate response is to show that person both the seriousness of sin and the love of Christ. I've been called out countless times for my sinful behavior by others who care about me (most often my wife). When it happens, my first instinct is always to swell up with pride and resist, but in retrospect, it's always exactly what I needed. Jesus called us to live in the ambiguous tension of simultaneous truth and love, and we feel that tension in these verses as well.

As for your last question, I do think faithful Christians are on paths of continual—but not continuous—fruit-bearing and improvement. That's because the fruit-bearing and improvement might look like straying off the path for a little while, gaining new realizations of your status before God, and getting back on the path better than ever. There have been numerous times in my life when I've been self-obsessed for months at a time (like, more than normal, because it's honestly all the time), repented, and found myself in better relationship with God than I ever have been. I'm pretty sure this is not good theology, but I always look back and am grateful I went so far off the path because of the lessons I learned. Or maybe it is good theology:

*"Therefore, I tell you, her many sins have been forgiven—as her great love has shown. But whoever has been forgiven little loves little."* (Lk 7:47)

**Victoria:** Those were great answers. I liked the baseball analogy; it's a relatable reminder that love is an action. I also liked the phrase, "ambiguous tension of simultaneous truth and love." It can be so hard to be open to the truth about ourselves.

Regarding Lk 7:47, I'd been thinking about the concept of forgiveness lately. I remember first hearing the phrase, "To err is human, to forgive divine," when I was a kid and being confused by it. There were so many good traits and actions—to love, to honor, to obey, etc.—so why was forgiveness specifically highlighted as divine? But as I've gotten older, I've realized just how hard it is to forgive. Even when I strive toward forgiveness, I'm not always completely there. It's made me realize the depth of love and weight behind forgiveness and how amazing it is that God forgives.

## JOHN 15:18–27

**Victoria**: This section can come across as discouraging. It did for me when I first read it (a couple of years ago?). I remember thinking, *why be a disciple, then, if you know you're going to be hated*? But then it can be comforting to read:

> *Do not be afraid of those who kill the body but cannot kill the soul. Rather, be afraid of the One who can destroy both soul and body in hell.* (Mt 10:28)

Verse 22 is interesting; why wouldn't people have been guilty of sin before Jesus came? Wasn't the point of animal sacrifices before then to cleanse people of their sins? As for verse 25, why would it be written into law to hate someone without reason? Is that referring to something in the Old Testament? In verse 26, what does it mean for the Holy Spirit to testify about Jesus?

**Steve**: Yes! To be a disciple of Jesus, we have to fight this constant desire to be liked. I see it work out to my own mental detriment in so many ways (i.e., worry, stress, anxiety, etc.) when I choose the approval of others over Jesus. And it plays out in so many subtle ways in my life and this world. Believe it or not, I was a huge heavy metal fan in my youth. There was this whole vibe of "We hate the world" or "We don't care what anyone thinks about us." But the only reason any of us were saying that was so that the likeminded people around us would approve of us. That world-hating persona then led to general anger issues that hurt and delayed positivity and healthiness in every human relationship I had for years. (To be clear, I'm not blaming heavy metal; I still like the genre but had to move away from the negative stuff.) I realize now that if I really wanted to be a rebel, I should've just loved my neighbor. Sometimes, loving my neighbor like Jesus wants me to will make people hate me. I hate being hated, but it goes back to whether I want to be liked or useful.

In verse 22, Jesus is not saying that people weren't guilty of sin before (e.g., the animal sacrifices you mentioned). In the surrounding context of the persecution of himself and his disciples, the Robinson Translation says, "I've made it clear by this point who I am, so if they're fighting us in the face of all that, they're compounding their sins":

> *"The servant who knows the master's will and does not get ready or does not do what the master wants will be beaten with many blows. But the one who does not know and does things deserving punishment will be beaten with few blows. From everyone who has been given much, much will be demanded; and from the one who has been entrusted with much, much more will be asked."* (Lk 12:47–48)

In verse 25, by saying it was "written in their Law," he was—in the height of irony—saying that his persecutors' own scriptures (which they revered) prophesied their own hatred of the one whom the scriptures were all about. Many Old Testament prophecies (like this one) weren't like a lady with a crystal ball predicting the future (OK, none were like that, but that tends to be how we think about prophecy). Instead, Jesus often refers to himself as the fulfillment of scripture (or a particular scripture), which just simply means that it has its ultimate meaning in him. For example, David wrote Ps 35:69 and 69:4, and in their immediate context, he appears to be in great distress due to his enemies, who hated him for no reason. Now Jesus steps in and says (Robinson Translation), "Those verses were ultimately about me. Do you see how I'm now walking in David's shoes and bearing the same burdens he had and you will have?"

The testimony of the Holy Spirit in verse 26 refers to his presence in us, continually leading us back to the truth about Jesus:

> *Therefore I want you to know that no one who is speaking by the Spirit of God says, "Jesus be cursed," and no one can say, "Jesus is Lord," except by the Holy Spirit.* (1 Cor 12:3)

**Victoria**: I like that statement: "I realize now that if I really wanted to be a rebel, I should've just loved my neighbor." That's more challenging than just hating the world and everything else around us.

Regarding verse 22, the Robinson Translation makes more sense than the literal reading, also in context with Luke 12:47–48.

# CHAPTER 34: JOHN 16

### JOHN 16:1-15

**Victoria:** Compared to earlier passages, this one talks more about the Holy Spirit, which is still kind of mysterious to me. So here, the "Advocate" is the Holy Spirit who *proves* the world to be in the wrong (verse 8), but how is that actualized? Also, on verse 11, how does Jesus' going to the Father lead the prince of the world (Satan?) to stand condemned when Satan is still active in the world? Is it because Jesus' bearing the world's sins calls for accountability of all sins, but the reckoning doesn't come until later (e.g. charged and convicted but not yet sentenced)? Verses 13–14 in light of verse 15 kind of make it seem like the Holy Spirit is a "lesser" rank than Jesus and the Father, though I would guess this isn't the case.

**Steve:** Yes, the Holy Spirit is mysterious to all of us. My big-picture view is usually just "God guiding my conscience." When we look at the types of verbs used to describe the Holy Spirit's actions in our lives—prove, convict, guide, glorify, reveal—those are things going on in my heart and mind. Clearly, the Jewish unitary understanding of God could accomplish the same thing, but there's something different going on here with a constant indwelling compared to the spottiness of the Sprit's presence in the Old Testament. The work of Christ for our justification allows God to live with us in a new, personal way. My thinking is that the Holy Spirit is the allowance of that while still maintaining the holy separateness of God the Father. (Yikes, I have no idea if that's right.)

Jesus says that the Holy Spirit actualizes that proof about sin, righteousness, and judgment, and all three of these will happen through our understanding of Jesus. Let's take them one at a time, and if we're going to "prove the world wrong," we need to know what the world thinks first. If you watch the news about all of the responses to racial injustice going on now, there is virtually *nothing* about the human condition (i.e., nothing about *sin*). Sure, there are actual steps being taken to help improve the situation (or make it worse), such as pouring money into minority communities, examining police brutality, defunding the police, tearing down statues, changing sports teams' nicknames, rethinking hiring practices, etc. Some are good ideas, and some might ultimately cause more hostility. But no one (in the media at least) is saying that every person on both sides has a humanly unfixable heart problem. No one is saying that both sides should be in a race for submission to each other. It's like we all know there's a huge problem with the world, but no one will say what it is: that we have all chosen ourselves over God. And here's the key: we can't get along with each other until we realize we all have the same problem. So Jesus is saying,

"No one understands what sin is or how to fix it, because they haven't believed in me. The Holy Spirit will reveal a new understanding to you."

As far as righteousness, we will understand real righteousness when we see it in Jesus, and it will be proven to us by his resurrection and ascension ("going to the Father"). The world's view of righteousness is one's own political opinion. For example, "I'm righteous because I believe in the freedom of humankind, and that freedom just might play out in my right to own assault weapons." "No, wait, *I'm* righteous because I believe in strict gun control, because guns have been responsible for the murders of thousands of innocent people in random shootings." Both sides often see the other side as not just wrong, but evil. The Holy Spirit will allow you to see truth in both sides of an argument, because your goal is to work for a solution rather than demonize other people because you don't understand what righteousness is:

> *For our struggle is not against flesh and blood, but against the rulers, against the authorities, against the powers of this dark world and against the spiritual forces of evil in the heavenly realms.* (Eph 6:12)

Jesus isn't here to condemn us, but to rescue us (if we want to be rescued):

> *For God did not send his Son into the world to condemn the world, but to save the world through him.* (Jn 3:17)

So Jesus is saying that the world is completely blind to both who he is (and by extension, what sin is) and how to relate to God and others (i.e., righteousness). He's going to take care of it by defeating Satan, who, as you said, is charged and condemned, but the sentence hasn't started yet. That's the judgment part; in contrast, the world believes that we get to be the final judges:

> *In those days Israel had no king; everyone did as they saw fit.* (Judg 17:6)

I've seen it said well that...

> Sin is the truth about man, righteousness is the truth about God, judgment is the inevitable combination of these two truths.[1]

As for the last few verses, no, we do not believe in any certain rank of the members of the Trinity, especially in light of what Jesus said here:

---

[1] David Guzik, "John 16 – The Departing Jesus' Final Teaching," *Enduring Word Bible Commentary*, enduringword.com/bible-commentary/john-16/.

*Then he said to them, "Whoever welcomes this little child in my name welcomes me; and whoever welcomes me welcomes the one who sent me. For it is the one who is least among you all who is the greatest."* (Lk 9:48)

That is, in Jesus' view, the ones who submit and build up others are actually the greatest, so the narrative of "The Holy Spirit only works to make Jesus look great, therefore he's the least" doesn't work. However, this is nuanced, as usual.[2]

**Victoria**: It's reassuring that the Holy Spirit has a constant presence instead of a spotty one. A unitary god would feel much less like a personal god.

That commentary on racial injustice expresses my thoughts exactly! A couple of weeks ago I watched the documentary *13th*, and I couldn't help but feel sad about the consequences of different groups of people prioritizing their own desires: e.g., political leaders making harmful promises to gain power, or incarceration rates influenced by those in the private prison industry seeking personal wealth. On the surface level, individual actions don't seem to cause much direct harm but altogether contribute to the large problem of systemic racism. Hmm, that may exemplify your point about the Holy Spirit revealing new understanding about the world. I think most people can clearly see the immorality in these systemic issues, but the underlying issue of sin, as you said, is not even hinted at—and, of course, there are those who don't believe in the inherent sinfulness of the human heart.

So the Holy Spirit proves the world to be in the wrong by revealing this new understanding. Does that mean that those who do not have the presence of the Holy Spirit don't have this same revelation of the wrongness of the world? But yet those people may be the ones who need to be most aware? Seems a bit like a "preaching to the choir" situation.

I really like that quote from David Guzik; it's concise and descriptive. Thinking about the Trinity in the perspective of Lk 9:48 is interesting. I always interpreted it as applied to human living, that is, calling people to have humility and serve others. But as we've discussed before, the Holy Spirit is not an "it," but a person, so I guess I can see how this verse applies to the relational entities of the Trinity.

I read through the *Got Questions* footnote, which differentiated economic and ontological subordination. I can see why there is no ontological subordination of the Trinity. The economic/relational subordination seems lopsided though, since the Father sends the Son who sends the Holy Spirit, but the Father himself does not get sent.

**Steve**: Yes, Jesus is saying that the Holy Spirit gives Christians a new understanding. I agree that it is somewhat of a preaching-to-the-choir situation, with two caveats. First, I still veer off into wrong thinking like

---

[2] "How can there be subordination/hierarchy in the Trinity?" *Got Questions*, www.gotquestions.org/subordination-Trinity.html.

anyone else, so when the Holy Spirit leads me, it's not as if I'm always eager to follow. That is, I can easily be a choir member who's not real happy with the preacher. Second, it's the presenting of this new information by the Holy Spirit that leads unbelievers to Christ, so it's definitely not always directed to the choir. In any case, this indwelling of the Holy Spirit allows one to see things how they really are, and while we often think of it as pertaining to individuals, the collective cooperation of Christians can bring light into seemingly intractable issues like systemic racism.[3]

As for the subordination of the Son and the Holy Spirit, yes, there does seem to be some kind of ordering, but I tend to think of it as just the best way to get things done. For example, on a professor/student level, there is a certain understood hierarchy. In no way would I consider myself inherently superior to my students (especially since one of them could be my boss one day), but I have to maintain a level of authority to keep the integrity of the system intact (e.g., an employer or graduate school having confidence that I appropriately judged a student's abilities). Thus, on a practical level, I want to know (*especially* if I were a 1st-century Jew, but now also as a 21st-century Gentile) that Jesus is conforming and submitting to the God of Israel I know, love, and obey. That practical side makes me often feel that the labels of Father, Son, and Holy Spirit were given for our understanding more than being a complete description of the nature of God (in the same vein as God carrying a masculine label to begin with).

### JOHN 16:16–33

**Victoria**: I thought the childbirth analogy in verse 21 was particularly suitable for Jesus' impending crucifixion. In verse 24, when Jesus says nothing had been asked in his name up to that point, were his disciples supposed to have known to do so? Or is he just saying essentially that they hadn't because he wasn't known of very long before? In verse 33, what does it mean for Jesus to overcome the world? Is that synonymous with bearing the weight of the world's sins?

**Steve**: We're nearing the end of Jesus' life here, so these verses are meant to encourage the disciples. (Of course, they weren't verses when he said them, ha ha. I just thought of how funny it would be if Jesus said, "Verse 20..." and how everyone would have looked around at each other like "What?") They're obviously clueless as to what's going to happen, and I imagine their cluelessness extends to verse 24 as well. My interpretation of that verse is that 1) they're finally going to understand who he is and that he is worthy of being prayed *to*, not just someone to be prayed *with* or who prayed on their behalf, and 2) they'll realize that their ability to pray to God at all has been and will be predicated on the

---

[3] "Christian abolitionism," *Wikipedia*, en.wikipedia.org/wiki/ Christian_abolitionism.

crucifixion. I think it would be a lot to ask anyone to understand everything that was going to happen, so I think this falls into the typical way that Jesus sees all of us: really wanting us to "get it," but having incredible patience when we don't. (And yes, there is the practical side of Jesus' public ministry only being three years, so one's ability to know him intimately would be fairly limited at this point.)

I love Jn 16:33. Ten or so years ago, when I was really starting to grow in my faith, I was struggling to gain an understanding of the resurrection. I understood why it was important, but had no idea how it pertained to me. (I'm still trying to learn that maybe everything doesn't have to pertain to me, but this particular issue really bothered me.) On an Easter Sunday, when my family was almost ready to leave for church to celebrate the resurrection I was confused about, I heard a running-water noise. After a few minutes of inspection, I went in my crawl space in my church clothes and discovered that my water heater was spewing water everywhere. I was *mad*. Here I was, struggling with the resurrection but ready, willing, and even excited to go to church to worship God and possibly gain a little more perspective on what I was missing, and *this* happens? It felt like I was doing my part to know him more, but he wasn't doing his part. The water heater needed to be fixed immediately, so I skipped church and drove to the store to buy the part I needed. While I was fuming at God in the car, I happened to begin listening to a sermon on the radio. It was an Easter sermon, but instead of using the typical Easter passages at the ends of the gospels, the preacher focused on Jn 16:33. He explained that this verse, as you said, refers to Jesus destroying the system of this world and its slavery to sin. I had mostly already understood that theology, but then he explained how this verse takes on so much more additional meaning in our daily lives. If someone insults you, Jesus' opinion of you overcomes it. If you're terminally ill, the prospect of eternal life with him overcomes your diagnosis. If you're depressed, Jesus' promise of the deepest joy in the middle of despair (e.g., verses 20–22) overcomes it. If you're frustrated, the knowledge that God can use it to build your character overcomes it. If you go through hard times, your ability to minister in the future to people who have gone through similar issues overcomes them. When your comfort is stripped away, being able to finally see God as your only real comfort overcomes it. So, now here I was, being punched in the face by this sermon because, while I was whining about everything, God was simultaneously helping me understand what it meant for Jesus to rise from the dead: not only overcoming the world and death itself and showing me a promise of my own future resurrection, but showing me that if he can do that, then he can give me a new perspective on all the relatively minor frustrations I deal with on a daily basis (e.g., broken water heaters):

*He who did not spare his own Son, but gave him up for us all—how will he not also, along with him, graciously give us all things?* (Rom 8:32)

I have rarely consciously experienced the tenderness of God so much as in that car ride; that while I was angry at him, he was gently and compassionately teaching me the life-altering lesson I had been praying for:

*But God demonstrates his own love for us in this: While we were still sinners, Christ died for us.* (Rom 5:8)

It's these types of things that allow me to make cold, theological arguments about topics such as the omnibenevolence of God.

**Victoria**: I can see how it could be harder to see Jesus as one worthy of being prayed to from the perspective of a disciple. Going through life with Jesus, one would see all of his humanness, but thousands of years later when we see his life through scripture, it's easier to see him as divine. Though I suppose it's also important to not see him during his time on earth as "not human" or "beyond human."

That's a profound interpretation of Jn 16:33. It's incredibly personal and relevant to our day-to-day problems and worries in life. Not that saving us from our sins isn't personal, but it's the little things in life that can get so overwhelming. Does Jesus' overcoming require individual repentance? For example, if you said something mean about someone behind their back and then regretted it, is that only overcome by repenting to God?

**Steve**: It's interesting that you would say that it's *easier* to see Jesus as divine now rather than at the time of his earthly ministry. I think most people would say the opposite because they wish they had the same sort of proof (i.e., miracles and teaching) that the disciples had. But you make a good point, because honestly, if I saw a guy perform a miracle and then the next week, he's puking from a stomach virus (not that that's in scripture, but it seems possible), I would have my doubts. The Israelites were the same way, going from experiencing their miraculous delivery from the Egyptians to completely doubting that God was going to take care of them in no time:

*And when the Israelites saw the mighty hand of the LORD displayed against the Egyptians, the people feared the LORD and put their trust in him and in Moses his servant.* (Ex 14:31)

*The Israelites said to them, "If only we had died by the LORD's hand in Egypt! There we sat around pots of meat and ate all the food we wanted, but you have brought us out into this desert to starve this entire assembly to death."* (Ex 16:3)

My wife and I were joking the other day about how we can do the same thing to each other. We've been married 21 years, and our relationship is better than ever and still improving. I feel like we have an unbreakable bond founded on rock-solid Christian principles. But if one of us does or says something really annoying, the other immediately feels like everything is lost, and the last 21 years meant nothing. Early in our marriage, those feelings might have lasted a week or more, but now we can *usually* get over it in a couple of hours or so (or immediately on our best days). Three years with Jesus (as a disciple or a modern-day Christian) would make the relationship just as rocky and full of doubt as a three-year-old marriage.

As far as Jesus' overcoming involving our repenting, yes! I don't think Jesus is going to overcome much in our lives without our willingness to conform to him.

> Imagine yourself as a living house. God comes in to rebuild that house. At first, perhaps, you can understand what He is doing. He is getting the drains right and stopping the leaks in the roof and so on; you knew that those jobs needed doing and so you are not surprised. But presently He starts knocking the house about in a way that hurts abominably and does not seem to make any sense. What on earth is He up to? The explanation is that He is building quite a different house from the one you thought of—throwing out a new wing here, putting on an extra floor there, running up towers, making courtyards. You thought you were being made into a decent little cottage: but He is building a palace. He intends to come and live in it Himself.[4]

Here's an example. About ten years after I graduated high school, I was looking through my yearbooks and was reminded of some pretty awful things I said to or about people. It immediately hit me that I outwardly claimed to be a Christian in high school and how poorly I had represented Christ to others. I felt really guilty and knew this was something that would eat me up if I didn't deal with it. I knew in my head that I was forgiven for what I had done, but I had neither repented nor attempted to remedy it. (Side note: I believe that regular repentance is foundational to any Christian's walk, but in the knowledge that I have committed sins I've forgotten or not properly recognized as sins, I have no choice but to rest in the blood of Christ without an ability to specifically repent of some things.) So I knew this thing wasn't taken care of: even though Jesus had already overcome this particular sin on the cross, if I wanted my guilty feelings and others' animosity to be overcome, I had to do my part. Or to put it another way, if I wanted this

---

4 C. S. Lewis, *Mere Christianity* (New York: HarperCollins, 2015).

thing to be absolutely destroyed, I had to submit to the Holy Spirit's prompting. The problem was that I had no contact and lived 2000 miles from everyone I went to school with (this was near the very beginning of social media). I was eventually able to get some contact information and proceeded to apologize to the people I could remember hurting. I don't recall how many people I contacted now, but I do remember one responding that every time she thought of me over the previous ten years, she thought of the word ******* (I'll let you use your imagination there), but now she could move on and had changed her opinion of me. Another said she had no idea I had said such terrible things about her but appreciated me reaching out and understood why I would do so. There was one whom I have never been able to find, and it still bothers me, but I can't do anything about it and have to move on. So, yeah, in summary, if I wanted Jesus to overcome my sin, guilt, poor representation of him, and broken relationships, I had to not only repent but take action. It might look like I'm the one doing the overcoming in that story, but there is zero chance I would do any of that without Jesus' teaching and leading. And not only that, but those types of examples have allowed Jesus to overcome even my personality to become quicker to repent and make amends, allowing me to live free from the slavery of guilt.

**Victoria**: Ha ha! Or if he was seen picking his nose. That would make him seem very human.

I think there's something human about overemphasizing the present state of mind. A bad situation in the present can feel like it has lasted and will last much longer than it actually did/does. When I was in one of my depressive states before, I've felt that I would never experience the feeling of happiness again.

I like that house interpretation. I've heard similar stories about people who reached out to others in their past, like you did, in the process of repentance. That speaks a lot to a changed life. On a side note, what if someone repents in general terms without seeing (or without being willing to see) the weight of their sins? Would they not be fully forgiven?

**Steve**: Yes, I suppose that's what depression is: 20% "I feel bad right now" and 80% "I'm never going to feel better." I think Christianity allows us to get rid of (or at least chip away at) that 80%.

As far as repentance goes, we have to be really careful here. If salvation comes through faith alone,

> *For it is by grace you have been saved, through faith—and this is not from yourselves, it is the gift of God—not by works, so that no one can boast.* (Eph 2:8–9)

then we can't say that it also requires really good repenting, because that would be a work. In other words, apart from the repentance needed to have faith at all, I think heaven will be full of terrible repenters (including me). However, I do think there is a dividing line which you alluded to in your parenthetical statement with the word *willing*. As I mentioned earlier, it is often necessary for us to repent in general terms because we are unaware of sins we have committed, but that is completely different from being unwilling to repent. I think the following is spot on:

> I cannot pray but I sin. I cannot hear or preach a sermon but I sin. I cannot give an alms or receive the sacrament but I sin. Nay, I cannot so much as confess my sins, but my very confessions are still aggravations of them. My repentance needs to be repented of, my tears need washing, and the very washing of my tears needs still to be washed over again with the blood of my Redeemer.[5]

I'll try to make it concrete. I grew up in the rural South around almost exclusively white people, a few of whom were outwardly, blatantly racist (including a few of my own relatives), but most of whom were just generally prejudiced without knowing it (including me). I don't remember it being a conscious thing for me, and I never really realized I had biases until I started attending a Bible study in college in which I was the only white person. I was shown a lot of love where I thought there would be animosity, and that changed my mind about a lot of things. So in the context that I believe that the Bible is crystal clear about God being anti-racist,

> *Then Peter began to speak: "I now realize how true it is that God does not show favoritism but accepts from every nation the one who fears him and does what is right."* (Acts 10:34–35)

then I can say the following for myself. When I was young and didn't know that I had certain biases, I still would've openly and genuinely acknowledged that racism is wrong and could've properly repented for it (i.e., in a general way). That is, if Jesus had shown up at my door and said, "Steve, you're a racist, and here's why...," then—assuming I'm on my best behavior—I would've said, "Yes, you're correct; I've been doing and thinking wrong things, and I will change." My entire mindset would be one of submission. But if I said, "I don't care what you think," or "Yeah, but did you see what those people did?" or "I don't think the Bible can be trusted on this issue" (and I've done all three), then I've made it all about me and am asking God to submit to me instead. In such a case, my relationship with him is in shambles, because Jesus correlates our relationships with other people with our relationship with him:

---

[5] William Beverage, *Private Thoughts Upon Religion and a Christian Life* (London: Forgotten Books, 2018)

*"Therefore, if you are offering your gift at the altar and there remember that your brother or sister has something against you, leave your gift there in front of the altar. First go and be reconciled to them; then come and offer your gift."* (Mt 5:23–24)

*But if you do not forgive others their sins, your Father will not forgive your sins.* (Mt 6:15)

Importantly, though, I think both of those passages (and others like it) are describing a mentality/worldview rather than a single act. That is, I don't believe in, "Well, you lived a faithful Christian life but didn't forgive that girl in 3rd grade, so off to hell with you." To say it a different way, repentance is so much more about "Am I *willing* to give up everything about myself—especially my own self-righteousness—to make Jesus king in my life?" than actually succeeding at it (understanding, of course, that true willingness leads to real action). Bad repentance looks like arguing with and justifying oneself to God. The whole foundation of Christianity is so much more about humility/pride rather than repenting the right way or having exact knowledge of my sins or anyone's sins.

It's easy to talk about myself as being sinful in the past, so let's talk about now. I hate racism. I hate sexism. I think they are part of the foundation of the world's problems and have been as long as humans have been around. I want no part of them, and I think they're evil and disgusting. Am I sometimes racist? If racism is, at minimum, making incorrect assumptions about someone based on their race, then yes; we all are.[6] Am I sometimes sexist? By the same token, yes; we all are.[7] So proper repentance for me looks like both acknowledgement of my problems (to God and others) and being intentional about fixing them. In other words, I have to continually ask myself the question, "If you agree with God that these things are evil, that the Bible is explicit about it, and that you do them, then what are you doing about it?" If the answer is "nothing" (or worse, "celebrating"), then I'm not repenting. I heard an apologist (Frank Turek) put it like the following when he is confronted by a skeptic (paraphrased): "If I were to convince you of the truth of Christianity, would you become a Christian?" If the answer is no, then that person has a repentance problem. (And I strongly believe we should all answer "yes" to *any* question posed as "If you were convinced

---

[6] Agustín Fuentes, "We're All a Bit Racist," *Psychology Today*, July 18, 2016, www.psychologytoday.com/us/blog/busting-myths-about-human-nature/201607/we-re-all-bit-racist.

[7] Oliver Burkeman, "Sexist? Bigoted? Aren't we all?", *The Guardian*, January 18, 2019, www.theguardian.com/lifeandstyle/2019/jan/18/sexist-bigoted-examine-own-behaviour-oliver-burkeman.

of the truth of X, would you align your life with X?") Maybe that's the best way to think about repentance; it's just agreeing with God and living that agreement out. Since that can be fuzzy, then while salvation is an either/or thing, a Christian's relationship with God (and, thus, satisfaction) is on a spectrum depending on his/her repentance and obedience, although, again, I would say that being way over on the wrong side of obedience might be a sign of being on the wrong side of salvation:

> *Whoever says, "I know him," but does not do what he commands is a liar, and the truth is not in that person.* (1 Jn 2:4)

**Victoria**: I've never heard so much on repentance before! Usually when repentance is mentioned, it's usually in the context of, "Just do it, and here's why." It's interesting to see that repentance isn't something to be overly stressed about if it's done in earnest.

On the non-submission mindsets of "I don't care what you think," / "Yeah, but did you see what those people did?" / "I don't think the Bible can be trusted on this issue," I think your explanation on this really seems to emphasize that if you're not with God, then, at some level, you're against God. These three gut-reaction-thoughts don't directly come across as antagonistic, but by not deferring to God's authority, I can see how that would be synonymous to insisting that God submits instead (even though probably most people would never directly issue directives to God).

I like the way you phrased this: "Jesus correlates our relationships with other people with our relationship with him." It seems almost second nature to be judgmental and critical of others, but that kind of thinking probably falls into one of those gut-reaction thoughts above.

I also particularly liked this statement: "The whole foundation of Christianity is so much more about humility/pride." In the last chapter, I mentioned how I found it surprising that forgiveness is "divine," where forgiveness seems to be emphasized instead of other positive qualities. Similarly, I wouldn't have expected the foundation of Christianity to be so much about pride (or lack thereof) compared to other negative qualities like anger or greed.

On the question, "If you were convinced of the truth of X, would you align your life with X?" I wholeheartedly agree that the answer to that question should be yes. Tangentially, I recently saw on social media a similar question but applied to the political party divide. In the case of politics, I think a lot of people align themselves to what they see as the "lesser evil," as opposed to what is good or what reflects truth because that's what's available.

"Maybe that's the best way to think about repentance; it's just agreeing with God and living that agreement out." Simple and practical.

**Steve**: You're correct in seeing this through a with-or-against God lens. Jesus said as much:

> *"Whoever is not with me is against me, and whoever does not gather with me scatters."* (Mt 12:30)

> *"... for whoever is not against us is for us."* (Mk 9:40)

These verses seem to contradict each other (or, at the very least, not clarify the results of half-heartedness), but they *are* in different contexts and need to be interpreted as such.[8] But regarding what we're talking about, in full acknowledgement that many Christian ideas can be put on a spectrum (e.g., sin, faithfulness, theology, etc.), this still seems to be a black-and-white issue to me: do we desire to be on his team or not?

Regarding politics, yes, aligning yourself with X and Y can be very difficult when one party is pro-X, anti-Y and the other is anti-X, pro-Y. I feel that exact frustration about numerous political issues, but if I don't think that politics is the solution anyway, then it's not that big of a deal to have a hard time aligning with a party. One should align oneself to the truth in both one's thoughts and personal actions, but perfect alignment will probably be impossible in terms of political options. Even more (and I can't stress this enough), the biggest danger is saying, "I belong to this political party; therefore, I support this and that." That's just a foolish way to go through life.

**Victoria**: I recently heard in a podcast about the *AND Campaign*,[9] whose goals are to fight party loyalty in favor of applying biblical principles when engaging in politics.

**Steve**: Yes! We need so much more of *that*. Can I vote for the *AND Campaign* for President?

---

[8] *Real Truth. Real Quick.*, "Is Jesus Contradicting Himself In Mark 9:40 and Matthew 12:30?" *YouTube*, March 2, 2020, youtu.be/6Yp02DN6ppk.

[9] *AND Campaign*, andcampaign.org.

# Chapter 35: John 17

## John 17:1-5

**Victoria:** The phrasing here is interesting, because it reminds me of what we talked about in the last chapter regarding the hierarchy of the Trinity. Specifically, I'm more familiar with the Son glorifying the Father compared to the Father glorifying the Son.

**Steve:** Yes, and it has everything to do with the crucifixion and resurrection. There's never been a time in which God's glory was on display like those events, and Jesus was the central figure.

Along those lines, Jesus defines eternal life in verse 3 in the same strange way as 1 Jn 5:20. It isn't "living forever in heaven with puppies," but is entirely about knowing God. It completely changes the way we view our future. We tend to think, "If I do good things, I will have a good end." Jesus changes the focus to, "If you want to know God, you will know him in the end."

**Victoria:** This makes sense with my understanding. It also relates to what we talked about in Chapters 5-6, about hell being an "existence without God" rather than necessarily being a physical location with literal fire and brimstone.

**Steve:** Yes, but wouldn't such a place be a great lab setting for chemists? Seriously, though, although I prefer the "existence without God" interpretation as we've discussed, I think if we understand God correctly, that's the worse of the two options (or three if you count annihilationism[1]).

**Victoria:** Ha! The beach parking lot near where I live has such a strong, persistent smell of sulfur because of the sewage line. I can barely stand to walk through that area for a few minutes every day, let alone a whole lifetime of it.

## John 17:6-19

**Victoria:** In verse 9, why does Jesus say that he isn't praying for the world when he also later asks God to forgive those who crucify him? In verse 12, did Jesus know from the start who this "doomed" disciple would be? In verse 15, this clarification is unexpected to me, that Jesus says he does not pray for them to be taken out of the world.

**Steve:** This whole passage is particularly a prayer for his followers, so my understanding is that he's clarifying what he's saying for the benefit of those (humans) listening. In other words, he's not saying, "I'm not the kind of guy who prays for the world," but is rather saying, "My followers need special help, so that's the focus of this prayer."

As for the betrayal of Judas, I think it's hard to say. We have these:

---

[1] "Annihilationism," *Wikipedia*, en.wikipedia.org/wiki/Annihilationism.

*Even my close friend, someone I trusted, one who shared my bread, has turned against me.* (Ps 41:9)

*Then Jesus replied, "Have I not chosen you, the Twelve? Yet one of you is a devil!" (He meant Judas, the son of Simon Iscariot, who, though one of the Twelve, was later to betray him.)* (Jn 6:70–71)

*For he knew who was going to betray him, and that was why he said not every one was clean.* (Jn 13:11)

*"I am not referring to all of you; I know those I have chosen. But this is to fulfill this passage of Scripture: 'He who shared my bread has turned against me.'"* (Jn 13:18)

It's clear that he knew at some point before it happened. From the perspective that Jesus is God and/or it was predicted 1000 years earlier that someone would betray him, yes, he knew *something* from the start (here's another interesting link[2]). From the perspective that he knew his mission and what would happen to him, yes, he knew *something* from the start. But from the perspective that he was a man who sometimes didn't know things (as we talked about earlier), one might make a reasonable case that, no, he didn't know specifically that it would be Judas who betrayed him. I tend to fall into the camp that Jesus had a regular brain like mine (i.e., the "man" side of him) but also had an extremely close communicative relationship with God in which things were revealed to him (i.e., the "God" side of him). In that respect, we just don't always know exactly what he knew.

I think verse 15 is a big deal. Jesus is shortly going to be victorious over sin, death, and Satan, and he's going to turn his little group of followers into a world-changing force. But he's not going to do it by just taking his followers into heaven and zapping everyone else. He's going to use you and me! On the surface (and I say this quite often to myself), I want to just go ahead and leave this world:

*I eagerly expect and hope that I will in no way be ashamed, but will have sufficient courage so that now as always Christ will be exalted in my body, whether by life or by death. For to me, to live is Christ and to die is gain. If I am to go on living in the body, this will mean fruitful labor for me. Yet what shall I choose? I do not know! I am torn between the two: I desire to depart and be with Christ, which is better by far; but it is more necessary for you that I remain in the body.* (Phil 1:20–24)

---

[2] "Is Zechariah 11:12-13 a Messianic prophecy?" *Got Questions*, www.gotquestions.org/Zechariah-11-12-13-Messianic.html.

But there's also something deep inside me that knows I have a role in an awesome *Lord of the Rings* type adventure—that God himself has given me a part to play in his kingdom and his transformation of this world into something amazing. It's that knowledge that gives me motivation to live for him (and sometimes to just get out of bed).

**Victoria**: That makes sense, thanks for those explanations! I suppose it would be preferable for Jesus not to pray for his disciples to be taken out of the world; otherwise, the impact of his life, work, and mission becomes significantly lessened in the years immediately following his death.

I've heard something along those lines before of wanting to leave this world and be with God instead. But isn't suicide a grave sin, especially as it's centered around the person's desire? (Not that the people I heard this from were actually talking about taking their own lives.)

**Steve**: In the context that murder is wrong, and committing suicide is murdering oneself, yes, it's wrong. In the context that heaven is going to have plenty of murderers in it (e.g., Moses,[3] David,[4] Paul,[5] and countless others), I do believe there is still eternal hope for those who commit suicide.[6] But regarding Philippians, we need to understand it in the limitations of our language. For example, in the context of what's been promised to me, I *want* to die (to be clear, though, I'm not suicidal). Meeting God and other Christians and having no more sorrow, sickness, or pain sounds pretty good; dying sounds like the best option in that sense. But I also *don't* want to die. I, like Paul, feel like I haven't completed my work here. It would also create a lot of difficulty and sadness for my family (I hope!). And although I haven't met anyone with a firsthand account, dying doesn't seem real enjoyable. One might look at those things and conclude that suicide is the best solution: I would get to end my suffering and make the process quick and painless. But that thought process is ignoring the fact that I would be destroying something of great value (what in this universe is worth more than a human?) that isn't mine:

> Do you not know that your bodies are temples of the Holy Spirit, who is in you, whom you have received from God? You are not your own; you were bought at a price. Therefore honor God with your bodies. (1 Cor 6:19–20)

---

[3] Ex 2:12

[4] 2 Sam 11:15

[5] Acts 8:1

[6] John Piper, "Suicide and Salvation," *Desiring God*, May 29, 2014, www.desiringgod.org/interviews/suicide-and-salvation.

So, yes, I would agree that suicide is ultimately a selfish act. But in the few times I've been able to counsel suicidal students, I'm way more focused on the fact that 1) they matter to someone else (God first and foremost, but also other people), 2) suicide creates more problems than it solves, and 3) there really is hope in the gospel.

**Victoria**: Ah, it's the same kind of language extremes/limitations applied to the verse about hating one's father, mother, etc.:

> *If anyone comes to me and does not hate father and mother, wife and children, brothers and sisters—yes, even their own life—such a person cannot be my disciple.* (Lk 14:26)

I don't usually think about suicide as murdering oneself, but I suppose that's true, especially in light of 1 Cor 6:19–20.

### JOHN 17:20–26

**Victoria**: The header for this section says, "Jesus prays for all believers," which I read as him praying for those who *are* believers, but considering verse 20, he is also praying for those who *will be* believers. That makes "who becomes a believer" seem deterministic—we've talked about this idea before when discussing Calvinism vs. Arminianism. Verses 22 and 24: once again, the direction of glory being given is interesting (I'm starting to see this everywhere). Verse 26: "will continue to make you known"—does that refer to his future death and resurrection? Also verse 26: "I myself may be in them"—isn't that more the realm of the Holy Spirit?

**Steve**: I'll get to your questions in a moment, but I first wanted to say that 20–23 is literally the hardest passage in the Bible for me to deal with. Here's why. First, it seems like we've failed monumentally in this regard over the last 2000 years. We've split into three main branches—Catholic, Protestant, and Eastern Orthodox—(or four if you count the persecuted church just hanging on with their Bibles) with countless denominations under those. I suppose you could say that everyone under the umbrella of Christianity believes the same foundational things, but from a fleshed-out doctrinal standpoint, Jesus' prayer was not answered very well at all. In fact, there are things that other branches and denominations believe and do that I think threaten the root of Christianity (e.g., salvation by faith alone in Christ alone). To make it worse, this was a problem from the very beginning:

> *You foolish Galatians! Who has bewitched you? Before your very eyes Jesus Christ was clearly portrayed as crucified. I would like to learn just one thing from you: Did you receive the Spirit by the works of the law, or by believing what you heard? Are you so foolish? After beginning by means of the Spirit, are you now trying to finish by means of the flesh?* (Gal 3:1–3)

Second, even within a single denomination, church, or Christian organization, we have all kinds of disunity: racial, political, doctrinal, moral, etc. Paul himself even places unity on the back burner to prioritize discipline:

> But now I am writing to you that you must not associate with anyone who claims to be a brother or sister but is sexually immoral or greedy, an idolater or slanderer, a drunkard or swindler. Do not even eat with such people. (1 Cor 5:11)

So we have Jesus praying this final prayer about what the church is supposed to look like, making it clear that unity both brings vitality and bears witness to the world, and it looks to me like we've failed from the start. One might say that unity is not the same thing as uniformity, so we shouldn't all be in lockstep, and I would definitely agree with that. One might also say that unity is sometimes achieved by meting out Paul's church discipline (or Jesus'[7]), so that unity doesn't mean that everyone gets along. I would also agree with that. So I guess my real difficulty is the practical side of balancing the hard parts of Christianity (truth and discipline) with the fun parts (love and unity), and I just have a really hard time pulling it off. I probably look like I'm doing it on the outside, but my mind is still pulled in several directions. It's not so bad at my church, where I definitely have political disagreements with others but get along fairly well in terms of doctrine. It's harder working at an ecumenical Christian university with a wider set of beliefs and having to wrestle with simultaneous secular priorities (e.g., free speech, budgets, careers, etc.). I'm sure there are colleagues of mine who would have issues with my doctrine, and I theirs, and I'm OK with that. It's just difficult in general to know when unity takes priority over "taking a stand." And now that I've written all of this, I'm reminded of the following:

> "When you are brought before synagogues, rulers and authorities, do not worry about how you will defend yourselves or what you will say, for the Holy Spirit will teach you at that time what you should say." (Lk 12:11–12)

I imagine Jesus said this to people like me in response to "What do we do when Thing X happens?" And his answer was probably something like this:

> Give us today our daily bread. (Mt 6:11)

---

[7] Mt 18:15–17

So there isn't an "always" answer for truth vs. love or discipline vs. unity (unless you want to say the answer is always "both," which I suppose would be correct). He's saying, "Trust me now. Don't worry about tomorrow. I'm in charge, not you. I'll help you when the time comes." I don't like that answer, but I love the answerer.

OK, I hope you've enjoyed the digression into my internal dialogue; back to verse 20. Yes, it's wonderfully odd that he's talking about us! He does it later, too:

> *Then Jesus told him, "Because you have seen me, you have believed; blessed are those who have not seen and yet have believed." (Jn 20:29)*

If it were me, I'd be wondering this whole time if the dying-on-the-cross thing was actually going to work, but he seems pretty confident here that more believers are coming. But I don't think predestination is an issue here for two reasons. First, I wouldn't go so far as to say these believers have to be specific. For example, I could easily and confidently pray, "God, be with the persecuted believers in North Korea" without knowing any of them. Thus, he doesn't have to be talking about anyone in particular. Second, as a proponent of Molinism, I would say that God has sovereignly created an optimal world in which some people will freely choose him, so that the salvation of some is guaranteed (i.e., it will happen) but not inevitable (i.e., it must happen). In other words, Jesus has a right to be confident that believers are on the way because he knows how he set up the world, but it doesn't follow that any specific person had no choice in his/her salvation. (To be more specific, God has knowledge of how everyone would freely respond to his offer of salvation and created an optimal world based on that knowledge.)

As for verses 22 and 24, glory everywhere! "Triangle of Glory" doesn't sound quite as good as Trinity, though. (Way-off-topic side note but related to words: I was doing a little Hebrew inspection of a verse the other day and again realized that English didn't even begin until about 500 years after the New Testament was written. Then I imagined meeting Paul in heaven and trying to speak to him and him looking at me like I was an alien. I'm pretty sure it doesn't work that way, though.)

Regarding verse 26, yes, Jesus knows he's going to die soon but says he's going to continue doing stuff. It reminds me of Is 53, a whole chapter of prophecy about Jesus, and specifically this verse that says he's going to die but then see his offspring:

> *Yet it was the LORD's will to crush him and cause him to suffer, and though the LORD makes his life an offering for sin, he will see his offspring and prolong his days, and the will of the LORD will prosper in his hand. (Is 53:10)*

The "I myself may be in them" phrase is just another way of Jesus expressing the Trinity. It's patently obvious that Jesus-the-man can't live inside someone (except Mary when he was much smaller), so he's using this language to describe his presence with us. I would agree that the correct idea is that the Holy Spirit is actually the one living inside a Christian, but even that is just figurative language. The Holy Spirit isn't "living" in any biological sense we can understand, and "inside us" implies some finite spatial state that doesn't make a lot of sense, either. And then, of course, we know that even though Jesus and the Holy Spirit are distinct, they're also both God. So when we say something like "Jesus lives in me," we just mean "God's helping me out."

**Victoria**: All the denominations and labels and sublabels in Christianity was off-putting to me when I didn't know a thing about Christianity. If Christians can't figure out what they believe (collectively), then it certainly doesn't give confidence to non-believers. You said that Jesus said that "unity both brings vitality and bears witness to the world." But I don't get the ordering of this statement. Isn't unity supposed to come from belief in God and following Jesus for each person? In other words, isn't God the priority over unity, such that when Paul places unity on the back burner, it's because the people need to prioritize God before they can be unified?

"I'm sure there are colleagues of mine who would have major issues with my doctrine, and I theirs." I find this interesting since I once would have thought, "well, Christian is Christian," also considering the fact that you all are highly educated. Wasn't Belmont not ecumenical not that long ago but associated with the Southern Baptists? That being said, I guess I wouldn't be surprised if people in the same church had slightly different beliefs in doctrine.

"God has knowledge of how everyone would freely respond to his offer of salvation and created an optimal world based on that knowledge." That sounds like an insane optimization problem.

**Steve**: Ugh. I was really hoping you'd say that, as a non-Christian, you never really noticed how Christians couldn't get it together. But your statement is such an indictment of how Christianity has played out in the last 2000 years. Verse 23 could not be clearer: the world will not come to know God if Christians are not unified. (Reading that verse again, I see an element of unity meaning "unified with God," but I don't think one can throw off the "unified with each other" interpretation.) How many people have not come to know Jesus because of our/my pettiness?

As for your first question, yes, God is the priority over unity (and everything), and unity is the natural result of a community of believers with a right relationship with God. But that's the very issue I have. When I see disunity, it makes me question whether we're right with God, but I'm not sure that's the right conclusion. The trouble I have is in discerning whether disagreement counts as disunity. With Belmont in particular, I love my colleagues. They've been very kind and loving to me, and I am comforted by the fact that we do have a common core belief that guides us and gives us a purposeful direction. I also wholeheartedly agree that "Christian is Christian:"

> *If you declare with your mouth, "Jesus is Lord," and believe in your heart that God raised him from the dead, you will be saved.* (Rom 10:9)

But we still have varying beliefs about important theology and the consequential appropriate social actions to take. I think that's great in many ways, because we really are one body with many parts.[8] But I'm not sure when diversity of thought (a good thing) turns into disunity (a bad thing), and the line between the two seems so fine. I guess I just really want to know whether Jesus would think we're (i.e., Christians in general) succeeding at unity, especially since he puts such a priority on it. If I'm convinced that his answer is "yes," then I fully embrace what we're doing. If I'm convinced that his answer is "no," then I feel both defensive about my own positions and compelled to change others'. (This all leads to a few tangential thoughts. First, I would love for his answer to be "yes" for my own mental rest. Second, I am well aware that defensiveness and trying to change others are not Christian ideals. Third, maybe I think I'm more important than I am in this regard, and it's really not my place to make these kinds of decisions and judgments.) More succinctly, I apparently have no idea what he meant by "unity" in his prayer. That's why I feel OK with what I said above about him helping me figure it out on a case-by-case basis when the time comes. That seems to be his way.

**Victoria**: I suppose the first two paragraphs of my response were somewhat at odds with each other. I think you bring up an important nuance, that disagreement or diversity may not always be the same as disunity.

You said that "defensiveness and trying to change others are not Christian ideals." Isn't the act of evangelizing (which is a Christian ideal?) trying to change others?

**Steve**: Evangelism's goal is conforming someone to Jesus (and is a Christian ideal). Politics' (and egotism's) goal is conforming someone to myself. I was referring to the latter. I really don't need or want more people like me except in the ways I'm like Jesus.

---

8 1 Cor 12:12–29.

# CHAPTER 36: JOHN 18

## JOHN 18:1–14

**Victoria**: Ah, now we're at the betrayal. Verse 6: why would they fall to the ground? Verse 9: what about the people who were believers who stop believing? It looks like this references Jn 6:39, but we didn't discuss this verse earlier. Regarding verse 14, weird question, but are Judas and Caiaphas equally guilty more or less?

**Steve**: This whole passage adds some perspective on our unity discussion; immediately after Jesus prays for unity, one of his disciples turns him over to be killed. Well, then.

As for verse 6, it's hard to tell why they might have fallen down. I've heard some say that this was a clear demonstration of the power of God in him that supernaturally pushed them over. But I think it could be as mundane as the confidence and authority he showed combined with their surprise that he was finally caught that made them step back. Maybe there was a clumsy guy up front who stepped back and tripped on someone and made them fall over like dominoes. I really want replays of some of this stuff in heaven.

Speaking of verse 9, I think it's speaking of the 11 disciples who stayed the course until the end. But since John is referencing a more general thought in Jn 6:39, a Calvinist would say that there are no believers who stop believing. That is, there are some who have the external appearance of belief but were never true believers. I think that completely discounts the numerous genuine stories I've heard from people who say, "I was a believer but stopped believing," so I don't favor that explanation. Again, I would favor the Molinist interpretation that people can freely choose to believe or not believe, but God has set up the world so that those who would ultimately freely choose him will have that opportunity in the end. In that way, people simultaneously have both self-determining free will and are under the complete and total sovereignty of God. Thus, I have no problem with Jesus saying that none are lost who are given to him *and* that some people genuinely believe and then stop believing. In that sense, "given to him" means "divinely ordained to freely choose him in eternity" rather than "forced to believe by God."

It's come up a few times, so let me try to explain Molinism in clearer terms. Before God laid out the universe, he knew all future things because he's God. Also, because he's God, he knows all possible things, not just those things which will be actualized. For example, these verses show that God knew a possible future which never actually took place:

> *"Will the citizens of Keilah surrender me to him? Will Saul come down, as your servant has heard? L*ORD*, God of Israel, tell your servant." And the L*ORD *said, "He will." Again David asked, "Will the citizens of Keilah surrender me and my men to Saul?" And the L*ORD *said, "They will." So David and his men, about six hundred in number, left Keilah and kept moving from place to place. When Saul was told that David had escaped from Keilah, he did not go there.* (1 Sam 23:11–13)

We have similar types of knowledge (e.g., if I punch this guy, he's going to be angry), but obviously it isn't certain or complete like God's. Now if we apply this knowledge to salvation, God knows who is going to exist and whether they will eternally choose (i.e., willfully forever submit to) him. I would go so far as to say that this eternal choosing is independent of anything on this earth (e.g., culture, age, disability, knowledge, etc.), in that there is an eternal version of us who is the "real" us much more than the earthly us we know now. The question is then whether this "real" version of us (you might call it a soul) wants God or not, and God knew this answer (which we freely choose) before the creation of the universe. Then, he created a world in which those for whom the answer is "yes" will be placed in situations in which they will have the ability to freely choose him on this earth. For example, suppose I'm not a fraud and I really do want God forever. Then he will set me up in a position to hear the gospel and accept it:

> *From one man he made all the nations, that they should inhabit the whole earth; and he marked out their appointed times in history and the boundaries of their lands. God did this so that they would seek him and perhaps reach out for him and find him, though he is not far from any one of us.* (Acts 17:26–27)

It is quite possible, though, for someone to—for all kinds of reasons—freely become convinced that Christianity is correct and then later become convinced that it's not, while still being under God's sovereignty the whole time. You might wonder why God would create a world like this, and I think it hinges on two massively important points: 1) he's completely in charge and in control, and 2) the love relationship he pursues with us is made exponentially better and complete when we choose each other rather than coercion being involved. So, in my mind, I can't shake either God's sovereignty or our free will (there are so many Bible passages that clearly point to both), and Molinism provides the best explanation. It doesn't answer all of my questions, but it beats Calvinism and Arminianism.

As for the responsibility of Jesus' death, yes, it's pretty easy to put Judas, Caiaphas, and Pontius Pilate at the top of the list. But then you have to add the entire Roman system and the Sanhedrin. Then there's the crowd who chanted to crucify him. But when you read something like this,

> *"He himself bore our sins" in his body on the cross, so that we might die to sins and live for righteousness; "by his wounds you have been healed."* (1 Pet 2:24)

then it's pretty evident that we all had a role in it. It seems like such an abstract idea, that my sins cost a man his life 2000 years ago, but that's the inevitable conclusion we have to come to. There's been a lot of unfortunate anti-Semitism based on the idea that the Jews were ultimately responsible for the death of Jesus. I think that's just such a twisted way to view the whole thing in the light of the entirety of scripture. So instead of thinking whether anyone in particular was responsible for betraying Jesus, I have to think of the high likelihood that I would've done the same in their shoes (betrayal, denial, indifference, chanting, etc.) and put my hope in some of Jesus' final words:

> *Jesus said, "Father, forgive them, for they do not know what they are doing."* (Lk 23:34a)

Finally, stepping back to verse 10, we have Peter trying to kill a man and immediately being rebuked by Jesus! If you ever feel like you just don't get it, you've gone too far, or you're just dumb, remember that Jesus made this guy the founder of the Christian church and let him write a couple of books of the Bible:

> *And I tell you that you are Peter, and on this rock I will build my church, and the gates of Hades will not overcome it.* (Mt 16:18)

(Peter is the translation of the Greek "petros," meaning "rock."[1] His actual name was Simon.) No one is beyond the reach of Christ, and no one is beyond being used by Christ.

**Victoria**: Ha ha! I'd like to see those replays, too.

Okay, so the Molinist view of verse 9 was a bit hard to wrap my mind around since it seems to imply that the number of those God gave to Jesus isn't fixed (to allow for personal choice). But it still is fixed in a sense because God knows what each disciple's personal choice will be without interfering with or forcing their actions.

"God knew a possible future which never actually took place." Reading those verses, wouldn't a critic just say God was wrong, though? What if God really didn't know whether Saul would come down or not?

---

[1] "Strong's Greek: 4074. Petros," Bible Hub, biblehub.com/greek/strongs_4074.htm.

That critique probably wouldn't be consistent with other descriptions of God, though.

The idea of there being an eternal version of us that is independent of everything on earth is interesting. Whether or not this independent eternal being chooses God or not can't be independent of earthly influences though, right? Otherwise, we would know and want nothing. This talk of our "real" versions reminds me of *The Matrix*. I re-watched the series not too long ago and couldn't help but see a lot of parallels between it and Christian living.

Regarding verse 10, I like that analysis. It's encouraging.

**Steve:** I think something can be fixed in one sense and not fixed in another, and I think physics can help a little in this regard. The Big Bang introduced time itself as we know it; that is, we understand time as a part of the bigger spacetime picture that governs the entire structure of the universe. Thus, if God was the author of the Big Bang, then he created time and must in some sense exist independent of it. Now imagine that you are a one-dimensional creature living on a line. Your ability to see ahead of you or behind you is limited by your immediate surroundings. But if I'm a two-dimensional creature, I can move off your line and get a bigger perspective than you can, seeing much further up and down your line from the side (think about being on the $y$-axis looking at the $x$-axis). In the same way, if time is sort of this one-dimensional world that we live in, then our perspective is going to be limited, but God can step off this time axis and see the whole picture (e.g., our future). But that doesn't mean that he has to be controlling it; he might choose to just see it. So I think that we are both freely choosing along our timeline (i.e., our salvation is not fixed) *and* God knows what we will freely choose (i.e., our salvation is fixed) without conflict. As far as "the number of those God gave to Jesus," I suppose that *would* be some specific number that he already knew, but it would not be a number that he decided to arbitrarily set in advance. (Arbitrarily deciding a number in advance is my view of Calvinism. A Calvinist would assert that God does nothing arbitrarily, but I don't see a way around it, especially with the stipulation that one's salvific election is unconditional.)

I don't think one could say that God was wrong about 1 Sam 23:11–13. If I said, "If Donald Trump gets elected a second time, lots of people will be angry," but then he doesn't get elected, that doesn't make me wrong.

Regarding whether God really didn't know whether Saul would go to Keilah, we barely touched on it earlier, but this is the idea of "open theism." In that view, the future doesn't actually exist and is completely open to possibilities, so God would not know whether Saul would go or not. Some open theists might argue that that doesn't diminish God's sovereignty because he can will the future to be whatever he wishes as we move through time. In my mind, however, that seems problematic, because he then still knows how it's going to turn out, thereby refuting the idea of open theism. Thus, I think open theism is probably not compatible with God's complete sovereignty. It also has God riding along the time axis with us, which I think doesn't work with the Big Bang. (I admittedly haven't thought this through completely, and I'm sure an open theist would have lots to say.)

By saying that our eternal choosing of God is independent of earthly influences, I mean that I have a really hard time thinking that, for example, my Americanness is going to carry over into heaven in some way. In a deeper sense, I find it very difficult to think that the only reason I chose God is because I happen to live in a free country with easy access to the gospel. I think verses like Acts 17:26–27 imply that God put me here in this place at this time because we love each other in some bigger-than-this-life sense. If one accepts that premise, then I'm perfectly fine with saying that my salvation was heavily influenced by the environment in which I grew up, namely because God set it up that way. So like I believe that fixed and unfixed salvation can be true at the same time, I think that my salvation can simultaneously be both independent of and heavily dependent on my environment.

I love the analogy with *The Matrix*. I find myself noticing all kinds of parallels between art and Christianity like that which may or may not have been intended by the art's creator.

**Victoria**: That was an illustrative explanation. I don't know if you've seen *Flatland: The Movie*, but I was picturing that throughout. That's a good point regarding what seems like a necessarily arbitrary decision by God from the Calvinist viewpoint.

On your response about 1 Sam 23:11–13, I agree that the Donald Trump statement is not wrong, but that's because there are both supporters and opponents of him. Isn't God saying more definitive (less conditional) statements in those verses? Connecting to open theism—whether or not it accurately describes God, how can God be omniscient but not know what will happen in the future?

That sounds good regarding salvation being independent and dependent on environment.

**Steve**: Yes, it is true that God's statement is less conditional than my statement. I don't *know* that people will be angry after an election, but I can surmise it based on past experience. God, on the other hand, *knew* that David would be captured if Saul went to Keilah. This is probably the main justifiable contention that one might have with Molinism: how could God come to have such certain knowledge? I don't have a great answer for that except to throw it in my massive pile of "How can God [anything]?" questions. Still, my belief in Molinism relies on your last question: I believe in God's omniscience, in which knowing *everything* includes things which may not be. For an open theist, the future is not a knowable thing, so God *can't* know it (much like he can't know what a square circle looks like). An open theist might say that God knew what kind of people Saul and the citizens of Keilah were and could then accurately predict what they would do without that reality ever coming to pass. (As another example, an open theist would claim to have no problem with the book of Revelation, because a God who doesn't know the future can still be certain that he may will the future to be whatever he wishes.)

All of this just made me think of the many-worlds interpretation of quantum mechanics,[2] in which every possible outcome creates another universe. I'm not a big fan of that interpretation at all, but it does make me think of God not only looking down our timeline but looking down all of our possible timelines. That makes my brain hurt.

**Victoria:** Oh, okay. I think I was reading those verses wrong. *If* David had stayed in Keilah, all that would have happened, but since he didn't, those foreseen events did not come to pass.

It's like each of us contains many worlds in ourselves.

**Steve:** Yes! There are many such passages. For example,

> *"Woe to you, Chorazin! Woe to you, Bethsaida! For if the miracles that were performed in you had been performed in Tyre and Sidon, they would have repented long ago in sackcloth and ashes."* (Mt 11:21)

> *None of the rulers of this age understood it, for if they had, they would not have crucified the Lord of glory.* (1 Cor 2:8)

### JOHN 18:15–27

**Victoria:** Peter's denials. Honestly, I feel like it would be hard not to revert to instinctive self-preservation in his situation.

**Steve:** So much of what I read about Jesus is hard to believe because it feels so different than my normal, everyday experience: a radical man who performs miracles, doesn't care what anyone else thinks, and speaks with incredible wisdom and authority. This whole passage is the exact opposite of that. This seems so real, believable, and like my life and world that it gives me a lot of confidence in the authenticity of the scriptures. In addition, it's so embarrassing, both for Jesus and Peter, that I would not have included it if I were just making stuff up. I mean, even the biggest skeptic has to admit that John claiming that Jesus is God in one chapter and then having him slapped in another is a little odd.

**Victoria:** I agree that the unbiased reporting is convincing.

### JOHN 18:28–40

**Victoria:** I've seen this scene from *The Passion of the Christ* often (like every Easter). Verse 28: The Jewish leaders' desire for cleanliness here is ironic. Verse 31: Why do they say we have no right to execute anyone when they go at lengths to persecute Jesus?

---

[2] "Many-worlds interpretation," *Wikipedia*, en.wikipedia.org/wiki/Many-worlds_interpretation.

**Steve**: Yes, their desire for cleanliness is ironic, but Jesus saw right through them:

> *"Woe to you, teachers of the law and Pharisees, you hypocrites! You are like whitewashed tombs, which look beautiful on the outside but on the inside are full of the bones of the dead and everything unclean. In the same way, on the outside you appear to people as righteous but on the inside you are full of hypocrisy and wickedness.* (Mt 23:27–28)

The scary part is that he sees right through me as well. My biggest danger is finding my righteousness in all of this theology that I think I have figured out. My subconscious thought process usually goes like this: 1) I am a terrible sinner, 2) God must be awfully proud of me for knowing that, and 3) he therefore thinks I'm pretty good. I have to constantly catch myself with that attitude and put a stop to it. I *am* righteous, but it comes solely by Jesus' work on the cross, not by my proper understanding of Jesus' work on the cross. (It's also a personally destructive and God-dishonoring thought pattern: it makes it seem that God will only be satisfied if I feel appropriately ashamed.)

As for verse 31, this was effectively a way to slough off responsibility. Hardly anyone was in favor of the Roman occupation, but if it provided a way to let someone else do the dirty work they didn't want to do or weren't allowed to do, the Pharisees found it useful. They felt they could push an issue to the brink of being responsible but not go over some imaginary line. It's easy to do that with politics even today: "All I did was vote for the guy; I didn't tell him to do Bad Thing X." Or in the workplace: "My job description doesn't involve helping you in this way, so go find someone else." Or in the military: "Hey, I don't really *want* to kill these Jews in gas chambers; I'm just following orders." Or everyday life: "I'm not the one making people work in sweatshops; I'm just buying a shirt."

Pilate's response of "What is truth?" is in all the movies, too, but I'm struck by the fact that he asked it and then immediately walked out. He didn't care about the answer. This is our society in a nutshell: wondering if truth exists but always diverting our attention to the latest thing, not really caring if questions have answers.

**Victoria**: Politics has been on my mind lately with the presidential election coming up. Something that bemuses me is how there is a sizable portion of White evangelicals who support Trump. It's probably some interplay of (what they might see as) the lesser of two evils, cultural vs. Biblical Christianity, and/or them wanting to maintain social power. But I would guess that a large influence is probably due to people behaving like the Pharisees did in Mt 23:27–28—too preoccupied with single issues of abortion or the economy that they're not thinking about the bigger picture.

Which do you think would be worse: having that kind of three-step subconscious thought process, or being arrested at step one and not realizing you are a total sinner?

On your response about verse 31, that makes sense. Facing the truth and taking responsibility is difficult and uncomfortable.

This reminds me of the phrase "bread and circuses." Why dig for the truth when your life is going okay (rhetorically speaking)?

**Steve:** I hold two thoughts in tension when it comes to politics: first, that the intermingling of Christianity and politics makes Christianity look unrecognizable, and second, Christians should be involved and vote their consciences on what they think are the most pressing issues in this world. There are so many different reasons that someone might vote for a candidate that it is unfair for anyone to jump to inappropriate conclusions about a voter's morality. I've known Christians who always voted for Democrats because Franklin Roosevelt led them out of the Great Depression. I also know Christians who believe that abortion is the barbaric murder of innocent human beings, and while they might recognize that Democrats align more closely with their other views on human life and human rights issues (e.g., death penalty, gun rights, immigration, etc.), the state sanctioning of abortion trumps (no pun intended) all of the other issues combined; thus, they will never vote for a Democrat. It all goes back to each American having to decide what an "optimal world" looks like in the face of an unfortunate two-party political system. Yes, sometimes that "optimal world" is too single-issue minded. Sometimes that "optimal world" really just means "what's best for me." And sometimes that "optimal world" just means reveling in the fact that the other party is really sad.

What I see from Jesus is that he refuses to join in. We talked about it a little, but I want to bring this passage back up:

> *Later they sent some of the Pharisees and Herodians to Jesus to catch him in his words. They came to him and said, "Teacher, we know that you are a man of integrity. You aren't swayed by others, because you pay no attention to who they are; but you teach the way of God in accordance with the truth. Is it right to pay the imperial tax to Caesar or not? Should we pay or shouldn't we?" But Jesus knew their hypocrisy. "Why are you trying to trap me?" he asked. "Bring me a denarius and let me look at it." They brought the coin, and he asked them, "Whose image is this? And whose inscription?" "Caesar's," they replied. Then Jesus said to them, "Give back to Caesar what is Caesar's and to God what is God's." And they were amazed at him.* (Mk 12:13–17)

The crowd wanted him to answer a political question: as God-fearing Jews, should they pay taxes to an oppressive pagan government? Surely we think there is a correct answer here, and we might know it by watching whether Jesus paid his taxes or not. But instead of saying "yes" or "no," and by looking at the inscription which probably said, "Caesar Augustus Tiberius, son of the Divine Augustus,"[3] he effectively answered their question with, "Caesar is not God." If you understand that Caesar is not God, then it suddenly makes it not a big deal to pay your taxes to him, because you're not necessarily saying anything *about* Caesar by doing it.[4] That is, Caesar thinks he gains our allegiance by imposing his will, but Jesus says it is simultaneously possible to obey Caesar on the outside (because God put him there anyway[5]) and maintain our true, internal allegiance to God. Another example is here:

> *If anyone forces you to go one mile, go with them two miles.* (Mt 5:41)

If a Roman soldier made you carry his gear for a mile, he's doing so to exert his authority over you. By volunteering to go even longer, you ironically show him that he has no authority over you. Or this:

> *But I tell you, do not resist an evil person. If anyone slaps you on the right cheek, turn to them the other cheek also.* (Mt 5:39)

If I do what comes naturally, I'll punch the person who slapped me, but that's such a predictable response that I would be effectively showing the slapper that he can control me (i.e., he knows that his action will cause me to react in a certain way). If I then let him slap me on the other cheek, I'm again showing him that he cannot control what I do or say.

All of this has been to say the same thing about politics. If the current President makes me mad, he/she has complete control over me. It's true for policy issues as well. I have very strong opinions about abortion, LGBT rights, immigration, gun control, climate change, vaccinations, the size of the government, capitalism, free speech, taxes, and a thousand other issues. But if my main concern is whether those policies get enacted the way I want them to, I am no longer free; I am a slave to the whims of politicians. According to Jesus, I can still be completely free even if all of my First Amendment rights are taken away:

> *So if the Son sets you free, you will be free indeed.* (Jn 8:36)

The other consequence with politics is that eternal people are turned into temporary issues; e.g., whether LGBT rights are enacted or not, it doesn't change the fact that Jesus requires me to love the LGBT people I actually interact with on a daily basis. In summary, vote your conscience, let other people vote theirs, and walk away from the polling

---

[3] "Tribute penny," *Wikipedia*, en.wikipedia.org/wiki/Tribute_penny.
[4] Rom 13:6–7.
[5] Rom 13:1.

booth knowing that you've been given an unbelievable freedom that you can keep no matter who gets elected or what policies get enacted. It may feel like you're doing the noble thing by defending others when you vote for their causes, but the people you're defending can have this greater freedom if you tell them about Jesus instead of supporting their movement. In fact, supporting their movement might only enable their political slavery.

If I understand your question about the subconscious thought process, I think the latter is worse. Christianity is built upon seeing oneself as desperately in need of salvation. Knowing that truth but falling into occasional pride is better than not knowing it at all. It's like the difference between having a car without an engine and having a car with an engine that needs to be fixed.

**Victoria**: Good food for thought throughout. If I could ever live by Mt 5:39, my life would be a lot more stable, at least emotionally. You mention a couple of Romans verses which basically say that authority has been established by God. Was this only true then? Is it true now? Was it true in Hitler's time?

**Steve**: I believe it's always true that authority is established by God. It was true in 1 Sam 8 when Israel asked for a king, God said it was a bad idea, and then he gave them what they wanted. It was true when Paul wrote Romans, and Nero—one of the most wicked people to ever live—was Caesar. (Think about that for a second: Paul wrote that Nero's authority was given to him by God, and Paul was executed under Nero's reign. That's exactly the kind of "You can't defeat me because I'm already submitting to you" attitude I've been talking about.) It was true when Hitler became Chancellor of Germany. And it will be true when whoever wins this election becomes President. Of course, this brings up the question of what "establishes" means, and, as usual, the best answer is probably found in some balance. Namely, I don't believe that God put people in a trance so that they pushed the Trump button on November 8, 2016, but I also don't believe that the results caught him off guard. The exact reasons and timing of God's intervention in this world are often invisible to us until well after the fact (or we may never know). For example, an overbearing British monarchy in the 1700s led to the formation of the United States, which I believe has been a net positive for the world. But if you were living under Henry VIII in the 1500s, you never would have seen the future good on its way. In the same way, I believe the devastation wrought by Hitler made society more tolerant and hesitant to engage in utter destruction (e.g., it probably kept the Cold War "cold"). If God wants to use a leader to bring peace or judgment on a nation, that's his prerogative, because he sees the greater ultimate good that we can't:

*Make your motions and cast your votes, but GOD has the final say.*
(Prov 16:33, MSG)

# CHAPTER 37: JOHN 19

### JOHN 19:1–16

**Victoria:** I almost feel bad for Pilate. He doesn't really want to be in that position, it seems (verses 6 and 12). In verse 7, what law are the Pharisees referring to that he must die? In verse 11, is that Judas? Or the Pharisees?

**Steve:** I've been watching *The Chosen*[1] (I can't recommend it enough) and they do a great job of showing the relationship between the Romans and Jews of that place and time. I imagine that these types of issues were annoyances for the Romans leaders in that area. In their minds, having to settle disputes regarding a god they didn't believe in was just a part of crowd control. (Sudden thought: how much of modern politics is simply crowd control? Yikes.)

As for verse 7, as the Pharisees believed Jesus was a blasphemous false prophet, I think they could be referring to either of these laws:

> ... *anyone who blasphemes the name of the* LORD *is to be put to death. The entire assembly must stone them. Whether foreigner or native-born, when they blaspheme the Name they are to be put to death.* (Lev 24:16)

> *"But a prophet who presumes to speak in my name anything I have not commanded, or a prophet who speaks in the name of other gods, is to be put to death."* (Deut 18:20)

When someone says that Jesus never claimed to be God, verses like verse 7 make it quite difficult to explain why the Pharisees were so angry and thought he should be killed.

Verse 11 is exactly what we discussed in Jn 18. We can't understand that God planned the crucifixion to happen unless we also understand that God established Pilate as an authority (which could've happened in a million ways, ranging from Pilate's great-great-grandfather deciding to move to Italy 100 years earlier to Pilate making the right decision about a construction project that resulted in his promotion).

My first thought is that Jesus is referring to Judas at the end of verse 11 just because of the simple explanation and singular pronoun. But people who know Greek a lot better than me have all kinds of interpretations:[2] Judas, Caiaphas, any generic Pharisee, Satan, and all of

---

[1] *The Chosen*, studios.vidangel.com/the-chosen.
[2] "What is the cause of the 'greater sin' in John 19:11?," *StackExchange*, hermeneutics.stackexchange.com/questions/13762/what-is-the-cause-of-the-greater-sin-in-john-1911.

us, and even that the authority "from above" could be God (which I favor), Caiaphas, or Caesar. It's a difficult verse to figure out and makes me wonder if Jesus was pointing toward the sky or a priest or a statue of Caesar when he said it. Given all of that, I think the message is still pretty clear as a response to Pilate's power play in verse 10: Jesus is saying, "Although you're really messing up here, you're an unwitting pawn in someone else's game, so you're neither as important nor responsible as you think you are."

Verse 15 is stunning. Going from "Is it right to pay the imperial tax to Caesar or not?" to "We have no king but Caesar" is unbelievable.

**Victoria**: I hadn't heard of *The Chosen* before; I'll check it out!

How did they decide who was a real blasphemous prophet back then, anyway? Maybe whoever consistently and correctly predicted the future was a strong contender. I wonder if the Pharisees believed deep down inside that there was more truth to Jesus than they were willing to admit.

On verse 11 and God's establishment of authority, it sounds like some complex butterfly effect at work.

On Pilate being "neither as important nor responsible as [he thinks he is]," is the corollary of that statement pretty much that everyone is more responsible than we think we are?

**Steve**: A prophet isn't necessarily someone who predicts the future, but more generally someone who delivers a message from God. For example, when Paul says that some have the gift of prophecy,[3] he isn't saying that Christianity breeds fortune tellers. (In the modern day, I generally think of this gift of prophecy as being an ability to take the whole of scripture and turn it into a concise message that provides some benefit. For example, a pastor might use the gift of prophecy to help a couple through a difficult marriage by applying biblical wisdom. The couple might not see how their specific issues are addressed by the Bible, but the pastor can speak on God's behalf using his gift and knowledge of scripture—all with the help of the Holy Spirit.) Now, there is some clarity about testing those who claim to have messages from God:

> *If what a prophet proclaims in the name of the LORD does not take place or come true, that is a message the LORD has not spoken. That prophet has spoken presumptuously, so do not be alarmed.* (Deut 18:22)

> *"Watch out for false prophets. They come to you in sheep's clothing, but inwardly they are ferocious wolves. By their fruit you will recognize them. Do people pick grapes from thornbushes, or figs from thistles?"* (Mt 7:15–16)

---

[3] 1 Cor 12:10.

*... but every spirit that does not acknowledge Jesus is not from God.* (1 Jn 4:3a)

For example, orthodox Christianity would say that the Prophet Muhammad failed the latter test and—considering that he received his revelation from an angel—this one as well:

*But even if we or an angel from heaven should preach a gospel other than the one we preached to you, let them be under God's curse!* (Gal 1:8)

Of course, this lends itself to circular reasoning because one might simultaneously say, "I believe the Bible because it was given by God through his prophets," and "I believe God's prophets because they're supported by the Bible." This is why we have to rely on extra-biblical evidence, reason, self-consistency, and experience to come to conclusions about the veracity of scripture to begin with. (Of course, Jesus had the benefit of being able to perform miracles to verify his claims.) I have a hard time trusting people who say they trust God's word because it's God's word.

I don't think the Pharisees were crazy and probably did think there was more to Jesus than they were willing to admit. But their issues were 1) a too-narrow focus on the scripture they liked that ignored texts like Is 53 and Dan 7:13–14 and 2) the threat that Jesus' way of thinking posed to their way of life. So... basically the same issues that every human has.

As to the butterfly effect, I don't mean to imply that either of those hypothetical scenarios would be random like the flapping of a butterfly's wings. Maybe God made Pilate's great-great-grandfather's crops fail so that he freely decided to move. Or maybe he created a universe in which those crops would fail 13.8 billion years later. I'm basically just saying that we don't have to think about God's providence as narrowly as God directly stepping in in some free will-altering way every time he wants to accomplish his will. It goes back to my belief that I probably understand God's actions as well as my cat understands mine. I used to have a lot of questions about how God could keep track of so much stuff, but the more I learn about the size of the universe, the less I wonder if God is capable of figuring all that out.

As to responsibility for the crucifixion, I suppose if you think about it as a zero-sum game, then the lessening of Pilate's responsibility would indeed put it more squarely on the rest of us. But I think it's a little more nuanced than that, in that Pilate the Roman official was just kind of unlucky to be there, but Pilate the human sinner falls in with the rest of us in bearing the weight. Thus, whomever we might think bore the greatest responsibility for Jesus' death is mostly irrelevant. Judas and

Hitler and Mother Teresa and Nelson Mandela all play a part in that perspective. (I just thought of how funny it would be if you thought that I thought that *only* those four people were responsible, and what a strange group that would be.)

**Victoria**: Hmm, would you say there are prophets who exist today?

On the point about the veracity of scripture, I would think most people use reason, self-consistency, and experience to reach their beliefs. On extra-biblical evidence though, how often do you feel the need to seek this out or refer to such sources? We've brought up many extra-biblical references throughout this discussion, but I assume by extra-biblical evidence that you mean contemporary evidence for Scripture.

Ha ha! I'm sure one could come up with common denominators for the four besides being human.

**Steve**: 1) In the sense I mentioned of prophecy being a gift of God to help communicate his message (i.e., scripture) to others, yes, I could call those people prophets. Of course, in normal conversation, throwing that word around has serious connotations, so I would avoid it (and do). 2) In the sense of a prophet delivering a message from God that isn't in scripture (something like, "Vickie, God is telling me that you should avoid driving on the interstate today"), I would have serious doubts. 3) I do think there could be a gentle nudge from the Holy Spirit along the lines of "I feel like God is telling me to reply to Vickie's email to talk to her about Jesus" (which actually happened). In that sense, it was just a mental "push" to do something that might make both of us uncomfortable but felt like the right thing to do. I have known many people who claim to feel such a thing on a regular basis. I wouldn't call them "prophets," but it's hard to dispute them. 4) In the sense of a prophet like Isaiah or Jeremiah hearing directly from God, predicting the future, and creating new books of the Bible, absolutely not (i.e., I believe the scriptural canon is closed). So overall, I would say I believe in modern prophecy in the sense of the Holy Spirit imparting guidance to some with the intention of revealing it to others, but not in the sense of any kind of new revelation. Or to put it another way, I would say it is a gift to elaborate on what's already been given. In the most general sense, every (good) sermon is a prophecy, although I am well aware that we rarely use the word that way, so again, I would avoid it.

I would like to think that most people use reason, self-consistency, and experience to reach their beliefs, but when I read/watch the news, it usually looks like pure emotion. As for extra-biblical resources, I would say they should be a tool which every believer should keep in their back pocket. It may not be necessary to attain salvation or live a faithful life, but they can sure be handy in times of doubt. When I feel like, "Is any of this real?", it can be grounding to know that I have legitimate reasons to believe. I've been doing this long enough now to not be shaken in my core beliefs, so I often just *enjoy* apologetics as much as I *need* apologetics.

**Victoria:** I like the way you laid out those four points. I think the connotation of prophets is much more along the lines of (2) or (4) than (1). It would be hard for me to think about anyone I know being a prophet, but perhaps that isn't so different from people who knew Jesus not being able to believe he was the Son of Man. I would also agree with (3) and your overall conclusions based on empirical evidence from experiences I've had and heard about.

## JOHN 19:17–27

**Victoria:** No comments here.

**Steve:**

> *There is a way that appears to be right, but in the end it leads to death.* (Prov 14:12)

**Victoria:** What does that mean here?

**Steve:** It means that if I were a Pharisee or in the crowd or a Roman official, I almost certainly would've concluded, "We are doing the right thing." Not just right in the sense of efficiency, criminal justice, or crowd control, but that we were actually, legitimately morally right, and that God (or the gods) would be pleased with me. That sense of moral rightness would have been the most wrong I've ever been, and it ended in someone's death. Jesus generalizes this to our potential spiritual death as well:

> *"Not everyone who says to me, 'Lord, Lord,' will enter the kingdom of heaven, but only the one who does the will of my Father who is in heaven. Many will say to me on that day, 'Lord, Lord, did we not prophesy in your name and in your name drive out demons and in your name perform many miracles?' Then I will tell them plainly, 'I never knew you. Away from me, you evildoers!'"* (Mt 7:21–23)

**Victoria:** Maybe it's the clarity of hindsight and the way it's presented in the Bible, but it seems pretty clear today that the Pharisees were not in the right. And as we talked about in the previous section, they probably had at least a bit of understanding that what they did was against, rather than for, God. Beyond the Pharisees though, Mt 7:21–23 seems kind of paranoia-inducing, because what if you are living a life that you legitimately think of as a good life and don't get feedback to suggest otherwise, yet in the end God says he doesn't know you? How to be saved (i.e., Rom 10:9) seems like such a simple concept in theory.

**Steve:** Mt 7:21–23 can be a little unsettling, but I think a genuine believer has no need to worry. Jesus is addressing those who have all the appearances of belief on the outside but have no love or relationship on the inside. They might do this for a lot of different reasons (money, status, guilt, fitting in, etc.), but notice that he takes their external actions to the extreme (they are by no means mundane). He's using hyperbole to point out that even the most fantastic appearances mean nothing to him without an inner connection. Rom 10:9 still remains a simple concept; *you* know if you love God and believe that Jesus is Lord, and you can rest in that.

### JOHN 19:28–37

**Victoria**: In verse 35, is this testimony generally known or was it only recorded in the Gospel?

**Steve**: John is referring to himself (which he often does in the third person[4]) and his eponymous account. He's just clearly stating that he's giving an eyewitness account, not hearsay.

### JOHN 19:38–42

**Victoria**: In verse 38, why was it that Joseph and Nicodemus took and buried Jesus' body instead of his disciples? Because they were of higher power and wealth than the disciples?

**Steve**: Yes, I think that's right. It's generally thought that the disciples were both poor...

> *As they were walking along the road, a man said to him, "I will follow you wherever you go." Jesus replied, "Foxes have dens and birds have nests, but the Son of Man has no place to lay his head."* (Lk 9:57–58)

and gone:

> *Then everyone deserted him and fled.* (Mk 14:50)

So just when we thought we had the Sadducees and Pharisees figured out, two of them show up at the last minute to take care of business. It's another huge reminder to me to think of people as individuals rather than predict their behavior based on what group I think they belong to.

Lastly, I wonder what I would have done or where I would've been at this point if I were a follower of Jesus. My best guess is that I would've run away to 1) avoid Jesus' fate and 2) wallow in embarrassment for believing a fraud. Would I have ever come back? Would I believe the stories about his resurrection if I only heard them from afar? Believing after getting the whole story and theology behind it two thousand years after the fact seems so much easier than if I had been there in person and missed the resurrection. Amazingly, the disciples *didn't* run away and didn't have to deal with that possibility. As easy as it is to make fun of them, they at least had the courage to stick around at this point.

---

[4] Jn 13:23, 19:26, 21:7.

**Victoria**: Yeah, I can imagine also being pretty mortified if everyone I knew saw me devote my life to someone who ended up being a sham. I suppose how one would handle news of the death and resurrection would depend on how convinced one was about Jesus. If your faith is all-encompassing, maybe you hold out hope even after running away.

Tangentially from that thought, a negative possible result of being convinced no matter what happens is that people could end up in cults. (I've been listening to a podcast which has a cult series focus, so it's fresh on my mind.) A lot of cult groups seem to start out for good reasons, such as for religion, self-help, or drug rehabilitation. But then the leader takes it to the extreme, perhaps misled by power and money. Followers may have had an initial or ongoing benefit from involvement in the group, which can blind them to the faults and wrongdoings of the leader. When it comes to Christian-in-name cults, biblical concepts can get twisted (e.g., predictions of the end times), leading people to slide down the slippery slope of denying oneself for the benefit of the cult rather than for the benefit of having God central to one's life. For example, if a church says one should marry someone within their specific church, is it because they're overzealous in making sure their constituents have godly marriages, or is it because they want to keep track of and limit people's outside relationships? On a related note, last summer while I was doing research in Sweden, I attended this small house church which I really liked, with insightful teachings and lively praise. However, I found out afterwards that their parent church may be a cult (?!). It was a jarring realization of how things can seem so normal at first, but you don't know if you're a frog in a pond or a pot of boiling water.

**Steve**: Yes, absolutely. As you've experienced, it can be an attractive, mesmerizing, and eventually scary thing. A faithful Christian should always be asking him/herself, "Who am I actually following?" Genuine Christian leaders let people think on their own but continually point their followers to Jesus, not themselves:

> What I mean is this: One of you says, "I follow Paul"; another, "I follow Apollos"; another, "I follow Cephas"; still another, "I follow Christ." Is Christ divided? Was Paul crucified for you? Were you baptized in the name of Paul? I thank God that I did not baptize any of you except Crispus and Gaius, so no one can say that you were baptized in my name. (1 Cor 1:12–14)

Verses like that give me confidence that Paul was not a cult leader like the ones you warn about.

# CHAPTER 38: JOHN 20

### JOHN 20:1–10

**Victoria**: Verse 8: what it is that he believed? I would have thought he believed that Jesus rose, but verse 9 seems to say otherwise.

**Steve**: First, if the events in this chapter (i.e., John 20, not the chapter we're writing) are true, these are the most important words ever written. If not, you and I are complete fools:

> *And if Christ has not been raised, your faith is futile; you are still in your sins. Then those also who have fallen asleep in Christ are lost. If only for this life we have hope in Christ, we are of all people most to be pitied.* (1 Cor 15:17–19)

I'm not trying to be dramatic, but this is why it's so important to come to an informed, reasonable conclusion on this issue; fortunately, there are a lot of great resources.[1] The minimal-facts approach addressed here[2] and here[3] are good starting places.

I think verses 8–9 could be read in three ways:

1. Verse 9 could be placed chronologically before verse 8 and be an after-the-fact explanation. Something like, "Vickie was surprised when her cat jumped into her lap. She still didn't know that cats could jump."
2. They could be read as, "John believed that Jesus was raised from the dead, but still didn't see how it connected to the Old Testament."
3. As you mentioned, John might have believed that Jesus' body was gone but had not yet believed that he was raised from the dead.

The following verse could be interpreted to support any of those explanations:

---

[1] Josh McDowell and Sean McDowell, *Evidence for the Resurrection: What It Means for Your Relationship with God* (Ventura, CA: Regal, 2009); Gary R. Habermas and Michael Licona, *The Case for the Resurrection of Jesus* (Grand Rapids: Kregel Publications, 2004); N. T. Wright, *The Resurrection of the Son of God (Christian Origins and the Question of God, Vol. 3)* (Minneapolis: Fortress Press, 2003); Lee Strobel, *The Case for the Resurrection* (Grand Rapids: Zondervan, 2010); Frank Morison, *Who Moved the Stone?* (Grand Rapids: Zondervan, 1987).

[2] Aaron Brake, *The Minimal Facts of the Resurrection*, March 5, 2018, crossexamined.org/the-minimal-facts-of-the-resurrection/.

[3] Gary Habermas, *Minimal Facts on the Resurrection that Even Skeptics Accept*, September 28, 2018, ses.edu/minimal-facts-on-the-resurrection-that-even-skeptics-accept/.

*Peter, however, got up and ran to the tomb. Bending over, he saw the strips of linen lying by themselves, and he went away, wondering to himself what had happened.* (Lk 24:12)

**Victoria**: From one of the references you brought up regarding the minimal-facts approach, I thought it was interesting that Christianity "is the *only* [emphasis added] religion which bases its faith on an empirically verifiable event." I would've thought that other religions such as Judaism, Islam, or Buddhism also rely on empirically verifiable events.

**Steve**: I will start by saying that *any* person's attempt to summarize any religion to which they do not adhere will often be fraught with errors of bias and mischaracterization, so I'll try to tread lightly here. Even more so, the adherents of any religion frequently disagree amongst themselves about what's really important (e.g., does it really matter if Job was a real person or if Jonah was really swallowed by a whale?). Still, if we take the four major religions by population (Christianity, Islam, Hinduism, and Buddhism) and add Judaism because of its strong ties with Christianity, I would tend to agree with the reference you mentioned: not in an absolute sense, but in a sense of *degree*. In other words, I would say that every religion is founded on some (at least perceived) historical element, but removing that historical element now may not affect the religion in its current state as would happen with Christianity. For example, if the Buddha had never existed as a real person, would the Four Noble Truths or Noble Eightfold Path still carry the same weight? Yes, I think they would; there are some timeless life- and world-changing ideas in rightly acknowledging that this world is filled with suffering and that "right view, right resolve, right speech, etc." can address it. Would the Torah mean less if the Israelite exodus were a metaphor instead of a reality? Even though learning such a fact would make me question some of my beliefs about the Bible, there would still be great truth regarding the providence of God contained in those books. If the Earth was not actually created in six days as Gen 1:31 and Quran 50:38 state, are Judaism, Christianity, and Islam doomed? No; we all appreciate symbolism as a valuable way of writing, speaking, and gleaning truth. Similarly, the Upanishads are full of teaching, stories, philosophizing, and thinking about the world in ways that are generally independent of whether they are grounded in a verifiable historical reality. All of this is true of many other smaller religions and philosophies as well. I'm not saying it's OK to turn any religion into just a bunch of symbolism, but I am claiming that history or a lack thereof usually does not trump theology.

But Jesus is different. As a Christian, I can unequivocally state that if the stories about Jesus' life, death, and resurrection (especially the latter) never really happened, then everything I believe falls apart. Here's why: 1) The Bible says that Jesus himself claimed to be God. If those words (or inferences, if you prefer) never came out of his mouth, then the most important things I believe about Ultimate Reality are wrong. This is nuanced because other faiths claim very important ideas as well, but Christianity depends on a real flesh-and-bones man who lived in a certain area of the world at a certain time and *claimed to be God*, not someone just philosophizing about the way the world is or should be or what God is like. You may have noticed that much of the Bible is simply stories written as historical events or arguments written to historical people, not Aristotelian treatises trying to logically persuade us. 2) The Bible claims that Jesus was raised from the dead. Every ounce of life and hope in me rests on that claim. If he was not physically raised to life after he died, what hope do I have? I'm already convinced that I don't have what it takes to rest on my good deeds to get me into any other religion's heaven, so if this event didn't actually happen, I'm toast (not necessarily in the "burning in hell" physical sense, but more in the "I have no coherent worldview on which to ground my life" mental sense).

Also, think about this: if Jesus was raised from the dead, everyone on Earth should convert to Christianity regardless of whether they initially agree with any other part of it: *a man raised himself from the dead!* If not, no one should be a Christian because it's utter nonsense and Jesus was a complete fraud. What other *debatable* historical question has that kind of dichotomous influence? (I acknowledge that other historical questions might have huge ramifications, but none that can be investigated in any modern sense with external sources, consistency of facts, plausibility arguments, reason, etc., and none that splits the world into two camps like the resurrection. For example, Muhammad actually receiving the Quran from the angel Gabriel would indeed change the world, but do we have any solid way to historically investigate such a claim? No. Would anything be very different if maybe he heard God's voice instead of an angel's? No, not really. Does a Muslim place all of his/her hope in the historical truth of this encounter? Nope—as far as my understanding goes, a Muslim prioritizes the Quran over the historicity of the creation of the Quran.) Now, I'm not saying that Christian apologetics is *only* based on historical argument (there are many other reasons to believe Christianity is true), but it is still the case that all Christian truth claims are founded on whether the resurrection happened or not. It's more important than any other story in the Bible. In fact, I would argue that it's more important than the Bible itself and even (along with the crucifixion) the central point of all history.

Finally, we are all partially influenced by what we *want* to believe and should remember that this is a debate, not a lab experiment or math problem. A person should not approach the resurrection with the idea that proof one way or the other will emerge. Rather, one should ask, "Given *everything* I know (science, reason, evidence, morality, experience, etc.), is an actual resurrection the most plausible explanation of the events?" If you approach that question with only your science hat on, the answer is clearly "No; people don't resurrect," but that would be ignoring all of the other non-scientific things about you and reality that you know to be equally valid. (Notice that I'm avoiding saying, "Just believe." That's a caricature of Christianity that doesn't work if you encounter a thinking Christian.) If accounting for everything still gives the answer of "no," fine. But if the answer is "yes," it changes everything.

**Victoria:** "If Jesus was raised from the dead, everyone on Earth should convert to Christianity regardless of whether they initially agree with any other part of it." I would agree this should be convincing in itself. It probably would be more convincing if the past weren't so easy to forget or ignore.

"Finally, we are all partially influenced by what we want to believe and should remember that this is a debate, not a lab experiment or math problem." Right; as Bayes' theorem has it, if you mentally allow a zero prior probability for some outcome, then you will see that outcome as never having occurred—a zero posterior probability. Being logically open-minded would mean admitting that the outcome that one thinks is *not* true can still have a non-zero probability even if that probability is minuscule.

### JOHN 20:11–18

**Victoria:** This is one of those significant events that I've long been familiar with from growing up in the South. No comments/questions, except a rhetorical musing as to why the angels were there.

**Steve:** I actually listened to a sermon this morning on this very text. The word "stood" in verse 11 is the Greek word εἰστήκει,[4] which is a past perfect verb tense designed to indicate a completed action. In other words, Mary didn't just happen to be standing there; she was absolutely resolved: "He *said* he was going to be raised from the dead, and darn it, I'm going to wait here because I believe it." That's admirable and/or foolish, depending on the result.

Also, the angels, "one at the head and the other at the foot," seems to be a direct callback to the mercy seat[5] on the Ark of the Covenant:

> *Make one cherub on one end and the second cherub on the other; make the cherubim of one piece with the cover, at the two ends.* (Ex 25:19)

It represented both God's presence and the atonement for sins. (There are hundreds of such Old Testament connections in the New Testament that we 21st-century Gentiles completely miss, but to a 1st-century Jewish reader, facts like this would be eye-popping and the parallels

---

[4] "Strong's Greek: 2476. histémi," Bible Hub, biblehub.com/greek/2476.htm.
[5] "Mercy seat," *Wikipedia*, en.wikipedia.org/wiki/Mercy_seat.

would be obvious. *BibleProject*[6] and *That the World May Know*[7] are top-notch resources on these sorts of things.)

It's also funny that she confused Jesus for the gardener. Maybe he and Jesus looked alike? Maybe Jesus looked different for some reason? (I imagine being crucified and resurrected could change your appearance somewhat.) Maybe he was kind of far away? Maybe it was too dark (verse 1)? Maybe she couldn't fathom that her belief came true? Maybe Jesus thought it would be funny to surprise everyone? (We don't get to see the comedic side of Jesus very much, but given how much we like humor, it's hard to imagine that he wasn't funny.) I don't know, but it seems to be common that people don't recognize him at first:

> *As they talked and discussed these things with each other, Jesus himself came up and walked along with them; but they were kept from recognizing him.* (Lk 24:15–16)

**Victoria**: It's interesting (and kind of unfortunate) how all that connotation gets lost in translation.

That's a helpful explanation regarding the angels. Speaking of *BibleProject*, I actually started a Bible reading plan from them since I liked their videos. Pairing the videos with reading helps tie together concepts and highlight big-picture details.

Ha ha, I didn't pay much attention to Mary thinking Jesus was the gardener. You would think if she had the resolve to stay there and wait that she'd be prone to recognize him when he showed up.

My brain can't imagine Jesus/God being funny, but I would certainly love to witness that.

**Steve**: It's harder to see with only written text in front of us, but Jesus uses irony and hyperbole in a way that would certainly make us laugh (even if just nervously) if we were in his audience. For example, in his parable about forgiveness in Mt 18:21–35, one man owed the king (i.e., God) about 150,000 years' worth of wages.[8] In Mt 15:21–28, Jesus plays right into an offensive stereotype of his day to test a woman's resolve.[9] (That one's tricky, but I view it in the same way as a woman saying something like, "I'll explain this in a way even a man can understand." That's funny.) In Mt 19:23–26, he uses an absurdity to reveal God's mercy. In Mt 12:1–3, he asked *the Pharisees* if they had read scripture. In Jn 10:31–32, he asked people which good thing he had done was worthy of them killing him. There are tons of verses like this which I normally interpret in a

---

[6] *BibleProject*, bibleproject.com/.

[7] *That the World May Know*, www.thattheworldmayknow.com/.

[8] "The Parable of the Talents," *St. John Chrysostom Orthodox Church*, www.orthodoxyork.org/the-parable-of-the-talents.html.

[9] Darren Huckey, "Are Gentiles Really Dogs?" *Emet HaTorah*, www.emethatorah.com/blog/2019/february-01/are-gentiles-really-dogs.

serious manner but upon reflection would've been pretty funny in person.

## JOHN 20:19–23

**Victoria**: In verse 21, is he "sending you" to share the Gospel? Also, what is the point of what he said in verse 23?

**Steve**: Yes, we can view verse 21 in the same light as the Great Commission:

> *Therefore go and make disciples of all nations, baptizing them in the name of the Father and of the Son and of the Holy Spirit, and teaching them to obey everything I have commanded you. And surely I am with you always, to the very end of the age."* (Mt 28:19–20)

Verse 23 is tough. A plain reading would indicate that Jesus is imputing the power of God's ability to forgive onto the disciples. But once, when the teachers of the law confronted him on a similar issue,

> *"Why does this fellow talk like that? He's blaspheming! Who can forgive sins but God alone?"* (Mk 2:7)

he answered not by saying that anyone can do God's job of forgiving sins, but that he was uniquely given this authority:

> *But I want you to know that the Son of Man has authority on earth to forgive sins."* (Mk 2:10)

So, I do not believe—as this verse has been interpreted by some—that Jesus is giving God-like authority to normal schmoes. Rather, I think it is better to see it in the context of how the book of John has already defined sin:

> *When [the Holy Spirit] comes, he will prove the world to be in the wrong about sin ... because people do not believe in me.* (Jn 16:8–9)

That is, in Jesus' mind, the most foundational definition of sin is "not believing in him;" therefore, belief is synonymous with having one's sins forgiven. The Greek root of the words translated as the first two "forgives" here is ἀφίημι (aphiémi),[10] which actually means "to release." Similarly, the second two "forgives" is actually from κρατέω (krateó),[11] which means "to hold." Of course, when they refer to the object "sin," then "forgive" is not a bad translation. But I think that word is a little too

---

[10] "Strong's Greek: 863. ἀφίημι (aphiémi)," *Bible Hub*, biblehub.com/greek/strongs_863.htm.

[11] "Strong's Greek: 2902. κρατέω (krateó)," *Bible Hub*, biblehub.com/greek/strongs_2902.htm.

inflexible given the context of Jesus' previous words in Jn 16:8–9. Thus, I would argue that "releasing" someone from their sins or "holding" someone to their sins is the exact same thing as presenting the gospel (with the "releasing" or "holding" depending on whether their response is favorable or unfavorable). Thus, the Robinson Translation might say (including verse 21), "Go preach the gospel, which will hold people accountable or release them from their sins as determined by their choice to believe or not." Confer with this:

> "If I had not come and spoken to them, they would not be guilty of sin; but now they have no excuse for their sin." (Jn 15:22)

**Victoria**: Huh. I definitely would not have gotten to the Robinson Translation from a straight reading of verse 23. The explanation makes sense though. So the "you" is much less of the "doer" in this scenario, since "you" is more of a conduit for the message. Trying to put the translation more in parallel with what the NIV has, would this be a valid interpretation: "If you preach the gospel to people who are receptive, they will be released from their sins. If you do not preach the gospel to people (and they don't receive it elsewhere), they will not have the option to be released from their sins" ... not that they would be *held* to their sins according to Jn 15:22?

**Steve**: I am almost always opposed to what I did to produce the Robinson Translation here. We are in grave danger of making the Bible say what we want it to say by overthinking or academizing its plain message, becoming too "smart" for our own good:

> Where is the wise person? Where is the teacher of the law? Where is the philosopher of this age? Has not God made foolish the wisdom of the world? (1 Cor 1:20)

For example, one of my least favorite passages in the Bible is...

> "If your right eye causes you to stumble, gouge it out and throw it away. It is better for you to lose one part of your body than for your whole body to be thrown into hell. And if your right hand causes you to stumble, cut it off and throw it away. It is better for you to lose one part of your body than for your whole body to go into hell." (Mt 5:29–31)

Now, I don't think Jesus here intends for us to take what he said literally (or I wouldn't have any body parts left). But the message is clear: sin will absolutely destroy us in both this life and the next, and we should do whatever we can to avoid it. If I try to lessen the forcefulness of this message by doing a Greek word study or reading all kinds of commentaries in the hopes of turning Jesus into someone who actually approves of us no matter what we do, then I've done major damage to my own and potentially someone else's life and understanding. But here in John 20:23, I think this verse is so clearly different from the context of the rest of scripture that we have to pause and wonder if this concise translation can be expanded for clarity. So, yes, I'm all for the Lim Translation. As for your last question (if I understand it correctly), I think it's a matter of semantics. If a person does not choose to be released from their sins, then they *will* be held to them; i.e., both God and the person play a role.

**Victoria**: It's also about self-consistency, right? It seems that Bible studies can often involve Greek word studies or other commentaries to try to understand the message as it was intended. But how one would know whether some message was strengthened or lessened in forcefulness, or otherwise distorted, would depend on one's prior understanding of God and the Bible. I suppose I can see that in my own thinking in the past few years. Without knowing very much before, I could believe various interpretations and messages even if contradictory. That's partly why the Bible seemed so unreliable to me at first: anyone could take some verse and twist it for their own agendas. Now I can parse out a little better what makes sense and what's baloney.

**Steve**: Yes, you absolutely nailed it! It's not hard to find entire websites devoted to showing why the Bible and Christianity are wrong and which are full of snippets of claimed problematic and contradictory scripture and theology.[12] It takes a lot of work to see the big picture, which goes back to my main message: if one sees that they have a problem that needs to be solved, they'll put in the work to see what Christianity really teaches. If they don't, they won't. If they need/want a king and savior, they'll do whatever it takes to follow and find him. If they want to be their own king and savior, they won't take the first step. This is why evangelism and discipleship work so much better when you care enough about someone to spend considerable time with them. Yelling at an unbeliever that the Bible is true and that they'd better believe it or else is exactly what creates those types of websites. It's very similar to learning physics. When I first took it in college, it seemed to be a thousand equations jumbled together (some of which appeared contradictory), and I believed it was my job to figure out how each equation applied to every possible scenario. Now having been immersed in it for over 20 years, I have a much simpler and more coherent understanding; it's just particles and spacetime, their interactions, and their symmetries. This then allows me to see difficulties in a new theory or experiment in light of the bigger underlying truths without feeling the need to panic or throw everything out.

---

[12] *The Christian Myth*, www.thechristianmyth.com.

## JOHN 20:24-29

**Victoria**: I would probably have had the same response as Thomas in verse 25. A skeptic could take this further: e.g., what if he didn't die at all? I think that's addressed in the minimal-facts argument mentioned in the previous section. Verse 29 is a commonly heard verse, though there's belief, and then there's conviction.

**Steve**: I agree regarding verse 25, and I think the label "doubting Thomas" is a little unfair (especially since he bravely showed his devotion for Jesus in Jn 11:16). Yes, a skeptic might wonder if Jesus died at all (or it might be outright denied as in Quran 4:157), but the crucifixion of Jesus is really not a debatable fact according to the scholarship I've looked at, even by people who are actively opposed to Christian thought.[13]

It's interesting that you say, "there's belief, and then there's conviction." What do you mean?

**Victoria**: The minimal-facts argument also discussed the potential objection that Jesus didn't die by quoting from the *Journal of the American Medical Association*: "Accordingly, interpretations based on the assumption that Jesus did not die on the cross appear to be at odds with modern medical knowledge."[14]

The way I think about it is that belief is a superset of conviction. One can believe *x* without being convicted that *x* is true. Believing without conviction doesn't necessarily lead to anything positive. It reminds me of the verse that says that even the demons believe in God (Jas 2:19) or that even the stones cry out (Lk 19:40). Obviously, they're not following Jesus.

## JOHN 20:30-31

**Victoria**: No comments here.

**Steve**: The New Testament is often discounted as historical evidence because the people who wrote it had a Christian belief. I understand and sympathize with that objection, but it's hard to imagine what else someone convinced of these truths could have done. None of the New Testament writers had a Christian upbringing, there was no surrounding Christian culture to impress, and they gained nothing positive from their writings. The simplest explanation to me, then, is that they went from unbelief to belief *because* of the evidence and then simply recorded that evidence, much in the same way that any historical writer would see the need to record *anything*.[15]

---

[13] "Crucifixion of Jesus: Historicity" *Wikipedia*, en.wikipedia.org/wiki/Crucifixion_of_Jesus#Historicity.

[14] "On the Physical Death of Jesus Christ" *JAMA*, jamanetwork.com/journals/jama/article-abstract/403315.

[15] Richard Bauckham, *Jesus and the Eyewitnesses* (Grand Rapids: Eerdmans, 2008).

**Victoria**: That's true. It's hard to see an ulterior motive for why this would've been written (and later accepted as canon) other than to note what happened and share the information.

# Chapter 39: John 21

### John 21:1-14

**Victoria:** I forgot that the fish scene was after Jesus resurrected. On verse 7, regarding "the disciple whom Jesus loved," I think this phrasing came up before, but the emphasis is strange to me. Doesn't Jesus love everyone? Also, I figured if "the beloved disciple" was anyone, it would be Peter, since isn't he the rock of the church (Mt 16:18)?

**Steve:** Yeah, the fish scene is great. The resurrected Jesus is often portrayed in paintings and stained-glass windows as floating and glowing with his hands up. Here, we have a guy with a real, physical body eating fish with his friends (who admittedly still have some hesitancy). Surely someone has made a "Jesus at a potluck" stained glass. The story of Peter jumping into the water is typical Peter behavior, but I love it. I'm not a Peter type at all, but I know people who are. They're loud, emotional, and reactive and often beat themselves up for it. But we introverts desperately need people like Peter who jump out of the boat without a second thought so we can say, "Alright, let's go, too."[1]

There's pretty strong consensus that John is so wrapped up in his identity as a Christian that he prefers to refer to himself in terms of how Jesus views him rather than use his own name. It's a beautiful picture of not only humility but of how a Christian's identity is transformed under the lordship of Jesus. Especially with a national election coming up in four days, what a joy it is to say that my identity and purpose are not in any way tied to the results thereof. I am simply a disciple whom Jesus loves.

**Victoria:** Agreed. I wouldn't want to live in a world full of only INTJs. I think other personality types love and enthuse better.

I guess that transformation applies to one's identity in relation to other people, too. For example, Christian identity can lead one from initially thinking, "Why doesn't this person love me like they are socially contracted to?" to realizing that we're all human, sinners, and in need of Christ who loves us unconditionally.

**Steve:** Wow, wow, wow, yes! The Beatles sang *All You Need Is Love*, and that's the world's message as well: that if we just love each other, then everything will be fine. But the world is missing that we do not have the capacity to love each other outside of God's love for us:

*We love because he first loved us.* (1 Jn 4:19)

---

[1] John Ortberg, *If You Want to Walk on Water, You've Got to Get Out of the Boat* (Grand Rapids: Zondervan, 2014).

Or to put it another way, the secular humanist path our society is on wants...

> "'Love your neighbor as yourself.'" (Mk 12:31)

without:

> "'Love the Lord your God with all your heart and with all your soul and with all your mind and with all your strength.'" (Mk 12:30)

But they were put in the order they were for a reason. If 1) I define love as wanting the best for someone and acting accordingly, and 2) God is the best for everyone, then I can't fully love my neighbor without leading them to God. That doesn't necessarily mean in-your-face evangelism but can be as subtle as showing them *why* they matter as opposed to only *that* they matter.

In addition to that, you're so right that our identity (and thus, mental health) is heavily dependent on this right way of thinking. Our culture often views love as a means to a personal end. I "love" tacos, but only in that I'm going to devour and destroy them, and I might "love" my wife in the same way (i.e., taking advantage of our contract to use her for my own personal gain, benefit, and pleasure). In such a case, her well-being is actually lessened by my "love." But if we do this marriage thing right, then 1) her identity is in Jesus, completely independent of me, and 2) my love for her looks like Jesus' love for me: sacrificial and working for her good. That's gotten lost in our culture's debate about marriage; we tend to think it's as simple as a contract (and that's OK, I suppose, as far as legality goes), but the biblical picture is meant to be an earthly representation of our "marriage" to Jesus. That is, it should be two people submitting to each other, continually forgiving each other, working for each other's good, living in obedience to scripture, and complementing each other to bring God's kingdom into their sphere of influence. My marriage is on a solid foundation not because we think that each other is the greatest, but because we know each other to be the worst. In that context, given how God has treated us individually, then my wife and I know how to treat each other; this is what Eph 5:21–33 is all about. (In some ways, this mindset *should* be easier to manage with people we don't sleep next to, but the lack of a common goal can often make it much harder.) Our culture (on its good days) views marriage as a high ideal. I agree that it is a noble goal (while forcefully stating that there's nothing wrong with remaining single.[2]) But Jesus doesn't let it reach his standard of what matters (i.e., things that last forever):

---

[2] 1 Cor 7:8.

> Jesus replied, "The people of this age marry and are given in marriage. But those who are considered worthy of taking part in the age to come and in the resurrection from the dead will neither marry nor be given in marriage, and they can no longer die; for they are like the angels. They are God's children, since they are children of the resurrection." (Lk 20:34–36)

As much as I love my wife and can't imagine life without her, Jesus says she and I are done with each other when we die. Apparently, this whole till-death-do-us-part thing was just preparation for what's to come.

So coming back full circle to John's perspective of his identity, if I can't define myself in terms of one of society's highest ideals, what do I have left?! Sure, I'm a white, southern, nerdy, conservative-leaning, married father, but if I wake up thinking, "This is how I should act today because I'm these things," then I'm setting myself up for a world of confusion, stress, guilt, fear, pride, etc., because everyone has a different opinion on what those things mean and what I should be doing. Namely, my mental health suffers because I don't really know who I am. But if take John's approach here and just say, "My identity is a disciple whom Jesus loves," then all pressure is off. What can trump that identity? Who can question it? When does it end? Is there a greater purpose? Nothing. No one. Never. No. *I know who I am and what I'm about.*

**Victoria**: I really like that last paragraph on how we see ourselves in relation to how others in society view us. It reminds me of leaders not being able to please everyone and how important it is to keep our ethics intact, i.e., not replacing "good and bad with better or worse."[3]

Regarding marriage, that sounds really great, but what about the people who never find their "soulmate"? What if someone wants that kind of relationship based on individual identities in Jesus leading to mutual sacrificial love, but that person only finds poor substitutes? I suppose none of us are owed anything in life, but would it be unreasonable for said person to settle on a good enough "contractual" relationship?

On how marriages are done for in the afterlife, that seems kind of sad to me after spending decades or so building lives together. Though, if being with God is super amazingly wonderful, I guess you won't really need to miss anyone else.

**Steve**: Neither my wife nor I believe in soulmates, and what's more, neither of us is naturally the kind of person who easily does this mutual, sacrificial love thing. In fact, we're two of the most prideful and pigheaded people I know, and it was revealed in some very unfortunate

---

[3] Maya A. Jones, "Dave Chappelle tells Allen University audience you 'gotta keep your ethics intact'" *The Undefeated*, www.theundefeated.com/features/dave-chappelle-tells-allen-university-audience-you-gotta-keep-your-ethics-intact/.

ways in the first seven or so years of our marriage. But what we did and do have is 1) Jesus and 2) a strong desire to make this thing work *no matter what*. As much as we have been frustrated and occasionally despondent through our 21 years of marriage, divorce was simply never an option and never will be. That decision has not only made a world of difference in our marriage, but it comes from the same line of thinking we have in our faith: I've chosen Jesus, and I'm sticking with him *no matter what*. (Of course, if I had compelling evidence that Christianity is wrong or that my real wife had been switched out for a body double, I would absolutely leave my faith and/or marriage, but I'm talking about working through extreme difficulties, not "this is objectively different than I thought it was" circumstances.) To put it another way, when we got married, we were simultaneously madly in love with each other but secretly terrified that we had picked the wrong person (I don't believe it's possible to go into a marriage without second thoughts). But even while wondering if this was the right person, we were committed to *making* this the right person. In other words, the "over the hump" moment we both had many years into our marriage was realizing that this wasn't going to work if we kept trying to change each other; it was only going to work if we changed ourselves. Practically speaking, that looks like "I'm going to continue to clean this apartment—over and over and over again—even when she continues to make a mess of it." Or it might look like, "Even though he seems to care more about the neatness of this apartment than actually showing me affection, I'm going to continue to show him affection over and over and over again." *Anyone* can argue about organization, money, affection, sex, kids, jobs, family, food, time, and all of the things that married couples argue about, all the while saying and/or thinking things like "I'm the only one who really cares." That's easy. The difficult thing is saying, "The problem in my marriage is *me*, and I'm going to make this thing work by changing myself (with God's help), regardless of what he/she does." (Obviously, I'm not talking about abusive situations here). It's extraordinarily difficult to pull off that mindset, but having a Christian understanding of who you are absolutely helps.

All of this is why Paul says that Christians should only marry Christians:

> *A woman is bound to her husband as long as he lives. But if her husband dies, she is free to marry anyone she wishes, but he must belong to the Lord.* (1 Cor 7:39)

> *Do not be yoked together with unbelievers.* (2 Cor 6:14a)

The picture in the second verse is of two side-by-side (i.e., yoked together) oxen plowing a field, but one has a different goal than the other. If they're not pulling in the same direction, they'll veer off course and/or tire each other out because they're not working together. We can get along great with and love our non-Christian friends, coworkers, and family, but marriage requires something on a completely different level: hence, Paul's command. (By the way, none of this gives permission for divorce when a believer and non-believer *are* married to each other; see 1 Pet 3:1.) So to finally answer your question, I definitely don't think it's wise to enter into marriage for contractual reasons alone. But I do think that two Christians who are 70% sure that this is the right thing to do but 100% sure that they're going to do what it takes to make it work can absolutely have a God-honoring, healthy, happy, lasting marriage. On that note, as clearly as I've expressed the difficulties faced in my own marriage, I wouldn't trade them for anything. Because of them, I've gotten a front-row seat in seeing God turn two people who worshipped themselves and demanded submission from the other into two people whose entire reason and purpose for existence is to love and honor God (and if they can use their marriage to do that even better, then so much the better).

As for your last comment, I think you've kind of answered it with your previous comment. I *am* a poor substitute for that mutual, sacrificial love you mentioned, and so is my wife. A human spouse (not that I recommend any other kind) can be nothing *but* that, so Jesus has something much better for us in store. (Besides, it would be a little strange for there to be married people alongside single people in heaven, and then there's the whole "what to do with people who were married multiple times" conundrum.) We're by no means perfect, and we still have issues and mess up, but there's nothing like moving beyond all of the pettiness of who's right or wrong and whether we've been offended to "I love you and preemptively forgive you for whatever you're about to say/do." I have no clue how to do that apart from the cross. My marriage has revealed my sinfulness more than anything else. Jesus lets me look at that objectively and, instead of denying it or running away from it, I can acknowledge it and fix it with my wife's help. It might take the full 60+ years of marriage we hopefully have, but we're on our way.

Finally, marriage isn't for everyone. There are both those who want to get married and don't find someone suitable, as well as those who wish to remain single. There's nothing wrong with either of those types of people. My wife and I lost as much freedom in getting married as we've gained, and it's a ton of mental, emotional, and physical work. It is not a Christian ideal: Jesus was single! My wife's and my main ministry is to each other, and that necessarily means that we've left a lot of people out that could've received our help if we had remained single. It is not a moral success or failure—nor does it say anything about one's worth— to get married or stay single. All one really needs to ask are two questions: 1) Do I and this person want to get married to each other? 2) Are we committed to using our marriage to further God's kingdom? If the answer to both of those is "yes," then get married! If you're waiting for the "right" person to come along, then you'll *never* get married, because Rom 3:10–18 is more than just a theological statement; it's a prediction of how two people living in the same house will treat each other. That is, everyone who's married is married to a depraved sinner! But if the answer to either question is "no," then run away as fast as you can because you're heading for personal and spiritual disaster.

### JOHN 21:15–25

**Victoria**: It's nice to see a happy ending here as far as Peter's relationship with Jesus goes. I suppose this is Jesus forgiving Peter for denying him even though he doesn't say so explicitly? The emphasis on one disciple versus another (verses 20–22) catches my attention since, without prior knowledge of Jesus or his followers, I would have assumed them to be more on equal footing with each other. It seems to be otherwise, though—some are known positively, others negatively, and others relatively unknown.

**Steve**: Yes, I think it's pretty clear that Jesus has forgiven Peter here. I'm so glad this story is in the Bible, because even if I were to totally convince myself of all of this theology we've been discussing for years, there would still be a part of me wondering 1) if he really loves me beyond the fact that I agree with him (i.e., the way our world works) and 2) whether I've screwed up so badly that he'll finally tire of me and say, "Forget it." Jesus blasts those thoughts to smithereens. His incredible gentleness here is palpable, considering that he was betrayed by one of his best friends during his most dire moment. Not only that, but to then give Peter a mission is noteworthy. It's one thing to forgive someone; it's another to completely welcome them back in and trust them with such an enormous task.

It's commonly thought that Jesus did have a sort of inner circle: Peter, James, and John. For example,

> *After six days Jesus took Peter, James and John with him and led them up a high mountain, where they were all alone. There he was transfigured before them.* (Mk 9:2)

I think about this in a similar way to Paul writing about the fact that not everyone has the same role in God's kingdom,[4] and that our personalities aren't just the result of random genetic configurations but serve a spiritual purpose. These three weren't ontologically greater than the others; they just had a different calling, for reasons that were more apparent to Jesus. The same sort of thing applies to the call to pastoral ministry in 1 Tim 3:1–7. Pastors aren't better people or "more saved" than anyone else, but they are called to a higher standard. For

---

[4] 1 Cor 12:12–27, Rom 12:3–8, Eph 4:11–13.

example, many churches have removed leaders for sexual misconduct, but it's less common to kick someone out who merely attends; the Bible backs up that double standard:

*Not many of you should become teachers, my fellow believers, because you know that we who teach will be judged more strictly.* (Jas 3:1)

Salvation is freely available to everyone and is a very low bar to cross, but not everyone is qualified to take leadership roles. When I've been asked, "Will Sin X disqualify me being a Christian?" my answer is "No, but it might 1) severely harm your relationship with God, your ability to effectively do his work, and your joy, and 2) lead you down a path in which you find yourself permanently enjoying said sin more than Jesus, at which point you're no longer a Christian (or never were, depending on your soteriology)."

In that view, Jesus still has an inner circle: those who consistently follow and obey him, whether they are known by the world or not. So while I feel secure in the saving power of Jesus apart from my own effort and morality, still from a daily, walking-with-Jesus sort of way, I'm going to get out of Christianity what I put into it:

*Whoever sows to please their flesh, from the flesh will reap destruction; whoever sows to please the Spirit, from the Spirit will reap eternal life.* (Gal 6:8)

One more thing that stuck out to me here is verse 19; one's reaction to this verse will be quite telling. Jesus knew that Peter would die an unpleasant death, but 1) he did nothing to stop it, and 2) he (or least John) recognized that it would glorify God. If you're the type of person who expects God to provide you a comfortable life and follow a standard of morality you pulled out of thin air, then Christianity is not for you. But if you see God as everything and the only thing worth pursuing and are willing to suffer in life and death for his glory, then that kind of faith won't and even *can't* waver. You'll see that he is good even when he told Abraham to kill his son,[5] accommodated the Israelites to hold slaves,[6]

---

[5] Gen 22:1–19; S. Kierkegaard, *Fear and Trembling* (London: Penguin Classics, 1986).

[6] Lev 25:44–46; Mt 19:3–9; 1 Tim 1:8–11; "Does the Bible endorse slavery?" *YouTube*, www.youtube.com/watch?v=0uBqkZ-m3XI; "The Contemporary Conflation of Slavery in the Bible," *YouTube*, www.youtube.com/watch?v=1OZMeXCG-c8; "Accommodation (religion)," *Wikipedia*, en.wikipedia.org/wiki/Accommodation_(religion).

commanded them to wipe out the Canaanites,[7] and even killed his own son for our benefit.[8] You'll believe that he was justified in flipping over the tables at the temple,[9] ripping the Pharisees to shreds,[10] and letting Lazarus die so that he could raise him back from the dead for his own glory.[11] You'll think that this confusing and messy world and Bible are actually part of his plan to use humans to make things right one day, forever and ever.[12] You'll realize that his demand that you follow his rules is for your own good.[13] You'll understand that not getting that thing you really want is teaching you what to really want.[14] You'll know that your terminal illness that he refuses to cure is just the beginning of the best thing that can happen to you.[15] The world will claim you're morally depraved, insane, on the wrong side of history, unenlightened, and backward, and they will insult and attack you and the God you love.[16] You'll know that he calls us to love, joy, peace, forbearance, kindness, goodness, faithfulness, gentleness and self-control[17] because he *is* those things in a way the world can't understand.[18] But you'll join the throngs for whom it was said:

*The world was not worthy of them.* (Heb 11:38a)

Then one day,

*When the Chief Shepherd appears, you will receive the crown of glory that will never fade away.* (1 Pet 5:4)

*No longer will there be any curse. The throne of God and of the Lamb will be in the city, and his servants will serve him. They will see his face, and his name will be on their foreheads. There will be no more*

---

[7] Deut 7:1–6; "Why Did God Command the Invasion of Canaan?" *BibleProject*, March 5, 2020, bibleproject.com/blog/why-did-god-command-the-invasion-of-canaan-in-the-book-of-joshua/.
[8] Rom 5:8.
[9] Jn 2:13–17.
[10] Mt 23.
[11] Jn 11:1–44.
[12] Heb 1:1–2.
[13] 2 Tim 3:16–17.
[14] Phil 3:1–14.
[15] Jn 11:21–27.
[16] Lk 21:12–13; Acts 26:24; "Persecution of Christians in the New Testament," *Wikipedia*, en.wikipedia.org/wiki/Persecution_of_Christians_in_the_New_Testament; "Persecution of Christians," *Wikipedia*, en.wikipedia.org/wiki/Persecution_of_Christians.
[17] Gal 5:22–23.
[18] 1 Cor 1:18.

*night. They will not need the light of a lamp or the light of the sun, for the Lord God will give them light. And they will reign for ever and ever.* (Rev 22:3–5)

# Epilogue

We were both changed by this conversation. It was mentally taxing on both of us to spend as much time as we did on this given our general busyness. It was also just as spiritually taxing for both of us. Imagine having someone whose intellect you respect question your every fundamental belief which ultimately governs your every word, thought, and action, and doing this for years. But we did this because we care about the truth, however uncomfortable that may be. Each of us will give a recap here of what this process was like and some final thoughts.

## Victoria

When we started this conversation over three years ago, I didn't know what I was getting myself into. I don't think Dr. Robinson did, either.

I wasn't on the market for a new set of beliefs. I always found the topic of religion to be slightly uncomfortable, especially when I was on the receiving end of proselytizing. It felt like being sold a car that I didn't need or want by some salesman with a quota. Additionally, in this dialogue, I did not set out to prove or disprove anything, for myself or for Dr. Robinson. I wanted to challenge Dr. Robinson's beliefs not for mere debate but for my own understanding of how and why they came to be. I cared about pursuing the truth, and I was curious to understand the reasoning of someone who held ardent beliefs when it came to religion.

I approached this conversation in the same way I approached a new PhD project—with curiosity and an open mind. I had an endless number of questions, some which were repeated in different contexts in different chapters. In hindsight, I'm surprised by how much there was to explore in the greater theme of "Who is God, really?" We discussed many details about Christian beliefs and practices, but I realized that it could all be boiled down to a few key points, such as sin being a problem of pride.

Over the course of the discussion, I discovered an implicit bias in myself regarding the association between science and Christianity. I used to believe that one had to make concessions in either science or Christianity in order to fit both into one's life. While this bias wasn't directly addressed in this book, Dr. Robinson set a strong example of how one doesn't have to throw away logic and rationality when examining the truths of the Bible. Rather, one of the constant themes that emerges is how doubt can be a powerful tool to strengthen conviction:

> *Consider it pure joy, my brothers and sisters, whenever you face trials of many kinds, because you know that the testing of your faith produces perseverance.* (Jas 1:2–3)

God doesn't want us to be mindless believers.

For someone who knows little about the basis of Christianity, it's easy to think that Christianity is for the weak, the less educated, or the needy. I myself thought that way. But through this conversation, my mindset has transformed due to a greater self-awareness,

*As it is written: "There is no one righteous, not even one; ..."* (Rom 3:10)

a willingness to acknowledge indisputable events in history and their implications,

*"He himself bore our sins" in his body on the cross, so that we might die to sins and live for righteousness; "by his wounds you have been healed."* (1 Pet 2:24)

and God's love and mercy:

*"No one can come to me unless the Father who sent me draws them, and I will raise them up at the last day."* (Jn 6:44)

I cannot overemphasize God's involvement in leading me to this point. Despite being surrounded by other Christians growing up, attending a Christian university, and even selecting a PhD advisor who I didn't realize was Christian, I had no interest in pursuing Him. Fortunately, He didn't feel the same way in his pursuit of me:

*But because of his great love for us, God, who is rich in mercy, made us alive with Christ even when we were dead in transgressions—it is by grace you have been saved.* (Eph 2:4–5)

There were two stretches of time while writing back and forth that I felt tired, disinterested, and unwilling to continue. The first was approximately a year and a half from when we started. At the time, Dr. Robinson had said, "Let's give this thing a rest; you sound weary. If you want to resume it at some point, send me an email and I'd be happy to pick it back up again. If you never want to mention it again, that's fine, too." I genuinely believed that it would be the end of the conversation. It seemed a disappointing and premature ending, but I also didn't have any expectation of how it should have gone differently. Three months later, I reached out to Dr. Robinson to see if we could resume where we left off, in the Bible study in John. I couldn't articulate a good reason for why, when asked, but I just felt the need to keep on, at least to finish the book of John for the sake of completeness.

The second hiatus was about two years from when we began. My increasing disengagement became particularly evident around the discussion of John 12–13. I was in my 4th year of the PhD at this time, and my research was taking its toll. Everything around me seemed bleak, but not for lack of trying. I felt like I was spending an inordinate amount of time and effort, yet not realizing any fruits from my labor. In the context of learning about God, the personal aspect seemed missing. I didn't doubt Jesus' existence or claims, but I didn't feel particularly moved to change my life. If there was truth to be acted upon, I saw my reception to it like seeds sown on a bed of thorns:

> *"Listen! A farmer went out to sow his seed. As he was scattering the seed, some fell along the path, and the birds came and ate it up. Some fell on rocky places, where it did not have much soil. It sprang up quickly, because the soil was shallow. But when the sun came up, the plants were scorched, and they withered because they had no root. Other seed fell among thorns, which grew up and choked the plants, so that they did not bear grain. Still other seed fell on good soil. It came up, grew and produced a crop, some multiplying thirty, some sixty, some a hundred times." Then Jesus said, "Whoever has ears to hear, let them hear."* (Mk 4:3–9)

This point also seemed like it would be the end of the conversation and the end of any "spiritual journey" I might have been on.

It came as a surprise, then, when I had a change of heart five months later at a ministry retreat. I realized that I was held back by fear: fear of being alienated by my family, fear of being judged by those I knew personally and professionally, and fear of losing comfort and control over my life. I counted the opportunity cost of following Christ, but I didn't fairly consider the costs of turning away:

> *For whoever wants to save their life will lose it, but whoever loses their life for me and for the gospel will save it.* (Mk 8:35)

If God is the eternal Creator to whom I owe everything and to whom I will ultimately be held accountable, how could I continue living my life guided by such temporal fears? I couldn't hold onto anything I gained or anyone I knew in this world, but I could place my faith and trust in the sovereignty of God. As intimidating as it was to make that decision, I wasn't called to do it alone:

> *So do not fear, for I am with you; do not be dismayed, for I am your God. I will strengthen you and help you; I will uphold you with my righteous right hand.* (Is 41:10)

It's been a long road, but a worthwhile one:

> *Let perseverance finish its work so that you may be mature and complete, not lacking anything.* (Jas 1:4)

My hope is that this book will open up the doors to conversation for you, dear reader, whether you are seeking or not, a believer or nonbeliever, sharing the Gospel or learning about God. I didn't quite believe it myself, but:

*"Ask, and it will be given to you; seek, and you will find; knock, and it will be opened to you."* (Mt 7:7)

### STEVE

This has been an incredible experience which I will never forget. As someone who likes to question everything, I spend a lot of time thinking about what I think. However, it is quite a different experience to have someone else continually probe the very foundations of your entire worldview from every angle. Vickie is unequivocally not only one of the most intelligent people I know, but also one of the best question-askers (they often go together, I suppose). I saw it in her from the first day she stepped in my classroom: she wants to know answers, she wants to know them exactly, and she's going to keep asking until she's satisfied. I felt reasonably confident in my faith entering this conversation, but it's a scary thing having someone like Vickie examine your every belief to see if it holds water. There were numerous times in which I would reflect on what I had written and had to ask myself, "Wait, do I really believe that, or am I just saying what a 'good' Christian should say?" Vickie's eventual approval (or lack thereof) of certain conclusions of mine has played a huge role in my confidence in the intellectual side of Christianity over the last few years, because if *she* thinks something I said makes sense, then it probably makes sense. In addition, I have seen firsthand how the mind and the heart work together or fight against each other, both in my life and in Vickie's. I love my students, but I never thought a typical student-professor encounter would turn into a deep, meaningful friendship with one of them. It takes very special kinds of humility, patience, and dedication to jump into this the way Vickie did.

My ultimate goal as a Christian cannot ever be to convert people, because I have very little control over that process and will usually end up disappointed. That being said, I cannot express the happiness I have felt in playing a small part in the journey of a new believer in Christ. There's nothing like knowing that someone will see the world in a new way, watching Jesus work in them in both explicit and subtle ways, and gaining a common bond over the thing you hold most dear. I love my little sister in Christ and am forever grateful for getting to know her. Thank you, Vickie.

As for the future, I imagine this work will translate into further conversation with others. I am now 42 years old, and I have been seriously questioning and wrestling with my faith since I was about 15. Many dismiss apologetics as irrelevant to the Christian faith, but it has been absolutely essential for not only my mental progress, but also in giving me the confidence to really live out my faith to serve others. If I'm confident in my faith and theology, what's going to stop me from having *any* conversation?

What's going to keep me from serving meals to the poor? What's going to hinder me from getting on my knees and having a chat with my Father in heaven? In other words, apologetics and action are not two different aspects of Christianity; they are intertwined and inseparable, and I love others because I know God. Still, I believe God has rescued me for a purpose, and while I don't always know exactly what that's going to entail, I know he's going to walk with me through it until my time is up, and that's worth more than *understanding* anything. So like theologian Karl Barth (but with much less clout), I can summarize my life and life's work as "Jesus loves me, this I know, for the Bible tells me so." Maybe there will be more of this in the future. Maybe there won't. I don't know, but I know that I love God and am thankful for what he's done in and with me so far.

Finally, I would like to address you, the reader. First, thank you for reading these hundreds of pages. Second, in writing this much about so many controversial issues both in and out of Christianity, I have undoubtedly said many things with which you've disagreed. I almost certainly said some things which I wish I might have said differently. And I probably said a few things that I don't even agree with now. (For example, I spent most of my life in subconscious Arminianism, began this book near the end of a brief tryst with Calvinism, quickly headed toward uncertainty, and ended it as a fairly confident Molinist.) So I thought I would use a little space here trying to present my beliefs as concisely and clearly as possible in two ways: first, regarding my understanding of God and, second, how that translates to my relationships with people.

~~~~~~~~

On my most clearheaded days, I see that I am absolutely bent on loving and exalting myself. Every waking hour is spent thinking about what I want and need. When Jesus says,

*"Love your neighbor as yourself."* (Mt 22:39)

then I don't have to wonder what he means; I love myself unconditionally and look out for all of my short- and long-term needs. Some of this shows up in clearly sinful ways, but most of it appears benign at first; for example, I need to eat. But when I realize that I'm rarely in tune with whether other people need to eat, my eyes are opened to my self-obsession. Now, that doesn't mean that I need to immediately drop everything and turn my life upside down to feed starving people; they might benefit more by my steady employment and financial contribution. But that doesn't change the fact that my natural, evidential position is apathy; that is, I have to *fight* to come to any other conclusion. As another example, I frequently find myself defending my theological and political positions—and basically any potential argument I could have—to ... *no one in particular.* Yes, these are mental arguments I have with imaginary people who suddenly confront me about my most deeply held beliefs. And, boy, are those people wrong. They are *so* wrong, and I know exactly why. And that pretty much makes me right about ... *everything*. In its most dastardly form, my pride shows up as depression—the times when I am most inwardly focused on my failures and shortcomings, completely aware of everything about *me*, not having a care in the world about what God or the people who love me think.

Now, if you met me, you would usually see a strongly subdued version of this inner person; even if you thought I was proud, you would have no idea how much worse it really is. I've gotten pretty good at pretending I'm humble (see, I even think highly of my abilities to trick you!), but sometimes this inner person makes his way out with devastating consequences. The bottom line is not that I believe or am convinced, but that I *know* that I am absolutely full and overrunning with pride. In light of everything this book presents, I am actually more certain that I am self-consumed than that I even exist. I've just given a few examples out of thousands that prove me right in this regard (see, there it is again!). There aren't too many places where our secular culture and the Bible agree, but one of them is that self-obsession, which is naturally married to a disregard for others, is just plain wrong. The Bible would go much further than just "wrong," but, either way, I simply can't escape the fact that the most clear, evident thing about myself is contradictory to every good thing in this world. This is not a guilt complex, because I generally don't feel *any* guilt about my pride; rather, it's just an acknowledgment of a fact staring me in the face.

This has been discussed at length, but the recognition that the word *wrong* has *any* meaning is a recognition that there are standards beyond me. In the context of my apparent consciousness and free will paradoxically existing in a deterministic and incomprehensibly vast and complex universe—that is, given that my existence is evidently owed to something that almost any religion would call God—then my self-importance is not only a moral failing, but a direct affront to God himself. If this is a universally accepted wrong, then God himself, the standard by which all things are measured, must not be happy with it. But even worse, this particular sin is the only one which directly opposes God. For example, if I steal something, I'm directly taking it from someone else, not from God. (One could argue I'm stealing from God because he owns all things, but if you take that position, I'm still not stealing from him because he never lost it.) But with pride, I am saying that I am the most important thing around, when that title clearly belongs to God. It is this reason that all other sins are rooted in pride; they result from self-importance and self-justification over God. This is the second fact staring me in the face: the most fundamental thing about me is the worst possible thing there could be about anyone.

The third obvious fact is that I don't have fitting consequences for my devastating problem. My pride has damaged numerous relationships and caused me severe mental anguish. However, if I were God, someone like me would've been destroyed or punished long ago; yet here I am, breathing, thinking, and typing. The only conclusion I can draw from this is that God is not like me—he is merciful and good.

The fourth and final evident fact is that I am going to die one day. This makes me wonder if God, an eternal being, is withholding judgment on me only temporarily or forever. It's not that I believe that God is just an angry tyrant waiting for me to mess up so that I can be punished. Rather, when I look at this world, it appears to me that justice has not yet been served, and I wonder if that day is coming. It seems the only way I could possibly know is if he revealed it; there is no scientific method or process of reason to discern such an answer. There are many such claimed revelations in this world, and I encourage you to research as many as you can. First, however, think of whether you would agree that my presented "facts" apply to you as well:

1. I'm self-obsessed, and...
2. That's bad.
3. I'm doing OK now, but...
4. I will die.

If not, Christianity isn't going to make a lot of sense. But if so, out of all of the claimed revelations, I have found the Bible's account, especially with regard to Jesus, to be the most explanatory and satisfying with regard to those four statements. Hopefully, this book has aided you in understanding why I might think that. With regard to my understanding of God, I am admittedly ignorant in many areas (there's that false humility again), but I can honestly say the following with no qualms or possibility of wavering.

Jesus is my only hope. He's all I want. He's all I have. He's all I need. He's all I am. And there has never been a time in my life when I could identify more with Peter:

> "You do not want to leave too, do you?" Jesus asked the Twelve. Simon Peter answered him, "Lord, to whom shall we go? You have the words of eternal life. We have come to believe and to know that you are the Holy One of God." (Jn 6:67–69)

Indeed.

~~~~~~~~

I have come to terms with my position before God. My bigger difficulty, rather, is in how I daily live in this world. Much of what I will say arises from a modern American perspective, but I imagine there are parts that will apply to people everywhere.

We each live our lives based on some sort of identity: how I define myself determines how I live and interact with God and others. There has never been a time in history in which people have attached so many labels to themselves and others: Democrat, Republican, Libertarian, Christian, Muslim, Jew, Hindu, Buddhist, atheist, agnostic, introverted, extroverted, healthy, sick, disabled, LGBT, non-LGBT, fascist, anti-fascist, racist, sexist, capitalist, Marxist, open-minded, closed-minded, addicted, criminal, patriotic, (insert every nationality here), pro-life, pro-choice, black, white, brown, other, ROYGBIV, male, female, neither, autistic, artistic, analytical, married, single, divorced, old, young, tall, short, smart, dumb, fast, slow, peacemaking, hotheaded, fat, skinny, fit, happy, morose, creationist, evolutionist, flat-earther, urban, suburban, rural, industrious, lazy, attractive, ugly, abused, heretical, optimistic, pessimistic, wise, foolish, funny, boring, crazy, famous, irrelevant, rich, poor, environmentalist, informed, uninformed, oppressor, oppressed, victim, depressed, anxious, good, bad, sinner, saint, winner, loser, neat, sloppy, articulate, annoying, humble, proud, and all the others I left out (so I'll add forgetful, ignorant, and offensive to the list, as well). I fit many of those labels, and some might put labels on me I do or don't want. Any given label might have a positive or negative connotation depending on who you ask. Our self- and politically-obsessed culture is bent on making sure that all *my* labels get the same respect and treatment as all *your* labels. That is—in the right context—a noble goal. But it's an impossible goal. It's impossible because politics attempts to put a bandage on the outside when our insides are rotten. If I'm a funny, patriotic criminal, I might be forbidden by law from firing a boring, healthy environmentalist just because of their identity. That's a good thing. But *nothing* can make me love that person, and if I don't have love for someone, they're never going to get the respect they deserve from me as someone made in the image of God.

So I don't look to politics as a solution to much at all, because it won't solve the problems that need to be solved: the ones *inside* of us. Don't get me wrong; I have very strong political opinions and preferences, but I don't need them to work out to find my happiness, fulfillment, or sense of justice—or anyone else's, for that matter.[1] Three things are simultaneously true: God wants me to act for justice, he wants me to recognize that I don't have the ability to create ultimate justice, and he wants me to understand that I *cannot* be just until I follow him:

*Learn to do right; seek justice. Defend the oppressed. Take up the cause of the fatherless; plead the case of the widow.* (Is 1:17)

*Do not take revenge, my dear friends, but leave room for God's wrath, for it is written: "It is mine to avenge; I will repay," says the Lord.* (Rom 12:19)

*Evildoers do not understand what is right, but those who seek the* LORD *understand it fully.* (Prov 28:5)

---

[1] If you really want to know, my most basic political stances are 1) every piece of legislation is a moral stance, and 2) it is possible to simultaneously have strong moral convictions and not legislate others to abide by them.

Thus, my sense of rightness in this world is always founded upon a right relationship with God, which plays into what I prioritize. For example, on a societal level, I believe it is more productive for a Christian to evangelize the owner of a company so that he/she understands that God expects him/her to pay a reasonable wage than for our society to continually help his employees with money, food, etc. This treats the cause rather than the symptoms. (Of course, if the cause can't be easily changed, then the symptoms need to be addressed.) And just as I don't see answers in politics, I don't look to religion for answers, either. Religion, including my own, has caused innumerable harms throughout history, both on a personal and societal scale, and I don't want to be associated with those problems.

We tend to see the biggest problems the world faces as poverty, discrimination, disease, war, hatred, destructive ideologies, etc. But Jesus said that with regard to sin (i.e., the problems the world faces), the Holy Spirit's main point of conviction (i.e., the biggest problem he's trying to address) is that the world doesn't believe in Jesus:

> When [the Holy Spirit] comes, he will prove the world to be in the wrong about sin ... because people do not believe in me. (Jn 16:8–9)

So with regard to solving the world's problems, I look to a *person*: Jesus Christ. It is by and through him—and him only—that *all* things are made just,

> For God was pleased to have all his fullness dwell in him, and through him to reconcile to himself all things, whether things on earth or things in heaven, by making peace through his blood, shed on the cross. (Col 1:19–20)

and *all* people are made equal:

> There is neither Jew nor Gentile, neither slave nor free, nor is there male and female, for you are all one in Christ Jesus. (Gal 3:28)

Paul does a clever thing here. He uses labels to say that some labels are both real and accurate but simultaneously don't matter at the foot of the cross. So you want to be a skinny, agnostic Republican? Fine, you're in the same boat as that smart, famous fascist over there. You, too, sick, short extrovert. We have nothing to offer God, because he's not impressed with our labels:

> But the LORD said to Samuel, "Do not consider his appearance or his height, for I have rejected him. The LORD does not look at the things people look at. People look at the outward appearance, but the LORD looks at the heart." (1 Sam 16:7)

I don't need any of them or my job, marriage, finances, social status, education, etc., to get me where I need to go, because where I need to go is collapsing in the arms of Jesus, and *anyone* can collapse. He just might want to change some of those labels I've been carrying around, but that's OK, because the alternative is more politics, more social media rants, more anger, more despair, and worst of all, more *me* and less *him*. I don't want more me. "Me" hasn't worked out so far.

At the same time, Jesus not only allows us, but *commands* us to love each other in a way that looks nothing like politics or Facebook rants:

> *"But I tell you, love your enemies and pray for those who persecute you."* (Mt 5:44)

A simple definition of an enemy is someone directly trying to harm you. But in the social climate in which we live, our "enemies" are usually just the people with different labels. Jesus said to love those people, but in recognizing that I have enemies, he's not saying I should agree with them. I tend to like a guy like that. He wants me to simultaneously hold fast to my convictions (i.e., if they're actually *his* convictions) and reach out a hand to those who don't have those same convictions. That's really important to me, because my tendency is to not like most of what he said, and yet, he's reached his hand out to me. Yes, there are undoubtedly marginalized people in this world, and he wants us to take care of them:

> *"The King will reply, 'Truly I tell you, whatever you did for one of the least of these brothers and sisters of mine, you did for me.'"* (Mt 25:40)

But not at any cost. Not at the cost of failing to realize that he's the only reason the marginalized have worth to begin with. Without that realization, we become betrayers of Jesus who look good on the outside but are rotten to the core:

> *But one of his disciples, Judas Iscariot, who was later to betray him, objected, "Why wasn't this perfume sold and the money given to the poor? It was worth a year's wages." He did not say this because he cared about the poor but because he was a thief; as keeper of the money bag, he used to help himself to what was put into it. "Leave her alone," Jesus replied. "It was intended that she should save this perfume for the day of my burial. You will always have the poor among you, but you will not always have me."* (Jn 12:4–8)

This is why secular humanism (the idea that we can find morality and fulfillment apart from God) doesn't work. As William Lane Craig has pointed out, if God exists, then objective morality exists and we should follow it, not secular humanism. If God does not exist, then nihilism naturally follows (as Nietzsche was concerned), and secular humanism has no meaning or purpose. God either does or does not exist; therefore, secular humanism should not be followed. That is, the idea that we're all going to just figure out how to get along with each other without God is flat-out wrong.

So, yeah, I've got labels. Sometimes I put them on others. Sometimes others put them on me. Sometimes I put them on myself. They're awfully burdensome, but Jesus said he'd take mine and yours off and give us a new one:

> *"Come to me, all you who are weary and burdened, and I will give you rest."* (Mt 11:28)

> *So in Christ Jesus you are all children of God through faith.* (Gal 3:26)

My label is "child of God." And as a child of God, I am called to love and serve other children of God as well as those who are indifferent or even hate our family.

Christianity is a race to the bottom. In our status before God, we're already there. But in our relationships with other people, we are called to the most difficult thing imaginable:

> *Do nothing out of selfish ambition or vain conceit. Rather, in humility value others above yourselves, not looking to your own interests but each of you to the interests of the others.* (Phil 2:3–4)

Protests are fine. Marches are fine. Slogans are fine. Hashtags are fine. Voting is fine. Laws are fine. Bumper stickers are fine. Depending on the issue, maybe I'm with you. But this world will not change for the better until we act like our example, one person at a time:

> *In your relationships with one another, have the same mindset as Christ Jesus: Who, being in very nature God, did not consider equality with God something to be used to his own advantage; rather, he made himself nothing by taking the very nature of a servant, being made in human likeness. And being found in appearance as a man, he humbled himself by becoming obedient to death—even death on a cross!* (Phil 2:5–8)

Our mandate is to lower ourselves to love others, and I don't know how (or want) to love a political party or policy. But I have a pretty good idea how to love individuals: to want the best for them and act accordingly. *Sometimes* that means disagreeing with them, but it *always* means that every person has dignity and worth given to them by God—that their value (and *your* value, reader) has already been determined and displayed by the Ultimate Decider of such things:

> *But God demonstrates his own love for us in this: While we were still sinners, Christ died for us.* (Rom 5:8)

~~~~~~~~

If Jesus sounds appealing to you and you are not currently a Christian, consider the following. In Lk 14:25–35, Jesus asked us to determine the cost of being his disciple before choosing to follow him. Dietrich Bonhoeffer stated, "When Christ calls a man, he bids him come and die." For this gospel, are you *willing* to

- trust scripture over your own opinions? (2 Tim 3:16–17)
- devote yourself to prayer? (1 Thess 5:16–18)
- regularly meet with other Christians? (Heb 10:24–25)
- love God and other people with everything you have? (Mk 12:28–31)
- commit yourself to a holy life? (1 Thess 4:1)
- have Christ alone as your master? (Mt 6:24)
- live it out publicly and boldly? (Rom 1:16)
- be different than the world? (Rom 12:2)
- have unity with other Christians you don't like? (Jn 17:22–23)
- love your enemies? (Mt 5:43–48)
- forgive everyone who has wronged you? (Eph 4:32)
- look foolish? (1 Cor 1:18)
- abandon every political ideal you have? (Mk 12:17)
- trade your own desires in for suffering? (Mt 16:24–26)
- turn away from the most comfortable and important things in your life? (Lk 9:57–62)
- give up your friends and family? (Mk 3:31–35)
- suffer shame, embarrassment, and even death? (Heb 11:35–40)

If your answers are yes, the Bible says,

> *If you declare with your mouth, "Jesus is Lord," and believe in your heart that God raised him from the dead, you will be saved.* (Rom 10:9)

If you can genuinely say you've done these two things in the context of the acknowledgement and repentance of your sins, welcome to the family! You have a long road ahead, and it should begin by finding a local Bible-teaching church. We would love to hear from you personally as well.

# APPENDIX

**Steve**: In the middle of our conversation, when I felt like I was not doing a good job communicating a sense of purpose, I sent Vickie the following email.

~~~~~~~~~

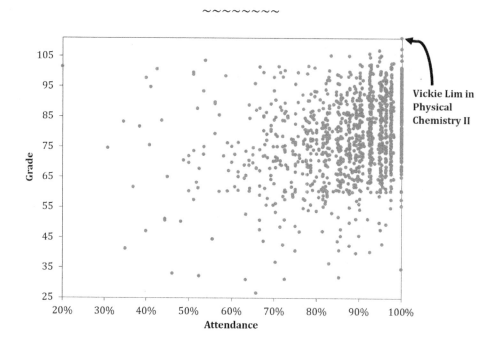

Vickie Lim in Physical Chemistry II

I just finished submitting all of my grades for the semester. I keep track of all kinds of statistics in my classes, and I've now given 1047 grades. I've attached my updated graph of all of my grades vs. attendance, so it includes everything from easy classes like freshman seminar all the way to quantum mechanics and physical chemistry. I didn't send it to you as a compliment (although it certainly could be) but rather as a wake-up call. This is where you are. Do you feel fulfilled? No? Then what will fulfill you? What could possibly make you feel meaning and purpose in life if this graph doesn't? The same graph but with grad students? A PhD? A job? A Nobel Prize? A family? You know better than that by now.

But maybe life doesn't have meaning or purpose. Then what on earth are you doing at the top right of that graph? What made you do that?! Don't live as if things matter but then not try to find out why they matter.

God matters and he loves you. Therefore, you matter. And when you matter, that little blue dot at the top right of that graph matters. It aids your research, which can help people who also matter because God loves them, and God matters. But more importantly, your brains are a reflection of your creator, and when you acknowledge that, he gets the credit he deserves. When you see your life as always pointing back to an infinite being with infinite purpose, now it has meaning, and daily life takes on a new perspective.

We probably don't need two separate conversations happening, so don't feel compelled to respond. I just saw that little blue dot and thought of you.

# ACKNOWLEDGEMENTS

## VICTORIA

In this conversation, it was mentioned that "You can tell what God is doing in your life by the people he's put in your life." Thank You God, for Your grace and mercy, for not giving up on me, and placing these people in my life that led me to You.

Thank you, Dr. Robinson, for reaching out to me. Thank you for all you put into this conversation: countless hours, thoughtful responses, vulnerable moments, never-ending patience, and personally challenging me to explore the truth for myself.

I've also spent many hours discussing Christianity with my PhD advisor, David Mobley, and his wife, Maura Mobley. These chats shaped my understanding of God and of His desire to relate to us. Thank you, David and Maura, for inviting me into your home and sharing this time with me.

Thank you to Gracepoint Church and specifically the UC Irvine International Graduate Student Ministry. There are too many to acknowledge individually, but in particular, I want to thank Pacie Lei, Irene Heung, Grace Pan, Sharon Kim, and Cindy Yan for your guidance and encouragement.

I also appreciate my temporary church home in Stockholm, filled with kind and fervent individuals. Thank you to everyone there and especially to Ashley Tambaur, Elizabeth Whitaker, and Kristin Kivi-Justineviciene.

Many others have influenced my beliefs and nudged me in the right direction over the years. Thank you to Dr. Daniel Biles, Hannah Baumann, Léa El Khoury, and my Belmont friends. I also particularly appreciate the authors who have caused me to stop and think. These include Timothy Keller, Francis Collins, David Gregory, Josh and Sean McDowell, and C. S. Lewis.

More generally, I am incredibly grateful to my family: my parents, my siblings, my cat, and my partner, Justin Smith. To mom and dad, thank you for your love, care, and support over all these years. It wasn't easy to start new lives as immigrants and refugees from Vietnam, but you have shown by example time and time again what it means to persist and persevere. To William and Kristina, thanks for keeping life interesting, and thanks for being there when life gets rough. It sucks that we live far away from each other, but I'm always only a phone call away. To my cat, Mia, who cannot read this, I am so happy to have you in my life ever since the days you were a tiny, timid ball of fur. I don't think I could understand why God would love me if I didn't love you so dearly and without expecting anything in return. Finally, thank you Justin, for your companionship and support in this life journey. From the minutiae of everyday living to life's momentous highs and lows, it's all better experienced with you, with your unwavering stability, your good-natured humor, and your thoughtful intellect. You make me a better version of myself.

### STEVE

Many writers and speakers outside of the Bible whom I do not personally know have positively influenced my thinking in various ways. These include Tedashii Anderson, Anselm of Canterbury, Thomas Aquinas, Augustine of Hippo, William Barefield, Dietrich Bonhoeffer, William Branch, Justin Brierley, Kevin Burgess, Virgil Byrd, Christine Caine, Francis Chan, Matt Chandler, Francis Collins, Cruz Cordero, William Lane Craig, David Crowder, Luis de Molina, Fyodor Dostoevsky, Jonathan Edwards, John Eldredge, Tony Evans, Cleveland Foat, Brady Goodwin, Billy Graham, Hank Hanegraaff, Brant Hansen, Matthew Henry, Juan James, Søren Kierkegaard, John Lennox, C. S. Lewis, Max Lucado, Martin Luther, Sherri Lynn, Tim Mackie, Sean McDowell, J. Vernon McGee, Alister McGrath, Herman Melville, Andy Mineo, Lecrae Moore, John Piper, David Platt, John Polkinghorne, Nabeel Qureshi, Dave Ramsey, Francis Schaeffer, Charles Spurgeon, John Steinbeck, Chuck Swindoll, J. R. R. Tolkien, A. W. Tozer, Frank Turek, Travis Tyler, Ray Vander Laan, John Walton, Rick Warren, John Wells, Jen Wilkin, David Wood, N. T. Wright, and many others I've forgotten.

On an organizational level, the American Scientific Affiliation and BioLogos have been instrumental in helping me see God in science. The Christian ministries Cure, Open Doors, and Voice of the Martyrs have given me perspective in this world.

In addition to these, throughout my life, I have leaned heavily on many people while wrestling with my faith. These are the people I know and love, although in most cases there are too many of you to name individually.

- Thank you to my colleagues and students at Belmont; I spend as much time with you as just about anyone, and you make work not only enjoyable, but meaningful.
- Thank you to my teachers and academic leaders, especially my graduate advisors, Drs. John Tucker and T.-C. Shen, for pushing me to continue down the path of curiosity, even if it had nothing to do with pursuing a degree.
- Thank you to my teachers, pastors, and friends at my past and current churches who have truly provided a continual refuge from the raging storm of this world.
- Thank you to my Bible study at Belmont, especially James Maxwell; each one of you has played a significant role in my spiritual formation.
- Thank you to most of my neighbors and neighborhood for making my home life less stressful.
- Thank you to Vickie Lim. This conversation required the kind of humility and open-mindedness on your part that I often find lacking in myself.

- Thank you to my mom, dad, stepdad, brothers, in-laws, and extended family. I know of no other place where I can be myself as I can around you.
- Thank you to my kids: Olivia, Mark, and Jack. There's nothing like seeing a baby turn into a woman or man of God to give a person a different perspective on life. You are a large chunk of the evidence I have that God is real and loves me.
- Thank you to my wife, Windee. You, more than any other person on this planet, have been the catalyst for my spiritual development. In my attempts to mentor students in deep, one-on-one conversations (like this book), you have given foundational guidance to me, supporting me with openness and wisdom. You love the gospel more than your life, and you are the best Christian I know. Even when we're not married in heaven, I'm still going to love you forever.
- Finally, thank you, thank you, thank you Jesus. I don't know why or how you put up with me. I hope you like our book; it's not as good as your book, but we tried our best for you.

# About the Authors

## Victoria

Victoria Lim lives in Southern California where she works as a technical writer for a software company. She obtained her BS degree from Belmont University with a double major in chemistry and mathematics. She completed her MS and PhD degrees in chemistry at the University of California, Irvine. Victoria's PhD research focused on the development and application of molecular simulations for drug discovery. She became a Christian during her time in graduate school.

## Steve

Steve Robinson is a Professor of Physics at Belmont University in Nashville, Tennessee, where he has worked since 2007. He received BS degrees in electrical and computer engineering at North Carolina State University before pursuing MS and PhD degrees at the University of Illinois at Urbana-Champaign, where he performed research in nanoelectronics. He became a Christian at the age of twelve and is married with three children.

Printed in Great Britain
by Amazon

24122235R00205